SNORRI STURLUSON
HEIMSKRINGLA

VOLUME II

The printing of this book is made possible by a gift to the University of Cambridge in memory of Dorothea Coke, Skjæret, 1951

SNORRI STURLUSON
HEIMSKRINGLA

VOLUME II
ÓLÁFR HARALDSSON (THE SAINT)

TRANSLATED BY

ALISON FINLAY

AND

ANTHONY FAULKES

© VIKING SOCIETY 2014

ISBN: 978-0-903521-89-5

Corrected 2016, 2023

The cover illustration is from a fresco by the Isefjord Master (c. 1460–1480) in the church at Tuse, north-west Sjælland, Denmark. Photograph by Peter Bondesen, © Hideko Bondesen http://www.nordenskirker.dk/

Printed by Short Run Press Limited, Exeter

CONTENTS

INTRODUCTION vii
   Óláfs saga helga vii
   Earlier Texts and Sources... ix
   The Separate Saga and Heimskringla x
   This Translation xii

BIBLIOGRAPHICAL REFERENCES xiii

HEIMSKRINGLA II 1
   Óláfs saga ins helga 3
   Passages from Snorri's Separate Óláfs saga helga not in
      Heimskringla... 279

INDEX OF NAMES 313

Introduction

Óláfs saga helga

Óláfr Haraldsson, born c. 995, son of the petty king Haraldr grenski of Vestfold in Norway and allegedly a great-great-grandson of Haraldr hárfagri,[1] ruled Norway from 1015 to 1028, before his death in battle at Stiklastaðir in 1030 after a period of exile in Russia. *Óláfs saga helga*, which chronicles this short though admittedly eventful life, is the longest saga in *Heimskringla*, making up more than a third of the whole, and occupying a dominant position at its centre. Clearly the justification for the scale of this saga is the framing of Óláfr's death as a martyrdom, and his future role as the patron saint of Norway, the *perpetuus rex Norvegiæ* 'perpetual king of Norway' as he is dubbed in the twelfth-century *Historia Norwegiae* (*A History of Norway* 2001, 17). The political dimension of the saint's cult is reflected in the Succession Law introduced in Norway with the coronation of Magnús Erlingsson in 1163, whereby all subsequent kings were to be considered as vassals holding Norway as a fief from St Óláfr. In *Heimskringla* the influence of St Óláfr after his death is registered by occasional miracles occurring during the reigns of subsequent kings and attributed to his sanctity (e.g. *Magnús saga ins góða* ch. 27; *Haralds saga Sigurðarsonar* chs 14, 55; *Haraldssona saga* chs 24–25). *Óláfs saga ins helga* in *Heimskringla* is a fairly close revision of the free-standing saga of the king, known as the *Separate* (or *Great(est)*) *Saga of St Óláfr*, written by Snorri probably shortly before the composition of *Heimskringla*; in the *Separate Saga* these miracle stories are mostly collected together at the end of that text. The relationship between *Heimskringla* and the *Separate Saga* will be considered in more detail below.

It is often said that the saga of Óláfr Haraldsson 'developed from the confluence of two lines of historical writing in medieval Norway and Iceland, the religious-historical tradition of saints' lives and the secular-historical tradition of royal biography' (Heinrichs 1993, 447), but it is hard to draw a hard and fast line between the hagiographical and the historical in even the earliest texts about the king and his cult. Snorri's own account is generally categorised by scholars as a 'profane saga' (Widding et al. 1963, 328) and Snorri credited (from a modern historian's point of view) with rationalising his source material by omitting or toning down the miraculous (e.g. Whaley 1991, 120, 131; see Phelpstead 2000, 297–98; 2007, 134–38 for discussion of this issue). But Sverrir Tómasson makes a case for the reading of the saga as hagiography (e.g. 1994); and the length and strategic placing of the saga as the climax of *Heimskringla* in itself suggests the endowment of Óláfr

---

[1] The authenticity of Óláfr's descent from Haraldr hárfagri is called into question by some critics (Krag 1989 and 2002).

with a significance beyond that of other, merely secular kings. That this was Snorri's deliberate choice can be seen by the contrast with the treatment of Óláfr in other texts such as *Fagrskinna*, in which 'no special prominence is given to his story' (Heinrichs 1993, 448).

Carl Phelpstead argues that Snorri's approach is 'dialogic', representing a deliberate juxtaposition of historical and hagiographical viewpoints, in order to capture contradictions in the king's own story: 'hagiographic and non-hagiographic genres are juxtaposed within the text so as to provoke reflection on the nature of Óláfr's sainthood' (2000, 294; 2007, 132). Other scholars too have noted the contradictions in Óláfr's transitions from youthful viking to energetically proselytising king to saint and martyr. For Gabriel Turville-Petre they are successfully reconciled: Óláfr 'became a saint gradually as he faced the trials of this life' (1953, 222); for Sverre Bagge, unresolved: 'Snorri does not describe a development. He describes three successive characters with no real link between them' (1991, 182). These contradictions arise surely from the rapidity with which Óláfr's cult was established, so that the hagiographical materials attached to the cult developed side by side, and in dialogue with, with the poetic record which was based ultimately on eyewitness accounts and personal memories of the king's life.

Óláfs saga ins helga itself gives an account of the establishment of the cult of St Óláfr, just over a year after the king's fall; Þórarinn loftunga's poem *Glælognskviða*, despite being introduced by Snorri as 'about Sveinn Álfífuson', dwells on Óláfr's elevation to sanctity and the miracles he has achieved; dated by its location within the short reign of Óláfr's unpopular Danish successor Sveinn Álfífuson to between 1030 and 1034, it stands as the first surviving text to refer to Óláfr as a saint. The cult soon established itself in Niðaróss (now known as Trondheim), where his body was enshrined, and was associated with the archbishopric founded there in 1152/53, with authority over Norway, Iceland and other areas of Norse settlement. Another early poem, Sigvatr Þórðarson's *Erfidrápa Óláfs helga*, which refers to Óláfr's sanctity and some of the miracles attributed to him, is dated to around the time of the return of Óláfr's son Magnús from exile to claim the throne of Norway in 1035. Einarr Skúlason's poem *Geisli*, composed for the dedication of the new cathedral in 1152/53, provides further poetical testimony to the by then well established cult, praising Óláfr's warlike qualities as well as the miracles attributed to him, and recording his death at Stiklastaðir, the subsequent enshrinement of his body and the establishment of the archdiocese. The cult was quick to spread; evidence of the earliest liturgy for the saint's feast day is preserved from c. 1050 in England, probably as a result of the re-establishment there of Grímkell, Óláfr's *hirðbiskup* 'household bishop', who was the prime mover, according to *Heimskringla*, in establishing the king's sanctity after his fall (chs

243–44). According to Adam of Bremen, Óláfr had brought Grímkell from England to assist in the strengthening of Christianity in Norway and beyond (1959, 94); he became bishop of Selsey in 1038/39.

Earlier Texts and Sources

Turville-Petre writes: 'it is probable that the clerks of Niðaróss had begun to keep records of the miracles worked through the agency of their patron soon after his relics were translated in 1031' (1953, 171). Einarr Skúlason's poem recounts fourteen miracles attributed to the saint; eight of these are also related in surviving collections of miracle stories dated to the later twelfth century, in Latin versions now called the *Acta Sancti Olavi* and the *Passio et miracula beati Olavi*, with a translated version in the *Old Norwegian Homily Book*. This suggests that by 1152/53, when Einarr's poem was composed, a written collection of miracles was already in existence and was the poet's source. Some at least of this material is attributed to Archbishop Eysteinn of Niðaróss. One such collection, or more than one, is mentioned by Theodoricus, the author of one of the three synoptic histories from the late twelfth century that represent the earliest surviving records of the writing of what is classified as the secular history of Norway (Theodoricus monachus 1998, 33). Theodoricus refers not only to miracles performed by Óláfr but to the exhumation and enshrining of his body at Niðaróss, material deriving from the short *passio* or *vita* that accompanied the miracle stories. Lessons for the saint's feast day were derived from these texts and widely disseminated.[2] An extract from the *Passio sancti Olavi* gives a flavour of the rhetoric adopted by the hagiographers, styling Óláfr as the blameless preacher of God's word and his death as martyrdom (*A History of Norway* 2001, 30–31):

> The martyr of Christ chanced to come into that district to preach God's grace to the unbelieving people. When the enemies of the truth learnt this, they summoned a wicked council and gathered together against the Lord and his anointed. For his preaching of salvation was entirely opposed to them and their works. Some of them were corrupted by the bribes of his enemy, a certain Knútr; some were prompted by malice alone and, further, were unwilling to receive a new religion, contrary to their ancestral laws. So they assembled an army and gave battle to the king at the place now called Stiklarstaðir, catching him unawares and at some little distance from his own men. But the most illustrious martyr was unafraid in the face of the multitude, his thoughts wholly centred on things celestial and in his innermost being desirous of attaining heaven through the crown of martyrdom . . . So in order to crown him with greater glory, God permitted the glorious martyr to fall by the spears of the wicked.

[2] A full account of these texts and their relationships can be found in Phelpstead 2001; for a recent addition to scholarship on this subject, see Jiroušková 2010.

Only six fragments, dating from about 1225, survive of what is believed to be the earliest extended life of the king, known as *The Oldest Saga of St Óláfr*, and thought to have been written in Iceland at the end of the twelfth century. What survives is anecdotal, notably including stories of the king's encounters with poets, and incorporating six complete and one fragmentary skaldic stanza; chronologically, the fragments derive from the middle part of the saga, excluding the king's early viking exploits and his death in battle. Although this text is otherwise lost, the surviving *Legendary Saga of St Óláfr*, a slightly abridged Norwegian redaction written in or near Trondheim probably in the mid-thirteenth century, can be seen by comparison with the existing fragments to be closely based on it. As the modern title suggests, the bias of the *Legendary Saga* is hagiographical (from the specialised use of *legend* to mean 'written saint's life'), including uncritical accounts of miracles performed throughout Óláfr's life as well as posthumously. Two interpolations of material not derived from the *Oldest Saga*—a list of miracles close to those found in the *Norwegian Homily Book* and an account of Óláfr's missionary activity in Guðbrandsdalar—intensify this emphasis. Turville-Petre characterises the genesis of the *Oldest Saga*, and its descendant the *Legendary Saga*, as a coming together of foreign hagiographical form and native, largely poetical material: 'Although lives of foreign saints might suggest a form for the biographer of S. Óláfr, they could not supply the material, for which the author must rely on native sources' (1953, 179)—largely the verses made by skalds patronised by the king himself, or composed soon after his lifetime.

Snorri may well have known the *Oldest Saga*, but it is another now lost work, a *lífssaga* 'biography' by his older contemporary Styrmir inn fróði 'the Learned' Kárason, that is believed to have been the source he used most extensively, not least because Styrmir was Snorri's close associate. Fragments of Styrmir's saga survive in the form of eleven 'articles' appended to the version of Snorri's *Separate Saga* included in the fourteenth-century compilation Flateyjarbók; many of the expansions made to Snorri's saga in Flateyjarbók and other later redactions have also been shown to derive from Styrmir's text (Rowe 2005, 264–70).

The Separate Saga and Heimskringla

In this translation, as in the edition of Bjarni Aðalbjarnarson on which it is based, the main text (that of *Óláfs saga helga* in *Heimskringla*) is followed by those passages from the *Separate Saga* that do not appear in *Heimskringla*. Comparison of these passages with the *Heimskringla* version shows how the *Separate Saga* was adapted for inclusion in the compendium. The *Separate Saga* has a structure of its own, surrounding the saga of St Óláfr proper with summaries of the reigns that preceded and followed that of the saint himself;

but the text of the greater part of the saga is comparable enough to that of *Heimskringla* to be considered a redaction of the same work. In a sense this is how it was treated by medieval scribes, since in two of the major branches of manuscripts of *Heimskringla*, those deriving from Fríssbók and those from Jöfraskinna, the saga of St Óláfr is omitted entirely, perhaps because the scribes or their commissioners already had access to manuscripts of the *Separate Saga*; in the case of Jöfraskinna an abbreviated version of the *Separate Saga* was added later. Other scribes blended the *Separate Saga* and *Heimskringla* versions in copying the saga (Whaley 1991, 41–42). The now lost manuscript Kringla is considered to be the closest to Snorri's archetype of *Heimskringla*, and seventeenth-century transcripts of this are used for the edition of *Óláfs saga* as for the rest of *Heimskringla*.[3] The *Separate Saga* is found in a comparatively large number of manuscripts; the edition of Johnsen and Jón Helgason (1941) gives variant readings from twelve manuscripts in addition to the oldest and only complete version, that of Perg 4to nr 2 in the Royal Library Stockholm, from 1250–1300. The editors also make use of ten, such as Flateyjarbók (mentioned above), which have interpolated texts based on the *Separate Saga*.

The *Separate Saga* begins in some manuscripts with a Prologue, which exists in a shorter and a longer version. That translated here is the longer version, found in the main manuscript and in some other manuscripts; the shorter version is found in two manuscripts, and there are others that seem never to have had a Prologue (Whaley 1991, 55). Both versions are generally agreed to be reworkings by later redactors of Snorri's Prologue to the whole of *Heimskringla* (Sverrir Tómasson 1988, 383). Thus, for instance, the Prologue to the *Separate Saga* reproduces the references to the Age of Burning and the Age of Mounds (*Heimskringla* I, 4) relevant only to *Ynglinga saga*; and most of its material is shared with the *Heimskringla* Prologue, reordered and abbreviated. Significant differences are that Óláfr helgi is specifically introduced, and the inclusion of information about Icelanders defended on the ground that they brought first-hand accounts of Óláfr to Iceland: 'I know that it will seem, if this account comes abroad, as though I have said a great deal about Icelandic people, but the reason for this is that Icelandic people who saw or heard about these events, carried these accounts here to this country, and people have afterwards learnt about them from them' (422). The implication that oral narrative other than verse has been used as a significant, though less verbally fixed and therefore less reliable, source is also evident in the more detailed statement in this Prologue about the use of skaldic and other sources, as Theodore Andersson has pointed out (Andersson 2008).

[3] Bjarni Aðalbjarnarson notes the occasional use of readings from *Separate Saga* manuscripts where those of *Heimskringla* are clearly incorrect (*Hkr* II, cvii).

This Translation

Like *Heimskringla* I, published by the Viking Society in 2011, this translation is based on the *Íslenzk fornrit* edition of *Heimskringla* by Bjarni Aðalbjarnarson (*Íslenzk fornrit* XXVI–XXVIII, *Hkr* I–III). *Óláfs saga helga* occupies the whole of *Hkr* II. Page numbers of this edition appear here in square brackets, and internal page references as well as those in the index and introduction are to this edition. The prose has been translated by Anthony Faulkes and the verses by Alison Finlay, who also wrote this Introduction. Both have contributed footnotes, but as in vol. I, many of these are closely based on those of Bjarni Aðalbjarnarson.

To the right of each verse is noted, as in *Heimskringla* I, the name of the poem and the stanza number, but in this volume these are based on the attributions in the new edition of the skaldic corpus, of which the relevant volume has recently been published, *Skaldic Poetry of the Scandinavian Middle Ages* I. *Poetry from the Kings' Sagas* 1: *From Mythical Times to c. 1035* (*Skald* I) . These attributions sometimes differ slightly from those in the older edition of Finnur Jónsson (FJ), which was used in *Heimskringla* I. The page number on which the verse appears in the new skaldic edition is also noted here, and can be referred to for full information on the meaning and manuscript status of each verse. This edition has proved invaluable for the interpretation of the verses in this translation, and in specific instances the editors of particular poems have been acknowledged in the footnotes. The interpretations sometimes differ, however, since our translation has followed manuscripts of *Heimskringla* that are not always the ones chosen as primary manuscripts by the editors of the skaldic edition.

The verses sometimes preserve archaic spellings of names, appropriate to the presumed date of composition of the verse, thus 'Óleifr' for 'Óláfr' and 'Hǫkon' for 'Hákon'. Although these are more often the reconstructions of editors than spellings found in surviving manuscripts, they are retained here in accordance with the conventions used in the *Íslenzk fornrit* edition. Similarly, when names appear in alternative forms in the text (such as Fiðr/ Finnr), the identity of the characters is made clear in the Index of names.

We are most grateful to Carl Phelpstead for reading a proof of this book, and for the many useful suggestions he has made.

Bibliographical References

This bibliography incorporates that published in Volume I, with the addition of references made in this volume.

1GT = *The First Grammatical Treatise* 1972. Ed. Hreinn Benediktsson. Reykjavík.
3GT = *The Third Grammatical Treatise*. In *Den Tredje og Fjærde Grammatiske Afhandling i Snorres Edda*. 1884. Ed. Björn Magnússon Ólsen. København, 1–119.
Adam of Bremen 1959. *History of the Archbishops of Hamburg-Bremen.* Trans. Francis J. Tschan. New York.
Ágrip = *Ágrip af Nóregskonunga sǫgum. Fagrskinna—Nóregs konunga tal* 1984. Ed. Bjarni Einarsson. Reykjavík, 1–54. *ÍF* XXIX.
Ágrip 2008 = *Ágrip af Nóregskonunga sǫgum*. 2008. Ed. M. J. Driscoll. London.
A History of Norway and The Passion and Miracles of the Blessed Óláfr 2001. Trans. Devra Kunin. Ed. with introduction and notes by Carl Phelpstead. London.
Andersson, Theodore M. 1993. 'Snorri Sturluson and the Saga School at Munkaþverá'. In *Snorri Sturluson. Kolloquium anläßlich der 750. Wiederkehr seines Todesdages*. Ed. Alois Wolf. Tübingen, 9–25. ScriptOralia 51.
Andersson, Theodore M. 2008. 'The Oral Sources for *Óláfs saga helga* in Heimskringla'. *Saga-Book* XXXII 5–38.
Andersson, Theodore M. and K. E. Gade (trans.) 2000. *Morkinskinna: The Earliest Icelandic Chronicle of the Norwegian Kings (1030–1157)*. Ithaca and London. Islandica LI.
Anglo-Saxon Chronicle = *Two of the Saxon Chronicles Parallel* 1892–99. Ed. John Earle and Charles Plummer. Oxford.
Ármann Jakobsson 2005. 'Royal Biography'. In *Companion to Old Norse-Icelandic Literature*. Ed. Rory McTurk. Oxford, 388–402.
Ásgeir Blöndal Magnússon 1989. *Íslensk orðsifjabók*. Reykjavík.
Bagge, Sverre 1991. *Society and Politics in Snorri Sturluson's Heimskringla*. Berkeley.
Boulhosa, Patricia Pires 2005. *Icelanders and the Kings of Norway. Mediaeval Sagas and Legal Texts*. Leiden and Boston. The Northern World 17.
Clunies Ross, Margaret 1999. 'From Iceland to Norway. Essential Rites of Passage for an Early Icelandic Skald'. *Alvíssmál* 9, 55–72.
Dillmann, François-Xavier 2000. 'Pour l'étude des traditions relatives à l'enterrement du roi Halfdan le Noir'. In *International Scandinavian and Medieval Studies in Memory of Gerd Wolfgang Weber*. Ed. Michael Dallapiazza *et al*.Trieste, 147–56.
Edda Magnúsar Ólafssonar 1979. Ed. Anthony Faulkes. Reykjavík.
Egils saga Skalla-Grímssonar 1933. Ed. Sigurður Nordal. Reykjavík. *ÍF* II.
Ellis Davidson, Hilda 1943. *The Road to Hel. A Study of the Conception of the Dead in Old Norse Literature*. Cambridge.
Fagrskinna. In *Ágrip af Nóregskonunga sǫgum. Fagrskinna—Nóregs konunga tal* 1984. Ed. Bjarni Einarsson. Reykjavík, 55–364. *ÍF* XXIX.
Falk, Hjalmar 1912.'Altnordisches Seewesen'. *Wörter und Sachen* 4, 1–122.
Falk, Hjalmar 1914. *Altnordische Waffenkunde*. Kristiania.
Farrell, R. T. 1972. *Beowulf, Swedes and Geats*. London.

Faulkes, Anthony 1966. *Rauðúlfs þáttr. A Study*. Reykjavík. Studia Islandica 25.
Faulkes, Anthony (ed.) 2011. *Two Icelandic Stories*. London. Viking Society Text Series IV.
Fell, Christine 1981. 'Víkingarvísur'. In *Speculum norroenum. Norse Studies in Memory of Gabriel Turville-Petre*. Ed. U. Dronke et al. Odense, 106–22.
Fidjestøl, B. 1982. *Det norrøne fyrstediktet*. Øvre Ervik. Universitet i Bergen Nordisk institutts skriftserie 11.
Finlay, Alison 2011. 'Risking one's Head. *Vafþrúðnismál* and the Mythic Power of Poetry'. In *Myths, Legends, and Heroes. Essays on Old Norse and Old English Literature*. Ed. Daniel Anlezark. Toronto, 91–108.
FJ = Finnur Jónsson (ed.) 1912–15. *Den norsk-islandske skjaldedigtning* A I–II, B I–II. København.
Flb = *Flateyjarbók* I–IV 1944–45. Ed. Sigurður Nordal. Reykjavík.
Foote, Peter 1978. 'Wrecks and Rhymes'. In *The Vikings*. Ed. T. Andersson and K. I. Sandred. Uppsala, 57–66. Reprinted in Peter Foote 1984. *Aurvandilstá. Norse Studies*. Ed. M. Barnes, H. Bekker-Nielsen and G. W. Weber. Odense, 222–35. The Viking Collection 2.
Foote, Peter and David Wilson 1970. *The Viking Achievement*. London.
Fóstbrœðra saga. In *Vestfirðinga sǫgur* 1943. Ed. Björn K. Þórólfsson and Guðni Jónsson. Reykjavík, 119–276. *ÍF* VI.
Frank, Roberta 1984. 'Viking Atrocity and Skaldic Verse: The Rite of the Blood-Eagle'. *English Historical Review* 99, 332–43.
Fritzner, Johan 1886–96. *Ordbog over det gamle norske Sprog* I–III. Kristiania.
Fsk = *Fagrskinna*.
Grettis saga Ásmundarsonar 1936. Ed. Guðni Jónsson. Reykjavík. *ÍF* VII.
Grønlie, Siân (trans.) 2006. *Íslendingabók, Kristni saga. The Book of the Icelanders, The Story of the Conversion*. London. Viking Society Text Series XVIII.
Gylf = *Gylfaginning*. In Snorri Sturluson 2005. *Edda. Prologue and Gylfaginning*. Ed. Anthony Faulkes. London.
Hálfs saga ok Hálfsrekka 1981. Ed. Hubert Seelow. Reykjavík.
Halldór Halldórsson 1954. *Íslenzk Orðtök*. Reykjavík.
Hallfreðar saga. In *Vatnsdœla saga. Hallfreðar saga. Kormáks saga* 1939. Ed. Einar Ól. Sveinsson. Reykjavík, 133–200. *ÍF* VIII.
Háttatal = Snorri Sturluson 2007. *Edda. Háttatal*. Ed. Anthony Faulkes. London. [Referred to by stanza and, where appropriate, line no.]
Heimskringla 1893–1901 = Snorri Sturluson. *Heimskringla* I–IV. Ed. Finnur Jónsson. København.
Heinrichs, Anne 1993. 'Óláfs saga helga'. In *Medieval Scandinavia. An Encyclopedia*. Ed. Phillip Pulsiano et al. New York and London, 447–48.
Hemings þáttr Ásláksssonar 1962. Ed. Gillian Fellows Jensen. Copenhagen. Editiones Arnamagnæanæ B 3.
Historia Norwegie 2003. Ed. Inger Ekrem and Lars Boje Mortensen. Trans. Peter Fisher. Copenhagen.
Hkr = Snorri Sturluson 1941–51. *Heimskringla* I–III. Ed. Bjarni Aðalbjarnarson. Reykjavík. *ÍF* XXVI–XXVIII.
ÍF = *Íslenzk fornrit* I ff. 1933– . Reykjavík.
Íslendinga saga. In *Sturlunga saga* I.

Íslendingabók = Ari Þorgilsson 1968. *Íslendingabók*. In *Íslendingabók. Landnámabók*. Ed. Jakob Benediktsson. Reykjavík, 1–28. ÍF I.

J = Jöfraskinna (See vol. 1, p. xiii).

Jesch, Judith 2001. *Ships and Men in the Late Viking Age. The Vocabulary of Runic Inscriptions and Skaldic Verse*. Woodbridge.

Jiroušková, Lenka 2010. 'Textual Evidence for the Transmission of the Passio Olavi Prior to 1200 and its Later Literary Transformations'. In *Saints and their Lives on the Periphery: Veneration of Saints in Scandinavia and Eastern Europe (c. 1000–1200)*. Ed. Haki Antonsson and Ildar H. Garipzanov. Turnhout, 219–39.

Johnsen, A. O. and Jón Helgason (eds) 1941. *Den store saga om Olav den hellige*. Oslo.

Jóms (291) = *Jómsvíkinga saga* 1969. Ed. Ólafur Halldórsson. Reykjavík [ÁM 291 4to].

Jóms (510) = *Jómsvíkinga saga (efter cod. AM 510, 4to) samt Jómsvíkinga drápa* 1879. Ed. Carl af Petersens. Lund.

Jón Hnefill Aðalsteinsson 1997. *Blót í norrænum sið. Rýnt í forn trúarbrögð með þjóðfræðilegri aðferð*. Reykjavík.

Jónas Kristjánsson 1977. '*Egils saga* og konungasögur'. In *Sjötíu ritgerðir helgaðar Jakobi Benediktssyni, 20 júlí 1977*. Ed. Einar G. Pétursson and Jónas Kristjánsson. Reykjavík, 449–72.

Jónas Kristjánsson 1990. 'Var Snorri Sturluson upphafsmaður íslendingasagna?' *Andvari* 115, 85–105.

Jørgensen, Jon Gunnar 1995. '"Snorre Sturlesøns Fortale paa sin Chrønicke". Om kildene til opplysningen om *Heimskringlas* forfatter'. *Gripla* 9, 45–62.

Jørgensen, Jon Gunnar 2007. *The Lost Vellum Kringla*. Trans. Siân Grønlie. Copenhagen. Bibliotheca Arnamagnæana 45.

K = Kringla (see Introduction p. xi).

Keraliunas, Simas 1994. 'The Information on the Aistians in Olafs saga Tryggvasonar and its Importance for the History of the East Baltic Region'. In *Samtíðar sögur*. Preprints of the ninth International Saga Conference II, 450–54. Akureyri.

Knýt = *Knýtlinga saga*. In *Danakonunga sǫgur* 1982. Ed. Bjarni Guðnason. Reykjavík, 91–321. ÍF XXXV.

Krag, Claus 1989. 'Norge sem odel i Harald hårfagres ætt'. [Norwegian] *Historisk tidsskrift* 68, 288–302.

Krag, Claus 2002. 'Myten om Hårfagreættens odel—et svar til Knut Dørum'. [Norwegian] *Historisk tidsskrift* 81, 381–94.

Landn = *Landnámabók*. In *Íslendingabók. Landnámabók* 1968. Ed. Jakob Benediktsson. Reykjavík, 29–397. ÍF I.

Laws of Early Iceland I 1980. Trans. Andrew Dennis, Peter Foote and Richard Perkins. Winnipeg.

Legendary saga = *Ólafs saga hins helga. Die 'Legendarische saga' über Olaf den Heiligen (Hs. Delagard. saml. nr. 8¹¹)* 1982. Ed. Anne Heinrichs, Doris Janshen, Elke Radicke and Hartmut Röhn. Heidelberg.

Leland, Charles Godfrey 1892. *Etruscan Roman Remains in Popular Tradition*. New York and London.

Lind, E. H. 1920–21. *Norsk-isländska personbinamn från medeltiden*. Uppsala.

Lindow, John 2007. 'St Olaf and the Skalds'. In *Sanctity in the North: Saints, Lives, and Cults in Medieval Scandinavia*. Ed. T. A. DuBois. Toronto, 103–27.

Lindquist, I. 1929. *Norröna Lovkväden från 800- och 900-Talen*. Lund.

LP = Sveinbjörn Egilsson 1931. *Lexicon Poeticum Antiquæ Linguæ Septentrionalis*. Rev. Finnur Jónsson. Copenhagen.

Maríu saga 1871. Ed. C. R. Unger. Christiania.

Mork = *Morkinskinna* 2011. Ed. Ármann Jakobsson and Þórður Ingi Guðjónsson. *ÍF* XXIII.

Mork (Flb) = Passages in *Flb* taken to be derived from the original *Morkinskinna*, printed in *Mork* (and other editions of *Morkinskinna*).

NGL = *Norges gamle love indtil 1387* 1846–95. Ed. R. Keyser et al. Christiania.

NN = E. A. Kock 1923–44. *Notationes Norrænæ* I–XXVIII. Lund. [References are to paragraph numbers]

Oddr = Oddr munkr Snorrason 2006. *Óláfs saga Tryggvasonar*. In *Færeyinga saga*. *Óláfs saga Tryggvasonar eptir Odd munk Snorrason*. Ed. Ólafur Halldórsson. Reykjavík, 123–380. *ÍF* XXV.

O'Donoghue, Heather 2005. *Skaldic Verse and the Poetics of Saga Narrative*. Oxford.

ÓH = *Den store saga om Olav den hellige* 1941. Ed. O. A. Johnsen and Jón Helgason. Oslo.

Ólafur Halldórsson 1965. 'Flutningur handrita milli Íslands og Noregs fyrr á öldum'. *Tíminn*, 17th June. Reprinted in *Grettisfærsla. Safn ritgerða eftir Ólaf Halldórsson gefið út á sjötugsafmæli hans 18. apríl 1990*. 1990. Reykjavík, 339–47.

Ólafur Halldórsson 1979. 'Sagnaritun Snorra Sturlusonar'. In *Snorri: átta alda minning*. Reykjavík, 113–38. Reprinted in *Grettisfærsla. Safn ritgerða eftir Ólaf Halldórsson gefið út á sjötugsafmæli hans 18. apríl 1990*. 1990. Reykjavík, 376–95.

Oldest saga of St Óláfr = Anhang. In *Olafs saga hins helga. En kort saga om kong Olaf den hellige fra anden halvdeel af det tolfte aarhundrede* 1849. Ed. R. Keyser and C. R. Unger. Christiania, 90–95.

Olrik, Axel 1909. 'At sidde paa Hoj'. *Danske Studier*, 1–10.

ONP = *Ordbog over det norrøne prosasprog* at http://onp.ku.dk

Orkn = *Orkneyinga saga* 1965. Ed. Finnbogi Guðmundsson. Reykjavík. *ÍF* XXXIV.

ÓTM = *Óláfs saga Tryggvasonar en mesta* I–III 1958–2000. Ed. Ólafur Halldórsson. Copenhagen. Editiones Arnamagnæanæ A 1–3.

Phelpstead, Carl 2000. 'In Honour of St Óláfr. The Miracle Stories in Snorri Sturluson's *Óláfs saga helga*'. *Saga-Book* XXV, 292–306.

Phelpstead, Carl 2001. 'Introduction'. In *A History of Norway*.

Phelpstead, Carl 2007. *Holy Vikings. Saints' Lives in the Old Icelandic Kings' Sagas*. Tempe.

Poetic Edda = *Edda. Die Lieder des Codex Regius* I 1962. Ed. Hans Kuhn. Heidelberg.

Rauðúlfs þáttr: in *ÓH* 655–82; normalised text with notes and translation at www.vsnrweb-publications.org.uk/Raudulfs%20thattr.%20text.pdf

Rowe, Elizabeth Ashman 2005. *The Development of Flateyjarbók. Iceland and the Norwegian Dynastic Crisis of 1389*. Odense. The Viking Collection 15.

Separate Saga of St Óláfr = *ÓH*.

Skald I = Diana Whaley (ed.) *Skaldic Poetry of the Scandinavian Middle Ages*. I. *Poetry from the Kings' Sagas* 1: *From Mythical Times to c. 1035*. 2012. Turnhout.

Skald II = Kari Ellen Gade (ed.). *Skaldic Poetry of the Scandinavian Middle Ages*. II. *Poetry from the Kings' Sagas* 2. *From c. 1035 to c. 1300* 2009. Turnhout.

Skáldsk = Snorri Sturluson 1998. *Edda. Skáldskaparmál.* Ed. Anthony Faulkes. London.
Skjǫldunga saga: in *Danakonunga sǫgur* 1982. Ed. Bjarni Guðnason. Reykjavík, 3–90. *ÍF* XXV.
SnE II = *Edda Snorra Sturlusonar* II 1852. Ed. Jón Sigurðsson et al. Hafniæ.
Snorri Sturluson 1987. *Edda*. Trans. Anthony Faulkes. London.
Stefán Karlsson 1976. 'Kringum Kringlu'. *Landsbókasafn Íslands: Árbók*, 5–25. Reprinted in *Stafkrókar. Ritgerðir eftir Stefán Karlsson gefnar út í tilefni af sjötugsafmæli hans* 2000. Reykjavík, 253–73.
Stefán Karlsson 1979. 'Islandsk bogeksport til Norge i middelalderen'. *Maal og minne*, 1–17. Reprinted in *Stafkrókar. Ritgerðir eftir Stefán Karlsson gefnar út í tilefni af sjötugsafmæli hans* 2000. Reykjavík, 188–205.
Straubhaar, Sandra Ballif 2002. 'Ambiguously Gendered. The Skalds Jórunn, Auðr and Steinunn'. In *Cold Counsel. Women in Old Norse Literature and Mythology*. Ed. Sarah M. Anderson and Karen Swenson. New York and London, 261–72.
Sturlunga saga I–II 1946. Ed. Jón Jóhannesson et al. Reykjavík.
Sverrir Tómasson 1994. 'The Hagiography of Snorri Sturluson, especially in the Great Saga of St Olaf'. In *Saints and Sagas: A Symposium*. Ed. Hans Bekker-Nielsen and Birte Carlé. Odense, 49–71.
Sverrir Tómasson 1998. *Formálar íslenskra sagnaritara á miðöldum. Rannsókn bókmenntahefðar*. Reykjavík.
Theodoricus monachus 1998. *An Account of the Ancient History of the Norwegian Kings*. Trans. David and Ian McDougall. London.
Turville-Petre, E. O. G. 1953. *Origins of Icelandic Literature*. Oxford.
Turville-Petre, E. O. G. 1976. *Scaldic Poetry*. Oxford.
Turville-Petre, Joan 1988. 'A tree dream in Old Icelandic'. *Scripta Islandica* 39, 12–20.
de Vries, J. 1977. *Altnordisches etymologisches Wörterbuch*. 2nd revised edition. Leiden.
Wanner, Kevin J. 2008. *Snorri Sturluson and the Edda. The Conversion of Cultural Capital in Medieval Scandinavia*. Toronto.
Whaley, Diana 1991. *Heimskringla. An Introduction*. London.
Whaley, Diana (ed.) 1998. *The Poetry of Arnórr jarlaskáld*. London.
Widding, Ole, Hans Bekker-Nielsen and L. K. Shook 1963. 'The Lives of the Saints in Old Norse Prose. A Handlist'. *Mediaeval Studies* 25, 294–337.
Örvar-Odds saga. In *Fornaldarsögur norðurlanda* 1950. Ed. Guðni Jónsson. Reykjavík, II 199–363.

SNORRI STURLUSON

HEIMSKRINGLA

II

[3] Óláfs saga ins helga

CHAPTER ONE

Óláfr, son of Haraldr inn grenski (the Grenlander), was brought up with his stepfather Sigurðr sýr (Pig) and his mother Ásta. Hrani inn víðfǫrli (the Far-Travelled) was with Ásta. He fostered Óláfr Haraldsson. Óláfr soon became an accomplished man, handsome-looking, of middling height. He was sensible and soon a good speaker too. Sigurðr sýr was a very enthusiastic farmer and kept his men very busy, and he frequently went himself to see to his fields and meadows or animals, to building work, or wherever men were busy at something.

CHAPTER TWO

It happened on one occasion that King Sigurðr was going to ride out of the farm when there wasn't a man in at the farm. He told his stepson Óláfr to saddle a horse for him. Óláfr went to the goat-shed and from there took the biggest buck there was and led it to the house and put on it the king's saddle, and then went and tells the king that now he had got a mount ready for him. Then King Sigurðr went along and saw what Óláfr had done. He said:

'It is obvious that you are deliberately frustrating my orders. No doubt your mother thinks it proper that I should make no demands on you that are not to your liking. It is obvious that we are not both going to turn out [4] to have the same disposition. You are going to be much more arrogant than I am.'

Óláfr made little response and laughed at him and went away.

CHAPTER THREE

Óláfr Haraldsson, when he grew up, was not tall, a medium man and very sturdily built, physically strong, his hair light brown, broad in the face, light and ruddy of complexion, with exceptionally fine, handsome and keen eyes, so that it was fearful to look into his eyes if he was angry. Óláfr was a very accomplished man in many ways, he knew well how to use a bow and was a good swimmer, most skilled with a javelin, an able craftsman with a good eye for all kinds of craftsmanship, both his own work and other people's. He was known as Óláfr digri (the Stout). He was bold and eloquent in speech, matured early in every way, both physically and mentally, beloved of all his kinsmen and acquaintances, competitive in sports, wanting to outdo everyone, as befitted his status and birth.

CHAPTER FOUR

Óláfr Haraldsson was twelve years old at the time he boarded a warship for the first time. His mother Ásta put Hrani, who was known as King-

Fosterer, in charge of the force and alongside Óláfr, for Hrani had often been on viking expeditions before. When Óláfr took over the force and the ships, then his followers gave him the name of king, as it was the custom that the rulers of troops who were on viking expeditions, when they [5] were of royal blood, then they immediately took the title of king, even though they ruled no lands. Hrani sat at the rudder-control.[1] This is why some people say that Óláfr was an oarsman, but he was still king over the force. They took their course eastwards along the coast and first of all to Denmark. So says Óttarr svarti (the Black), when he made a poem about King Óláfr:[2]

1.	Young, you launched, king bold in battle,	*Hǫfuðlausn* 3
	the blood-of-land stallion[3]	*Skald* I 745
	on course to Denmark; you've become	
	accustomed to fine valour.	
	From the north, most fruitful	
	your faring grew; now power	
	you've gained, king, from such keenness;	
	clearly I heard of your venture.	

CHAPTER FIVE

So when autumn came, he sailed east along the coast of the realm of the Svíar, then began to ravage and burn the land, since he felt he had to pay the Svíar back for their total hostility in [6] taking his father's life. Óttarr svarti says it in plain words, that he then went east from Denmark:

2.	East with vessels oar-decorated	*Hǫfuðlausn* 4
	you pressed over the salt sea.	*Skald* I 746

[1] A rope or thong holding the upper part of the shank of the rudder to the side of the ship. It could be removed to swing the lower part of the rudder up to allow the ship to sail in shallow water.

[2] The Icelandic poet Óttarr svarti, of unknown family except that Snorri identifies him as the maternal nephew of the poet Sigvatr Þórðarson (see ch. 91), is said to have composed for five patrons beside Óláfr helgi, including King Sveinn tjúguskegg and King Knútr inn ríki of the Danes and King Óláfr sœnski of the Swedes. Parts of poems in honour of the latter two are preserved, as well as twenty stanzas of Óttarr's *Hǫfuðlausn* 'Head-Ransom' in honour of Óláfr helgi. A story preserved in Flateyjarbók explains the origin of this title (which was also applied to poems by Egill Skalla-Grímsson and Þórarinn loftunga), suggesting that Óttarr had offended the king by composing a love poem for the king's wife Ástríðr, and was forced to compose the praise-poem in recompense. It is worth noting that Snorri does not give the poem this title in *Hkr*.

[3] *vengis dreyra blakkr*: 'horse of the blood of the field, land (sea)', ship.

From the land, shields of limewood,
land-guard,[4] onto ships you carried.
You used sails and set them
sometimes before the sea-thrower.[5]
Many much-rowed oars cut into
the mighty swell beneath you.

3.   Great fear befell people   *Hǫfuðlausn* 6
from your journey, battle-snake's   *Skald* I 748
swan's feeder;[6] then you started
to stain red Svíþjóð's headlands.

CHAPTER SIX

That autumn near Sótasker (Sóti's rocks) Óláfr fought his first battle. It is among the Svíasker. There he fought against vikings, and the one that was their leader is named as Sóti.[7] [7] Óláfr's force was much smaller and his ships larger. He positioned his ships between some rocks, and it was difficult for the vikings to attack. But the ships that lay closest to them, they (Óláfr's men) got grappling hooks onto them and hauled them in to themselves and then disabled the ships. The vikings stood off and had lost much of their troop. The poet Sigvatr tells of this battle in the poem in which he enumerates King Óláfr's battles:[8]

4.   Long, it bore out the youthful   *Víkingavísur* 1
offspring of princes[9] to the channel—   *Skald* I 535
the folk were then fearful—
the flood-beam[10]—of the king's anger.

---

[4] *landvǫrðr*: 'land-guardian', king.

[5] *sundvarpaðr*: 'thrower of the sea', storm.

[6] *dolglinns svanbrœðir*: 'feeder of the swan (raven) of the snake of battle (sword)', warrior.

[7] The names 'Sóti' and 'Sótasker' are clearly derived from Sigvatr's verse (st.4), where the place-name is broken up as 'sker Sóta'. The names are not found in any other historical source, although a viking called Sóti is mentioned and located in Svíasker in the legendary *Ǫrvar-Odds saga* (see Fell 1981).

[8] For the background and early life of the Icelandic poet Sigvatr Þórðarson, see ch. 43 below. He was the best known and most prolific of the poets of Óláfr helgi, and composed also in honour of other leaders of the time, including enemies of Óláfr such as Knútr inn ríki of the Danes and the *hersir* Erlingr Skjálgsson, and Óláfr's son Magnús inn góði. The poem whose modern title is *Víkingavísur* 'Verses on Viking Activities', of which 14½ stanzas survive, enumerates Óláfr's early raiding adventures. These considerably predate Sigvatr's first appearance at Óláfr's court, and must have been composed retrospectively.

[9] *jǫfra kundr*: 'descendant of princes', king, man of royal birth.

[10] *sæmeiðr*: 'tree or beam of the sea', ship.

> I know further what men about much
> remember; that first time, in
> the east, wild, he washed red
> the wolf's foot, off Sóti's skerry.

CHAPTER SEVEN

King Óláfr then laid his course east along the coast of Svíþjóð and sailed into Lǫgrinn and ravaged both shores. He sailed right on up to Sigtúna and lay off Old Sigtúnir. The Svíar say that the piles of stones that Óláfr had made [8] under the ends of his jetty are still there. And when autumn came, then King Óláfr heard this, that King Óláfr of the Svíar was mustering a great army, and also this, that he had put chains across Stokksund and positioned troops by it. And the king of the Svíar thought that King Óláfr would have to stay there until the frosts came, and the king of the Svíar was unimpressed by King Óláfr's army, since he had few troops. Then King Óláfr went out to Stokksund and could not get out there. There was a fortification to the east of the sound, and an army of men to the south. And when they learned that the king of the Svíar has embarked and had a great army and numerous ships, then King Óláfr had a channel cut out through Agnafit to the sea. Then it rained hard. And all over Svíþjóð all the running water flows into Lǫgrinn, but there is just one mouth to the sea out of Lǫgrinn, and so small that many rivers are wider. But when there is heavy rain and thawing snow, then the water flows so furiously that there is a torrent out through Stokksund, and Lǫgrinn rises so much over the land that there are widespread floods. But when the canal came out to the sea, then the water and the stream ran out. Then King Óláfr had all the rudders on his ships detached and the sails hoisted to the tops of the masts. They steered with the oar, and the ships ran swiftly out over the shallows and all safely reached the sea. And then the Svíar went to see King Óláfr of the Svíar and told him that Óláfr digri had now got out to the sea. The king of the Svíar strongly reprimanded those who should have seen to it that Óláfr did not get out. It is now known as Konungssund (the King's Sound), and large ships cannot go along it except when the water is flowing most violently. But according to some people's account, the Svíar found out [9] when Óláfr's men had dug out the channel through the meadows by the lake and the water was flowing out, and also that the Svíar then went up with an army of men and were going to prevent Óláfr from going out, but when the water had undermined it on both sides, then the banks collapsed and all the people as well, and a large number of troops was lost there. But the Svíar contradict this and say it is nonsense that men perished there. King Óláfr sailed in the autumn to Gotland and started to lay it waste. But the Gotlanders met together there and sent men to the king and offered him tribute from the country. The king accepted it and took tribute from the country and spent the winter there. So says Óttarr:

> 5. From troops of Gotland, tribute   *Hǫfuðlausn* 7
> you took, sailors' supporter;[11]   *Skald* I 749
> men dared not defend from you
> the folk's lands with the shield-rim.
> They ran, Eysýsla people;
> plenty possess less daring
> than the king; I heard wolves had their
> hunger, in the east, lessened.

CHAPTER EIGHT

Here it says that King Óláfr went, when spring came, east to Eysýsla and ravaged it, invaded there, and the people of Eysýsla came down and fought a battle with him. There King Óláfr won victory, pursued the fleeing army, ravaged and laid waste [10] the land. So it is said that to begin with, when King Óláfr and his men entered Eysýsla, then the landowners offered him tribute. But when the tribute came down, then he advanced against them with a fully armed force, and it turned out differently from what the landowners had intended, for they went down, not with tribute, but with weapons of war and fought with the king, as was stated above. So says the poet Sigvatr:

> 6. There again it was that Ǫleifr—   *Víkingarvísur* 2
> unconcealed was trickery—   *Skald* I 537
> held further, in sacked Eysýsla,
> assemblies of weapon points.[12]
> Their feet to thank had farmers
> who fled away for their lives
> once more; few stood waiting
> for wounds there, great ruler.

CHAPTER NINE

Afterwards he sailed back to Lappland and ravaged there and went ashore, but all the inhabitants fled to the woods and emptied their settlement of all their property. The king went up into the interior a long way and through some woods. Some of the valley-dwellers were there. There it is called Herdalar. They found little property, but no people. Then it got late in the

---

[11] *flotna gildir*: 'one that makes seafarers doughty', ruler, sea captain.
[12] *odda þing*: 'meeting(s) of (weapon) points', battle(s).

day, and the king turned back down to his ships. But when they entered the wood, then forces rushed at them from all sides and shot at them and attacked hard. The king bade them save themselves and fight back as far as they [11] could manage. But this was difficult, because the Lapps used the wood as protection for themselves. And before the king came out of the woods, he lost many men, and many were wounded; afterwards, in the evening, he reached his ships. During the night the Lapps caused furious weather by magic, and a storm at sea. But the king had the anchors weighed and the sails hoisted and during the night they sailed along the coast close to the wind. Then again as on other occasions, the king's good fortune had more power than the magic of the Lapps. During the night they managed to sail close to the wind past Bálagarðssíða and so out to the open sea. But the army of Lapps went along the coast on shore, as the king went along in the sea. So says Sigvatr:

7.	There on the taxing trip to Herdalar took place the third harsh tempest of steel[13] of the king's descendant,[14] strong, in meeting the Finnish. And the sea by the shore unshackled ships of vikings in the east; Alongside the surf-skis'[15] stems lay Bálagarðssíða.	*Víkingarvísur* 3 *Skald* I 538

[12] CHAPTER TEN

Then King Óláfr sailed to Denmark. There he met Jarl Sigvaldi's brother Þorkell inn hávi (the Tall), and Þorkell joined forces with him, for he was just then ready to go on a viking expedition. So they sailed south along Jótlandssíða and to a place called Suðrvík, and they overcame many viking ships. And vikings who were constantly at sea and were leaders of large forces assumed the title of king even if they had no lands to rule. There King Óláfr had an engagement. There was a great battle there. King Óláfr gained victory there and much booty. So says Sigvatr:

8.	Again, they said the beginnings of Gunnr's chant[16] the king caused— I heard of glory for the good defender gained—for the fourth time,	*Víkingarvísur* 4 *Skald* I 540

[13] *stáls hríð*: 'storm of steel', battle.
[14] *fylkis niðr*: 'descendant of a ruler', here Óláfr.
[15] *brimskíð*: 'surf-ski', ship.
[16] *Gunnar galdr*: 'chant, spell of Gunnr (valkyrie)', battle.

when no little peace between the
princes' troops was sundered,
out in (known to the Danish)
dangerous Suðrvík.

[13] CHAPTER ELEVEN

Then King Óláfr sailed south to Frísland and lay off Kinnlimasíða in biting weather. Then the king went ashore with his forces, and the men of the country rode down against them and fought with them. So says the poet Sigvatr:

9. You fought, foe of pilferers,[17]   *Víkingarvísur* 5
    the fifth battle, hard on helmets;   *Skald* I 541
    bows suffered a storm off
    steep Kinnlimasíða,
    when down to the ships of the ruler
    rode the army, grandly,
    and to war against warriors
    went the troop of the leader.

CHAPTER TWELVE

King Sveinn tjúguskegg (Forkbeard) of the Danes was at this time in England with an army of Danes and had then stayed there for a while and held King Aðalráðr's land. The Danes had then spread widely across England. As a result, King Aðalráðr had fled the land and gone south to Valland. [14] The same autumn, when King Óláfr got to England, the news got round that King Sveinn Haraldsson had died suddenly at night in his bed, and that, according to Englishmen, St Edmund had killed him in the same way as St Mercurius had killed Julian the Apostate.[18] And when King Aðalráðr of the English heard this, he immediately turned back to England. And when he got back to the country, he sent word to all those men who were willing to take money to help him win back the land. Then large numbers flocked to him. Then King Óláfr came to support him with a great force of Norwegians. [15] Then they first of all made for London and up into the Thames, but the Danes were holding the city. On the other

[17] *hlenna hneigir*: 'oppressor of thieves', just king.
[18] This probably refers to the expedition of Þorkell the Tall to England in 1009–12 (Anglo-Saxon Chronicle, C version), in which Óláfr Haraldsson may have taken part. Sveinn Forkbeard came to England in July 1013 and died of sickness in February 1014. One of the Englishmen that knew this legend about St Edmund (the martyr, king of East Anglia, killed by vikings in 869) was Florence of Worcester. Cf. *Anglo-Saxon Chronicle* II 192. The legend of Julian the Apostate being killed by St Mercurius appears, among other places, in *Maríu saga* 1871, 72–73 and 699–702.

side of the river there is a large market town that is called Southwark. There the Danes had done a lot of work, digging a great ditch and placing inside it a wall of timber and stones and turf and keeping inside it a great troop. King Aðalráðr ordered a strong attack, but the Danes defended it, and King Aðalráðr achieved nothing. There were arched bridges there over the river between the city and Southwark so wide that wagons could be driven over them in both directions at once. There were fortifications, both strongholds and wooden breast-works on the downstream side that came up waist-high. And under the arches were stakes, and they stood down in the river just under the surface. And when the attack was made, then the army stood on the arches all over them and guarded them. King Aðalráðr was very worried about how he should win the bridge. He called all the leaders of his army to a council, and tried to work out a plan with them for bringing the arches down. Then King Óláfr said that he would try to bring up his force, if the other leaders would attack as well. At this conference it was decided that they should bring their army up under the arches. Then each one got his force and his ships ready.

CHAPTER THIRTEEN

King Óláfr had great hurdles made of withies and of wet branches and had wicker-work houses taken to pieces and had these put across his ships far enough to reach over both sides. Underneath he had poles put that were thick and high enough for it to be possible to fight from underneath and for it to withstand stones [16] if they were dropped on top. And when the army was ready, then they rowed forward along the river to attack from below. And when they got close to the arches, then both weapons and stones were thrown down on them, so heavily that nothing could withstand them, neither helmets nor shields, and the ships themselves were seriously damaged. Then many drew away. But King Óláfr and the force of Norwegians with him rowed right up under the arches and put chains round the posts that supported the arches, and they took hold of them and rowed all the ships downstream as hard as they could. The posts were dragged along the bottom right on until they were loose under the arches. And because an armed host was standing packed together on the arches, a lot of stones and many weapons were there, and the posts were broken below; as a result the arches collapse and many of the people fall down into the river, and all the rest of the force fled from the arches, some into the city, and some into Southwark. After this they brought an attack against Southwark and won it. And when the citizens saw this, that the river, the Thames, was won, so that they could not prevent the passage of ships up inland, then they became fearful of the passage of ships and gave up the city and received King Aðalráðr. So says Óttarr svarti:

10.	Further, you broke bridges, battle-snake's user,[19] daring in Yggr's storm,[20] of London; lands you have turned out to win. Much in demand in battle, moving were shields; warfare waxed with that, and ancient iron rings[21] burst asunder.	*Hǫfuðlausn* 8 *Skald* I 750 *1GT* 226

[17] And again he uttered this:

11.	You brought to the land and made landed, land-guardian,[22] Aðalráðr. This the counsellor of soldiers,[23] strengthened with power, owed you. Hard was the battle by which you brought Játmundr's kinsman[24] to enter a land of peace; the family's pillar[25] had previously ruled the country.	*Hǫfuðlausn* 13 *Fsk* 168 *Knýt* 99 *Skald* I 756

Again, Sigvatr tells of this:

12. [18]	It is so that the sixth battle— the swift prince offered the English Yggr's strife[26]—was where Óleifr attacked London's bridges. Frankish swords fought, but vikings defended the ditch there. Some of the troop had shelters on the Southwark flatlands.	*Víkingarvísur* 6 *Fsk* 168 *Legendary saga* 10 *Skald* I 542

CHAPTER FOURTEEN

King Óláfr stayed for the winter with King Aðalráðr. Then they had a great battle on Hringmara heath in Úlfkell's country. This realm was at that time ruled by Úlfkell snillingr (Master). There the kings were victorious. So says Sigvatr:

[19] *éla linns kennir*: 'user of the snake (sword) of storms (battles)', warrior.
[20] *Yggs veðrþorinn*: 'daring in the (stormy) weather of Yggr (Óðinn)', i.e. in battle.
[21] *íarnhringar*: 'iron rings', mailcoat, or swords.
[22] *láðvǫrðr*: 'guardian of land', king.
[23] *rekka rúni*: 'confidant of warriors', king.
[24] *Játmundar niðr*: 'kinsman of Edmund', Ethelred (Aðalráðr), father of Edmund Ironside.
[25] *áttstuðill*: (elsewhere *ættstuðill*): 'pillar of a family', leader of a clan, king.
[26] *Yggs at*: 'conflict of Yggr (Óðinn)', battle.

13.	Again he set a seventh time	*Víkingarvísur* 7
	sword-assembly[27] in motion	*Skald* I 545
	once more, in the land of Ulfkell,	
	Óleifr, as I tell the story.	
	All over Hringmara heath stood	
	—a host fell there—Ella's	
	kin,[28] where the keeper of Haraldr's	
	bequest[29] caused hard labour.	

[19] Also Óttarr says this about this battle:

14.	King, I heard that heavy	*Hǫfuðlausn* 9
	heaps of corpses far from the ships	*Skald* I 752
	your host piled up; Hringmara	
	heath with blood was reddened.	
	To the earth ere it ended	
	the English force, the landsfolk,	
	cowered before you in shields' clamour[30]	
	quickly, though many fled.	

Then the country again became subject to King Aðalráðr, but housecarls[31] and Danes held many cities, they then still controlled large areas of the country.

[20] CHAPTER FIFTEEN

King Óláfr was commander of the army when they made for Canterbury and fought there, right on until they won the place, slaying there many troops and burning the city. So says Óttarr svarti:

15.	Lord, you made a great onslaught	*Hǫfuðlausn* 10
	on the offspring of princes.	*Skald* I 753
	Gracious king, broad Canterbury	
	you coloured red[32] in the morning.	
	Fire and smoke played fiercely—	
	you framed, son of chieftains, victory—	
	on houses; I have heard you	
	harmed the lives of people.	

[27] *sverðþing*: 'sword-meeting', battle.
[28] *Ellu kind*: 'kin of Ella', the English.
[29] *arfvǫrðr Haralds*: 'guardian of the inheritance of (i.e. son of) Haraldr', Óláfr.
[30] *randa gnýr*: 'clash of shields', battle.
[31] *þingamenn* (probably an adaptation of Old English *þeningmenn* 'servingmen') no doubt means the same as *húskarlasveit* 'company of housecarls', a term used of the personal following of some Danish kings in England in Anglo-Saxon times.
[32] *rauðtu*: K (the main manuscript of *Hkr*), i.e. 'you caused to glow red with fire'. *ÍF* 27 follows the reading of the *ÓH* manuscripts, *tóktu* 'you captured'.

Sigvatr reckons this to be the eighth of King Óláfr's battles:

16. I'm aware that the war-confronter,[33]   *Víkingarvísur* 8
 to Wends dangerous, his eighth battle   *Fsk* 169 (1st half)
 —strong, the troop's protector[34]   *Legendary saga* 13 (1st half)
 attacked the fortress—fought there.   *Skald* I 546
 City reeves could not—sorrows
 on the splendid Partar
 bore hard—ban from Canterbury,
 their borough, Ǫleifr.

[21] King Óláfr was in charge of the defence of England and took warships round the coast and sailed up into the Nýjamóða—they found there a troop of housecarls—and held a battle there, and King Óláfr won victory. So says the poet Sigvatr:

17. The young king gave, eager,   *Víkingarvísur* 9
 Englishmen red haircuts.   *Skald* I 548
 And brown blood appeared
 on blades in the Nýjamóða.
 Now of battles I have numbered   *Fsk* 169
 nine, eastern fear-raiser.[35]   *Legendary saga* 13
 The Danish host died where
 darts flew most at Ǫleifr.

[22] King Óláfr then travelled widely round the country and received tribute from people, but otherwise laid it waste. So says Óttarr:

18. No power had people,   *Hǫfuðlausn* 11
 prince wide-famed, of English stock   *Skald* I 754
 to withstand you, unyielding one,
 where you took tribute.
 Men gave the gracious ruler
 gold not seldom.
 I heard of treasures at times
 taken down shorewards.

King Óláfr stayed there on that occasion for three winters.

---

[33] *víga mætir*: 'meeter of battles', warrior.
[34] *verðungar vǫrðr*; 'protector of the troop', warrior, king.
[35] *austan ógnvaldr*: 'causer of terror or battle', warrior, from the east (i.e. Norway); but Finnur Jónsson takes *austan* to refer to the Danish army (*Skj* B I 215).

CHAPTER SIXTEEN

But in the third spring King Aðalráðr died. His sons Eaðmundr and Eaðvarðr took over the kingdom. Then King Óláfr travelled southwards over the sea and then he fought in Hringsfjǫrðr and stormed a castle at Hólarnir, which vikings were occupying. He demolished the castle. So says the poet Sigvatr:

> 19. A decade, with a battle-wall blizzard[36]   *Víkingarvísur* 10
> in beautiful Hringsfjǫrðr,   *Skald* I 549
> was completed; the company
> at the king's bidding went there.
>
> [23] On Hóll a high building
> he had—vikings held it;
> they asked not afterwards
> any such luck—demolished.

CHAPTER SEVENTEEN

King Óláfr led his force westwards to Gríslupollar and fought there with vikings off Viljámsbœr. There King Óláfr was victorious. So says Sigvatr:

> 20. Ǫleifr, you fought, young sapling,[37]   *Víkingarvísur* 11
> the eleventh fight, where princes   *Skald* I 550
> fell; clear from that encounter
> you came, at Gríslupollar.
> I heard that in that battle, fought briskly
> by the town of Jarl Viljálmr
> the steadfast, destroyed were helmets—
> that story is told most quickly.

[24] Next he fought in the west in Fetlafjǫrðr, as Sigvatr says:

> 21. Fame's follower[38] the twelfth time   *Víkingarvísur* 12
> tooth of she-wolf reddened,   *Skald* I 552
> there fell a life-forfeit,
> in Fetlafjǫrðr, on people.

From there King Óláfr travelled all the way south to Seljupollar and had a battle there. There he won the city that was called Gunnvaldsborg—it was large and ancient—and there he captured a jarl who was in charge of the city, and who was called Geirfiðr. Then King Óláfr held a parley with the citizens. He imposed a ransom on the town and on the jarl for his release,

---

[36] *folkveggs drífahregg*: 'driving storm of the battle-wall (shield)', battle.
[37] *þollr*: 'tree', would normally be the base word in a kenning for a man.
[38] *tírfylgjandi*: 'follower of glory', glorious warrior.

twelve thousand gold shillings. The amount of money that he imposed was paid to him by the city. So says Sigvatr:

> 22. His thirteenth fight the Þrœndir's— *Víkingarvísur* 13
> that was woe to the fleeing— *Skald* I 552
> skilled lord[39] fought south in
> Seljupollar, a famed one.
> Up the king ordered them
> all to old Gunnvaldsborg,
> and the jarl to be captured,
> called Geirfiðr, in the morning.

[25] CHAPTER EIGHTEEN

After that King Óláfr led his force westwards to Karlsár and laid waste there, holding a battle there. And while King Óláfr was lying in Karlsár and waiting for a fair wind and planning to sail out to Nǫrvasund and from there out to Jerusalem, then he dreamed a remarkable dream, that there came to him a remarkable and handsome and yet terrifying man and spoke to him, telling him to abandon that plan, of going to distant lands.

'Go back to your ancestral lands, for you will be king over Norway for ever.'

He understood this dream to mean that he and his kinsmen would be king over the land for a long time.

CHAPTER NINETEEN

As a result of this revelation he turned back from his voyage and made for Peituland and laid waste there and burned a market town there called Varrandi. Óttarr speaks of this:

> 23. War-glad king, you were able *Hǫfuðlausn* 12
> young to ravage Peita. *Skald* I 755
> The painted targe you tested
> in Túskaland, ruler.

[26] And also Sigvatr says this:

> 24. The sword's mouth-reddener,[40] the Mœrir's *Víkingarvísur* 14
> master,[41] when he came northwards, *Skald* I 554
> fought his way where ancient spears
> were shattered, up by the Leira.

---

[39] *Þrœnda dróttinn*: 'lord of the Þrœndir', i.e. king of Norway, Óláfr.
[40] *malms munnrjóðr*: 'reddener of the mouth (edge) of the metal (sword)', warrior.
[41] *Mœra hilmir*: 'chief of the Mœrir', king of Norway.

> For warfare-Nirðir,[42] Varrandi—
> so named is the town, distant
> from sea in settled land—was
> set on fire, in Peita.

CHAPTER TWENTY

King Óláfr had been raiding in the west in Valland for two summers and one winter. By then thirteen winters had passed since the fall of King Óláfr Tryggvason. At this time there were two jarls in Valland, Viljálmr and Roðbert. Their father was Ríkarðr Rúðujarl (jarl of Rouen). They ruled over Normandy. Queen Emma, who had been married to King Aðalráðr of the English, was their sister. Their sons were these, Eaðmundr and Eatvarðr inn góði (the Good), Eatvígr and Eatgeirr. Ríkarðr Rúðujarl was son of Viljálmr[43] langaspjót's (Longspear's) son Ríkarðr. He was son of Jarl Gǫngu-Hrólfr (Walker-), who conquered Normandy. He was son of Rǫgnvaldr inn ríki (the Great) jarl of the Mœrir, as is stated above.[44] From Gǫngu-Hrólfr the jarls of Rúða are descended, and they for a long time afterwards claimed kinship with rulers of Norway and honoured them for this for a long time afterwards and were all the time very great friends of the Norwegians, [27] and all Norwegians found a welcome there who wanted one. In the autumn King Óláfr came to Normandy and stayed the winter there on the Seine and was welcomed there.

CHAPTER TWENTY-ONE

After the fall of Óláfr Tryggvason, Jarl Eiríkr gave Eindriði Styrkársson's son Einarr þambarskelfir (Bowstring-shaker) quarter. So it is said, that Einarr has been the strongest of all men and the best bowman there has ever been in Norway, and his strength in shooting was superior to that of all other men. He shot with an archery bolt through a raw oxhide that was hanging on a beam. He was better than anyone at skiing. He was a man of very great accomplishments and valour. He was of high lineage and wealthy. Jarl Eiríkr and Jarl Sveinn gave Einarr their sister Bergljót Hákonardóttir in marriage. She was a quite outstanding person. Their son was called Eindriði. The jarls gave Einarr very great revenues in Orkadalr, and he became the most powerful and noblest man in Þrœndalǫg, and he was a very great support to the jarls and a close friend.

---

[42] *víga Nirðir*: 'Nirðir (plural of Njǫrðr, a god) of battles', warriors, men (here, townspeople).

[43] All manuscripts of the separate *Óláfs saga helga* wrongly have Roðbert here. Cf. *Haralds saga ins hárfagra* (vol. I), ch. 24.

[44] vol. I, 123.

[28] CHAPTER TWENTY-TWO

Jarl Eiríkr was displeased that Erlingr Skjálgsson should have so much power, and he appropriated to himself all the royal property that King Óláfr had granted to Erlingr.[45] But Erlingr carried on the same as before, receiving all the land rents throughout Rogaland, and the inhabitants were often paying double land rents, for otherwise he laid waste the settlement. The jarl got little from fines and penalties as the bailiffs could not stay on there, and the jarl only went round collecting his dues if he had a large following. Sigvatr speaks of this:[46]

> 25. Erlingr treated the offspring *Flokkr* about Erlingr Skjálgss. 9
> of jarls[47] as the king couldn't, *Skald* I 640
> so that he awed them, kinsman[48] of Ǫleifr
> the worthy son of Tryggvi.
> Next the keen lord of land-dwellers[49]—
> life's good fortune that was
> for Úlfr's sire[50]—his second
> sister gave to Rǫgnvaldr.

The reason Jarl Eiríkr did not venture to fight with Erlingr was [29] that the man came from a large and great family, and was powerful and popular. He always kept a large following as if it was a royal court. Erlingr often spent the summer on raids and got himself wealth, for he carried on his established custom as to his grand style and munificence, though he had now fewer and less profitable revenues than in the time of his brother-in-law King Óláfr. Erlingr was of all men the handsomest and tallest and strongest, better than anyone at fighting and in all accomplishments most like King Óláfr Tryggvason. He was a clever man and energetic in everything and a very great warrior. Sigvatr speaks of this:

> 26. No one other than Erlingr *Flokkr* about Erlingr Skjálgss. 10
> of the landed men *Skald* I 642
> liberal, held more battles,
> though barren of following.[51]

---

[45] I 307.

[46] This and the following stanza are attributed to a poem by Sigvatr about Erlingr Skjálgsson, a powerful chieftain whose clashes with and eventual death at the hands of the king are related later in the saga. These two stanzas of general praise of Erlingr conclude the poem as it is reconstructed by editors.

[47] *jarla ótt*: 'lineage of jarls', jarls.

[48] *mágr*: brother-in-law.

[49] *búþegna harri*: 'lord of husbandmen', king, i.e. Óláfr Tryggvason.

[50] *Úlfs faðir*: 'Úlfr's father', i.e. Rǫgnvaldr.

[51] *stoð þorrinn*: 'deprived of support' (from the king?)

Generous, his courage he carried
to conflicts, to the utmost,
in many fights first to enter
the fray, and last to leave it.

People have always said that Erlingr has been the noblest of all landed men[52] in Norway. These were Erlingr and Ástríðr's children: Áslákr, Skjálgr, Sigurðr, Loðinn, Þórir and Ragnhildr, who was married to Þorbergr Árnason. Erlingr always had ninety or more free men in his following, and both winter and summer there was a set amount of drink served at the morning meal, and at the evening meal drink was served without restriction. But when jarls were in the neighbourhood, he kept two hundred[53] or more men with him. He never travelled with less than a twenty-benched ship [30] with a full complement. Erlingr had a great warship with thirty-two benches, though a large one at that. He took it on raids or previously planned expeditions, and it held two hundred[54] men or more.

CHAPTER TWENTY-THREE

Erlingr always also had thirty slaves in his establishment besides the rest of his household. He assigned day work to his slaves and gave them time after it and permission for each man who wanted to work for himself in the evening or at night, he gave them arable land to sow their own corn and to use the produce to enrich themselves. He set a price and redemption value on each of them. Many freed themselves in the first or second year, and all those that were any good freed themselves in three years. With the money thus gained Erlingr would buy himself other slaves, and some of his freedmen he put into herring fishing and some into other profitable occupations. Some cleared woodland and set up dwellings there. He enabled all of them to get on in some way.

CHAPTER TWENTY-FOUR

When Jarl Eiríkr had ruled over Norway for twelve winters, there came to him a message from his brother-in-law King Knútr of the Danes, saying that Jarl Eiríkr was to go west to England with him taking his army, for Eiríkr was very renowned for his warfare, having won victory in the two battles that had been the fiercest in the Northern lands, one being when Jarl Hákon and Eiríkr fought with the Jómsvikings, the other when Eiríkr fought with King Óláfr Tryggvason. Þórðr Kolbeinsson speaks of this:[55]

[52] A *lendr maðr* 'landed man' was one who held land in fief from the king. He was next in rank to a jarl in Norway.

[53] i.e. probably 120. The long (duodecimal) hundred is generally meant in early texts.

[54] i.e. probably 240.

[55] For Þórðr Kolbeinsson and his *Eiríksdrápa*, see vol. I, note 473.

[31]	27. Again praise is raised, where people praise-renowned, I heard, land's leaders sent to the ruler seemly in helmet, a summons to the jarl, that with greatest urgency— I guess what the king said that he wanted—once more must Eiríkr attend a friendly meeting.	*Eiríksdrápa* 11 *Skald* I 504

The jarl did not want to ignore the king's message. He left the country, leaving his son Jarl Hákon behind in Norway to look after the country, putting him in the charge of his brother-in-law Einarr þambarskelfir for him to see to the government of the country on Hákon's behalf, since he was then no older than seventeen winters.

CHAPTER TWENTY-FIVE

Eiríkr got to England and met King Knútr and was with him when he won London. Jarl Eiríkr fought on the western side of London. There he laid low Úlfkell snillingr. So says Þórðr:

[32]	28. The gold-tester[56] joined battle— the billows' horse Þundr,[57] famous, won to land in warfare— west of London, together.[58] Ulfkell got—there ran[59] the rain of Þorinn's heroes[60]— terrible blows, where blades hovered blue over *þingamenn*.[61]	*Eiríksdrápa* 14 *Knýt* 117–18 *Skald* I 508

Jarl Eiríkr was in England for one winter and fought some battles. The following autumn he was going to set out on a pilgrimage to Rome, but then he died of a haemorrhage there in England.

[33] CHAPTER TWENTY-SIX

King Knútr had many battles in England with King Aðalráðr of the English's sons, and the outcomes varied. He came to England in the summer that

---

[56] *gullkennir*: 'tester, spender of gold', generous man, i.e. Eiríkr.

[57] *grœðis hests Þundr*: 'Óðinn (god) of the stallion of the sea (ship)', seafarer.

[58] *lét gunni saman bundit*: 'had battle bound together', joined battle.

[59] *rann*: 'flowed'. This is the reading of J, where K and other manuscripts have *rǫnn* 'houses'.

[60] *Þorinn's rekka regn*: 'rain of Þorinn's (dwarf's) men (dwarves)', poetry.

[61] *þingamenn*: a band of Scandinavian warriors established by Knútr in England.

Aðalráðr died. Then King Knútr married Queen Emma. Their children were Haraldr, Hǫrða-Knútr, Gunnhildr. King Knútr made peace with King Eaðmundr. Each of them was to have half of England. In the same month Heinrekr strjóna (Profit) killed King Eaðmundr. After that King Knútr drove all King Aðalráðr's sons from England. So says Sigvatr:[62]

29.	And quickly Knútr	Knútsdrápa 2
	quashed or exiled	Knýt 120
	Aðalráðr's offspring,	Skald I 652
	each one, indeed.	

CHAPTER TWENTY-SEVEN

King Aðalráðr of the English's sons came from England to Rúða in Valland to their maternal uncles the same summer as Óláfr Haraldsson returned from viking raids in the west, and that winter they were all in Normandy and they formed a league together on the [34] understanding that Óláfr was to have Northumberland if they won England from the Danes. Then in the autumn Óláfr sent his foster-father Hrani to England to raise forces there, and Aðalráðr's sons send him with tokens of authority to his friends and relations, and King Óláfr provided him with a great deal of money to attract forces to join them. And Hrani spent the winter in England and gained the confidence of many of the ruling class, and the people of the country were more disposed to have native kings over them, but even so the power of the Danes in England had grown so great that all the inhabitants had become subjected to their rule.

CHAPTER TWENTY-EIGHT

In the spring they all returned from the west together, King Óláfr and King Aðalráðr's sons, arriving in England at a place called Jungufurða, going up ashore with their forces and on to the city. There they found many of the men who had promised them support. They won the city and killed many people. But when King Knútr's men realised this, then they assembled an army that soon became numerous, so that King Aðalráðr's sons did not have the numbers to withstand them, and saw that their best course was to withdraw and return westwards to Rúða. So King Óláfr parted from them

---

[62] Sigvatr's *Knútsdrápa*, in honour of King Knútr inn ríki (the Great), may have been composed after Knútr's death in 1035 (some of its stanzas are cited in *Fsk*, which refers to it as an *erfidrápa* 'memorial poem'), or during an earlier visit made by Sigvatr to Knútr's court in England in 1027 (see Matthew Townend in *Skald* I 650–51). Eleven full or part stanzas survive, including sts 29 and 90–91, 96–100 below. On the verse form and metre of this poem see note 252 below.

and refused to go to Valland. He sailed north along the coast of England right on to Northumberland. He landed in the harbour known as off Valdi and fought there with the citizens, and gained the victory and much booty there.

[35] CHAPTER TWENTY-NINE

King Óláfr left his warships behind there and set out from there with two cargo ships and he then had two hundred and twenty (260) men with full coats of mail and very select. In the autumn he sailed northwards across the sea and had very rough weather at sea, so that their lives were in danger, but since they had good troops and the good luck of the king, all went well. So says Óttarr:

30.	From the west, swift in slain-fire storm,[63] two cargo-ships you readied. Often you raced into risk, kings' bench-mate.[64] The strong current could have, if a crew less hardy had stood on board, on the billow embroiled the trading vessels.	Hǫfuðlausn 14 Skald I 759

And also thus:

31. [36]	You feared not the ocean, over a great sea you travelled. No mighty ruler of men gets more capable warriors. Oft tested, the ship tossed from it the towering torrent, until you sailed, son of Haraldr, close to the wind to mid-Norway.	Hǫfuðlausn 15 Skald I 760

Here it says that King Óláfr came to land in the middle of Norway. And the island where they came to land is called Sæla, off Staðr. Then the king spoke, saying it must be their lucky day, since they had reached land at Sæla[65] in Norway, and said it must be a good omen, turning out like that. Then they went ashore onto the island. The king stepped ashore with one foot where there was some mud, and stopped himself from falling with the knee of his other leg. Then he said:

[63] *valfasta veðrǫrr*: 'one quick in storm (battle) of the fire of the slain (sword)', warrior.
[64] *skjǫldunga þopti*: 'bench-mate of kings', ruler.
[65] The common noun *sæla* means 'bliss, happiness'.

'I fell there,' says the king.

Then Hrani said: 'You did not fall, king, you are now taking your stand in the land.'

The king laughed at this, and said:

'It may be so, if God wills.'

Then they went down to the ships and sailed south to Úlfasund. There they heard news of Jarl Hákon, that he was south in Sogn, and was expected in the north as soon as there was a fair wind, and he had one ship.

CHAPTER THIRTY

King Óláfr kept his ships inside the shipping lanes when he got south past Fjalir, and turned into Sauðungssund and hove to, lying with one ship each side of the sound holding between them a stout cable. Just at that moment Jarl Hákon Eiríksson rowed up to the sound with [37] a manned warship, thinking that they were two merchant ships in the sound. They row forward into the sound between the ships. Now King Óláfr and his men haul the cables up under the middle of the warship's keel and drew it in with windlasses. As soon as it took hold somewhere it rose up at the stern and dived down in front so that the sea flowed in over the bows, filled the warship and next it capsized. King Óláfr took Jarl Hákon out of the water there and all those of his men that they managed to catch hold of, but some they slew and some sank down. So says Óttarr:

32.	You seized, wealthy food-server of the sea-of-wounds' dark osprey,[66] Hókon's craft, its fine equipment, and the crew themselves. Young, you sought here, sater of the seagull of Þróttr's meeting,[67] ancestral lands that you owned; the jarl could not prevent that.	*Hǫfuðlausn* 16 *Skald* I 761

Jarl Hákon was taken up onto the king's ship. He was of all men the handsomest that people had seen. He had long hair and beautiful as silk, tied round his head with a gold band. He sat down amidships. Then King Óláfr said:

---

[66] *brœðir blágjóða bengjálfrs*: 'feeder of the dark osprey (raven) of wound-sea (blood)', warrior.

[67] *Þróttar þings mógrennir*: 'feeder of the gull (raven) of Þróttr's (Óðinn's) assembly (battle)', warrior.

[38] 'It is no lie about your family, what handsome men they are to look at, but you have now run out of good luck.'

Then Hákon says: 'This is not bad luck that we have suffered. It has gone on for a long time that victory has gone, now to the one, now to the other of us. This is also how it has gone between your and my kinsmen, that now these, now those have been defeated. I am yet hardly emerged from childhood. We were now also not in a good position to defend ourselves, having no reason to expect hostility. It may be that on another occasion it will go better with us than this time.'

Then King Óláfr replies: 'Do you have no suspicion, jarl, that now it has so come about, that you will from now on have neither victory nor defeat?'

The jarl says: 'That is for you to decide, king, for the time being.'

Then says King Óláfr: 'What will you undertake to do, jarl, if I let you go, safe and unharmed?'

The jarl asks what he would require.

The king says: 'Nothing else but that you leave the country, and so give up your rule and swear oaths that you will not fight battles from now on against me.'

The jarl replies, saying that he would do that. Now Jarl Hákon swears oaths to King Óláfr that he will never again fight against him and not use warfare to keep King Óláfr out of Norway or attack him. Then King Óláfr grants him and all his men quarter. The jarl took back the ship he had had before. The men row off on their way. The poet Sigvatr speaks of this:

33.	The great king, keen for glory, declared that he needed to seek in ancient Sauðungs- sund to meet with Hǫkon.	Víkingarvísur 15 Skald I 555
[39]	There the mighty monarch met the young jarl whose rank was second, best descended of all whose speech was Danish.[68]	

CHAPTER THIRTY-ONE

After this the jarl sets out from the country as hastily as he can and sails west to England and there goes to see his maternal uncle King Knútr, telling him all about how things had gone between him and King Óláfr. King Knútr gave him an exceptionally good reception. He took him into his household

---

[68] *á danska tungu*: lit. 'in the Danish-speaking [region]', commonly used of the Scandinavian world in general. This is the earliest recorded use of the expression (Judith Jesch in *Skald* I 556).

and gives him great power in his realm. Jarl Hákon now stayed a long time there with Knútr.

While they, Sveinn and Hákon, were rulers of Norway, they came to an agreement with Erlingr Skjálgsson, and it was included in it that Erlingr's son Áslákr should marry Jarl Sveinn's daughter Gunnhildr. The father and son, Erlingr and Áslákr, were to have all the revenues that King Óláfr Tryggvason had granted Erlingr. Erlingr then became an absolute friend of the jarls, and they confirmed this between them with oaths.

CHAPTER THIRTY-TWO

King Óláfr inn digri turns eastwards along the coast and held meetings with the landowners in many places, and many submit to him, but some object who were kinsmen or friends of Jarl Sveinn. King Óláfr therefore went hastily east to Vík and keeps his forces within the Vík and beaches his ships, then makes his way up inland. And [40] when he got to Vestfold, then many people welcomed him there warmly, those who had been acquaintances or friends of his father. There were also many family connections of his there around Foldin. In the autumn he went up inland to see his stepfather King Sigurðr, and arrived there early one day. And when King Óláfr gets close to the farm, then some workmen ran ahead to the farmhouse and into the living room. King Óláfr's mother Ásta was sitting in there and some women with her. The workmen then tell her about King Óláfr's coming and also that he could be expected there soon. Ásta gets up straight away and told men and women to put things to rights there as best they could. She had four women see to the arrangement of the living room and to deck it out with hangings and get the benches ready. Two men spread the straw on the floor, two put up the table, two set out the food, two she sent away from the farmhouse, two brought in the ale, and all the others, women and men, went out into the courtyard. Messengers went for King Sigurðr, wherever he was, bringing him his robes of state and his horse with gilded saddle, and the bit decorated with enamel and gems and gilded all over. Four men she sent in four different directions round the district inviting all the important people to come to her and partake of a feast, as she was holding a welcome banquet for her son. All the other people that were present she made put on the best attire that they had, and she lent clothes to those who did not have any of their own.

[41] CHAPTER THIRTY-THREE

King Sigurðr sýr was at that moment stood out in a cornfield when messengers found him and told him what was happening and also everything that Ásta was having done back at the farmhouse. He had many men there. Some were reaping corn, some were binding, some were driving the corn home, some were piling up ricks or into barns. But the king and two men with him went now to the cornfield, now to where the corn was being stacked. About his dress it is said that he had on a dark tunic and dark leggings, high boots also tied round his legs, a grey cloak and broad grey hood and a cloth over his face,[69] a staff in his hand with a gilded silver cap on the top which had a silver ring on it. This is said about King Sigurðr's character, that he was a great man for work and always looking after his property and farm and managed his farming himself. He had no interest in finery in dress and was rather taciturn. He was of all men who were then in Norway the most sensible and the richest in money. He was peaceable and unambitious. His wife Ásta was liberal and imperious. These were their children: Guthormr was eldest, then Gunnhildr, then Hálfdan, then Ingiríðr, then Haraldr.

Then the messengers said: 'These words Ásta bade we should convey to you, that she thought it was now very important that you should behave nobly, and requested this, that you should take more after the line of Haraldr inn hárfagri (the Fine-Haired) in disposition than be like your maternal grandfather Hrani mjónefr (Thin-Nose) or Jarl Nereiðr the Old, though they have been great sages.'

The king says: 'Great news you bring me, [42] and truly you bring it with great gusto. Ásta has made a great fuss before over people to whom she owed less duty, and I see that she has still the same tendency. And she will be devoting great zeal to this, if she causes her son to be sent on his way with the same munificence as she is now welcoming him in with. But it seems to me, if that is how it must be, that those who stake a lot on this business will be doing no good to their wealth or their lives. This man, King Óláfr, is striving against great odds, and he will bring upon himself and his undertakings the wrath of the king of the Danes and the king of the Svíar, if he continues on this course.'

CHAPTER THIRTY-FOUR

Now when the king had said this, then he sat himself down and had his footwear pulled off and put on cordovan (soft goatskin) leggings and fastened them with gilded spurs, then took off his cloak and tunic and clad himself in silken clothes and on top a fine woollen cloak,[70] girded himself with an ornamented sword, put a gilded helmet on his head, then mounted his horse.

[69] Probably to keep off the midges.

[70] *skarlatskápa*, a cloak of expensive foreign material, often but not always scarlet in colour.

He sent labourers into the surrounding district and got himself thirty men, well fitted out, who rode into the farmstead with him. And [43] they rode up into the courtyard in front of the living room, then he saw on the opposite side of the courtyard, where swept forward King Óláfr's banner and with it there he himself and with him a hundred (120) men and all well fitted out. People were also arrayed everywhere between the buildings. King Sigurðr welcomed his stepson King Óláfr down from his horse, and his troop, and invited him in to drink with him, and Ásta went up and kissed her son and invited him to stay with her, and everything, lands and troops, that she could give him should be at his service. King Óláfr thanked her heartily for her words. She took his hand and led him in with her into the living room and to the seat of honour. King Sigurðr got men to look after their clothes and give corn to their horses, and he went to his seat of honour. And this banquet was held with very great zeal.

CHAPTER THIRTY-FIVE

Now when King Óláfr had been not very long there, then it happened one day that he called to speak with him and to a conference his stepfather King Sigurðr and his mother Ásta and his foster-father Hrani. Then King Óláfr began to speak:

'So it is,' he says, 'as you are aware, that I am come to this country having previously been for a long time abroad. I and my men have had for our maintenance all this while only what we have gained by raiding, and in many places we have had to risk both lives and souls to get it. Many a man who was innocent has had to lose his property, and some their lives as well, at our hands. But foreigners have taken over the possessions that my father and his father and one after another of our family had, and that I have an inherited right to. And they do not consider that to be enough, but they have taken control of the possessions of all us [44] kinsmen who are derived in the direct male line from Haraldr inn hárfagri. They share a little of it out with some, but with some nothing at all. Now I shall make known to you what has been for a very long time in my mind, that I intend to claim my patrimony, and I go to see neither the king of the Danes nor the king of the Svíar to beg of them any favours, though they have now for a while declared what was the heritage from Haraldr hárfagri their own possession. I intend rather, to tell you the truth about it, to pursue my patrimony with point and edge and invoke the support of all my relations and friends and all those who are willing to adopt this course with me. I shall also so set about this claim that one of two things will result, that I shall gain possession of all that realm to govern that they deprived King Óláfr Tryggvason of, or that I shall fall here on my patrimony. Now I expect as regards you, my stepfather Sigurðr, and other men in the land who have an inherited right to kingdoms here according to laws established by Haraldr hárfagri, it will not take so very much to make you rise up to get rid of this disgrace to your family that you will not put everything you have got into supporting the one who is willing to be your leader in restoring our family line. But whether or not you are willing to show any manhood in this matter, I do know the temper of the people, that they would all be eager to escape their subjection to foreign rulers as soon as there was someone to help them do it. The reason I have raised this matter with no one else before I have done so with you, is that I know that you are a sensible man and will have some good ideas about how this purpose can be implemented from the start, whether it should first of all be discussed on the quiet with a few people present, or whether it must be made public straight away before the people. I have now somewhat reddened my teeth [45] on them when I captured Jarl Hákon, and he is now fled the land, and he gave me with oaths the part of the kingdom that he had previously ruled. I think we will find it easier to deal with Jarl Sveinn on his own than it was when they were both here to defend the land.'

King Sigurðr now replies: 'It is no trifling matter you have on your mind, King Óláfr. This plan has more of zeal than forethought behind it, as far as I can see, and to be sure it is likely that there will be a large gap between my cautious attitude and this big idea that you seem to have, for when you were hardly more than a child, you were already full of eagerness and irresponsibility to the full extent of your power. You are also well experienced in warfare now and have modelled yourself on the ways of foreign rulers. Now you must have taken this affair so far that it will be no good trying to hold you back. It is also to be expected that such things will figure largely with those who are men of any spirit, when King Haraldr's whole family and kingdom is on the way down. But I will bind myself by no promises before I know the attitude and intentions of other kings in Upplǫnd. But you have done well to let me know of this plan before you announced it openly before the people. I will promise you my good offices with the kings and also with other men of rank and the rest of the people. Also my wealth will be at your disposal, King Óláfr, for your backing. But I am willing for us to put this to the people only when I can see the possibility of some success, or when some support is available for this great enterprise, for you must not forget that a great deal is being taken on if you are going to contend with King Óláfr of the Svíar, and with Knútr, who is now king both in England and in Denmark, and great precautions need to be taken against them if it is to be successful. But I think it is not unlikely that you will find good [46] support, for the people are eager for change. It was the same before, when

Óláfr Tryggvason came to the country, that everyone was pleased at it, and yet he did not enjoy the kingdom for long.'

When the discussion had come thus far, Ásta began to speak:

'My attitude, my son, is that I am pleased with you, and will be the most pleased if your advancement could be as much as possible. I will spare nothing within my power, though you can look to me for little in the way of helpful counsel. But I would rather, if there was the choice, that you should become supreme king in Norway, even if you lived no longer in your kingdom than Óláfr Tryggvason, rather than the alternative, that you were no greater a king than Sigurðr sýr and died of old age.'

And after these words they broke up the conference. King Óláfr stayed there for a while with all his following. King Sigurðr served them at table on alternate days with fish and milk, and every other day meat and beer.

CHAPTER THIRTY-SIX

At that time there were many kings in Upplǫnd who ruled over shires, and most of them were descended from the line of Haraldr inn hárfagri. Over Heiðmǫrk there ruled two brothers, Hrœrekr and Hringr, and in Guðbrandsdalar, Guðrøðr. There was also a king in Raumaríki. There was also that one king who had Þótn and Haðaland. In Valdres there was also a king. King Sigurðr sýr arranged a meeting with the shire kings up in Haðaland, and Óláfr Haraldsson was at that meeting. Then Sigurðr brought up before the kings he had arranged the meeting with his stepson Óláfr's proposal, and asks them for both support and advice and consent, setting out what need there was for them to get rid of this subjection that the Danes and Svíar have imposed on them, saying that now there is a man available who will probably be able to [47] take the lead in this enterprise, setting out the many great achievements that King Óláfr has done in his wanderings and raids. Then King Hrœrekr speaks:

'It is true that King Haraldr inn hárfagri's kingdom has declined, since no one of his line is supreme king in Norway. Now people in this country have experienced various things. Hákon Aðalsteinsfóstri (foster-son of Aðalsteinn) was king, and everyone was well content with that. But when Gunnhildr's sons ruled over the land, then everyone got tired of their tyranny and injustice, so that people preferred to have foreign kings over them and be more independent, for the foreign rulers were always far away, and cared little about what people did, taking such tribute from the country as they determined for themselves. But when they fell out, King Haraldr of the Danes and Jarl Hákon, then the Jómsvíkings raided Norway. And then all the commoners and hosts of people rose against them and drove this warfare away. People then urged Jarl Hákon to keep the country from the king of the Danes and defend it with point and edge. And when he felt he was secured in his power by the support of the people of the country, then he became so harsh and demanding towards the folk of the country that people could not put up with him, then the Þrœndir themselves slew him and then raised to power Óláfr Tryggvason who was entitled to the kingdom by birth and in all respects well fitted to be king. All the commoners rushed into wanting to have him as king over them and to raise up anew the kingdom that Haraldr inn hárfagri had gained for himself. But when Óláfr felt that he was secured in his power, then no one was independent of him. He went at it with us petty kings to claim in a domineering way all the dues for himself that Haraldr inn hárfagri had received here, and some things even more despotically, and people were so far the less independent from him in that no one could [48] decide what god he should believe in. And so, since he was removed from the land, we have now maintained friendship with the king of the Danes and we have had great support from him with everything that we need to ask for, and independence and a quiet life within the country and no oppression. Now there is this to say about my attitude, that I am well content with things as they are. I do not know whether, even if a kinsman of mine were king over the land, my situation will be improved thereby in any way, but if not, I shall have no part in this enterprise.'

Then his brother Hringr spoke:

'I will make known my attitude. It seems to me better, as long as I have the same power and possessions, that a kinsman of mine should be king over Norway rather than foreign rulers, if our family could again rise up in this land. But this is my feeling about this man, Óláfr, that his destiny and luck will decide whether he is going to achieve power or not, but if he becomes sole ruler over Norway, then he will think he is better off who has the larger share to count on from him in his friendship. Now in no respect does he have a better chance than any one of us, but rather the less in that we have some lands and power to employ, but he has none at all. We are also no less entitled to kingship by birth. Now if we should want to become such great supporters of him as to grant him the highest rank in this country and help him to this with all our resources, why should he not then reward this properly and long remember it with kindness, if he is so great in manhood as I think and everyone claims? Now we shall take this risk, if I have my way, of confirming friendship with him.'

After this one after another stood up and spoke, and the outcome was that most were keener on confirming friendship with King Óláfr. He promised them his absolute friendship and improvement of their condition if he became sole ruler over Norway. They then confirm their agreement with oaths.

[49] CHAPTER THIRTY-SEVEN

After this the kings appointed a meeting. Then King Óláfr put before the people this plan and the claim that he has to power there, asking the landowners to accept him as king over the country, promising them in return ancient laws and to defend the land from foreign armies and rulers, speaking about it long and eloquently. He got good applause for his address. Then the kings got up and spoke to each other, and all of them pleaded this case and proposal before the people. This came about then in the end, that Óláfr was given the name of king over all the land and land was awarded to him in accordance with Upplǫnd law.

CHAPTER THIRTY-EIGHT

Then King Óláfr immediately began his journey and ordered banquets for himself, wherever there were royal residences. He went first round Haðaland, and then made his way north into Guðbrandsdalar. It went then as Sigurðr sýr had guessed, that so many troops thronged to him that he thought he would scarcely need half of them, and he had now three hundred (360) men. Then the banquets that had been arranged turned out to be insufficient, for it had been the custom for kings to travel round Upplǫnd with sixty men or seventy, and never more than a hundred (120) men. The king went round quickly and stayed just one night in each place. And when he got to the mountain in the north, then he set out on his way, got north over the mountain and went on until he came down from the mountain on the north side. King Óláfr [50] came down into Uppdalr and stayed the night there. After that he went through Uppdalr Wood and came out in Meðaldalr, requested a meeting there and summoned landowners to him there. Then the king spoke at the meeting and asked the landowners to accept him, offering them in return the same rights and laws as King Óláfr Tryggvason had offered. The landowners did not have the power to keep up a quarrel with the king, and it ended with them granting the king acceptance and confirmed this with oaths. But they had previously, however, sent information down into Orkadalr and also into Skaun, letting them know about King Óláfr's movements and everything they knew about him.

CHAPTER THIRTY-NINE

Einarr þambarskelfir had an estate and farmstead in Skaun. And when information reached him about King Óláfr's movements, then he immediately had a war summons sent round and sent in four directions calling together freeman and slave fully armed, with the command with it that they were to defend the land from King Óláfr. The summons went into Orkadalr and also to Gaulardalr, and the whole army assembled together there.

[51] CHAPTER FORTY

King Óláfr took his forces down to Orkadalr. He travelled very quietly and peaceably. But when he came out to Grjótar, he met there the gathering of farmers, and they had more than seven hundred (840) men. He drew up his troops in battle formation, for he thought the farmers would want to fight. But when the farmers saw this, they found everything less straightforward, for it had not yet been decided who should be their commander. And when King Óláfr saw this, that the farmers were in disarray, then he sent Þórir Guðbrandsson to them, and when he came, Þórir says that King Óláfr does not want to fight with them. He named twelve men, the most senior in their number, to come and meet with King Óláfr. And the farmers agreed to this and come forward over a certain bluff that was there, to where the king's troops were lined up. Then King Óláfr said:

'You farmers have now done well, so that I now have a chance to talk with you, for I will tell you this about my business coming here to Þrándheimr. This to begin with, that I know that you have already heard that Jarl Hákon and I met together this summer, and the outcome of our negotiations was that he gave me all the dominion that he had here in Þrándheimr, and that is, as you know, the Orkadalr district and the Gaulardalr district and Strind district and Eynir district. And I have here men as witnesses, who were there and saw the jarl and me shake hands and heard the words and oaths and all the terms that the jarl granted me. I wish to offer you law and peace, in accordance with what King Óláfr Tryggvason offered before me.'

He spoke long and eloquently, and the conclusion of it was that he offered the farmers two choices, the one to submit to him and grant him [52] obedience, the other to engage in battle with him now. Then the farmers went back to their troops and told them the result of their errand, then asked for advice from the whole host, which alternative they should take. And although they debated this for a while among themselves, their choice was to submit to the king. This was then confirmed with oaths on the part of the farmers. The king then arranged his travels, and the farmers provided banquets for his reception. The king then went out to the coast and ordered ships there for himself. He got a longship, one with twenty rowing benches, from Gunnarr of Gelmin. Another ship, one with twenty rowing benches, he got from Loðinn of Vigg. A third ship, one with twenty rowing benches, he got from Angrar on Nes. This farm had belonged to Jarl Hákon, but there was a steward in charge of it there who is named as Bárðr hvíti (the White). The king had four or five light ships. He also travelled fast and made his way in along the fiord.

CHAPTER FORTY-ONE

Jarl Sveinn was just then inland in Þrándheimr at Steinker and was having preparations for his Yule banquet made there. There was a market town there. Einarr þambarskelfir learned that the people of Orkadalr had submitted to King Óláfr. He then sent informants to Jarl Sveinn. They went first to Niðaróss and took an oared ship that Einarr had. They then went inland along the fiord and arrived late one day in at Steinker and delivered this message to the jarl, telling him all about King Óláfr's movements. The jarl had a longship that was riding with tents up by the town. Straight away that evening he had his wealth and his people's clothing and drink and food loaded onto the ship, as much as the ship would take, and straight away during the night they rowed out and came at dawn into Skarnsund. There they saw King Óláfr rowing in along the fiord with his troops. The jarl then turned in to shore off Masarvík. There was thick forest there. They put in so close to the rock that foliage [53] and branches reached out over the ship. They cut great trees and set it all on the off side down in the sea so that the ship could not be seen for the foliage, and it had not become fully daylight when the king rowed in past them. The weather was calm. The king rowed in past the island, and when they got out of sight of one another, the jarl rowed out into the fiord and right on out to Frosta, there putting in to shore. This was within his own dominions.

CHAPTER FORTY-TWO

Jarl Sveinn sent men out into Gaulardalr for his brother-in-law Einarr. And when Einarr came to the jarl, then the jarl tells him all about his dealings with King Óláfr and also this, that he is going to muster troops and go against King Óláfr and fight with him. Einarr replies thus:

'We shall go into this sensibly, get information about what King Óláfr is planning to do. We will spread it around that we are just doing nothing. Then it may be, if he does not find out about our mustering of troops, that he will settle down inland at Steinker for Yule, since everything is all ready for it there. But if he hears that we have mustered troops, then he will lay his course straight out of the fiord and then we shall have lost him completely.'

It was done just as Einarr proposed. The jarl went travelling round staying with farmers up in Stjóradalr. King Óláfr, when he got to Steinker, took charge of the provisions for his entertainment and had them loaded onto his ships and got hold of some transport ships and took away with him both food and drink and set off as fast as he could and sailed all the way out to Niðaróss. There King Óláfr Tryggvason had had a market town set up, as was written above.[71] But when Jarl Eiríkr came to the country, he set up at Hlaðir, where his father had made his chief residence, but he did not maintain the buildings that Óláfr had had built by the Nið. They had now, some of them, collapsed, and some still stood [54] but were rather uninhabitable. King Óláfr took his ships up into the Nið. There he straight away had things put to rights in the buildings that were standing, and had those that had collapsed rebuilt, and employed large numbers of men in this, and also had both the drink and the food carried up into the buildings, intending to stay there over Yule. And when Jarl Sveinn and Einarr heard this, then they made their own plans elsewhere.

CHAPTER FORTY-THREE

There was an Icelandic man called Þórðr Sigvaldaskáld (Sigvaldi's Poet). He had been a follower of Jarl Sigvaldi for a long time, and later on of the jarl's brother Þorkell hávi, but after the jarl's fall Þórðr was a trader. He met King Óláfr, when he was on viking raids in the west [in the British Isles], and entered his service and after that became his follower. He was still a follower of the king when these events were taking place. Sigvatr was Þórðr's son. He was being brought up by Þorkell at Apavatn. Now when he was almost a full-grown man, then he went abroad with traders, and in the autumn the ship came to Þrándheimr and the men took lodgings in the district. This same winter King Óláfr came to Þrándheimr, as was written just above. And when Sigvatr heard that his father Þórðr was there with the king, then Sigvatr went to the king, meeting his father Þórðr and staying there for a time. Sigvatr was at an early age a good poet. He had made a poem about King Óláfr and invited the king to listen to it. The king says he doesn't want poems to be made about him, saying he cannot listen to poetry. Then Sigvatr said:

34.	Hear my poetry, harmer	*Skald* I 701
	of the horse, dark, of awnings,[72]	
[55]	most noble, for I can make it;	
	you must have one poet.	
	Even if you reject altogether	
	all other poets' tributes,	
	great ruler, still I'll give you	
	glorification in plenty.	

---

[71] *Óláfs saga Tryggvasonar* (vol. I) ch. 70. Instead of the last four words, the *Separate Saga of St Óláfr* has: 'and buildings erected for a royal palace where previously there had been premises for a single household on Niðarnes.'

[72] *myrkblás tjalda drasils meiðir*: 'harmer of the dark, black (tarred?) horse (ship) of awnings', sea warrior.

King Óláfr gave Sigvatr as a reward for poetry a gold ring weighing half a mark.[73] Sigvatr became a member of King Óláfr's following. Then he said:

> 35. I accepted your sword[74] gladly,   *Skald* I 702
> assault's Njǫrðr,[75] and will not later
> find fault; that occupation
> is fine; it is my pleasure.
> You've gained a true retainer,
> tree of the lair of the serpent's
> blood-brother,[76] and I—a bargain
> for us both—a good liege-lord.

In the autumn Jarl Sveinn had charged the ship from Iceland half the land dues, as has been customary before, since Jarl Eiríkr [56] and Jarl Hákon had been entitled to equal shares of these dues as of others there in Þrándheimr. But when King Óláfr came there, then he charged his own followers, claiming half the land dues from ships from Iceland, and they went to to see the king. They asked Sigvatr for help. Then he went before the king and said:

> 36. Greedily demanding the gladdeners   *Skald* I 704
> of Gunnr's vulture[77] will call me
> if I ask now for cloaks;[78] already
> I've accepted sea's fire.[79]
> Of the landing-tax, lessener
> of the lair of the meadow-flounder,[80]
> allow the cargo-ship to escape—
> I've again made a steep demand—half.

[57] CHAPTER FORTY-FOUR

Jarl Sveinn, together with Einarr þambarskelfir, gathered together a great army and went out to Gaulardalr by the inland route and made their way out to Niðaróss, having nearly two thousand men. Some of King Óláfr's men

---

[73] A *mǫrk* was eight *aurar* (ounces).

[74] That is, became the king's retainer.

[75] *sóknar Njǫrðr*: 'Njǫrðr (a god) of battle', warrior.

[76] *látrs linns blóða þollr*: 'tree of the lair of the serpent's brother (dragon, whose lair is gold)', generous man.

[77] *Gunnar gamteitendr*: 'gladdeners of the vulture (eagle) of Gunnr (valkyrie)', warriors, men.

[78] i.e. land dues, paid in skins.

[79] *ægis eldr*: 'fire of the sea', gold.

[80] *engilúru látrþverrandi*: 'one who diminishes the lair (gold) of the meadow-flounder (snake)', generous man.

were out on Gaularáss looking after the horses. They noticed the army going down from Gaulardalr and brought the king information at about midnight. King Óláfr immediately got up and had the troops roused. They straight away went on board their ships and carried out all their clothing and weapons and everything they could manage to take with them, then rowed out from the river. Just then the jarl's troop came to the town. They then took all the Yule provisions and burned all the buildings. King Óláfr went out along the fiord to Orkadalr and disembarked from their ships there, then went right up through Orkadalr to the mountain and eastwards over the mountain to Dalar. It is told about this, how Jarl Sveinn burned the town at Niðaróss, in the series of verses that was composed about Klœngr Brúsason:[81]

| 37. | Burned were the king's buildings— a blaze, I think, felled the dwelling, half-finished, hard by the Nið itself; fire showered the host with soot. | *Flokkr* about Klœngr 1 *Fsk* 173 *Skáldsk* 98 *Skald* I 241 |

CHAPTER FORTY-FIVE

King Óláfr then went southwards along Guðbrandsdalar and from there out to Heiðmǫrk, receiving the maintenance due to him as he went over the midwinter season, but mustered an army when spring came, and travelled out to the Vík. He got a large force from Heiðmǫrk that the kings [58] provided for him. From there many landed men came. Ketill kálfr (Calf) at Hringunes took part in the expedition. King Óláfr also got troops from Raumaríki. His stepfather King Sigurðr sýr came to join him with a large company of men. They then made their way out to the sea and got themselves ships and set out from in the Vík. They had a fine and large force. And when they had fitted out their forces, they sailed out to Túnsberg.

CHAPTER FORTY-SIX

Jarl Sveinn musters forces from all over Þrándheimr straight after Yule and calls out a levy, getting the ships ready too. At that time there was a large number of landed men in Norway. They were many of them powerful and of such high descent that they were come from lines of kings or jarls not many generations back; they were also enormously rich. The kings and jarls who ruled the land were entirely dependent on these landed men, for it was in every district as if the landed men ruled over the class of farmers. Jarl Sveinn was

[81] Klœngr Brúsason is not referred to elsewhere, and nothing more is known of this series of verses (*flokkr*). In *Fsk* this verse is attributed to Þórðr Sjáreksson, whose *Róðadrápa*, a memorial poem for King Óláfr, is cited as stanza 101 below. His *drápa* on Þórálfr Skólmsson is cited as stanza 78 of *Hkr* I.

on very friendly terms with landed men. He found it easy to get troops. His brother-in-law Einarr þambarskelfir was with him, as were many other landed men, and many of those who the previous winter had sworn oaths of loyalty to King Óláfr, both landed men and farmers. They sailed out of the fiord as soon as they were ready and went southwards along the coast and picked up troops from every district. And when they got south off Rogaland, then there came to join them Erlingr Skjálgsson, bringing a large troop, and with him were many landed men; then they sailed with the whole force eastwards to Vík. It was towards the end of Lent when Jarl Sveinn made his way into the Vík. The jarl took the force in through Grenmarr and stopped by Nesjar.

[59] CHAPTER FORTY-SEVEN

Then King Óláfr sailed his force out along the Vík. There was then only a short distance between them. They were aware of each other on the Saturday before Palm Sunday. King Óláfr had the ship that was called Karlhǫfði. A king's head was carved on its prow. He had carved it himself. This figurehead was for long after used in Norway on ships captained by rulers.

CHAPTER FORTY-EIGHT

On the Sunday morning, as soon as it got light, King Óláfr got up and dressed, went ashore, then had a horn blown to summon the whole force to go ashore. Then he made a speech to the troops and tells everyone that he has now heard that Jarl Sveinn cannot be far away.

'We must now,' he says, 'prepare ourselves, for it will not be long before we encounter them. Let men now arm themselves, and each man get himself ready and into his place to which he has earlier been assigned, so that then everyone may be ready when I have the horn blown for our departure. Then let us all row together, no one is to set off until the whole fleet is on the move, and no one is to stay behind when I row out of the harbour, for we have no means of knowing whether we shall encounter the jarl where he is now, or whether they will come to meet us. But if we come across them and a battle begins, then our men are to draw our ships close to each other and be ready to tie them together. Let us hold back to begin with and be careful with our missiles so that we do not let them fall into the sea or throw them uselessly. But once battle is joined properly and the ships have been fastened together, then attack as hard as you can, and everyone do as bravely as he can.'

[60] CHAPTER FORTY-NINE

King Óláfr had a hundred (120) men on his ship, and they all wore coats of ring-mail and French helmets.[82] Most of his men had white shields with the

---

[82] See Falk 1914, 40, 162.

Holy Cross depicted on them in gold, but in some cases they were coloured with red or blue paint. He had a cross drawn on the forehead of all helmets in white. He had a white pennant; it was a serpent.

Next he had prayers said before him, then went aboard his ship and told the men to have something to eat and drink. Next he ordered a horn to be blown and the ships to sail out of the harbour. And when they reached the harbour where the jarl had been lying, then the jarl's troops were armed and were about to row out of their harbour. But when they saw the king's troops, then they began to tie their ships together and put up flags and got ready. And when King Óláfr saw this, then they launched their attack. The king made for the jarl's ship. Then battle commenced. So says the poet Sigvatr:

38.	A strong assault on men	*Nesjavísur* 2
	the sovereign made, advancing—	*Skald* I 559
	blood fell red on Róði's	
	ride[83]—into harbour against Sveinn.	
	Brave, the king who brought the meeting	
	about steered his [ships] ruthlessly	
	forward, while Sveinn's forces	
	fastened their ships together.	

[61] Here it says that King Óláfr went into battle, but Sveinn was lying there in the harbour. The poet Sigvatr was there in the battle. He composed straight away in the summer just after the battle the series of verses that are called *Nesjavísur*, and it tells there in detail about these events:

39.	It's known to me how the knower	*Nesjavísur* 3
	of nail-points of frost[84]	*Fsk* 174
	caused to be placed Karlhǫfði	*Legendary saga* 76
	close to the jarl east of Agðir.	*Skald* I 561

The battle was very fierce, and for a long time one could not tell which way it would go. Many fell on both sides, and large numbers were wounded. So says Sigvatr:

40.	There was no cause to sneer at Sveinn	*Nesjavísur* 4
	for the swords' din,[85] nor at	*Skald* I 562
	war-glad Óleifr for the onslaught-moon's	
	osprey's fine tempest,[86]	

[83] *Róða rein*: 'the strip of land of Róði (a sea king)', the sea.
[84] *odda frosts kennir*: 'experiencer of frost of spear-points (battle)', warrior.
[85] *sverða gnýr*: 'clash of swords', battle.
[86] *sigmána gjóðs hríð*: 'storm of the osprey (raven) of the battle-moon (shield)', battle.

> for each side had to aim for
> the other's maiming—never
> was the army worse placed—
> where warriors did battle.

[62] The jarl had greater forces, but the king had a picked company on his ship which had followed him on raiding expeditions and was fitted out so excellently, as was said before, that each man had a coat of ring-mail. They did not get wounded. So says Sigvatr:

> 41.   Teitr,[87] I saw, in the splendid   *Nesjavísur* 5
>   squad of the ruler—bitter   *Skald* I 563
>   sword-clash[88] set in—cold mailcoats
>   cover the shoulders of us two,
>   and my black hair hid under my Frankish
>   helmet in the spear-storm;
>   thus I knew us both, benchmate,
>   for battle to be fitted out.

But when the men began to fall on the jarl's ship, and some of them were wounded, then the crew at the gunwales thinned out.

CHAPTER FIFTY

Then King Óláfr's men made a boarding assault. The flag was then taken up onto the ship that was next to the jarl's ship, and the king himself went along with the flag. So says Sigvatr:

> [63]   42.   The gilded standard preceded   *Nesjavísur* 7
>   the splendid prince where, under banners, *Fsk* 175 (1st half)
>   we givers of the din of Gǫndul's   *Skald* I 566
>   garment[89] went on the ships, furious.
>   Then it was not as if, on the rope-stallion,[90]   *Skáldsk* 81
>   to these ruler's pay-receivers[91]
>   a maiden were bearing mead before the
>   metal weapons' greeting.[92]

[87] *Teitr* could be an adjective meaning 'cheerful', but here is taken to be the name of the poet's companion, in line with the use of the dual pronoun *okkr*. This personal address has led Finnur Jónsson and others to class this as an occasional verse rather than include it in the *Nesjavísur* sequence, as Russell Poole does in *Skald* I (563).

[88] *hjǫrdynr*: 'sword-din', battle.

[89] *Gǫndlar serks gnýs greiðendr*: 'providers of the din (battle) of the shirt (mailcoat) of Gǫndul (a valkyrie)', warriors.

[90] *strengjar jór*: 'horse of the rope, cable', ship.

[91] *heiðþegi*: 'receiver of payment', retainer.

[92] *malma kveðja*: 'greeting of metal (weapons)', battle.

There was a keen battle there and Sveinn's men fell fast, while some leapt overboard. So says Sigvatr:

> 43. Keenly we crowded, where the noisy *Nesjavísur* 8
> clash of weapons sounded — *Skald* I 568
> reddened blades split shield-rounds —
> enraged, onto warships.
> Where they fought, wounded farmers —
> fitted ships were captured —
> fell overboard; no few corpses
> floated out[93] by the land-spit.

[64] And also this:

> 44. Men coloured crimson — *Nesjavísur* 9
> clearly seen was that by *Skald* I 569
> sharers of sword-clamour[94] —
> our shields that white had come there.
> There I think the young ruler
> that we followed onto the ship advanced
> where swords — the blood-bird[95]
> a battle-draught[96] got — were blunted.

Then the casualties began to mount in the jarl's forces. Then the king's men attacked the jarl's ship, and they were on the point of boarding the ship. But when the jarl saw what a bad state they had got into, then he gave orders to the men at the prow that they were to cut the cables and get the ships free. They did so. Then the king's men put grappling irons onto the bow posts and held on to them. Then the jarl gave orders that the men at the prow should cut off the bow posts. They did so. So says Sigvatr:

> 45. Sveinn himself had the swarthy *Nesjavísur* 10
> stem-posts cut off quickly — *Fsk* 176
> the rowing had almost reached him, *Skald* I 570
> raising our hopes of plunder —
> [65] when to the raven's benefit — bodies
> the black osprey of Yggr[97]
> gained in plenty — the host had
> hewn the prows of the vessel.

---

[93] *út* 'out': many manuscripts of *ÓH* have *ǫrt* 'swiftly'.
[94] *hljóms hringmiðlandi*: 'sharer of the clamour of the ring (i.e. sword) (battle)', warrior.
[95] *blóðs svǫrr*: '(a species of) bird of blood', raven or eagle.
[96] *gunnsylgr*: 'battle-drink', blood.
[97] *Yggs svartr gjóðr*: 'Óðinn's black osprey', raven.

Einarr þambarskelfir had positioned his ship on one side of the jarl's ship. They then threw an anchor onto the prow of the jarl's ship and so moved themselves then all together out into the fiord. After that all the jarl's forces took to flight and rowed out into the fiord. Bersi Skáld-Torfuson was in the position in front of the stern decking on Jarl Sveinn's ship. And as the ship floated forward away from the fleet, then King Óláfr called out aloud when he recognised Bersi—for he was easily recognised, the handsomest of men and fitted out exceedingly well with weapons and clothes:

'Farewell, Bersi.'

He said: 'Goodbye, king.'

So says Bersi in the series of verses that he composed when he fell into the hands of King Óláfr and was sitting in shackles:[98]

46.	You bade this skilful expert in praise,[99] farewell, and we were able so to answer the active war-fosterer.[100]	*Flokkr* about Óláfr helgi 1 *Skald* I 791
[66]	Unwilling, we sold those words of the well-born offerer of fires of the barque-god's borderland,[101] as I bought them from the mailcoat's tree.[102]	
47.	I have seen the sore trials of Sveinn—the cool bright tongues of swords[103] carolled keenly—when in company we went forward. I shall never follow in the future a finer man, an offerer	*Flokkr* about Óláfr helgi 2 *Skald* I 792

---

[98] The Icelandic poet Bersi Skáld-Torfuson plays a part in *Grettis saga* (*ÍF* VII, 42), which refers to his friendship with Jarl Sveinn. His metronymic indicates that his mother, Skáld-Torfa, was also a poet. He is said in *Skáldatal* to have composed for Sveinn and for King Knútr inn ríki, but only these three verses survive attributed to him. According to the fragments of Styrmir Kárason's life of St Óláfr, Bersi accompanied Sigvatr on his later pilgrimage to Rome; on his way back Bersi learned of Óláfr's death, returned to Rome and died of grief there.

[99] *hróðrs hagkennandi*: 'skilful teacher (or understander) of praise', poet.

[100] *gunnar snarrœkir*: 'brisk cultivator of war', warrior (here, Óláfr).

[101] *knarrar hapts úthauðrs elda boði*: 'offerer of fires (gold) of the outlying land (sea) of the god of the ship (seafarer)', generous man (Óláfr). This follows the reading of Kock (*NN* §684) and *ÍF* XXVII. Russell Poole takes *trauðir hapts* together meaning 'reluctant for hindrance', without delay (*Skald* I 791).

[102] *brynju viðr*: 'tree of the mailcoat', warrior (here, Óláfr).

[103] *rekninga svaltungur*: 'cool tongues of (inlaid) swords', sword blades.

of Elgr's tempest,[104] out on
any terms by waves' stallion.[105]

48. I slink not so, swinger   *Flokkr* about Óláfr helgi 3
of the snake of wounds[106]—this year   *Skald* I 794
for you I'm making ready
an Áti's ski,[107] no small one—
[67]   as to jettison, generous
general, or then to tire of—
young, I learned to know there[108]
your foe[109]—my loyal allies.

CHAPTER FIFTY-ONE

Now some of the jarl's men fled up ashore, some sued for quarter. Then Jarl Sveinn's party rowed out into the fiord and they brought their ships together, and the leaders held a discussion together. The jarl sought counsel from the landed men. Erlingr Skjálgsson recommended that they should sail to the north of the country and get themselves reinforcements and fight again with King Óláfr. But since they had lost a lot of their men, nearly all of them were keen for the jarl to leave the country to go to his brother-in-law the king of the Svíar, and reinforce his troops from there, and Einarr followed this course, because he felt they did not have the resources to fight with King Óláfr now. Then their forces dispersed. The jarl sailed south past Foldin, and with him Einarr þambarskelfir. Erlingr Skjálgsson and many other landed men too, who did not want to abandon their inherited lands, went north to their homes. In the summer Erlingr kept a large following by him.

[68] CHAPTER FIFTY-TWO

King Óláfr and his men saw that the jarl had gathered his ships together. Then King Sigurðr sýr urged that they should attack the jarl and fight it out with them. King Óláfr says that he wants to see first what course the jarl adopts, whether they keep their army together, or the troops leave him. Sigurðr said it was up to him.

[104] *Elgs hríðboði*: 'offerer of Elgr's (Óðinn's) tempest (battle)', warrior. This is the interpretation of Bjarni Aðalbjarnarson in *ÍF* XXVII, but depends on reading *elgr* 'elk' as a *heiti* for Óðinn, among other difficulties. See Diana Whaley in *Skald* I (793) for other possible readings.
[105] i.e. ship.
[106] *sára linns sveigir*: 'swinger of snake of wounds (sword)', warrior (here, Óláfr).
[107] *Áta ǫndurr*: 'ski of Áti (a sea-king)', ship.
[108] i.e. among the poet's former friends.
[109] i.e. Sveinn.

'But it is my feeling,' he says, 'considering your character and ambition, that you will never be able to trust those great lords, accustomed as they are to be always absolutely opposed to rulers.'

And nothing came of the attack. Then they soon saw that the jarl's troops were dispersing. Then King Óláfr had them search through the fallen. They lay there a few nights and divided the spoils. Then the poet Sigvatr spoke these verses:

> 49. I declare, moreover, that very many   *Nesjavísur* 11
> messengers of war[110] who came southwards   *Skald* I 572
> will have, in this harsh battle,
> their homecoming to forgo.
> From the swart swimming-horse[111]
> sank many to the bottom
> joined to the sun;[112] it's certain
> Sveinn out there we encountered.

[69]
> 50. This year the wise Innþrœnzk[113] maiden   *Nesjavísur* 12
> will not jeer at our effort,   *Fsk* 176
> this I thought certain, though smaller   *Skald* I 573
> the size of the king's forces.
> The girl will deride rather
> the ranks who lunged forward
> with their beards[114] — we stained scarlet
> the skerry's land[115] — should she choose either.

And also this:

> 51. His strength swells, for this launcher—   *Nesjavísur* 14
> Sveinn, you learned this—of plank-steed[116]   *Skald* I 575
> the Upplendingar are eager
> to aid into kingship.

---

[110] *morðǫrr*: 'messenger of killing', warrior.

[111] *syndiblakkr*: 'black, dark horse of swimming', ship.

[112] *sunnu samknúta*: 'one joined to the sun'? This obscure phrase was interpreted tentatively by Finnur Jónsson as 'bone of the sun of the sea (gold)', man (*Heimskringla* 1893–1901, IV 124–25); Jón Hnefill Aðalsteinsson sees it as a jibe at the men of Þrándheimr as pagan sun-worshippers (1997, 126–29). See further Russell Poole in *Skald* I 573.

[113] *innþrœnzk*: 'of inner Þrándheimr'.

[114] *sækja framm skeggi*: apparently a mocking expression for 'fall to the ground face down'.

[115] *skers fold*: 'land of the skerry', the sea.

[116] *þilblakks sendir*: 'launcher of the plank-horse (ship)', sea captain.

This is evident: the Heinir
are able to do more than
drink ale of the army leader:
we make the corpse-snake's journey.[117]

[70] King Óláfr gave gifts to his stepfather Sigurðr sýr at parting and also to other leaders who had supported him. He gave Ketill of Hringunes a carvel,[118] with fifteen benches, and Ketill transported the carvel up along the Raumelfr and right on up to Mjǫrs.

CHAPTER FIFTY-THREE

King Óláfr kept watch on the jarl's movements, and when he learned that the jarl had left the country, then he travelled westwards along the Vík. Men then flocked to him. He was accepted as king at assemblies. Thus he went right on to Líðandisnes. Then he learned that Erlingr Skjálgsson had gathered large numbers of men. He did not delay then in Norðr-Agðir, since he had got a strong fair wind. He went as fast as he could north to Þrándheimr because he thought that all the main part of the land lay there, if he could get it under his control while the jarl was out of the country. And when King Óláfr got to Þrándheimr, then there was no uprising against him, and he was accepted as king there and established himself in the autumn there in Niðaróss and he made preparations for staying the winter there and had a royal residence built and founded Clemenskirkja there in the place where it still stands. He marked out sites for dwellings and gave them to householders and merchants or to others as he thought fit and who wanted to set up houses. He stayed there with a large following, because he felt he would not be able to rely on the Þrœndir's loyalty, should the jarl come back into the country. This was most obvious in the case of the Innþrœndir, and from them he received no dues.

[71] CHAPTER FIFTY-FOUR

Jarl Sveinn went first to Svíþjóð to see his brother-in-law King Óláfr of the Svíar and told him all about his dealings with Óláfr digri, and sought for advice from the king of the Svíar as to what course he should take. The king says that the jarl shall stay with him, if he wants to, and have what land he thinks fitting for him to rule over there.

'And otherwise,' he says, 'I shall provide you with sufficient troops to get the land back from Óláfr.'

The jarl took the second option, because that was what all those of his men wanted that were there with him, many of whom had extensive possessions in Norway. And while they were deliberating over these plans, then it was

---

[117] *hrælinns fǫr*: 'expedition, journey of the corpse-snake (sword)', battle.

[118] On the use of the term 'carvel', see note 148 below.

agreed that they should the following winter set out to go the overland route through Helsingjaland and Jamtaland and so down into Þrándheimr, for the jarl felt he could rely best of all on the Innþrœndir for support and help, if he went that way. But yet they decide to go first raiding in the summer to the eastern Baltic and get themselves some wealth.

CHAPTER FIFTY-FIVE

Jarl Sveinn took his troops east to Garðaríki and made raids there. He spent the summer there, and when autumn came he turned back with his troops to Svíþjóð. Then he caught a disease which led to his death. After the jarl's death the troops that had been following him went back to Svíþjóð, though some went off to Helsingjaland and from there to Jamtaland and then west over Kjǫlr to Þrándheimr, and there they tell the news of what had happened during their travels. Then the death of Jarl Sveinn was accurately reported.

[72] CHAPTER FIFTY-SIX

Einarr þambarskelfir and the force that had followed him went during the winter to the king of the Svíar and stayed there and were treated well. There were also many others there who had followed the jarl. The king of the Svíar was extremely displeased with Óláfr digri for having established himself in his tributary land and driven away Jarl Sveinn. The king threatened Óláfr with the severest retribution for this as soon as he could bring it about. He says that Óláfr will not be so bold as to take control of the land that the jarl had ruled. Many of the king of the Svíar's men agreed that this would be the case. But when the Þrœndir learned for certain that Jarl Sveinn was dead and that he was not to be expected back in Norway, then all the ordinary people switched their allegiance to King Óláfr. Many people then went out from Þrándheimr to see King Óláfr and became his followers, and some sent word and tokens that they wanted to serve him. Then in the autumn he went in to Þrándheimr and held meetings with the farmers. He was then accepted as king in every district. Then he went out to Niðaróss and had all the royal dues taken there and made preparations for spending the winter there.

CHAPTER FIFTY-SEVEN

King Óláfr had a royal residence put up in Niðaróss. A large hall was built there for his following with doorways at both ends. The king's high seat was in the middle of the hall and further in from him sat Grímkell, his household bishop, and after that his other clerics, and further out from him his counsellors. In the other high seat opposite him sat his marshal, Bjǫrn digri (the Stout), after that the guests.[119] If high-ranking men visited the king, they were suitably accommodated. Ale would then be drunk by fires. He appointed [73] men to offices as was customary for kings then. He had sixty men in his personal following and thirty guests, and he established their salaries and rules. He also had thirty housecarls[120] who were to perform such duties within the residence as were necessary, and for when they moved away. He also had many servants. There was also in the residence a large apartment where the king's followers slept. There was also a large room in which the king held meetings with his men.

CHAPTER FIFTY-EIGHT

It was the king's custom to rise early in the mornings and dress and wash his hands, and then to go to church and hear morning prayers and matins and then to go to meetings and settle people's disputes or announce anything else that he thought necessary. He summoned to come to him the powerful and the humble and all those who were wisest. He often had recited before him the laws that Hákon Aðalsteinsfóstri had made in Þrándheimr. He made laws after consulting the wisest men, abolishing them or introducing new ones as he thought fit. But the Christian law he established with the guidance of Bishop Grímkell and other clerics and devoted all his mind to getting rid of heathendom and ancient practices that he thought injurious to Christianity. It came about that the farmers agreed to these laws that the king established. So says Sigvatr:[121]

52. Occupant of the wave-oxen's afterdeck,[122] you can lay down laws of the land that shall be lasting for all mankind.	*Óláfsdrápa* 1 *Skald* I 614

[74] King Óláfr was a virtuous man, very moderate, of few words, generous and avaricious. The poet Sigvatr was there with the king at this time, as was said above, and other Icelanders. King Óláfr enquired diligently how Christianity was observed in Iceland. It then seemed to him that it fell far short of being satisfactory, for they said about the observance of Christianity

---

[119] *Gestir* were royal retainers of inferior rank.
[120] members of the king's bodyguard.
[121] This single half-stanza is traditionally believed to belong to a *drápa* by Sigvatr in honour of Óláfr. Flateyjarbók refers to Sigvatr among skálds who composed about Óláfr's *lagastjórn* 'law-making' (*Flb* II 226).
[122] *unnar eykja loptbyggvir*: 'inhabitant of the *loptr* 'raised afterdeck' of the draught-beasts of the wave (ships)', sea captain, (here) Óláfr.

that it was permitted in the laws to eat horseflesh and expose children like heathen people, and still other things that were injurious to Christianity. They also told the king about the many great men who were then in Iceland. Skapti Þóroddsson held the office of lawspeaker[123] in Iceland then. He enquired of the men who had the closest knowledge about the practices of many lands and directed his questions mainly to Christianity, how it was observed both in Orkney and in Shetland and in the Faeroes, and he discovered that it must fall far short of being satisfactory in many places. He often discussed such matters as these or spoke about law or the law of the land.

CHAPTER FIFTY-NINE

That same winter there came from the east, from Svíþjóð, messengers from the Swedish King Óláfr, and they were led by two brothers, Þorgautr skarði (Harelip) and Ásgautr ármaðr (Steward), who had with them twenty-four men. And when they came from the east over Kjǫlr into Veradalr, then they called meetings with the farmers and spoke to them claiming dues and taxes on behalf of the king of the Svíar. But the farmers discussed it together and reached agreement that they would pay what the king of the Svíar asked provided that King Óláfr did not claim land dues from [75] them on his part, saying that they were not going to pay taxes to both of them. The messengers went off and out along the valley, and at every meeting that they held they got the same replies from the farmers, but no money, then went out into Skaun and held a meeting there and again demanded taxes, and everything went the same way as before. Then they went into Stjóradalr and requested meetings there, but the farmers would not come to them. Then the messengers saw that their mission was getting nowhere. Þorgautr then wanted to turn back east.

'I do not think we have carried out the king's business,' says Ásgautr. 'I want to go to see King Óláfr digri, even though the farmers are referring their case to him.'

He got his way, and they went out to the town and took lodgings in the town. They went to the king the following day—he was then sitting at table—, greeted him, saying that they were travelling on the king of the Svíar's business. The king told them to come the following day. The next day, when the king had heard prayers, he went to his meeting-house and had the king of the Svíar's men called and bade them put forward their business. Then Þorgautr spoke and says first on what business they were travelling and had been sent, and afterwards how the Innþrœndir had responded. After that he requested that the king should give a decision as to what the outcome of their mission there was to be. The king says:

[123] President of the Icelandic parliament.

'While jarls were ruling this land, it was not surprising that the people of the country should be subject to them, because they were native to this realm, and yet it would have been more proper for the jarls to have been subject to and in the service of the kings who had a true right to rule here, rather than being subservient to foreign kings and rising up with hostility against the true kings and driving them from the land. But as for the Swedish King Óláfr, who is claiming Norway, I do not know what claim he has that is just, [76] but this we have in mind, what loss of life we have suffered from him and his kin.'

Then Ásgautr says: 'It is not surprising that you are called Óláfr digri. You use very inflated words in your reply to the message of such a ruler. You cannot have a clear idea of how hard the king's anger will weigh upon you, and has done upon those who had more power behind them than it seems to me that you have. But if you are going to hang obstinately onto the kingdom, then your best course will be to go and see him and become subject to him. We shall then support you in begging him to grant you this kingdom on a lease.'

Then the king says, choosing his words with restraint:

'I shall give you some alternative advice, Ásgautr. Return now to your king and tell him this, that early in the spring I shall set out eastwards to the boundary which in former times separated the realms of the king of Norway and the king of the Svíar. He can then come there if he wants us to reach a settlement with each of us having the realm that we have an inherited right to.'

Then the messengers turn away and back to their lodgings and got ready to leave, but the king went to table. Then the messengers went to the king's residence, and when the doorkeepers saw this, they tell the king. He told them not to let the messengers in.

'And I do not wish to speak with them,' he says.

Then the messengers went away.

Then Þorgautr says that he and his men are going to turn back home, but Ásgautr says he wants to pursue the king's business. Then they part company. Þorgautr then goes inland to Strind, but Ásgautr and his twelve men turn up into Gaulardalr and so out to Orkadalr. He is planning to travel south to Mœrr and carry on the business of the king of the Svíar there. And when King Óláfr realised this, then he sent his guests out after them. They found them out at Steinn on Nes, captured them and took them in to Gaularáss, set up gallows there and hanged them there where they could be seen from the fiord from the sailing route. Þorgautr [77] heard what had happened before he left Þrándheimr. After that he continued his journey all the way back to see the king of the Svíar, and tells him what had happened on their travels. The king was very angry when he heard this told. There was no lack then of inflated words there.

CHAPTER SIXTY

The following spring King Óláfr called out troops from Þrándheimr and set out to go to the east of the country. Just then a ship for Iceland was getting ready to leave Niðaróss. Then King Óláfr sent word and tokens to Hjalti Skeggjason and summoned him to come and see him, and sent word to the lawspeaker Skapti and the other people who had most say in the laws in Iceland, that they were to abolish the laws that he thought were most injurious to Christianity. At the same time he sent friendly greetings to the population as a whole. The king travelled southwards along the coast and stopped in every district and held meetings with the farmers. And at every meeting he had Christian law promulgated together with the regulations appropriate to it. Thus he straight away abolished in the people many bad customs and heathen practices, because the jarls had well maintained the ancient codes and laws of the land, but had let everyone do as they pleased with regard to following Christianity. The situation now had come about that in most places in the coastal settlements people were baptised, but Christian rules were unknown to most people, and among the inland valleys and the mountain settlements many places were entirely heathen, because as soon as the ordinary people became independent, then their minds were mostly full of the beliefs they had learned in childhood. But the people that did not want to abide by the king's commands about Christianity he threatened then with harsh treatment, both the powerful and the humble. Óláfr was accepted as king everywhere in the country at every parliament. No one spoke against him at them. When he was lying in Karmtsund, [78] messages passed between him and Erlingr Skjálgsson proposing that they should come to terms, and a peace meeting was arranged on Hvítingsey. And when they met, they discussed terms of settlement in person. It seemed then to Erlingr that he could perceive something in what the king said rather different from what he had been told to expect, since he put forward his claim that he wanted to have all the revenues that Óláfr Tryggvason had granted him, and afterwards Jarls Sveinn and Hákon.

'I will then become subject and a loyal friend to you,' he says.

The king says: 'It seems to me, Erlingr, as though you would not be any worse off accepting from me just as many revenues as you received from Jarl Eiríkr, a man who had inflicted on you the greatest losses of men.[124] But I shall have you made the noblest man in the land, even if I decide to assign the revenues according to my own preferences without accepting that you landed men have an inherited right to my patrimonies, and even if I have to purchase your service at many times its value.'

[124] Cf. ch. 22 above.

Erlingr was not of a mind to ask the king for any changes in this, for he could see that the king was not easy to influence. He also saw that there were two choices available, the one being to make no settlement with the king and take his chance on how it would turn out, or alternatively to let the king have it all his own way, and he opted for the second, though he found it very much against his inclination, and said to the king:

'That service will be of most advantage to you that I offer to you of my own free will.'

They brought their discussion to an end. Afterwards Erlingr's kinsmen and friends went to him and urged him to give way and act with wisdom and not with stubbornness.

'You will,' they say, 'always be the noblest of landed men in Norway, in both your achievements and family and wealth.'

Erlingr realised that this was healthy advice and that they were motivated by goodwill, those who were saying these things. He acts accordingly, submits to the king on the terms that the king was resolved [79] to dictate; they went their separate ways after that and were nominally in agreement. Óláfr went his way eastwards along the coast.

CHAPTER SIXTY-ONE

As soon as King Óláfr reached the Vík and this became known, then the Danes went away, those who held offices there under the king of the Danes, and they made for Denmark and did not care to wait for King Óláfr. But King Óláfr travelled in along the Vík and held meetings with the farmers. All the native people submitted to him. He then received all the royal revenues and stayed in the Vík the whole summer. He went on eastwards over Foldin from Túnsberg and all the way eastwards across Svínasund. Then began the land subject to the king of the Svíar. He had set stewards over this area, Eilífr gauzki (Gautish, from Gautland) over the more northerly part, and Hrói skjálgi (Squint-Eyed) over the more easterly part right on as far as the Elfr. He held the two sides of the Elfr, and a large residence on Hísing. He was a powerful man and mightily wealthy. Eilífr was also from a great family. When King Óláfr had brought his troops into Ranríki, then he called a meeting with the local people there, and the people that lived on islands or near the sea attended. And when the meeting was in session, then Bjǫrn stallari (the Marshal) spoke up and told the farmers to accept King Óláfr as had been done elsewhere in Norway. Brynjólfr úlfaldi (Camel) was the name of a prominent farmer. He stood up and said:

'We farmers know what boundary is the most correct one from ancient times between the king of Norway and the king of the Svíar and the king of the Danes, that the Gautelfr has determined it from Vænir to the sea, and from the north Markir to Eiðaskógr, and from there Kilir all the way north to Finnmǫrk; and also that some from various sides have encroached on the territories of others. The Svíar have for long periods held power right down to Svínasund, and yet, to tell you the truth, I know it is the desire of many men to support the idea that it seems better to serve the king of Norway, but people don't have the courage to follow this through. The rule of the king of the Svíar is both [80] to the east of us and to the south, and it is likely that the king of Norway will soon go to the north of the country, where the main strength of the country lies, and we will not then have the resources to carry on a dispute with the Gautar. Now it is for the king to find a viable way forward for us. We would be very happy to become his subjects.'

Now in the evening after the meeting Brynjólfr was entertained by the king, and the next day as well, and they discussed many things privately between themselves. Then the king travelled eastwards along the Vík. And when Eilífr heard that the king was there, then he had a watch kept on his movements. Eilífr had thirty men with him, men from his district. He was in the district higher up by the forests and had assembled a body of farmers there. Many farmers went to see King Óláfr, and some sent messages of friendship to him. Then men passed between King Óláfr and Eilífr, and farmers begged both of them for a long time to make an arrangement for a meeting between themselves and agree on peace in some way, telling Eilífr that they could expect from the king, if his demands were not complied with, that there would be a prospect of harsh treatment from him, and declared that Eilífr should not lack support. It was then decided that they should come down and hold a meeting with the farmers and the king. And then the king sent Þórir langi (the Long), the leader of his guests, in a party of twelve in all, to Brynjólfr. They had coats of mail under their tunics and hoods over their helmets. The next day farmers came down with Eilífr in large numbers. Brynjólfr was then there in his troop with Þórir in his party. The king positioned his ships round where there was a rock that came out into the sea. He went ashore there with his troop, sat down on the rock, but there was level ground on the landward side, and the gathering of farmers was there, while Eilífr's men stood up within a wall of shields in front of him. Bjǫrn stallari spoke long and eloquently on behalf of the king. And when he sat down, then Eilífr stood up and began a speech, and at that moment Þórir langi stood up and drew [81] his sword and struck at Eilífr on the neck so that his head was cut off. Then all the gathering of farmers leapt up, but the Gautish men took to their heels. Þórir and his men killed a few of them. But when the crowd calmed down and the uproar abated, then the king stood up and said that the farmers should sit down. They did so. Much was said there, but in the end it came about that the farmers submitted to the king and consented to be ruled by him, and he promised them in return not to desert them and to remain there until he and King Óláfr of the Svíar had settled their differences one way or another. After that King Óláfr subjected to himself the more northerly part of the district and in the summer travelled all the way to the Elfr. He received all the royal dues along the coast and over the islands. And when the summer was drawing to a close, he turned back northwards into the Vík and took his ships up along the Raumelfr. There is a waterfall there that is called Sarpr. A headland goes out into the river up to the waterfall from the north. There King Óláfr had a wall built across the headland of stones and turf and timber and a ditch dug along the outside and built there a great earth fortress, and within the fortress he established a market town. He had a royal residence set up there and a St Mary's church built. He also had sites marked out there for other dwellings and got people to set up homes there. In the autumn he had provisions necessary for winter quarters brought there, and stayed there during the winter with a large following, and kept his men in all the districts. He banned all exports from the Vík up into Gautland, of both herring and salt. The Gautar found it hard to do without them. He held a great Yule[125] feast, inviting many leading farmers from surrounding districts to stay with him.

[82] CHAPTER SIXTY-TWO

There was a man called Eyvindr úrarhorn (Aurochs Horn) whose family came from Austr-Agðir. He was an important man and from a powerful family, spending every summer raiding, going sometimes over the sea to the west, sometimes to the eastern Baltic or south to Frísland. He had a ship with twenty benches, a cruiser (*snekkja*) and a well manned one. He had been at Nesjar and supported King Óláfr. And when they parted from each other there, then the king promised him his friendship, and Eyvindr the king his support, wherever he should request it. Eyvindr stayed the winter at a Yule feast with King Óláfr, and received good gifts at it from him. Also with him there at that time was Brynjólfr úlfaldi, and he got from the king as a Yule present a gold-ornamented sword and the farm known as Vettaland as well, and that is a very important manorial estate. Brynjólfr composed a verse about the gifts, and this is the conclusion of it:

> 53. The sovereign gave me *Skald* I 800
> a sword and Vettaland.

---

[125] As usual in Old Icelandic prose, Jól. Although originally the name of a pagan feast, this word has by now been fully Christianised and means Christmas.

Then the king gave him the title of landed man,[126] and Brynjólfr was always a very great friend of the king.

CHAPTER SIXTY-THREE

That winter Þrándr hvíti (the White) went from Þrándheimr east to Jamtaland to collect tax on behalf of King Óláfr digri. And when he had gathered the tax together, then the king of the Svíar's men came there and killed Þrándr and all twelve men of his party and took the tax and brought it to the king of the Svíar. King Óláfr heard about this, and he was displeased.

[83] CHAPTER SIXTY-FOUR

King Óláfr had Christian laws proclaimed round the Vík in the same way as in the north of the country and progressed well, for the people of the Vík were much better acquainted with Christian practices than the people in the north of the country, since both winter and summer there were large numbers of merchants there, both Danish and Saxon. The people of the Vík also went in for trading voyages to England and Saxland and Flæmingjaland or Denmark, while some were on viking expeditions and spent their winters in Christian lands.

CHAPTER SIXTY-FIVE

In the spring King Óláfr sent word that Eyvindr was to come to him. They spoke for a long time in private. Soon after this Eyvindr set off on a viking expedition. He sailed south along the Vík and came to land in Eikreyjar out from Hísing. There he learned that Hrói skjálgi had travelled north to Orðost and had there collected contributions to a defence force and land dues, and he was now expected back from the north. Then Eyvindr rowed in to Haugasund, and Hrói was just then rowing from the north, and they met there in the strait and fought together. There Hrói fell and nearly thirty men, but Eyvindr took all the goods that Hrói had had. Eyvindr then went to the eastern Baltic and was there on a viking expedition during the summer.

CHAPTER SIXTY-SIX

There was a man called Guðleikr gerzki (from Garðaríki). His family was from Agðir. He was a trader and a great merchant, wealthy and carrying out trading trips to various lands. He frequently went east to Garðaríki and he was for that reason often called [84] Guðleikr gerzki (from Garðaríki). That spring Guðleikr got his ship ready and was planning to go east to Garðar

---

[126] See note 52 above.

in the summer. King Óláfr sent him word that he wants to see him. And when Guðleikr came to him, the king tells him that he wants to enter into partnership with him, asking him to buy him valuables that are difficult to obtain in that country. Guðleikr says this arrangement shall be under the king's management. Then the king has money paid over to him, as much as he sees fit. In the summer Guðleikr went to the eastern Baltic. They lay for a while off Gotland. Then it happened as it often does, that not everyone kept their mouths shut, and the people of the country found out that on this ship was a partner of Óláfr digri. In the summer Guðleikr went to the eastern Baltic to Hólmgarðr and there bought splendidly fine cloths that he intended to be for the king for his robes of state, and also expensive furs and and an excellent table service as well. In the autumn, when Guðleikr returned from the east, then he had a contrary wind, and they lay for a very long time off Eyland. Þorgautr skarði had taken note of Guðleikr's travels. He came upon them there with a longship and fought with them. They defended themselves for a long time, but because the difference in numbers was so great, Guðleikr then fell and many of his crew, and many were wounded. Þorgautr took all their wealth and King Óláfr's valuables. Þorgautr and his men shared out all their booty equally, but he says that the king of the Svíar was to have the valuable items.

'And that,' he says, 'will count as a part of the tribute that he is owed from Norway.'

Þorgautr then went east to Svíþjóð. The news of these events spread quickly. Eyvindr úrarhorn came shortly afterwards to Eyland. And when he hears about this, then he sails eastwards after Þorgautr and his party, and they meet in Svíasker and fought. There Þorgautr fell and most of his troop, or else they leapt into the sea. Then Eyvindr took all the wealth that they had taken from Guðleikr, and also King Óláfr's valuables. Eyvindr [85] went back to Norway in the autumn. He then brought the king his valuables. The king thanked him warmly for his expedition and then again once more promised him his friendship. Now King Óláfr had been king in Norway for three winters.

CHAPTER SIXTY-SEVEN

That same summer King Óláfr made an expedition by sea and then again went east to the Elfr and lay there for a long time during the summer. Then messages passed between King Óláfr and Jarl Rǫgnvaldr and the jarl's wife Ingibjǫrg Tryggvadóttir. She set about supporting King Óláfr with all her energy. She was very keen indeed on this. There were two reasons for this, she and King Óláfr were closely related, and secondly, she could never get out of her mind about the king of the Svíar that he had been there at the fall of her brother Óláfr Tryggvason, and for that reason thought he had a claim to rule over Norway. As a result of her persuasive arguments the jarl became very inclined to friendship with King Óláfr. So it came about that the king and the jarl arranged to have a conference with each other, meeting by the Elfr and discussing many things there, and especially about the relations between the king of Norway and the king of the Svíar, and they both said this, which was true, that for both the people of the Vík and for the Gautar it was very damaging to the land that there should not be freedom to trade between their countries, and finally they established a truce between themselves until the next summer. They exchanged gifts at parting and made professions of friendship. Then the king went [86] north to the Vík, and he had now all the royal dues as far as the Elfr, and all the people of the land had now submitted to him. The Swedish King Óláfr conceived such great dislike of Óláfr Haraldsson that no one was to dare to call him by his proper name in the king's hearing. They called him the fat man and were always very critical of him when he was mentioned.

CHAPTER SIXTY-EIGHT

The farmers in the Vík discussed among themselves that the only thing to be done was for the kings to make a settlement and peace between themselves, and considered that they were in a bad state if the kings were going to be at war with each other, but no one dared to bring this complaint boldly before the king. Then they asked Bjǫrn stallari to do it, that he should put this request to the king that he should send men to see the king of the Svíar to offer terms on his part. Bjǫrn was reluctant for this and declined, but then, at the entreaty of many of his friends, he eventually promised to discuss this with the king, but said he had a strong feeling that the king would not lightly take to the idea of giving way in anything to the king of the Svíar. That summer Hjalti Skeggjason came abroad from Iceland in accordance with King Óláfr's message. He went straight away to see King Óláfr, and the king welcomed him, inviting Hjalti to stay with him and assigning him to a place next to Bjǫrn stallari, and they were table companions. A close friendship soon developed between them. On one occasion, when King Óláfr was holding a meeting with his men and with farmers and they were deciding political questions, then Bjǫrn stallari said:

'What plan do you have, king, as regards the hostilities that we have here between you and the king of the Svíar? Each side has now lost men at the hands of the other, but no decision has been made now any more than before as to how much each side is to have of the realm. You have stayed here in the Vík [87] one winter and two summers and you have turned your back on all the land north of here. Now people are getting tired of staying here, those who have possessions or patrimony in the north of the country. It is now the wish of landed men and of other of your followers and also of the farmers, that this matter should be settled in some way, and since truce and peace have now been established with the jarl and the Vestr-Gautar, who are our neighbours here, so people think the best thing to do is that you should send men to the king of the Svíar to offer terms of settlement on your part, and many men who are with the king of the Svíar will support this strongly, since it will be to the advantage of both parties, both those who live in this country and those who live in that.'

People responded to Bjǫrn's speech with great applause. Then the king said:

'This plan, Bjǫrn, that you have put forward here, it is most proper that you should have put it forward for yourself, and you shall undertake this mission. You will be the one to benefit if it turns out well, but if it proves to lead to deadly danger, then you yourself will be largely to blame. It is also your office to announce in public what I wish to have said.'

Then the king got up and went to church and had High Mass sung before him. Then he went to table.

The next day Hjalti said to Bjǫrn:

'Why are you downcast, man? Are you ill or upset at someone?'

Bjǫrn tells then what he and the king had said, and declares that this is a fatal mission. Hjalti says:

'That is how it is to serve kings, that such men have great honour and are thought more highly of than other men, but they frequently find themselves in mortal danger, and they have to be content with both. Kings' undertakings can be very propitious. Great benefit may result from this expedition now, if it succeeds.'

Bjǫrn said: 'You make light of the expedition. Would you like to go with me, for the king said I might take my comrades with me on the journey?'

Hjalti says: 'Certainly I shall go, if you wish it, for I shall find it difficult to get another such table companion if we part.'

[88] CHAPTER SIXTY-NINE

A few days later, when King Óláfr was at a meeting, Bjǫrn turned up in a party of twelve. He then tells the king that they were ready to set out on their mission and their horses were standing outside saddled.

'I now want to know,' says Bjǫrn, 'with what message I am to go, or what plan you are proposing for us.'

The king says: 'You shall bring to the king of the Svíar these words of mine, that I am willing to establish peace between our countries as far as the boundaries that Óláfr Tryggvason held before me, and it must be confirmed with undertakings that neither may go beyond them. But as to the lives that have been lost, no one need raise that issue, if agreement is to be reached, because the king of the Svíar cannot compensate us with money for the loss of men that we have suffered from the Svíar.'

Then the king stood up and went out with Bjǫrn's party. Then he brought out an ornamented sword and a gold finger ring and gave these to Bjǫrn.

'I give you this sword. Jarl Rǫgnvaldr gave it to me this summer. You shall go to him and bring him these words of mine, that he is to provide counsel and his support for you to achieve this mission. I think that you will have done well if you hear the king of the Svíar's words, and he says one thing or the other, yes or no. But give this gold ring to Jarl Rǫgnvaldr. He will recognise these tokens.'

Hjalti went up to the king and took his leave.

'And it is very important to us, king, that you give this expedition your blessing.'

And he bade him au revoir. The king asked where he would be going.

'With Bjǫrn,' he says.

The king says: 'It will be a great benefit to this expedition, that you are going with them, for you have often proved lucky. Be sure of this, that I am going to set my whole heart on this, if that makes any difference, and give you and your whole party my blessing.'

Bjǫrn and his party rode off on their way and came to Jarl Rǫgnvaldr's court. They were welcomed there. Bjǫrn was a renowned man, [89] known to many people by both sight and voice, to everyone who had seen King Óláfr, for Bjǫrn stood up at every assembly and announced the king's business. The jarl's wife, Ingibjǫrg, went up to Hjalti and embraced him. She recognised him, because she had been with her brother Óláfr Tryggvason while Hjalti was there. And Hjalti could claim kinship between the king and Hjalti's wife Vilborg. The two were brothers, sons of Víkinga-Kári (a landed man[127] on Vǫrs), Eiríkr Bjóðaskalli (Baldy of Bjóðar), King Óláfr Tryggvason's mother Ástríðr's father, and Bǫðvarr, Vilborg's father Gizurr hvíti's (the White's) mother Álof's father.

Now they stayed there with good entertainment. One day Bjǫrn and his party went to have a discussion with the jarl and Ingibjǫrg. Then Bjǫrn delivers his message and shows the jarl his tokens. The jarl asks:

'What have you done, Bjǫrn, to make the king want your death? It is the less possible for you to succeed with this mission, in that I think that there can be no one who speaks these words before the king of the Svíar who will

---

[127] See note 52 above.

get away unpunished. King Óláfr of the Svíar is much too high and mighty for anyone to be able to make speeches to his face that are contrary to his way of thinking.'

Then Bjǫrn says: 'I have not happened to do anything to cause King Óláfr to be angry with me, but there is many an undertaking he has planned both for himself and for his followers that will seem hazardous as to how it will turn out for those who are very timid, but all his plans up to now have turned out fortunately, and we expect it to carry on that way. Now this, jarl, I tell you truly, that I am going to see the king of the Svíar and not turn back before I have made him listen to every word that King Óláfr has asked me to bring to his ears, unless death prevent me or I am hindered so that I cannot proceed. That is what I shall do, whether you [90] want to pay any heed to the king's message or not.'

Then said Ingibjǫrg: 'I shall soon make my opinion known, that I wish you, jarl, to devote your whole mind to backing King Óláfr's message, so that this mission to the king of the Svíar may be fulfilled, however he may wish to respond to it. Though it incur the anger of the king of the Svíar or the loss of all our possessions or power, yet I will much rather risk that than that it should get around that you are ignoring King Óláfr's message out of fear of the king of the Svíar. You have the birth and the support of your kinfolk and all the resolution you need to have the freedom here in the Swedish realm to say anything you want that is honourable and everyone will consider worth listening to, whether many people or few, powerful men or humble are listening, even if the king himself is listening.'

The jarl replies: 'It is not difficult to see what you are urging. Now it may be that you will have your way in this, so that I shall promise the king's men to support them so that they manage to present their mission to the king of the Svíar, whether the king likes it or not. But I will have my plans carried out as to what procedure shall be followed, and I am not going rush into it with the recklessness of Bjǫrn or anyone else in such a problematic affair. I want them to stay with me until such time as seems to me something like most propitious for this mission to have some chance of success.'

And when the jarl had revealed that he would support them in this affair and put his backing behind it, then Bjǫrn thanked him warmly and said he was willing to abide by his advice. Bjǫrn and his party stayed with the jarl for a very long time.

CHAPTER SEVENTY

Ingibjǫrg was exceptionally good to them. Bjǫrn spoke of his business with her and felt unhappy that his journey should be delayed so long. They and Hjalti often discussed [91] it all together. Then Hjalti said:

'I shall go to the king, if you like. I am not a Norwegian person. The Svíar will have nothing against me. I have heard that there are Icelandic men there who are treated well, acquaintances of mine, the king's poets, Gizurr svarti (the Black) and Óttarr svarti. I shall then make enquiries, see what I can find out about the king of the Svíar, whether this matter can be as hopeless as it is now considered, or whether there are other possibilities. I will invent such reasons for going as I find suitable.'

This seemed to Ingibjǫrg and Bjǫrn a very smart idea, and they decided to settle on this among themselves. Ingibjǫrg then makes arrangements for Hjalti's journey and provided him with two Gautish men and instructed them that they should accompany him and be at his disposal for any service and also if he wanted to send them anywhere. Ingibjǫrg gave him for his expenses twenty marks by weight. She sent word and tokens with him to King Óláfr's daughter Ingigerðr that she was to devote every care to his affairs, whatever he might ask of her for his needs. Hjalti set out as soon as he was ready. And when he came to King Óláfr, then he soon met the poets Gizurr and Óttarr, and they were very pleased to see him and they immediately went with him before the king and they tell him that a person had arrived there who was a countryman of theirs and was a man of the highest regard there in that country, and bade the king that he should welcome him. The king then told them to take him and his companions into their companionship. And when Hjalti had stayed there for some time and made himself known to people, then he was highly thought of by everyone. The poets [92] were often in the king's presence, for they were bold of speech. They often sat during the daytime in front of the king's high seat, and Hjalti with them. They paid him the highest respect. The king then also became well acquainted with him in conversation. The king chatted with him a lot and asked for news from Iceland.

CHAPTER SEVENTY-ONE

It had happened, before Bjǫrn set out from home, that he had asked the poet Sigvatr to go with him—he was then staying with King Óláfr—but people were not keen to undertake that journey. Bjǫrn and Sigvatr were on very good terms there. He said:

54. Till now, on good terms with all the   *Skald* I 705
terror-bold king's good marshals
I've been, who at the knee of
our master have hovered.
Bjǫrn, you often earned me
at the king's hands, some favour;

good counsel, colourer of war-ice,[128]
can you give, knowing well how to.

And when they were riding up into Gautland, Sigvatr spoke these verses:

55. I was often glad when out there   *Austrfararvísur* 9
    on the fiords the storm fiercely   *Skald* I 596
[93] scraped the wind-blown sail of
    the Strindir's lord[129] in downpours.
    Keels carved Listi's necklace;[130]
    cantered the deep's horse[131] finely,
    when out to sea into action
    we urged on the warships.

56. We kept the brave king's vessel,   *Austrfararvísur* 10
    canvas-covered, hovering   *Skald* I 597
    in early summer, out by
    an island, opposite fine country.
    But when horses tread heathland
    hawthorn-grown in autumn,
    my lot was to ride; by ladies[132]
    I let various tasks be seen.

And when they were riding up across Gautland late in the evening, then said Sigvatr:

57. My horse runs long roadways,   *Austrfararvísur* 11
    ravenous, at twilight: *Skald* I 599
    [94] hoof tears ground hallwards;
    we have little daylight.
    Now 'tis the black steed bears me
    over burns, far from the Danish;
    in a ditch the hero's[133] horse lost—
    here day meets night—its footing.

---

[128] *íss gunnrjóðr*: 'reddener of battle-ice (sword)', warrior.

[129] *Strinda vísi*: 'lord of the Strindir (inhabitants of Strindafylki, a district in Þrándheimr)', king of Norway.

[130] *Lista men*: 'necklace of Listi (a district, almost an island, in Agðir, southern Norway)', sea.

[131] *kafs hestr*: 'horse of the deep', ship.

[132] *ekkjum*: '(to) ladies'; this reading, followed in *ÍF* 27, occurs (with minor variations, e.g. *ekkjur*, which must be vocative) in nearly all manuscripts other than K, which has *Ekkils*; *Ekkils hestar* means 'horses of the sea-king', i.e. ships, which 'tread the land' in autumn when they are drawn up on the shore (see *Skald* I 598).

[133] *drengs*: i.e. 'my'.

Then they ride into the market town at Skarar and along the street up to the jarl's residence. He said:

58. Outside elegant ladies in all haste will be gazing, women watch our dust, as we ride through Rǫgnvaldr's town. Let us spur our steeds so that a sage dame within the buildings may hear our horses racing to the house from a great distance.	*Austrfararvísur* 12 *Skald* I 600

[95] CHAPTER SEVENTY-TWO

One day Hjalti went before the king and the poets with him. Then Hjalti began to speak:

'So it is, king, as you know, that I have come here to see you and have travelled a long and difficult way. But since I came across the sea and heard about your grandeur, then it seemed to me foolish just to go back without having seen you and your splendour. Now it is the law between Iceland and Norway that Icelanders, when they come to Norway, pay land dues there. And when I came over the sea, then I collected the land dues of my crew, but since I know that the most just thing will be for you to possess the realm that is in Norway, so I travelled to see you to bring you the land dues.'

Then he showed the king the silver and poured into Gizurr svarti's lap ten marks of silver. The king said:

'Few have brought us anything like this from Norway for some time. I shall feel thankful and grateful to you for your having taken so much trouble to bring us the land dues rather than paying them to our enemies, and yet I would like you to accept them from me and my friendship as well.'

Hjalti thanked the king profusely. From then on Hjalti got to be on the most friendly terms with the king, and was often in conversation with him. It seemed to the king, as was true, that he was a clever person and a skilful speaker. Hjalti tells Gizurr and Óttarr that he has been sent with tokens for support and friendship to the king's daughter Ingigerðr, and asks them to get him an interview with her. They say that will be little trouble for them, and go one day to her residence. She was sitting there drinking with many people. She welcomed the poets, because they [96] were known to her. Hjalti brought her the jarl's wife Ingibjǫrg's greeting, saying that she had sent him to her for support and friendship, and brought out tokens. The king's daughter responded kindly and said he would be welcome to her friendship. They sat there drinking for a large part of the day. The king's daughter asked Hjalti the news about many things, and bade him come there often to chat with her. He did so, came there frequently and chatted with the king's daughter, then telling her in confidence about his and Bjǫrn's expedition, and asking what she thinks about how the king of the Svíar will take the proposal that peace should be made between the kings. The king's daughter speaks, affirming that she thought there was no point in pursuing the idea that the king should make peace with Óláfr digri, and said that the king had got so angry with Óláfr that he cannot bear to hear him named.

It happened one day that Hjalti was sitting before the king and chatting with him. The king was at the time very merry and quite drunk. Then Hjalti said to the king:

'Very great splendours of many kinds are to be seen here, and I can see with my own eyes what I have often heard spoken about, that there is no king in the Northern lands as illustrious as you. It is a very great pity that to get here we have such a long way to come, so difficult to travel, first the high seas, and then it being not peaceful travelling through Norway for those who want to get here in friendship. But do people make no attempt to carry proposals of peace between you and Óláfr digri? I have often heard it spoken of in Norway and also in Vestra-Gautland that everyone would be very eager for there to be peace, and I have been told as a fact about the words of the king of Norway that he would be eager to come to terms with you, and I know that one reason is that he must realise that he has much less power than you have. It was also said too, that he was intending to propose marriage with your daughter Ingigerðr, and that is also the most promising way to a full settlement, and he is a most distinguished man according to what I have heard reliable [97] people say.'

The the king replied: 'You must not speak of such things, Hjalti, though I will not take it amiss of you for what you have said, since you are not aware of what subjects must not be spoken of. That fat man must not be called king here in my court, and there is much less to be said for him than many claim, and you will find that the case if I tell you that this alliance could in no way be suitable, for I am the tenth king at Uppsalir with one after another of our kinsmen succeeding and being sole ruler over the realm of the Svíar and over many other extensive lands and all being supreme king over the other kings in the Northern lands. But in Norway there is little settlement, and even then very scattered. There have been petty kings there, though Haraldr inn hárfagri was the greatest king in that land, and he fought with the district kings and subjected them to himself. He found it his best course not to be greedy for the dominions of the king of the Svíar. Because of this the kings of the Svíar let him sit in peace, and another reason was that there was kinship between them. And when Hákon Aðalsteinsfóstri was in Norway, he then remained in peace until he raided in Gautland and Denmark, but afterwards a troop was raised against him and he was removed from his lands. The sons of Gunnhildr were also deprived of life as soon as they became rebellious to the king of the Danes. Then Haraldr Gormsson added Norway to his rule and laid tribute upon it. And yet we regarded King Haraldr Gormsson as inferior to the kings of Uppsalir, for our kinsman Styrbjǫrn cowed him into submission, and [98] Harald became his man, while my father Eiríkr inn sigrsæli (the Victorious) got the better of Styrbjǫrn when they put each other to the test. And when Óláfr Tryggvason came into Norway and called himself king, then we did not let him get away with that. King Sveinn of the Danes and I went and deprived him of life. Now I have gained possession of Norway and with no less power than you have now been able to gather, and gained it in no less convincing a way than by winning it in battle and defeating the king who had previously been ruling it. Now you, a sensible man, must realise that it will be far from the case that I am going to let go of that realm to that fat man. And it is surprising that he does not recall how he got with the greatest difficulty out of Lǫgrinn when we had trapped him in there.[134] I would have thought that he would have had other plans in his mind, if he got away with his life, than contending any more with us Svíar. Now you, Hjalti, must not have this talk on your lips any more in my presence.'

Hjalti thought it was beginning to look unlikely that the king would be willing to listen to proposals for a settlement. He then gave it up and turned to other subjects of conversation. Somewhat later, when Hjalti was chatting to the king's daughter Ingigerðr, he told her all about his talk with the king. She said she had expected such answers from the king. Hjalti asked her to say something to the king about it, saying that would be the most likely thing to help. She said the king would not listen, whatever she said.

'But I can speak about it,' she says, 'if you wish.'

Hjalti said he was grateful.

The king's daughter Ingigerðr was in conversation with her father one day, and when she found that he was in a good mood, then she said:

'What plans do you have about the dispute between yourself and Óláfr digri? Many people are now complaining about that problem. Some say they have lost money, some their kinsmen at the hands of the Norwegians, and none of your people can travel into Norway as things are. It was quite pointless of you to claim power in Norway. [99] That country is poverty-stricken and difficult to travel over, and the people are unreliable. The people in that country would rather have any other king than you. Now if I had my way, you would put aside your claim to Norway, and instead fight your

[134] See p. 8, ch. 7 above.

way to the power the earlier kings of the Svíar had in the eastern Baltic and which a little while ago now our kinsman Styrbjǫrn subjected to himself, and let Óláfr digri have what he has inherited from his kinsmen and make peace with him.'

The king says angrily: 'This is your plan, Ingigerðr, that I should give up my power in Norway, and give you in marriage to Óláfr digri. No,' he says, 'something else sooner than that. This rather, that this winter at the Uppsalir assembly I shall announce to all the Svíar that a levy shall be called out from the whole population before the ice clears from the lakes. I shall go to Norway and lay waste the land with point and edge and burn everything and thus repay them for their faithlessness.'

The king then got so furious that no reply could be made to him. Then she went away. Hjalti was looking out for her and went straight to see her. He then asked what was the outcome of her business with the king. She says that it had gone just as she had expected, that nothing could be put to the king and he responded with threats, and she asked Hjalti never to mention this matter before the king. Ingigerðr and Hjalti, when they chatted, frequently spoke of Óláfr digri. He often told her about him and his way of life and praised him as much as he could, and that was the same as telling as truthfully as possible. She was fully convinced. And on another occasion when they were chatting, then Hjalti said:

'May I, daughter of the king, have leave to say something to you that I have on my mind?'

'Speak on,' she says, 'so that I alone may hear it.'

Then Hjalti said: 'How would you respond if King Óláfr of Norway sent men to you with the mission to ask for your hand?'

She went red and replies hesitantly and composedly: 'I have not decided on what my reply to that would be, since I think I shall have no need to make such a reply, but if Óláfr is endowed in everything [100] as you have described him, then I would not be able to wish my husband any different, unless it is that you should have exaggerated his qualities in your praise in many respects.'

Hjalti says that he has described nothing about the king as better than it was. They spoke about this between themselves very frequently. Ingigerðr told Hjalti to be careful not to speak about this before other people,

'For the king will be angry with you if he finds out about it.'

Hjalti told the poets Gizurr and Óttarr all this. They said it would be a most happy plan if it could be put into effect. Óttarr was a man bold of speech and popular with people of high rank. He soon got to speaking with the king's daughter about this matter, and recounted the fine qualities of the king just as Hjalti had done. She and Hjalti and the others often spoke of this matter all together. And when they had spoken frequently and Hjalti had become convinced about how his mission would be concluded, then he sent off the Gautish men who had come there with him, making them go back to the jarl with the letters that the two of them, the king's daughter Ingigerðr and Hjalti, were sending to the jarl and Ingibjǫrg. Hjalti also dropped hints to them about the discussions that he had initiated with Ingigerðr, and also about her responses. The messengers came to the jarl a little before Yule.

CHAPTER SEVENTY-THREE

When King Óláfr had sent Bjǫrn and his party east into Gautland, then he sent other men to Upplǫnd with a commission to order entertainment for him, and he planned that winter to travel to quarters throughout Upplǫnd, for it had been the custom of previous kings to travel on a progress over Upplǫnd every third winter.[135] He began his journey in the autumn from Borg. The king first went to Vingulmǫrk. He arranged his journey like this, that he received entertainment [101] up near a forest district and sent for all the inhabitants of the district, and all those in particular who dwelt furthest from the main districts. He investigated concerning people's observance of Christianity, and where he felt there was need for improvement he taught them the right ways, and was so insistent (zealous) with this, if there were any that were unwilling to relinquish heathendom, that some he drove away out of the country, some he had mutilated in hands or feet or had their eyes put out, some he had hanged or beheaded, and no one he left unpunished who would not serve God. He travelled like this over all that district. He punished powerful and humble alike. He provided them with clergy and established these as densely in the districts as he saw most fitting. In this manner he went through that district. He had three hundred (360) fighting men when he went up into Raumaríki. He soon realised that the observance of Christianity was less the further he got up inland. Yet he continued in the same way, converting all people to the true faith and inflicting severe punishment on those who would not heed his words.

CHAPTER SEVENTY-FOUR

And when the king who was ruling over Raumaríki there heard about this, then he thought there was going to be great difficulty for him, because every day many people came to him complaining about these things to him, some powerful, some humble. The king adopted this plan, that he went up

---

[135] The king's 'progress' from landowner to landowner throughout his realm receiving board and lodging for himself and his following was a form of taxation which could alternatively be paid in kind or in money.

into Heiðmǫrk to see King Hrœrekr, for he was the most sensible of those kings who were there then. And when the kings had their discussion, then they reached agreement that they should send word to King Guðrøðr north in Dalar and also to Haðaland to the king who was there, and ask them to come to see King Hrœrekr and him. They did not put off this journey, and these five kings met in Heiðmǫrk at a place [102] called at Hringisakr. King Hrœrekr's brother Hringr was the fifth king there. These kings at first started making speeches one at a time. The one who was come from Raumaríki began talking first, and speaks about Óláfr digri's travels and the disturbance he was causing in both killing people and maiming people, driving some out of the country and seizing property from all those who opposed him at all, and travelling around the country with a host of men, and not with the numbers that the law provided for. He also says that he declares it is because of this disturbance he has fled to this place, also declaring that many other men of rank have fled their ancestral lands in Raumaríki.

'And though these difficulties have now affected us most, yet it will not be long before you will have to face the same, and so it is better that we all discuss together what plan should be adopted.'

And when he had finished his speech, then the kings turned to Hrœrekr for a response. He said:

'Now there has come to pass what I suspected would happen when we held a meeting in Haðaland and you were all eager to raise up Óláfr above our heads, that he was going to be hard to hold by the horns as soon as he had sole power over the land. Now there are two choices available, the one that we all go to see him and let him arrange and settle everything between us, and I think that is the best one to take, and the other to rise now against him while he has not travelled any further through the country. And although he has three or four hundred (360–480) men, still that is not an overwhelming force for us, if we are all of one mind. But most often those that are many of equal authority are less successful than the one that is sole leader over his troop, and it is my advice instead not to risk trying to match our luck with Óláfr Haraldsson's.'

And after that each of the kings spoke that which he thought fit. Some spoke against, and some spoke in favour, and there was no solution decided on, they pointed out the obvious disadvantages of both courses. Then Guðrøðr, [103] king in Dalar, began to speak and said as follows:

'It seems amazing to me that you are getting in such a tangle about a solution to this business, and you are totally afraid of Óláfr. There are five of us kings here, and none of us is of any worse descent than Óláfr. Now we have given him support in his fight with Jarl Sveinn, and he has with us behind him gained possession of this land. But if he wants now to begrudge each of us that little power that we held before, and treat us with oppression and tyranny, then I can say this of myself, that I shall get myself out of thraldom to the king, and I declare any one of you to be no man who flinches from this, that we should deprive him of life if we get him into our power up here in Heiðmǫrk, for I can tell you this, that we shall never hold up a free head while Óláfr is alive.'

And after this goading they all adopted this counsel. Then Hrœrekr spoke:

'It seems to me about this decision, that we shall need to make our alliance firm, so that no one may fail in loyalty to anyone else. Now you are planning, when Óláfr comes here to Heiðmǫrk, to make an attack on him at an arranged time. Now I do not want to have to rely on you for this, when you are some of you north in Dalar, and some out in Heiðmǫrk. I want, if this plan is going to be ratified between us, that we should stay together day and night, until this plan has been carried out.'

The kings agreed to this, to keep now all together. They have a feast prepared for them out at Hringisakr, and they drank with the cup passing round the whole company, but had watch kept for themselves out in Raumaríki, having one lot of watchers go out as soon as the other lot started back, so that they know day and night what is going on in Óláfr's travels and about his numbers. King Óláfr went on his visits [104] inland round Raumaríki, and always in the same manner as was previously described. And when the provisions did not last because of the large numbers, then he made the farmers in the area give contributions to lengthen the visits, when at times he found it necessary to stay on, but in some places he stayed a shorter time than had been intended, and his travels turned out quicker up to the lake than had been arranged. And when the kings had fixed their plan between themselves, then they send word and summon to them landed men and leading farmers from all those districts. And when they gather there, then the kings hold a meeting with them on their own and reveal the plan and appoint a day when this purpose is going to be put into effect. They decide on this, that each of the kings was to have three hundred (360) men. They then send the landed men back so that they could muster troops and come to meet the kings where it had been arranged. This plan pleased most people well, but yet it was the case, as they say, that everyone has a friend among his enemies.

CHAPTER SEVENTY-FIVE

At this meeting was Ketill of Hringunes. And when he got home in the evening, then he ate his supper, and then he and his domestic servants got dressed and went down to the water and took a carvel that Ketill owned, which King Óláfr had given him, launched the ship—all the tackle was in the boathouse—then set off and sit down to the oars and row out along the lake. Ketill had forty men, all well armed. They came early in the morning out to the end of the lake. Ketill then went with twenty men, but left the other twenty behind to guard the ship. King Óláfr was then at Eið in the upper part of Raumaríki. Ketill got there as the king was leaving matins. He welcomed Ketill. Ketill says that he wants to speak to the king urgently. They go and talk, the two of them together.

[105] Then Ketill tells the king what plans the kings have taken up, and what their intentions were that he had discovered. And when the king found this out, then he calls men to him, sends some into the settlement, telling them to get together mounts for him, some he sent to the lake to get what oared ships they could and bring them to meet him. And then he went to church and had Mass sung for himself, afterwards going straight to table. And when he had eaten, he got ready as quickly as he could and went up to the lake. Ships were coming there to meet him. He himself then boarded the carvel and with him as many men as the carvel would hold, and each of the others went aboard whatever ship they could. And in the evening, as it was getting late, they set out from the shore. The weather was calm. They rowed out along the lake. The king had then nearly four hundred (480) men. Before it dawned he got up to Hringisakr. The watchmen noticed nothing until the troop came up to the estate buildings. Ketill and his men knew precisely in which quarters the kings were sleeping. The king had all these quarters seized and guarded so that no one could get away, so awaited dawn. The kings had no forces for their defence, and they were all captured and led before the king. King Hrœrekr was a very intelligent man and determined. King Óláfr thought he was not to be depended on even if he made some sort of settlement with him. He had Hrœrekr blinded in both eyes and kept him with him, and he had the tongue cut out of Guðrøðr king in Dalar. But Hringr and the other two he forced to swear oaths to him and leave Norway and never return. And the landed men or farmers who were guilty of this treachery, some he drove out of the country, some were maimed, some he came to terms with. Of this says Óttarr svarti:

[106] 59. You have handed, harmer   *Hǫfuðlausn* 17
of hawk's land flames,[136] to   *Skald* I 762
the realm's rulers an ugly
recompense for all plotting.
You had, army-upholder,
the Heiðmǫrk kings rewarded
fitly, who formerly,
fine king, planned wrongs against you.

---

[136] *ifla folds branda lýtandi*: 'harmer of flames (gold) of the land of the hawk (hand)', generous man.

60. Away you have driven, wager *Hǫfuðlausn* 18
of war,[137] sword-reddener,[138] *Skald* I 763
the kings out of the country—
your courage than theirs was plainer.
Each king fled, as people
are aware, far from you.
Still later you restrained the
speech-reed[139] of the northernmost.

[107] 61. Now the ground you govern— *Hǫfuðlausn* 19
God with great victory *Skald* I 765
fortifies you—that formerly
five kings held sway over.
Broad lie, east to Eiðar,
ancestral lands beneath you.
Before, no forcer of Gǫndul's
fires[140] has held such a kingdom.

King Óláfr then subjected to himself the realms that these five kings had held, then took hostages from the landed men[141] and farmers. He took payments in lieu of entertainment from Dalar in the north and many parts of Heiðmǫrk and then turned back out to Raumaríki and then westwards to Haðaland. That winter his stepfather Sigurðr sýr died. Then King Óláfr went into Hringaríki and his mother Ásta held a great banquet to welcome him. Now Óláfr alone bore the title of king in Norway.

CHAPTER SEVENTY-SIX

So it is said, that King Óláfr was at the banquet with his mother Ásta and she led out her children and showed him. The king set his brother Guthormr on his knee, and on his other knee his brother Hálfdan. The king looked at the boys. Then he scowled and looked angrily at them. Then the boys' faces fell. Then Ásta brought her youngest son, who was called Haraldr, to him. He was at that time three years old. [108] The king scowled at him, but he looked up into his face. Then the king took hold of the boy's hair and pulled it. The boy reached up at the king's moustache and tugged at it. Then the king said:
  'You will be vengeful later on, kinsman.'

[137] *bǫðvar þreytir*: 'wager of war', warrior.
[138] *branda rjóðr*: 'reddener of swords', warrior.
[139] *orðreyrr*: 'word-reed', tongue.
[140] *Gǫndlar elda þrǫngvir*: 'forcer of Gǫndul's (valkyrie's) fires (swords)', warrior.
[141] See note 52 above.

The next day the king was outside strolling round the farm, and his mother Ásta with him. Then they walked over to a pond. The boys, Ásta's sons Guthormr and Hálfdan, were there then, playing. Large farms and large barns had been made there, many cattle and sheep. This was what they were playing with. A little way off beside the pond by an inlet made of clay was Haraldr, and he had got there some chips of wood, and a lot of them were floating near the shore. The king asked him what these were supposed to be. He said they were his warships. Then the king laughed at this, and said:

'It may be, kinsman, that the time will come that you will command ships.'

Then the king called Hálfdan and Guthormr over. Then he asked Guthormr: 'What would you like to have most, kinsman?'

'Cornfields,' he says.

The king said: 'How wide would you like to have your cornfields?'

He replies: 'I would like that headland that goes out into the sea to be all sown every summer.'

Ten farms stood there. The king replies:

'There could be a lot of corn standing there.'

Then he asked Hálfdan what he would most like to have.

'Cows,' he says.

The king asked: 'How many cows would you like to have?'

Hálfdan says: 'When they go down to the water, they must stand there all crowded as close as can be round the water.'

The king replies: 'It is large establishments you both want to have. That is just like your father.'

Then the king asks Haraldr: 'What do you most want to have?'

He replies: 'Housecarls,' he says.

The king says: 'How many would you like to have?'

'What I would like, is that they should eat up at one meal my brother Hálfdan's cows.'

The king laughed at this and said to Ásta:

'Here it must be a king you are bringing up, mother.'

No more of their conversation is recorded.

[109] CHAPTER SEVENTY-SEVEN

In Svíþjóð it was an ancient custom, as long as heathendom lasted there, for the chief sacrificial feast to be held at Uppsalir in Gói.[142] Sacrifices had to be offered at it for peace and victory for their king, and people had to attend it from all over Svíþjóð. Then there had also to be an assembly of all the

---

[142] Gói, according to the early pre-Christian calendar of Scandinavia, was the 'snow-month', mid-February to mid-March.

Svíar. There was also at the same time a market and meeting of traders and it lasted a week. And after Christianity came to be in Svíþjóð, then the legal assembly and market still continued there. But now since Christianity had become universal in Svíþjóð, and the kings stopped having their residence at Uppsalir, then the market was moved, and held at Candlemas.[143] That has continued ever since, and now it is held so that it lasts no more than three days. There is held the assembly of Svíar, and it is attended from all over the country.

The realm of the Svíar is divided into many parts. One part is Vestra-Gautland and Vermaland and Markir, and what belongs to these, and that is such a large realm that under the bishop who is in charge there, there are eleven hundred churches. Another part of the country is Eystra-Gautland. There is another bishopric in it. Gotland and Eyland now belong to it, and all that together comprises a much larger diocese. In Svíþjóð proper there is one part of the country that is called Suðrmannaland. That is one bishopric. [110] Then there is the area called Vestmannaland or Fjaðryndaland. That is one bishopric. Then the third part of Svíþjóð is called Tíundaland. Then the fourth part of Svíþjóð is called Áttandaland. Then the fifth is Sjáland and what belongs to it to the east along the coast. Tíundaland is the most splendid part and the most fully inhabited part in Svíþjóð. The whole realm defers to it. [That is where Uppsalir is.][144] The king's residence is there, the archbishop's see is there, and it is referred to as Uppsalaauðr (Riches of Uppsala). That is what the Svíar call the possessions of the king of the Svíar, they call it Uppsalaauðr. In each of these parts of the country there is a separate legal assembly, with its own jurisdiction over many things. Over each judicial area there is a lawman, and he is most influential with the farmers, for that must be the law that he decides to proclaim. But if the king or a jarl or bishops travel round the country and have meetings with the farmers, then the lawman replies on behalf of the farmers, and they all stand by him so that powerful rulers scarcely dare to attend their assemblies if the farmers and the lawman do not give them permission. But in every matter where the laws conflict, they must always give way to the law of Uppsalir, and other lawmen must all be subordinate to the lawman that is in Tíundaland.

[111] CHAPTER SEVENTY-EIGHT

In Tíundaland there was at that time the lawman who was called Þorgnýr. His father's name was Þorgnýr Þorgnýsson. Their forefathers had been lawmen in Tíundaland throughout the lives of many kings. At this time Þorgnýr was

---

[143] 2nd February.
[144] The words in brackets are from the *Separate Saga of St Óláfr*.

old. He had a large following. He was said to be the wisest man in the realm of the Svíar. He was related to Jarl Rǫgnvaldr and was his foster-father.

Now we must take up the story where the men that the king's daughter Ingigerðr, and Hjalti as well, had sent from the east came to Jarl Rǫgnvaldr. They presented their messages to Jarl Rǫgnvaldr and his wife Ingibjǫrg, and said this, that the king's daughter had often spoken before the king of the Svíar about a settlement between him and Óláfr digri, and she was a very great friend of King Óláfr, but the king of the Svíar got angry every time she mentioned Óláfr, and she thought there was no hope of a settlement as things stood. The jarl tells Bjǫrn what he had heard from the east, and Bjǫrn says the same thing again, that he will not turn back until he has seen the king of the Svíar, and says that the jarl has promised him this, that he shall accompany him to a meeting with the king of the Svíar. So the winter continues, and immediately after Yule the jarl set out on his journey and takes sixty men. Bjǫrn stallari went along with him and his companions. The jarl travelled eastwards all the way to Svíþjóð, and as he was making his way up inland, then he sent some of his men on ahead to Uppsalir and sent word to the king's daughter Ingigerðr that she was to set out to Ullarakr to meet him. She had a large residence there. And when the jarl's message reached the king's daughter, then she did not delay her journey, and she set out with a large number of men. Hjalti arranged to go with her. But before he started off, he went before King Óláfr and said:

'Occupy your throne as the most blessed of all kings! And to tell the truth, I have been nowhere [112] where I have seen such splendour as with you. I shall convey this conviction wherever I go from now on. I would like to ask you, king, that you should be my friend.'

The king replies: 'Why are you showing such eagerness to depart? Where are you off to?'

Hjalti replies: 'I am to ride out to Ullarakr with your daughter Ingigerðr.'

The king said: 'Farewell. You are a sensible person and well-bred and know well how to behave among people of rank.'

Then Hjalti went off. The king's daughter Ingigerðr rode to her residence out at Ullarakr, had a great banquet prepared for the jarl's coming. Then the jarl arrived there, and he was warmly welcomed. He stayed there a few nights. He and the king's daughter spoke of many things, and mostly about the king of the Svíar and the king of Norway. She tells the jarl that a settlement seems to her to look unlikely. Then the jarl said:

'How would you feel about it, kinswoman, supposing King Óláfr of Norway asked for your hand? It seems to us that it would be most conducive to a settlement if a relationship by marriage were to come about between the kings, but I shall not support the proposal if I know that is is directly contrary to your wishes.'

She says: 'My father will see to a match for me, but of my other kinsmen you are the one that I would most rather had a say about my future with regard to anything that I thought was of particular significance. So how advisable do you think this is?'

The jarl urged her strongly and recounted many things to King Óláfr's credit that were extremely honourable, telling her in detail about the events that had just recently taken place, when King Óláfr had captured five kings in one morning and deprived them all of their kingdoms, and laid their possessions and power under his control. They talked a lot about this matter and in all their discussions were in full agreement. The jarl left there when he was ready to do so. Hjalti went with him.

[113] CHAPTER SEVENTY-NINE

Jarl Rǫgnvaldr arrived one day in the evening at Lawman Þorgnýr's home. There was a large and magnificent estate there. Many men were there outside. They welcomed the jarl warmly and took charge of their horses and gear. The jarl went into the living room. There was a large number of people in there. In the high seat there sat an old man. Bjǫrn and his party had not seen so big a man. His beard was so long that it lay on his knees and spread over his whole chest. He was a handsome and splendid-looking person. The jarl went before him and greeted him. Þorgnýr welcomes him warmly and bade him go to the seat he usually sat in. The jarl sat on the other side opposite Þorgnýr. They stayed there a few nights before the jarl presented his business. He asked that he and Þorgnýr might go into his conference room. Bjǫrn and his companions went there with the jarl. Then the jarl began to speak and tells about this, that King Óláfr of Norway had sent some of his men to the east there to make peace, speaking at length about what a problem it was for the Vestr-Gautar that there was hostility between them and Norway. He also speaks about this, that King Óláfr of Norway had sent men there, and the king's messengers were there now and he had promised them to accompany them to a meeting with the king of the Svíar. And he says that the king of the Svíar took this business so bad-temperedly, that he would allow no one to speak in favour of this proposal.

'Now this is how it is, foster-father,' says the jarl, 'that I am not adequate to this undertaking. I have therefore now made my way to see you, and I was hoping for good advice and your support.'

And when the jarl ended his speech, then Þorgnýr was silent for a while. But when he started speaking, he said:

'You have a strange way of going on, you are eager to have noble titles, but do not know how to manage or see ahead when [114] you get into any difficulty. Why did you not realise before you promised this expedition, that you do not wield enough power to raise your voice against King Óláfr? It seems to me that one can have more self-respect by being of the number of farmers, and having freedom of speech to say what one wants even in the king's presence. So I shall come to the Uppsalir assembly and give you such support that you will be able to speak there without fear of the king whatever you like.'

The jarl thanked him warmly for this promise, and stayed with Þorgnýr and rode with him to the Uppsalir assembly. There were very large numbers there. King Óláfr was there with his following.

CHAPTER EIGHTY

The first day, when the assembly was inaugurated, King Óláfr was sitting on a throne and his following there round him. And on the other side at the assembly the two of them, Jarl Rǫgnvaldr and Þorgnýr, were sitting on a single seat, and there in front of them the jarl's following and Þorgnýr's body of retainers were sitting, and behind the seat and in a circle all round the crowd of farmers were standing. Some went up onto hillocks and mounds to listen from there. And when the king's announcements, those which it was customary to make at assemblies, had been proclaimed, and when that was finished, then Bjǫrn stallari stood up by the Jarl's seat and spoke in a loud voice:

'King Óláfr has sent me here with this charge, that he wishes to offer the king of the Svíar settlement and the division of the lands that existed formerly between Norway and Svíþjóð.'

He spoke in a loud voice so that the king of the Svíar heard clearly. But at first, when the king of the Svíar heard King Óláfr named, then he thought that the speaker was carrying out some business of his, but when he heard settlement and division of lands between Svíþjóð and Norway spoken of, then he realised from what roots it must have arisen. Then he leapt up and shouted in a loud voice that this man should be silent, and said that this would not do. Bjǫrn then sat [115] down. But when a hearing could be got, then the jarl stood up and spoke. He told about Óláfr digri's message and the offers of settlement to King Óláfr of the Svíar, and about this, that the Vestr-Gautar had sent King Óláfr every kind of verbal support for peace being made with the Norwegians. He recounted what a problem it was for the Vestr-Gautar to be without all the things from Norway which would supplement their own produce, and at the same time to be exposed to their attacks and raids whenever the king of Norway mustered an army and invaded them. The jarl also says that King Óláfr had sent men there with the message that he wishes to ask for the hand of his daughter Ingigerðr. And when the jarl stopped talking, then the king of the Svíar stood up. He replies bad-temperedly about the settlement, and reprimanded the jarl harshly and at length for his daring in having made a truce and peace with the fat man and having entered into friendship with him, declaring that he was guilty of treason against him, saying it would be proper for Rǫgnvaldr to be driven from the land, and says that he had got all this from the egging on of his wife Ingibjǫrg and declared that it had been the stupidest idea that he should have married such a woman for the sake of lust. He spoke long and harshly and then directed his words against Óláfr digri. And when he sat down, then at first there was silence. Then Þorgnýr stood up. And when he stood up, then all the farmers stood up, those who had previously been sitting down, and all those rushed up who had been in other places and wanted to listen to what Þorgnýr said. Then to begin with there was a great din from the crowd of people and weapons. But when a hearing could be got, then Þorgnýr said:

'Otherwise is now the temper of the kings of the Svíar than has been previously. My grandfather Þorgnýr remembered King Eiríkr Emundarson of Uppsalir, and said this of him, that while he was in his best years he took a levy out every summer and travelled to various countries and subjected to himself Lappland and Kirjálaland, Eistland and Kúrland and many places in the eastern lands. And there can still be seen the [116] earthworks and other great strongholds that he built, and he was not so high and mighty that he did not listen to people if they had someting important to speak to him about. My father Þorgnýr was with King Bjǫrn for a long period. His character was well known to him. Throughout Bjǫrn's life his rule lasted with great power and no lessening of it. He was easy with his friends. I can remember King Eiríkr inn sigrsæli and I was with him on many warlike expeditions. He increased the power of the Svíar, and defended it fiercely. It was easy for us to give him advice. But this king that we have now lets no one dare to say anything to him except just what he wants to have done, and devotes all his enthusiasm to that, but lets his tributary lands slip from his grasp through lack of energy and lack of determination. He desires to keep the realm of Norway subject to him, when no king of the Svíar has previously coveted it, and this causes trouble for many a man. Now this is what we farmers want, that you make a settlement with King Óláfr digri of Norway and give him your daughter Ingigerðr in marriage. But if you want to win back into your power those realms in the eastern Baltic that your kinsmen and forefathers have had there, then we will all support you in that. Should you be unwilling to accept what we demand, then we shall mount an attack against you and kill you and not put up with hostility and lawlessness from you. This is what our forefathers before us have done. They threw five kings into a bog at Múlaþing who had become completely full of arrogance like you with us. Say now straight away which choice you wish to take.' Then the people immediately made a clashing of weapons and a great din. The king then stands up and spoke, saying that he will let everything be as the farmers wish, says that is what all kings of the Svíar have done, let the farmers have their way with them in everything they wanted. [117] Then the grumbling of the farmers stopped. Then the rulers, the king and the jarl and Þorgnýr, talked together, and then made peace and settlement on the part of the king of the Svíar in accordance with what the king of Norway had previously sent his request for. It was at this assembly decided that King Óláfr's daughter Ingigerðr should be married to King Óláfr Haraldsson. The king handed over to the jarl the betrothal arrangements and commissioned him to negotiate all the details of this wedding, and they parted at the assembly with the business concluded thus.

And when the jarl went back home, then he and the king's daughter Ingigerðr met and talked about this business between themselves. She sent King Óláfr a long trailing robe of fine cloth and richly embroidered with gold and some silken puttees. The jarl went back into Gautland and Bjǫrn with him. Bjǫrn stayed there a short time and went back then to Norway with his troop of companions. And when he met King Óláfr and tells him the conclusion of his mission, how it had turned out, then the king thanked him warmly for his journey and says, as was true, that Bjǫrn had brought luck to bear in achieving the mission amid such hostility.

CHAPTER EIGHTY-ONE

King Óláfr went, when spring came, out to the sea and had his ships got ready and gathered troops round him and travelled in the spring right out along the Vík to Líðandisnes, and he went all the way north to Hǫrðaland, then sent word to landed men and summoned by name all the most powerful men from the districts and then set out in the finest style, when he went to meet his betrothed wife. The banquet was to be in the autumn east of the Elfr on the border between the countries.

King Óláfr took with him the blind King Hrœrekr. And when he had been healed of his wounds, then King Óláfr had provided him with two men to attend him and made him sit [118] on a throne next to himself and kept him in drink and clothes no whit worse than he had previously kept himself. Hrœrekr was untalkative and answered abruptly and curtly if people addressed words to him. It was his custom to have his servant lead him out in the daytime and away from other people. Then he began to beat the lad, and when he ran away from him, then he tells King Óláfr that the boy would not serve him.

Then King Óláfr exchanged servants with him, and it all went the same as before, no servant staying with King Hrœrekr. Then King Óláfr got to be with and to look after Hrœrekr a man who was called Sveinn, and he was a kinsman of King Hrœrekr and had been one of his followers previously. Hrœrekr carried on with the behaviour he had adopted before with regard to his cussedness and also his solitariness. But when he and Sveinn were just the two of them anywhere on their own, then Hrœrekr was cheerful and talkative. He called to mind many things as they had been previously, and also what had happened in his days, when he was king, and recalled his previous life, and also who it was that had brought it to an end, his power and his happiness, and made him into a beggar.

'But that, however, seems to me hardest of all,' he says, 'that you and my other kinsmen who should have turned out the finest of men, should now have fallen so low that no disgrace is to be avenged that has been inflicted on our families.'

He often expressed such lamentations. Sveinn replies and says that they had to deal with people that were much too powerful, and so they had little choice. Hrœrekr says:

'For what purpose shall we go on living in shame and mutilation except it should come about that I in my blindness might overcome them who overcame me in my sleep? My goodness, let us kill Óláfr digri. He has now no fears [119] for himself. I shall make the plans, and I would not hold back my hands if I was able to use them, but I cannot do that because of my blindness, and you must therefore make the attack on him. And when Óláfr is slain, then I can foresee that the kingdom will pass to his enemies. Now it may be that I might become king; then you shall be my jarl.'

His persuasion was so successful that Sveinn agreed to follow this infamous plan. The plan was that when the king set out for evensong, Sveinn would be standing out on the balcony before he got there and have a drawn cutlass under his coat. But when the king came out of the sitting room, then he got out sooner than Sveinn expected, and he looked at the king full in the face. Then he went pale and grew as white as a corpse and his hands failed him. The king noticed his terror and said:

'What is it now, Sveinn? Are you going to betray me?'

Sveinn threw down his coat and his cutlass and fell at the king's feet and said:

'Everything in God's hands and yours, Lord.'

The king told his men to seize Sveinn and he was put in irons. Then the king had Hrœrekr's seat moved to the other bench, and he pardoned Sveinn, and he left the country. The king then assigned Hrœrekr different quarters to sleep in from those that he slept in himself. There was a lot of his men that slept in those quarters. He got two of his men to be with Hrœrekr day and night. These men had long been with King Óláfr, and he had tried their loyalty to him. It is not told that they were men of high lineage. King Hrœrekr was changeable, he was silent on many days, so that no one could get a word from him, but sometimes he was so cheerful and merry that they found every word he spoke amusing, but sometimes he spoke a lot, but only what was unpleasant. It also happened sometimes that he drank everyone under the table, and made all those that were near him incapable, but generally [120] he drank little. King Óláfr gave him plenty of pocket money. Often what he did when he came into his quarters, before he lay down to sleep, was have mead brought in, several casks, and gave all the men in those quarters something to drink. As a result he was popular.

CHAPTER EIGHTY-TWO

There is a man called Fiðr litli (the Small), a man from Upplǫnd, but some say that he was a Lapp by descent. He was the smallest of all men and the fastest runner of all men, so that no horse could catch him up when running. He was the most skilled of men with skis and the bow. He had long been a servant of King Hrœrekr and often gone on errands for him that needed to be confidential. He knew the routes over the whole of Upplǫnd. He also knew many important men there to speak to. And when King Hrœrekr was put under the charge of a small number of men, then Finnr joined the group, and he generally kept company with boys and servants, but whenever he could, he got into the service of King Hrœrekr and often into speech with him, and the king was willing to talk with him for just short periods at a time and wanted to avoid any suspicion about their talks. And when spring drew to a close and they made their way out into the Vík, then Fiðr disappeared from the troop for a few days. Then he came back again and stayed for a while. Thus it happened often, and no notice was taken of it, for there were many vagabonds with the troop.

CHAPTER EIGHTY-THREE

King Óláfr came to Túnsberg before Easter and stayed there for a long time in the spring. Then many ships came there to the town, both Saxons and Danes and those from Vík in the east and from the north of the country. There was a very large number of people. [121] It was a good year and there was much drinking. It happened one evening that King Hrœrekr had come to his quarters and rather late and had drunk a lot and was now very merry. Then Finnr litli came in with a cask of mead, and it was mead with herbs in it and of the strongest. Then Hrœrekr had everyone that was in there given drink, going on until they all went to sleep in their seats. Finnr had then gone away. There was a light

burning in the room. Then Hrœrekr woke up the men who were accustomed to attend him, saying that he wanted to go into the yard. They had a lantern with them, but it was pitch dark outside. There was a large latrine in the yard and it stood on posts, and there were steps to get up to the doorway. And while Hrœrekr and the men were sitting in the yard, then they heard a man say:
'Strike down that fiend!'
Then they heard a crash and a thump, as if something had fallen. King Hrœrekr said:
'They must have drunk plenty, the ones who are fighting there. Go up quickly and separate them.'
They got ready quickly and ran out, but when they got to the steps, then the one that was in the rear was struck first, though they were both killed. It was King Hrœrekr's men that had come there, Sigurðr hít (Paunch?), who had been his standard-bearer, in a party of twelve. Finnr litli was now there. They dragged the bodies up between the buildings, but grabbed the king and took him with them, then leapt onto a boat that they had and rowed away.

The poet Sigvatr was asleep in King Óláfr's quarters. He got up in the night and his servant with him, and they went out to the great latrine. And when they were going to go back and down the steps, then Sigvatr slipped and fell on his knee and stuck his hands down and it was wet underneath. He said:
'I think that this evening [122] the king must have taken away the sea legs from many of us.'

And he laughed about it. But when they got into their quarters, where there was a light burning, then his servant asked:
'Have you scratched yourself, or why are you all covered in nothing but blood?'

He replied: 'I am not scratched, but this must mean something has happened.'

He then woke up his bedfellow, the standard-bearer Þórðr Fólason, and they went out, taking a lantern with them, and soon found the blood. Then they searched and soon found the bodies and recognised them. They also saw that there was a great tree stump lying there with a great gash in it, and it was discovered later that this had been done as a trick to entice out those that were slain. Sigvatr and the others told each other that it was essential for the king to know what had happened as soon as possible. They sent the lad straight away to the quarters where King Hrœrekr had been. There everyone was asleep, but the king was gone. He woke the men who were inside and said what had happened. Some men got up and went straight away to the place in the yard where the bodies were. But though they thought it essential for the king to know as soon as possible what had happened, no one dared to wake him. Then Sigvatr spoke to Þórðr:

'Which would you rather do, comrade, wake up the king or tell him what has happened?'

Þórðr replied: 'No way do I dare to wake him, but I can tell him what has happened.'

Then Sigvatr said: 'There is still much of the night to go, and it may be that before it is day, Hrœrekr will have got himself a hiding place where he will not easily be found, and they will still not have got far, for the bodies were warm. We must never fall into the disgrace of failing to let the king know of this treason. You, Þórðr, go up into the quarters and wait for me there.'

Then Sigvatr went to the church and woke up the bell-ringer and told him to toll the bell for the souls of the king's men, and he gave the names [123] of the men that had been killed. The bell-ringer did as he asked. And at the ringing the king awoke and sat up. He asked whether it was time for matins. Þórðr replied:

'The reason for it is worse than that. Something important has happened. King Hrœrekr has disappeared and two of your men are killed.'

Then the king asked about these events that had taken place there. Þórðr told him as much as he knew. Then the king got up and had a horn blown to summon a meeting of his followers. And when the troop assembled, then the king named men who were to go out in all directions from the town to search for Hrœrekr by sea and land. Þórir langi took a light ship and took thirty men, and when it got light they saw two small ships sailing ahead of them. And when they saw each other, each lot rowed as hard as they could. It was King Hrœrekr there and he had thirty men. And when they drew close to each other, then Hrœrekr's party turned towards the shore and all leapt up ashore there except for the king sitting up on the raised deck. He spoke, bidding them farewell and meet again in health. Next Þórir and his men rowed to land. Then Finnr litli shot an arrow, and it struck Þórir in the middle of his body, and he was killed—but Sigurðr and his men all fled into the woods—and Þórir's men took his body and also King Hrœrekr and carried them to Túnsberg. King Óláfr then took charge of King Hrœrekr. He had him guarded carefully and took great precautions against his treachery, getting men to watch him night and day. King Hrœrekr was then most cheerful, and no one could see any sign in him that he was not as pleased as could be.

[124] CHAPTER EIGHTY-FOUR

It happened on Ascension Day that King Óláfr was going to High Mass. Then the bishop walked in procession round the church leading the king, and when they came back into the church, then the bishop led the king to his throne on the north side of the entrance to the choir. And there next to him King Hrœrekr was sitting, as he usually did. He had his coat pulled over his face. And when King Óláfr had sat down, then King Hrœrekr felt his shoulder with his hand and squeezed. Then he said:

'You are wearing fine cloth now, kinsman,' he says.

King Óláfr replies: 'Now a great festival is being kept today in memory of when Jesus Christ ascended into heaven from earth.'

King Hrœrekr replies: 'I do not understand, so that it is fixed in my mind, what you say about Christ. Much of what you say seems to me rather incredible. Yet many things have happened in ancient times.'

And when Mass had begun, then King Óláfr stood up and held his arms up above his head and bowed towards the altar, and his coat hung back off his shoulders. King Hrœrekr sprang up quickly and forcefully. He then stabbed at King Óláfr with a dagger of the kind known as *rýtningr*. The thrust landed on the coat by his shoulder as he bent forward away from it. His clothes were much damaged, but the king was not wounded. And when King Óláfr felt this assault, then he leapt forward onto the floor. King Hrœrekr stabbed at him a second time with the dagger and missed him and said:

'You are running away now, Óláfr digri, from me, a blind man.'

The king told his men to take him and lead him out of the church, and they did so. After this incident people urged King Óláfr to have Hrœrekr killed.

'And it is,' they say, 'a very great tempting of your luck, king, to [125] keep him with you and spare him, such wickedness as he keeps committing, for he lies in wait day and night to bring about your death. But if you send him away from you, we do not know of anyone who would be able to guard him so that he had no hope of getting away. But if he goes free, then he will immediately raise a band and cause a lot of trouble.'

The king replies: 'What you say is right enough, that many have suffered death for doing less than Hrœrekr, but I am reluctant to spoil the victory that I gained over the kings of the Upplendingar, when I captured five of them in one morning, and so got control of all their realms without needing to become the slayer of any one of them, for they were all kinsmen of mine. But yet I can hardly see now whether Hrœrekr will force me to it or not, to have him slain.'

The reason Hrœrekr had felt King Óláfr's shoulder with his hand was that he wanted to know whether he was wearing a coat of mail.

CHAPTER EIGHTY-FIVE

There was a man called Þórarinn Nefjólfsson. He was an Icelandic man, his family were from the north of the country. He was not of high lineage and he was the most sensible of men and most intelligent of speakers. He was bold in speech with people of rank. He was a great trader and was abroad for long periods. Þórarinn was the ugliest of men, and the most extraordinary thing was how horrible his limbs were. He had large and ugly hands, but yet his feet were much uglier. Þórarinn was now located in Túnsberg when these events were taking place that have just been narrated. He and King Óláfr knew each other to speak to. Þórarinn now got a trading ship ready that he owned, and was intending to go to Iceland in the summer. King Óláfr had Þórarinn as a guest for a few days and had conversations with him. Þórarinn slept in the king's quarters. It was early one morning that the king was awake while [126] other men in the quarters were asleep. Just then the sun had come up a little, and it was very light indoors. The king noticed that Þórarinn had stretched out one foot from under the bedclothes. He looked at the foot for a while. Then the men in the quarters began to wake up. The king said to Þórarinn:

'I have been awake for a while, and I have seen a sight that has impressed me greatly, and that is a man's foot than which I think there cannot in this market town be one uglier.'

And he told other men to consider whether this did not seem to be true. And everyone who saw it agreed that it was so. Þórarinn realised what they were talking about and replied:

'There are few things so special that it cannot be expected that another such will be found, and it is very likely to be so in this case too.'

The king said: 'I am still prepared to assert that another foot as ugly as this will not be found, and even if I had to lay a wager on it.'

Then Þórarinn said: 'I am prepared to lay a wager with you on that, that I shall find an uglier foot in the town.'

The king says: 'Then whichever of us turns out to be right shall choose a favour from the other.'

'So it shall be,' says Þórarinn.

He then put his other foot out from under the bedclothes, and this was in no way more beautiful, and it lacked the big toe. Then said Þórarinn:

'See here now, king, another foot, and this is the uglier in that on this one a toe is missing, and I have won the wager.'

The king says: 'The other foot is the uglier, in that there are five hideous toes on that one, but on this there are four, and it is for me to choose a favour from you.'

Þórarinn says: 'One's lord's word outweighs others, so what favour do you wish to have from me?'

He says: 'This, that you carry Hrœrekr to Greenland and take him to Leifr Eiríksson.'

Þórarinn replies: 'I have not been to Greenland.'

The king says: 'A voyager like you, it is time you went to Greenland if you have never been there.'

Þórarinn made little response to this to begin with, but when the king persisted with this request, then Þórarinn did not [127] entirely reject it, and said as follows:

'I shall let you hear, king, the favour that I had intended to ask if I had won the wager, and that is, that I was going to ask you if I might become one of your men. And if you will grant me that, then I shall be the more obliged not to put aside what you desire to have commissioned.'

The king agreed to this, and Þórarinn became a member of his following. Then Þórarinn prepared his ship, and when he was ready, then he took charge of King Hrœrekr. And when they parted, King Óláfr and Þórarinn, then Þórarinn said:

'Now should it turn out, king, as is not unlikely and may often happen, that we are unable to complete the journey to Greenland, and we are carried to Iceland or to other countries, how shall I dispose of this king so that you may be pleased?'

The king says: 'If you come to Iceland, then you shall hand him over to Guðmundr Eyjólfsson or Lawspeaker Skapti or any other leading men who are willing to accept my friendship and tokens. But if you are carried to other countries that are nearer to here, then you must arrange it in such a way that you know for certain that Hrœrekr will never come back to Norway alive, and you are only to do this if you find there is no other alternative.'

Now when Þórarinn was ready and there was a favourable wind, then he sailed all along the outer route beyond the islands, and north of Líðandisnes he set his course out to sea. The winds were not very favourable, but he took care most of all to keep away from the shore. He sailed to the south of Iceland and could see signs of its closeness, and so west round the coast into the Greenland Sea. Then he encountered strong currents and much tossing about, and towards the end of summer he came to land in Iceland in Breiðifjǫrðr. Þorgils Arason then came up to them first of any men of rank. Þórarinn tells him about King Óláfr's message and the friendship and tokens that would accompany his taking charge of King Hrœrekr. Þorgils responded [128] well and invited King Hrœrekr to stay with him, and he stayed with Þorgils Arason for the winter. He was not happy there and asked Þorgils to have him taken to Guðmundr's, saying that he had heard that Guðmundr kept the highest state in Iceland, and that he had been sent into his keeping. Þorgils did as he asked, providing him with an escort and had him taken to the keeping of Guðmundr at Mǫðruvellir. Guðmundr welcomed him for the sake of the king's messages and he stayed the second winter with Guðmundr.

Then he could not bear it there any longer. Then Guðmundr provided him with lodging on a small farm called at Kálfskinn, and there were few servants there. Hrœrekr stayed there the third winter, and he said this, that since he had given up his kingdom, that was the place where he had stayed, that he had been most content, because there he had been most highly respected by everyone. The following summer Hrœrekr took a sickness that brought about his death. So it is said that this is the only king who lies buried in Iceland. Þórarinn Nefjólfsson spent a long time in trading voyages, but sometimes stayed with King Óláfr.

CHAPTER EIGHTY-SIX

That summer, when Þórarinn took Hrœrekr to Iceland, then Hjalti Skeggjason also went to Iceland, and King Óláfr sent him on his way with friendly gifts when they parted. That summer Eyvindr úrarhorn went on a viking voyage to the British Isles and came in the autumn to Ireland, to King Konofogor of the Irish. They met in the autumn in Úlfreksfjǫrðr, the king of the Irish and Jarl Einarr from Orkney, and there was a great battle there. [129] King Konofogor had much greater forces and won the victory, but Jarl Einarr fled on a single ship and got back to Orkney in the autumn having lost nearly all his troops and all the booty that they had gained. And the jarl was mightily displeased with his journey and blamed his defeat on the Norwegians who had taken part in the battle with the king of the Irish.

CHAPTER EIGHTY-SEVEN

Now the story must be taken up where we previously left off, that King Óláfr inn digri went on his bridal journey and to fetch his betrothed wife, King Óláfr of the Svíar's daughter Ingigerðr. The king had a great following, and it was so choice that all the men of rank that he could get hold of went with him, and each of the powerful men was accompanied by a choice troop, both as regards descent and those who were most accomplished. This host was fitted out with the finest equipment, both in ships and weapons and clothing. They took their troops eastwards to Konungahella. And when they got there, then there was no news of the king of the Svíar. Moreover there was no one come there on his behalf. King Óláfr stayed near Konungahella for a large part of the summer and made many enquiries as to what people could say about the king of the Svíar's movements or plans, but no one was able to tell him anything for certain about that. Then he sent some of his men up into Gautland to Jarl Rǫgnvaldr and had him asked if he knew what was the reason that the king of the Svíar had not kept the appointment that had been arranged. The jarl says that he did not know, 'but if I find out,' he says, 'then I shall immediately send my men to King Óláfr and let him know what it all means, whether this delay is for any reason other than because of the manifold business that can often bring it about that the king of the Svíar's travels are delayed more than he intends.'

[130] CHAPTER EIGHTY-EIGHT

King Óláfr Eiríksson of the Svíar had first of all a mistress who was called Eðla, the jarl of Vinðland's daughter. She had previously been captured in a raid and called the king's concubine. Their children were Emundr, Ástríðr, Hólmfríðr. They also had a son and he was born on the eve of St James's day.[145] And when the boy came to be baptised, then the bishop had him named Jákob. But the Svíar did not like this name, declaring that there had never been a king of the Svíar called Jákob. All King Óláfr's children were good-looking and very intelligent. The queen was haughty and did not treat her stepchildren kindly. The king sent his son Emundr to Vinðland, and he was brought up there with his mother's family, and he did not observe Christianity for a long time. The king's daughter Ástríðr was brought up in Vestra-Gautland with a high-ranking man called Egill. She was the most beautiful of women and very well spoken, cheerful in speech and modest, generous with her possessions. And when she came of age she often stayed with her father and was well liked by everyone.

King Óláfr was haughty and ungentle in speech. He was extremely displeased by the people having made an uproar at him at the Uppsalir assembly and threatened him with harsh treatment, and he blamed it mostly on Jarl Rǫgnvaldr. He had had no preparations made for the bridal journey, as had been agreed in the winter, for marrying his daughter Ingigerðr to King Óláfr digri of Norway and going that summer to the border between the two countries. And as time passed, many people became curious [131] as to what plans the king might have or whether he would observe his agreement with the king of Norway, or whether he would breach the agreement and also the peace. There were many that were very worried about this, but no one was so bold as to dare to raise the subject with the king. But many complained about it to the king's daughter Ingigerðr and asked her to find out what the king's intentions were. She replies:

'I am not keen to start a discussion with the king about the matters between him and Óláfr digri, for neither of them is a friend of the other. His response to me was unpleasant on the one occasion that I spoke on behalf of Óláfr digri.'

[145] The day before the feast of St James the Great (25th July). Jákob is the Swedish equivalent of James, so the child was effectively named after the saint.

This business caused the king's daughter Ingigerðr much anxiety. She was worried and gloomy, and became very concerned to know what the king was going to do. What she suspected more than anything else was that he would not fulfil his undertaking to the king of Norway, for it was evident that he got angry every time Óláfr digri was referred to as king.

CHAPTER EIGHTY-NINE

It was early one day that the king rode out taking his hawks and hounds and his men with him. And when they released their hawks, then the king's hawk killed in a single flight two grouse, and immediately afterwards he sent it off again and that time it slew three grouse. The hounds raced underneath and picked up each bird that hit the ground. The king rode after them and himself picked up his catch and boasted a great deal, saying:

'It will be a long time before most of you have such a catch.'

They agreed, saying that they thought that no king would have such great good fortune with his hawking. Then the king rode home, as did they all. The king's daughter was happy then, and came out of her room then, and when she saw that [132] the king was riding into the courtyard, she turned into it and greeted him. He welcomed her with a laugh and straight away brought out his birds, telling her of his catch and saying:

'Where do you know of the king who has got such a great catch in such a short time?'

She replies: 'This is a good morning's hunting, my lord, when you have taken five grouse, but it was a better one when King Óláfr of Norway captured five kings in one morning and took possession of all their realms.'

And when he heard this, then he leapt from his horse and turned towards her and said:

'Be sure of this, Ingigerðr, that however much love you have conceived for that fat man, you shall never enjoy him nor either of you the other. I shall wed you to some prominent man with whom I can be friends, but I can never be the friend of the man who has deprived me of my kingdom by force and caused me many a loss by plundering and killing.'

Thus they ended their talk, and each of them went their own way.

CHAPTER NINETY

The king's daughter Ingigerðr had now found out the truth about King Óláfr's intentions, and immediately sent men down into Vestra-Gautland to Jarl Rǫgnvaldr and had him told what the position was with the king of the Svíar, and that the whole treaty with the king of Norway was broken, and bade the jarl be on his guard, and the Vestr-Gautar, for they could not count on peace on the part of the people of Norway. And when the jarl learned of these events, he sends a message all round his realm bidding them be on their guard in case the people of Norway should decide to attack them. The jarl also sent messengers to King Óláfr digri and had him told the information he had received, and also that he wanted to keep his agreement and friendship with King Óláfr, and begged this too, that the king should not attack his realm. But when this message reached King Óláfr, he was very angry [133] and worried, and it was for several days that no one could get a word out of him. After that he held a meeting with his troops. Bjǫrn stallari then stood up first, and to begin with started his speech with how he had travelled east the previous winter to arrange a peace, saying how Jarl Rǫgnvaldr had welcomed him. He also says how perversely and harshly the king of the Svíar had received these proposals to begin with.

'But the settlement that was made,' he says, 'was more as a result of the power of the people and the influence of Þorgnýr and the support of Jarl Rǫgnvaldr than from any goodwill on the part of the king of the Svíar. And we therefore feel sure that the king must be the cause of the settlement being broken, but it will not be the jarl's fault. We found him to be a true friend of King Óláfr. Now the king wishes to know from the leaders and from other members of his following, what course he shall now adopt, whether he is to go up into Gautland and raid with the forces that we now have, or whether you prefer to adopt another course.'

He spoke both long and eloquently. After that many men of rank spoke, and it all came down to the same thing in the end, that everyone was against warfare, saying as follows:

'Though we have a large army, yet there are gathered together here leading men and men of rank, but for warfare young men are no less suitable, ones who are eager to gain wealth and fame. And it is also the practice of noblemen, if they are to go into fighting or battle, that they take with them many men for support and protection, and often those men do not fight any worse who have few possessions than those who are brought up wealthy.'

And as a result of their arguments it was the king's decision to break up the expedition, giving each man leave to go home, and announcing that the next summer he would call out a levy from the whole country and take them against the king of the Svíar and avenge this breach of his word. Everyone was very pleased at this. Then King Óláfr went north into the Vík and established himself in the autumn in Borg and had [134] all the provisions brought there that he needed for staying the winter, and stayed there with a large following for the winter.

CHAPTER NINETY-ONE

People spoke in very different ways about Jarl Rǫgnvaldr. Some considered that he was a true friend of King Óláfr, but some thought this hard to believe and said that he would manage to persuade the king of the Svíar to keep his word and the agreement between him and King Óláfr digri. According to what he said, the poet Sigvatr was a great friend of Jarl Rǫgnvaldr, and often spoke of this to King Óláfr. He offered the king to go to see Jarl Rǫgnvaldr and find out what he could discover about the king of the Svíar, and try if he could bring about some settlement. The king was well pleased at this, because he very much liked to talk frequently with his trusted friends about the king's daughter Ingigerðr. At the beginning of winter the poet Sigvatr in a party of three travelled from Borg and east across Markir and so on to Gautland. But then, before they parted, King Óláfr and Sigvatr, he spoke a verse:

62. Now sit sound till I come to *Skald* I 707
 claim fulfilment of your promise,
 and we meet in your mansion
 once more, King Ǫleifr.
 That the helm-storm's tree[146] keep hold of
 his life, is the skáld's prayer—
 here ends the eulogy;
 I close my verse—and this country.

[135] 63. Now are spoken—though speak further *Skald* I 708
 still we could of other matters—
 the words that of all others
 are to us, king, of most moment.
 May God let you, mind-bold
 monarch, guard your country,
 for you are born to it—
 I have that wish, truly.

After that they went eastwards to Eiðar and found a poor vessel to take them across the river, a kind of small ferry boat,[147] and managed with difficulty to get across the river. Sigvatr said:

64. I had dragged—for I dreaded, *Austrfararvísur* 2
 damp, turning back—the wobbly *Skald* I 585

---

[146] *hjalmdrífu viðr*: 'wood or tree of the storm of helmets (battle)', warrior.
[147] *eikjukarfi nǫkkurr*: cf. next note.

bark[148] to Eið; so badly
on the boat we managed.
[136]   Trolls[149] take that laughable
tub! I've seen no worse transport.
I took a risk on the sea-ram;[150]
it ran better than I looked for.

Next they went through Eiðaskógr. Sigvatr spoke a verse:

65.   It wasn't the first time—it's known widely—   *Austrfararvísur* 3
we met trouble; as through the forest   *Skald* I 587
twelve leagues and one extra,
angry, I ran from Eiðar.
I think, though, we travelled
there keenly that day, walking,
though sores made spots on both
soles of the king's followers.

Next they went across Gautland and in the evening reached the farm that is called Hof. The entrance there was shut and they could not get in. Those inside said that it was a sacred place. They turned away from there. Sigvatr said:

66.   I chose to aim for Hof;[151] the   *Austrfararvísur* 4
entrance was shut, but outside   *Skald* I 589
I made enquiries. Keenly
my curved-down[152] nose I thrust in.

[148] *karfi*: this word does not appear elsewhere in poetry, and it is difficult to translate it closely (Foote 1978, 59). The context suggests a small, unreliable craft (*bátr* 'boat' is used of it in l. 4, *hlægiskip* 'laughable ship' in l. 5). In prose it can suggest a larger vessel (see above, pp. 70, 104, 105, where it is translated (on the basis of perhaps spurious etymology) by 'carvel' (a small, light and fast ship), and where it is apparently used to carry Ketill and his 40 men. A word designating a larger, more impressive vessel could have been used ironically by Sigvatr of his inadequate tub. In the prose the boat is called *eikjukarfi*, here translated as 'a small ferry boat' (*eikja* on its own means a dugout oaken boat). Snorri may have based the form *eikjukarfi* on *karfi* in Sigvatr's verse.

[149] *hauga herr*: 'the grave-mounds army', trolls.

[150] *heims hrútr*: 'the ram of the sea', ship; *heimr* 'world, region' does not usually refer to the sea but may be part of an incomplete kenning. Many editions emend to *húms* (*húm* or *húmr* is a poetical word for the sea).

[151] *Hof* could be a farm name, as Snorri assumes, or a common noun meaning '(heathen) temple'. It is believed that in Iceland such place names denote places where there had been heathen temples in former times.

[152] *niðrlútt*: 'bent down'. This could be a description of the poet's nose (cf. *niðrbjúgt nef* in *Rígsþula* 10/5), or it could suggest he is bending down or thrusting his nose in over a low door.

[137] Small response I got there;
sacred they called it;[153] heathens
held me back; I bade ogresses
bandy words with them.

Then he came to another dwelling. The housewife was standing there in the doorway, told him not to enter there, saying that they were holding sacrifices to the elves. Sigvatr said:

67. 'Come not in,' cried the woman,   *Austrfararvísur* 5
'cursed fellow, any further.   *Skald* I 590
I fear Óðinn's
anger: we are heathens.'
They were holding, the hateful
hag said, she who drove me
off like a wolf, unyielding,
elf-sacrifice in her farmhouse.

The next evening he arrived at the house of three farmers, and each of them was called Ǫlvir, and they all drove him out. Sigvatr said:

[138] 68. Now three namesakes, who turned their   *Austrfararvísur* 6
napes against me,[154] have barred my   *Skald* I 592
way; the trees of the whetstone-base[155]
without honour are acting.
Yet above all I'm anxious
that every sea-ski loader[156]
named Ǫlvir from now on
us newcomers will drive out.

Then they travelled on again that evening and met the fourth farmer, and he was said to be the best host among them. This one drove him out. Sigvatr said:

69. I went later to look for—   *Austrfararvísur* 7
lavish treatment expecting—   *Skald* I 593
a wave-gleam breaker,[157] one who
warriors said was most friendly.
The pick's guardian[158] gazed at me,
glum; how bad the worst must be

[153] Either the place, or, possibly, the day.
[154] i.e. turned their backs on me.
[155] *heinflets þollr*: 'tree of the whetstone-floor (sword)', warrior.
[156] *hafskíðs hlæðir*: 'loader of the ocean-ski (ship)', seafarer, man.
[157] *bǫru bliks brjótr*: 'breaker of the wave's gleam (gold)', generous man.
[158] *grefs gætir*: 'keeper of the pickaxe', farmer, boor.

> (yet I don't spread far the foibles
> of folk) if he's the best one!

[139] 70. I missed, on the way east of   *Austrfararvísur* 8
        Eiðaskógr, the farm of   *Skald* I 594
        Ósta, when I asked the
        unchristian man for lodging.
        I met not the son of great Saxi;
        inside there was no fairness.
        I was, in one evening,
        ordered out four times over.

And when they got to Jarl Rǫgnvaldr's, then the jarl said they had had a hard journey. Sigvatr said:

71. Those sent by the king of Sygnir,[159]   *Austrfararvísur* 13
      who sought out the chieftains   *Skald* I 601
      with messages, have had a mighty
      mission on their hands.
      I spared myself little, but large is
      the luggage of men on the journey;
      the capable king of Norway
      decreed our route there southwards.

72. Eiðaskógr was arduous going   *Austrfararvísur* 14
      eastwards for fine fellows   *Skald* I 603
[140] to the lords' suppressor;[160] the prince's
      praise this fellow[161] strengthens.
      I shouldn't have been shooed off by
      shrubs of the slipway's bench's
      costly flame[162] of the ruler, before I
      reached my generous master.

Jarl Rǫgnvaldr gave Sigvatr a gold arm-ring. A woman said that he had travelled to some purpose with those black eyes of his. Sigvatr said:

73. To us[163] these Icelandic   *Austrfararvísur* 15
      eyes, the black ones, woman,   *Skald* I 604

---

[159] *Sygna gramr*: king of the Sygnir, inhabitants of Sogn in Norway, i.e. king of Norway.

[160] *jǫfra þrystir*: 'oppressor of kings or jarls', ruler, here Rǫgnvaldr?

[161] i.e. the poet.

[162] *hlunns bekkjar dýrloga runnr*: 'bush (man) of precious flame (gold) of the slipway-planks' bench (i.e. resting-place) (sea)', man.

[163] i.e. 'me'.

have shown a path, long and lofty,
leading to a bright arm-ring.
This foot of mine, mead-Nanna,[164]
most bravely has trodden
on ancient roadways
unknown to your husband.

And when Sigvatr got back to King Óláfr's and he went into the hall, he said, looking at the walls:

[141]
74. With helmets men of the household[165]   *Austrfararvísur* 16
who feed the wound-swan[166] and mailcoats   *Skald* I 605
furnish the king's hall; plenty
I find of both on the walls here.
So no young king has nobler—
no doubt there is about it—
hangings in his house to boast of;
the hall is fine in all ways.

After that he tells about his travels and spoke these verses:

75. I ask the great-hearted retinue,   *Austrfararvísur* 1
active prince,[167] to listen   *Skald* I 583
to the way I worked verses—
weathering hardship—about my journey.
I was sent up from the skis of
the swan-plain[168] on a long journey
east to Sweden—seldom after
I slept in the autumn.

And when he spoke to the king, he said:

[142] 76. I kept conscientiously,   *Austrfararvísur* 17
King Óleifr, to arrangements   *Skald* I 606
made with you, when I met the
mighty, excellent Rǫgnvaldr.

[164] *mjǫð-Nanna*: 'mead-goddess', woman (server of mead). The suffixed definite article on this word and *kona* 'woman' just above are used to give a vocative sense 'O woman', 'O Nanna'.

[165] *hirðmenn*: 'courtiers, retainers', an early borrowing of Old English *hīredmenn* 'household retainers'.

[166] *bens svanr*: 'wound's swan', carrion bird, that warriors feed with carrion.

[167] *hressfœrr jǫfurr*: manuscripts of the *Separate Saga*, followed by *Skald* I, have this phrase in the genitive: 'retainers of the vigorous prince'.

[167] *svanvangs ǫndurr*: 'ski of the swan-plain (sea)', ship.

I dealt with many matters,
metal-guardian,[169] in the courts of
the open-handed one; I've not heard of
a hired man's[170] speeches more loyal.

77. The jarls' kinsman requested you to   *Austrfararvísur* 18
keep well each housecarl   *Skald* I 608
of his, Rhine's sun's harmer,[171]
who may wander hither;
And each who wants to go eastwards,   *Fsk* 180
just as certainly, Listi's
prince,[172] of your people, will have
support there with Rǫgnvaldr.

[143] 78. Most people pondered, ruler,   *Austrfararvísur* 19
plans, whom Eiríkr's kinsman[173]   *Skald* I 609
had earlier urged to this treason,
as I travelled eastwards.
But I declare the aid of the jarls' kinsman
Ulfr's brother,[174] helped you
in this, to win the land, and likewise
what you took from Sveinn.

79. Wise Úlfr between you both had,   *Austrfararvísur* 20
Ǫleifr, peace terms accepted;   *Skald* I 611
we got sound answers; you both are
setting aside conflict.
Rǫgnvaldr caused those conflicts,
crusher of thieves' race,[175] to you to
be yielded, as if no bitter
breach had been engendered.

[144] At the beginning of winter the poet Sigvatr in his party of three travelled from Borg and east across Markir and so on to Gautland, and in that journey often had a poor reception. One evening he arrived at the house

---

[169] *málma vǫrðr*: 'guardian of weapons (made of metal)', warrior.
[170] *heiðmaðr*: a man who receives payment, here the king's subordinate, Rǫgnvaldr.
[171] *Rínar sólar søkkvir*: 'sinker (destroyer) of sun of the Rhine (gold)', generous man.
[172] *Lista þengill*: 'king of Listi (district of Norway)', i.e. king of Norway.
[173] *Eiríks ætt*: 'the family of Eiríkr (Jarl Eiríkr Hákonarson, defeated by King Óláfr at Nesjar)'; *ætt* could refer to one or more kinsmen of Eiríkr. The word is used here to indicate his brother Sveinn, mentioned in l. 6.
[174] *Úlfs bróðir*: Rǫgnvaldr's sons are named on p. 148 below as Úlfr and Eilífr.
[175] *þjófa aldar rýrir*: 'diminisher of the race of thieves', just ruler.

of three farmers, and they all drove him out. Then the poet Sigvatr uttered the *Austrfararvísur* about his journey.

The poet Sigvatr came to Jarl Rǫgnvaldr's and stayed there with good entertainment for a long time. Then he learned from letters sent by the king's daughter Ingigerðr that messengers of King Jarizleifr had come from the east from Hólmgarðr to King Óláfr of the Svíar to ask for the hand of the king's daughter Ingigerðr on behalf of Jarizleifr, and this too, that King Óláfr had received this very favourably. Then there also came to Jarl Rǫgnvaldr's court King Óláfr's daughter Ástríðr. Then there was held a great banquet there. Sigvatr soon gets on speaking terms with the king's daughter. She soon recognised who he was and his family background, for Sigvatr's sister's son, the poet Óttarr, he had been there for a long time on friendly terms with King Óláfr of the Svíar. Then a great deal was discussed. Jarl Rǫgnvaldr asked whether King Óláfr would be willing to marry Ástríðr.

'And if he is willing,' he says, 'then I suppose that about this match we shall not enquire of the king of the Svíar.'

The king's daughter Ástríðr said the same thing.

After this Sigvatr and his men went back and arrived shortly before Yule at Borg to see King Óláfr. Soon Sigvatr tells King Óláfr of the events he had heard about. The king was at first very gloomy, when Sigvatr tells about King Jarizleifr's proposal of marriage, and King Óláfr says that he could expect nothing but evil from the king of the Svíar—'whether or not we ever manage to repay him with something he may remember.'

But after a while the king asked Sigvatr a great deal about what was going on in the east in Gautland. Sigvatr tells him a lot about the good looks of the king's daughter Ástríðr and how well spoken she was, and also that everyone that was there said that she was in no way less well endowed than her sister Ingigerðr. The king was pleased to [145] hear this. Sigvatr told him of all the discussions that he and Ástríðr had had together, and the king was greatly impressed and said this:

'The king of the Svíar will not expect that I would dare to marry his daughter without his consent.'

But this affair was not revealed to anyone else. King Óláfr and the poet Sigvatr often spoke about this affair. The king asked Sigvatr in detail what he had found out about Jarl Rǫgnvaldr—'what sort of friend he is to us,' he says. Sigvatr says this, that the jarl was a very great friend to King Óláfr. Then Sigvatr said:

80. You must, mighty ruler,   *Austrfararvísur* 21
     with mighty Rǫgnvaldr firmly   *Fsk* 180 (1st half)
     keep the treaty; he kindly   *Skald* I 613
     cares for your needs night and day.

I know you have in him,
holder of meetings,[176] much
the best of allies in the east,
all along the green ocean.[177]

After Yule these two, the poet Sigvatr's sister's son Þórðr skotakollr (?-head) and secondly Sigvatr's servant lad, left the court secretly. They travelled eastwards into Gautland. They had travelled there with Sigvatr the previous autumn. And when they came to the jarl's court, they produced before the jarl the tokens that the jarl and Sigvatr had fixed with [146] each other at parting. They had also taken there the tokens that King Óláfr himself had sent the jarl in confidence. Forthwith the jarl immediately set out and with him the king's daughter Ástríðr, taking nearly a hundred (120) men and it was a choice troop both of his followers and of powerful farmer's sons, with all their equipment of the finest, both weapons and clothing and horses; they then rode north to Norway to Sarpsborg, getting there at Candlemas.[178]

CHAPTER NINETY-TWO

King Óláfr had had preparations made there. All kinds of drink were there, the best that could be got, and all other provisions of the best were there. He had also now summoned to come to him many men of rank from the districts round about. And when the jarl arrived there with his troop, then the king welcomes him exceptionally warmly, and the jarl was provided with spacious and fine quarters that were fitted out splendidly, and in addition with servants, and with people to ensure that nothing should be lacking that could enhance the banquet. And when this banquet had gone on for some days, then the king and the jarl and the king's daughter held a discussion, and the outcome of their talk was the decision that Jarl Rǫgnvaldr should betroth the king of the Svíar's daughter Ástríðr to King Óláfr of Norway with the dowry that had previously been stipulated that her sister Ingigerðr was to have brought with her from her home. The king was also to give Ástríðr the same bridal settlement as he was to have given her sister Ingigerðr. Then the banquet was extended, and then the wedding of King Óláfr and Queen Ástríðr was celebrated with great splendour. After that Jarl Rǫgnvaldr went back to Gautland, and at their parting the king gave the jarl good and great gifts and they parted the best of friends and stayed so as long as they both lived.

[176] *þinga kennir*: 'experiencer of meetings (both councils and battles)', king or warrior.
[177.] in the east (*á austrvega*) here means eastern Scandinavia, Sweden; the green ocean (*grœna salt*) is presumably Eystrasalt, the Baltic; cf. vol. I, st. 11.
[178] 2nd February.

[147] CHAPTER NINETY-THREE

The following spring King Jarizleifr's messengers came to Svíþjóð from the east, from Hólmgarðr, and went to take up the agreement whereby King Óláfr had the previous summer promised to give his daughter Ingigerðr to King Jarizleifr in marriage. King Óláfr spoke of this matter with Ingigerðr, saying that it was his wish that she should marry King Jarizleifr. She replies: 'If I am to marry King Jarizleifr, then I want,' she says, 'in my bridal gift Aldeigjuborg and the jarl's dominion that belongs with it.'

And the messengers from Garðaríki agreed to this on behalf of their king.

Then Ingigerðr spoke: 'If I am to go to the east, to Garðaríki, then I wish to choose someone from the Swedish realm that seems to me most suitable to go with me. I also wish to stipulate that he shall have there in the east no lower rank than here, and no worse or fewer rights or privileges in any way than he has here.'

The king agreed to this, and so did the messengers. The king pledged his troth to this arrangement, as did the messengers. Then the king asked Ingigerðr which person it is in his kingdom that she wishes to choose to accompany her. She replies:

'The person is my kinsman Jarl Rǫgnvaldr Úlfsson.'

The king replies: 'It is in a different way I had intended to reward Jarl Rǫgnvaldr for his treason in taking my daughter to Norway and handing her over there as a concubine to that fat man, one whom he knew to be our greatest enemy, and because of this he shall be hanged this summer.'

Ingigerðr then begged her father to keep the promise he had given her, and the result of her entreaty was that the king says that Rǫgnvaldr should leave the Swedish realm freely, and not come within sight of the king, nor return to Svíþjóð as long as Óláfr was king. Ingigerðr then sent men to see the jarl and had them tell him what had happened and gave him instructions [148] as to where they should meet. So the jarl immediately set out and rode up into Eystra-Gautland and got himself ships there and then went with his troop to meet the king's daughter Ingigerðr. They all travelled together in the summer east to Garðaríki. Then Ingigerðr was married to King Jarizleifr. Their sons were Valdamarr, Vissivaldr, Holti inn frœkni (the Brave). Queen Ingigerðr gave Jarl Rǫgnvaldr Aldeigjuborg and the jarl's dominion that belonged with it. Jarl Rǫgnvaldr stayed there a long time and was a man of renown. Jarl Rǫgnvaldr and Ingibjǫrg's sons were these two, Jarl Úlfr and Jarl Eilífr.

CHAPTER NINETY-FOUR

There is a man known as Emundr of Skarar. He was lawman there in western Gautland and was the wisest and most eloquent of men. He was of high lineage and had many kinsmen, was very wealthy. He was said to be crafty and not all that trustworthy. He was the most powerful person in Vestra-Gautland when the jarl was gone away. Then, the same spring as Jarl Rǫgnvaldr left Gautland, the Gautar held meetings among themselves and repeatedly debated between themselves what the king of the Svíar would decide to do. They heard that he was angry with them because they had made friends with King Óláfr of Norway instead of entering into conflict with him. He also brought charges against those [149] who had accompanied his daughter Ástríðr to Norway. Some said that they should seek support for themselves from the king of Norway and offer him their service. Some were against this and said that the Vestr-Gautar did not have the resources to enter into conflict with the Svíar.

'And the king of Norway is far away,' they say, 'for the seat of his power is far away, and the first thing to do is send men to the king of the Svíar and see if we can negotiate a reconciliation with him. And if that is not possible, then our course will be to seek support for ourselves from the king of Norway.'

Then the farmers asked Emundr to undertake this mission, and he agreed and took thirty men and came out in Eystra-Gautland. There were many of his kinsmen and friends there. He was kindly received there. He had discussion there with the wisest men about the problem, and they all reached agreement, and people considered that it was improper and unlawful, the king's treatment of them. Then Emundr travelled up into Svíþjóð and had discussion there with many powerful people, and the result was always the same. He then continued his journey until he reached Uppsalir late in the day. They got themselves a good lodging there and stayed the night. The next day Emund went to see the king while the king was sitting at an assembly and there were many people around him. Emundr approached him and bowed to him and saluted him. The king looked at him and greeted him and asked him for news. Emundr replies:

'There is not much news with us Gautar. But it seems to us something unusual, that last winter Atti inn dœlski (of the Dales/the Foolish) of Vermaland went up into the forest with his skis and bow. We declare him the greatest huntsman. On the mountain he had taken so many skins that he had filled his sledge to the maximum he could haul with it. [150] Then he turned home from the forest. He saw a squirrel in the wood and shot at it and missed. Then he got angry and let go the sledge and skied after the squirrel. But the squirrel kept on going where the forest was thickest, and sometimes among the roots of trees, sometimes up into the branches, then sailed between the branches into another tree. And when Atti shot at it, it always flew above or below, but the squirrel never went out of Atti's sight. He got so enthusiastic about this quarry that he skied after it all day, but even so could not get this squirrel. And when it began to get dark, he threw himself down in the snow, as he was accustomed to do, and lay there through the night. It was snowing in drifts.

The next day Atti went to search for his sledge and never again found it, and with that went home. Such is my news, Lord.'

The king says: 'Not much news, if there is no more to tell.'

Emundr replies: 'It also happened a little while ago, which may be said to be news, that Gauti Tófason went with five warships out along the Gautelfr, and while he was lying in Eikreyjar, then five large Danish merchant ships came there. Gauti's party quickly overpowered four of the merchant ships, losing no men, but winning a great deal of wealth, while the fifth ship got out to sea and managed to hoist its sail. Gauti went after it with just his one ship, and to begin with gained on them. Then the wind began to freshen, the merchant ship then went faster, making for the open sea. Then Gauti was going to turn back. Then a storm got up. He wrecked his ship off Hlésey, losing all its goods and the majority of the crew. But his associates were supposed to wait for them in Eikreyjar. Then Danes came upon them with fifteen merchant ships and slew them all and took all the wealth that they had previously won. That's how their greed served them.'

The king replies: 'That is significant news, and worth telling. But what is your purpose here?'

Emundr replies: 'I come, Lord, to seek a solution to a problem wherein our law [151] and the law of Uppsalir diverge.'

The king asks: 'What is the difficulty that you wish to raise?'

Emundr says: 'There were two men of noble birth, equal in descent but unequal in possessions and temperament. They had a dispute about land, and losses were inflicted on each by the other, more by the one that was wealthier, until their dispute was settled and arbitrated at a general assembly. The one that was previously the wealthier had to pay. And for the first instalment he paid a gosling for a goose, a piglet for an old pig, and for a mark of pure gold he paid half a mark of gold, and the other half mark of clay and mud. and moreover threatened the one who received this payment as his due with harsh treatment. What is your judgment in this case, Lord?'

The king says: 'Let him pay in full what was adjudged, and to the king three times that amount. And if it is not paid within one year, then let him forfeit all his possessions, half his wealth to go to the royal treasury, and half to the one whose claims he was due to compensate.'

Emundr appealed to all the people who had most say there to witness to this judgment, and cited the law that was valid at the Uppsalir assembly. After that he took his leave of the king and then went out. And then other men brought their suits before the king, and he was busy a large part of the day with people's business. And when the king sat down to his meal, then he asked where Lawman Emundr was. He was told that he was back at his lodging. Then said the king:

'Go and fetch him, he shall be my guest today.'

Next the special dishes were served, [152] and after that entertainers came in with harps and fiddles and musical instruments, and after that drink was served. The king was very merry and had many important people as his guests, and Emundr slipped from his mind. The king spent the rest of the day drinking and slept through the following night. But in the morning, when the king awoke, then he reflected on what Emundr had said the previous day. And when he was dressed, he had his advisers summoned to him. King Óláfr had about him twelve of the wisest men. They sat alongside him in courts of law and deliberated on difficult cases, but this was not without problems, for the king did not like it if judgments diverged from what was right, and it did not do to disagree with him. At this consultation the king began to speak and ordered Lawman Emundr to be summoned there. But when the messenger returned, 'Lord,' he said, 'Lawman Emundr rode away yesterday as soon as he had eaten.'

Then the king said: 'Tell me this, good lords, what did the legal question relate to, that Emundr asked about yesterday?'

They replied: 'Lord, you must have thought it out, if it meant something other than he said.'

The king said: 'The two men of noble birth that he spoke about then, who had been in dispute, though one of them was wealthier than the other, and had each inflicted losses on the other, in this he was talking about me and Óláfr digri.'

'So it is, lord,' they said, 'as you say.'

The king says: 'There was a judgment on our case at the Uppsalir assembly. But what was the reason for his saying that there was underpayment, a gosling for a goose, and a piglet for an old pig, and mud for half the gold?'

Arnviðr blindi (the Blind) replies: 'Lord,' he says, 'there is a very great difference between gold and mud, but the difference is greater between a king and a slave. You promised Óláfr digri your daughter Ingigerðr. She is of royal blood in every line of her descent, of the line of the Uppsvíar, which is the noblest in the Northern lands, for this line is descended from the gods themselves. But now King Óláfr has married Ástríðr, and though she is a child of a king, yet her mother is a concubine, [153] and moreover Wendish. There is a great difference between such kings, when one of them accepts this thankfully, and it is no surprise that one Norwegian should not be able to consider himself the equal of a king of Uppsalir. Let us all now give thanks for this, that this continues, for the gods have long taken great care of their loved ones, though now many do not care for that religion.'

There were three brothers, Arnviðr blindi—his sight was so poor that he was hardly able to fight, and he was the most eloquent of men; the second was Þorviðr stami (Stammerer)—he could not speak more than two words together; he was the boldest and most determined man there; the third was

Freyviðr daufi (the Deaf)—he could not hear very well. All these three brothers were powerful and wealthy, of high lineage and great wisdom and all of them dear to the king.

Then King Óláfr said: 'What does that mean, what Emundr spoke about Atti dœlski?' Then no one replied, and they all looked at each other. The king said: 'Speak now.' Then said Þorviðr stami: '"Atti":[179] aggressive, impetuous, malicious; "dœlskr": foolish.' Then spoke the king: 'Who is meant by this slight?' Then Freyviðr daufi replies: 'Lord, people will speak more openly if you give your leave.' The king said: 'Speak now, Freyviðr, by my leave, whatever you wish to say.'

Freyviðr then began his speech: 'My brother Þorviðr, who is reckoned the wisest of us, declares that it is all one, "Atti" and "atsamr" (aggressive), "dœlskr" and foolish. He calls a person this who dislikes peace, so that he contends for trifles and yet does not get them, but as a result loses important advantages. Now I am deaf like this, but so have many now said, that I have been able to understand that many, both powerful and of the common people, do not like it, lord, that you do not keep your word to the king of Norway, and what is still worse, that you have acted in defiance of the public decision that was made at the Uppsala assembly. You have no need to fear the king of Norway or the king of Denmark or anyone else, as long as the Svíar army will follow you, but if the people of the country [154] turn against you unanimously, then we, your friends, can see nothing that can be done that will do any good.'

The king asks: 'Who are making themselves leaders of this movement to try to unseat me from my kingdom?'

Freyviðr replies: 'All Svíar want to keep their ancient law and their full rights. Consider this, lord, how many leading men are sitting here now over your policy-making. I think it is true to say that there are six of us here that you call your counsellors, but all the others I think have ridden away and gone to the countryside, and are holding an assembly with the people of the country, and to tell you the truth, then a war arrow[180] has been raised and sent round the whole country and a criminal court has been summoned. All of us brothers have been asked to take part in this undertaking, but none of us wants to earn the name of traitor to our lord, for our father was none.'

The king then began to speak: 'What course shall we now take? We have a great problem on our hands. Offer now some advice, good leaders, as to

[179] cf. the past tense of *etja* 'to incite (someone) to fight' and the noun *at* 'fight'.
[180] An army could be mustered by sending a symbolic arrow round a district.

how I can hold on to my kingdom and my patrimony; but I do not want to have to contend with the whole Svíar army.'

Arnviðr blindi replies: 'Lord, this seems to me advisable, that you ride down to Áróss with those troops that are willing to follow you, and there take your ships and so go out into Lǫgrinn. Summon the people to meet you, do not use harshness, offer people law and traditional rights, have the war arrow lowered.[181] It will not yet have travelled far over the country, for the time has been short. Send your men, those whom you trust, to meet with these people who have this plan in hand, and try whether this discontent can be put down.'

The king says that he will accept this counsel.

'I want,' he says, 'you brothers to go on this mission, for I trust you best of my men.'

Then Þorviðr stami said: 'I will stay behind, but let Jákob go. He is necessary.'

Then Freyviðr spoke: 'Let us do, lord, as Þorviðr says. He does not want to part with you in this [155] danger, but Arnviðr and I shall go.'

This plan was carried out, that King Óláfr went to his ships, made his way out into Lǫgrinn, and his following then soon increased. But Freyviðr and Arnviðr rode out onto Ullarakr, taking with them the king's son Jákob, but concealed his presence in the party. They soon realised that there was a gathering in the offing and a rush to arms, as the farmers were holding an assembly day and night. And when Freyviðr and his party came across their kinsmen and friends there, then they say this, that they want to join their troop, and they all welcome this gladly. Then the decisions were straight away handed over to the brothers, and the crowds come to join them, and yet they are all unanimous, saying that they are not going to have Óláfr as king over them any longer and they are not willing to put up with this injustice and arrogance from him, when he will not listen to what anyone says, even when leading men tell him what is true. And when Freyviðr saw the vehemence of the crowd, then he realised what a fix they were in. Then he held meetings with the leading men of the country and addressed them, saying:

'So it seems to me, if this great undertaking is to go forward, deposing Óláfr Eiríksson from his kingdom, that we Uppsvíar shall be in charge. It has always happened thus here, that what the leaders of the Uppsvíar have established among themselves, then other people of the country have accepted those arrangements. Our forefathers have not needed to consult the Vestr-Gautar about their government. Let us now not be such degenerates that Emundr has to tell us what to do. I want us to unite our policies, kinsmen and friends.'

All agreed to this and considered it to have been well spoken. After that the whole mass of people entered into this league that the leaders of the

[181] Cf. note 180 above.

Uppsvíar set up among themselves. Then the leaders of the troops were Freyviðr and Arnviðr. But when [156] Emundr realised what had happened, then he became doubtful whether the plan would be carried out. So then he went to see the brothers, and they had a discussion together. Then Freyviðr asks Emundr:

'What do you propose should happen then, if Óláfr Eiríksson is put to death, what king do you want to have?'

Emundr says: 'The one that we consider best suited for it, whether he is of noble descent or not.'

Freyviðr replies: 'We Uppsvíar do not want the kingdom to pass from the line of forefathers of the ancient kings in our time, as long as there is such a good supply available as there now is. King Óláfr has two sons, and we want to have one or other of them as king, and yet there is a great difference between them. One is legitimately born and Swedish in every line of descent, but the other is son of a concubine and Wendish on one side.'

This opinion brought forth great applause, and everyone wants Jákob as king. Then Emundr said:

'You Uppsvíar have the power to get your own way in this for the time being, but I tell you this, which is what will happen, that some of those that at the moment want nothing other than that the kingship in Svíþjóð should stay in the ancestral line, they themselves shall now live to agree when the kingship shall pass to other lines, and that will be for the best.'

After this the brothers Freyviðr and Arnviðr had the king's son Jákob brought forward into the assembly and had him given the title of king, and at the same time the Svíar gave him the name of Qnundr, and so he was called afterwards as long as he lived. He was then ten or twelve winters old. After this King Qnundr got himself a following and chose leaders alongside himself, and they all had troops together, as many as he felt he needed, but then he gave the host of farmers leave to go home. After this envoys passed between the kings, [157] and the next thing was that they met in person and made their settlement. Óláfr was to be king of the country as long as he lived. He must also maintain peace and settlement with the king of Norway and likewise with all those men that had been involved in this plan. Qnundr was also to be king, and have that part of the land that was agreed between father and son, but was to be obliged to side with the farmers if King Óláfr does anything that the farmers would not put up with from him.

After this envoys went to Norway to see King Óláfr with this message, that he was to undertake a naval expedition to a conference at Konungahella to meet the king of the Svíar, and further that the king of the Svíar wishes them to make a firm settlement. And when King Óláfr heard this message, then he was again as before eager for peace, and he goes with his troop as had been arranged. Then the king of the Svíar arrived there, and when these kinsmen by marriage met, then they confirm the settlement between them and peace. King Óláfr of the Svíar was affable and courteous. So says Þorsteinn fróði (the Learned), that there was a settlement situated in Hísing that had at various times belonged to either Norway or Gautland. Then the kings discussed between themselves that they should cast lots for this property and throw dice for it. The one whose throw was the highest was to have it. Then the king of the Svíar threw two sixes and said that King Óláfr did not now need to throw. He said, shaking the dice in his hand:

'There are still two sixes on the dice, and it will still be a small matter for my Lord God to make them turn up.'

He threw, and got two sixes. Then King Óláfr of the Svíar threw, and again got two sixes. Then King Óláfr of Norway threw, and there was a six on one, but the other broke in two, and there was seven on the two parts. The settlement then became his. We have not heard of anything further that happened at this conference. The kings parted reconciled.

[158] CHAPTER NINETY-FIVE

After these events that have just been narrated, King Óláfr turned his troops back to the Vík, going first to Túnsberg and staying there a short while, and went northwards across the country and by the autumn all the way north to Þrándheimr, having winter quarters prepared there and staying there for the winter. Óláfr was now sole ruler over the whole realm that Haraldr hárfagri had had, and more than that, in that he was the only king over the country. He had now peacefully and by agreement gained the part of the country that King Óláfr of the Svíar had previously had, and the part of the country that the king of the Danes had had, he took by force and ruled over that part as over everywhere else in the country. King Knútr of the Danes at this time ruled over both England and Denmark, and he himself stayed mostly in England, and set up rulers to govern the country in Denmark, and made no claims in Norway at this time.

CHAPTER NINETY-SIX

So it is said, that in the days of King Haraldr inn hárfagri of Norway, Orkney was settled, but previously it had been a haunt of vikings there. The first jarl in Orkney was called Sigurðr—he was son of Eysteinn glumra (Rattle) and brother of Jarl Rǫgnvaldr of the Mœrir—and after Sigurðr, his son Guthormr for one winter. After him Jarl Rǫgnvaldr's son Torf-Einarr (Turf-) took the jarldom, and was jarl for a long time and a powerful man. Haraldr hárfagri's son Hálfdan háleggr (Long-Leg) went against Torf-Einarr and drove him out of Orkney. Einarr then came back and killed Hálfdan on Rínansey. After that King Haraldr went to Orkney with an army. Einarr then fled up into Scotland. King Haraldr made the people of Orkney transfer [159] all their patrimonies to him by oath. After this the king and the jarl were reconciled, and the jarl became his man and received the lands in fief from the king and had to pay no dues on them, because they were subject to a great deal of raiding there. Then the king made raids in Scotland as is told in *Glymdrápa*.[182] After Torf-Einarr his sons, Arnkell, Erlendr, Þorfinnr hausakljúfr (Skull-Splitter), ruled over the lands. In those days Eiríkr blóðøx (Blood-Axe) came from Norway, and the jarls were then subject to him. Arnkell and Erlendr fell while raiding, but Þorfinnr ruled the lands and reached a ripe old age. His sons were Arnfiðr, Hávarðr, Hlǫðvir, Ljótr, Skúli. Their mother was Jarl Dungaðr of Katanes's daughter Grélǫð. Her mother was Þorsteinn rauðr's (Red's) daughter Gróa. Towards the end of Jarl Þorfinnr's days Blóðøx's sons came from Norway after fleeing before Jarl Hákon. Their tyranny in Orkney was then very harsh. Jarl Þorfiðr died of sickness. After him his sons ruled the lands, and there are great stories about them. Hlǫðvir lived the longest of them and then ruled the lands alone. Sigurðr digri (the Stout) was his son, who took the jarldom after him. He was powerful and a great warrior. In his days Óláfr Tryggvason went from raiding in the British Isles with his forces and made for Orkney and captured Jarl Sigurðr on Rǫgnvaldsey. He was found lying there with a single ship. King Óláfr then offered the jarl as his ransom that he should accept baptism and the true faith and become his man and preach Christianity over the whole of Orkney. King Óláfr took as hostage his son who was called Hundi or Hvelpr. From there Óláfr went to Norway and became king there. Hundi was with [160] King Óláfr for a few winters, and he died there, but afterwards Jarl Sigurðr paid King Óláfr no homage. He then went and married King Melkólmr of the Scots's daughter, and their son was Þorfinnr. There were also Jarl Sigurðr's elder sons, Sumarliði, Brúsi, Einarr rangmuðr (Twisted Mouth). Five winters or four after the fall of Óláfr Tryggvason, Jarl Sigurðr went to Ireland, but he appointed his elder sons to rule his lands. He sent Þorfinnr to his mother's father, the king of the Scots. On this expedition Jarl Sigurðr fell in Brjánsorrosta.[183] And when this news reached Orkney, then the brothers Sumarliði, Brúsi, Einarr were taken as jarls, and they divided the lands into three parts between them. Þorfinnr Sigurðarson was now five winters old when Jarl Sigurðr fell. And when news of his fall reached the king of the Scots, then the king gave his

[182] See vol. I, notes 118 and 155.
[183] Brjánn's Battle (the Battle of Clontarf; cf. *Njáls saga* ch. 157) took place 23rd April 1014. The chronology of this passage is flawed: Óláfr Tryggvason fell in September AD 1000.

kinsman Þorfinnr Katanes and Suðrland and the title of jarl as well and got men to govern the realm with him. Jarl Þorfinnr was already in his early years soon mature in every aspect of development. He was big and strong, an ugly person. And when he grew older, it was evident that he was an impetuous man, tough and fierce and very wise. Arnórr jarlaskáld (Jarls' Poet) mentions this:[184]

81. No man younger than Einarr's brother[185] under the cloud-hall,[186] mind-bold, has said he was ready to safeguard his state and fight to win it.

   Þorfinnsdrápa 5
   Orkn 43
   Skald II 235

[161] CHAPTER NINETY-SEVEN

The brothers Einarr and Brúsi were unlike in character. Brúsi was gentle and a very compliant person, wise and eloquent and popular. Einarr was obstinate, reserved and unfriendly, impetuous and avaricious and a great warrior. Sumarliði was like Brúsi in character, and he was the eldest and lived for the shortest time of the brothers. He died of sickness. After his death Þorfiðr claimed his share of Orkney. Einarr replied with this, that Þorfinnr had Katanes and Suðrland, the realm that their father Jarl Sigurðr had formerly held, and he reckoned that was equivalent to much more than a third part of Orkney, and he refused to allow Þorfinnr a share. But Brúsi granted a share for his own part.

'And I do not wish,' he says, 'to covet more of the lands than the third part that I possess without dispute.'

Then Einarr took possession of two parts of the islands. He became a powerful man and had a large following, was often out raiding in the summer and levied a large force from the land, but the gains from viking raids turned out to be variable. Then the farmers grew tired of this business, but the jarl kept on inflexibly with all his demands and would allow no one to oppose him. Jarl Einarr was the most arrogant person. Now there came to be famine

[184] Arnórr Þórðarson jarlaskáld, from Hítarnes in western Iceland, was the son of another poet, Þórðr Kolbeinsson (see vol. I, note 473). His nickname refers to his spending several years in Orkney and composing the memorial poems *Rǫgnvaldsdrápa* and *Þorfinnsdrápa* for the Orkney jarls. He composed for the kings Magnús inn góði (*Hrynhenda*, in the innovatory *hrynhent* metre) and Haraldr Sigurðarson (*Blágagladrápa*) during their joint rule in Norway, and memorial poems for each (*Magnúsdrápa*, *Haraldsdrápa*). *Skáldatal* lists him as a poet of King Knútr inn ríki as well, and (according to one recension) Óláfr kyrri of Norway. He is also said to have composed poems about Icelanders. See further Whaley 1998, 41–47.

[185] Einarr's brother: Þorfinnr.

[186] *skýrann*: 'the hall of clouds', the sky.

in his realm as a result of the labour and expense imposed on the farmers. But in the part of the country that Brúsi had, there was much prosperity and an easy life for farmers. He was popular.

CHAPTER NINETY-EIGHT

There was a man called Ámundi, powerful and wealthy. He lived on Hlaupandanes in Sandvík on Hrossey. His son was called Þorkell, and he was the most accomplished of all men in Orkney. Ámundi was a most wise man and one of the [162] most highly thought-of men on the islands. It happened one spring, that Jarl Einarr called out a levy again, as he was accustomed to, but the farmers grumbled greatly and appealed to Ámundi, asking him to make representations on their behalf to the jarl. He replies:

'The jarl is obstinate,' and declares it will do no good to make any kind of request to the jarl about this. 'The friendship between me and the jarl is also good as things are, but it seems to me we are headed for disaster if we fall out, considering both our characters. I shall,' says Ámundi, 'not get myself involved.'

Then they discussed this with Þorkell. He was reluctant about it, and yet in the end promised at people's urging. Ámundi thought he had promised too soon. But when the jarl held an assembly, then Þorkell spoke on behalf of the farmers and begged the jarl to spare people the burdens and reckoned up people's difficulties. But the jarl replies in a kindly way, saying that he will pay great regard to what Þorkell says.

'I had just now planned to take six ships out to sea, but now I shall take no more than three. But you, Þorkell, do not ask for such favours again.'

The farmers thanked Þorkell warmly for his support. The jarl went on viking raids and returned in the autumn. But the following spring the jarl made the same demands as he was accustomed to do, and held an assembly with the farmers. Then Þorkell spoke again and begged the jarl to spare the farmers. Now the jarl replies angrily and says that the lot of the farmers would now worsen with his speech. He then got so angry and furious that he said that they should not both be well at the assembly the next spring. And so this assembly closed. And when Ámundi realised what had passed between Þorkell and the jarl, then he told Þorkell to go away, and he crossed to Katanes to Jarl Þorfinnr. Þorkell stayed there for a long time after that and grew fond of the jarl, since he was young, and he was afterwards known as Þorkell fóstri (Foster-Father), and he was a splendid man. There were other men of the ruling class who fled [163] their patrimonies in Orkney because of Jarl Einarr's tyranny. Most fled across to Katanes to Jarl Þorfinnr, but some fled from Orkney to Norway, and some to various countries.

Now when Jarl Þorfinnr grew up, then he advanced his claim to his brother Jarl Einarr, asking him for the realm he felt he was entitled to in Orkney, and that was a third of the islands. Einarr was reluctant to diminish his realm. And when Þorfinnr heard this, then he sets out with a force from Katanes and goes out to the islands. And when Jarl Einarr realised this, he musters a force and is going to defend his lands. Jarl Brúsi also musters a force and goes to meet them and carries messages of reconciliation between them. Their reconciliation was on these terms, that Þorfinnr was to have one third of the lands on Orkney, as he was entitled to. But Brúsi and Einarr combined their shares. Einarr was to have sole government of them, but if their deaths took place at different times, then the one that lived longest was to take the lands after the other. But this covenant now seemed unfair, since Brúsi had a son who was called Rǫgnvaldr, but Einarr was without a son. Then Jarl Þorfinnr set his men to look after the realm that he possessed in Orkney, but he was generally in Katanes. Jarl Einarr generally spent the summers raiding Ireland and Scotland and Bretland.

It happened one summer, while Jarl Einarr was raiding in Ireland, that he fought in Úlfreksfjǫrðr with King Konofogor of the Irish, and as was written above, Einarr suffered a great defeat and loss of men. The next summer following, Eyvindr úrarhorn (Aurochs-Horn) went from the west from Ireland and was making for Norway, but as the weather was rough and the currents impossible to negotiate, Eyvindr then turns into Ásmundarvágr and lay there for some time weatherbound. And when Jarl Einarr heard this, then he made his way there with a large force, captured Eyvindr and had him killed, but gave quarter to most of his men, and they went east to Norway in the autumn and came to meet King Óláfr and told him about the killing of Eyvindr. The king [164] makes little response, and it was evident that he felt this a great loss and done much to spite him, and he was reserved about most things that he felt to be contrary to his mind.

Jarl Þorfinnr sent Þorkell fóstri out to the islands to call in his dues. Jarl Einarr blamed Þorkell mostly for the rebellion in which Þorfinnr made his claim out onto the islands. Þorkell left the islands quickly and went over to Katanes. He tells Jarl Þorfinnr that he had found out for certain that Jarl Einarr had been planning his death if his kinsmen and friends had not brought him information.

'I shall not now,' he says, 'have any chance of bringing about a decisive encounter between us, but there is this alternative, to go further away and to somewhere where his power does not reach.'

The jarl was keen for Þorkell to go east to Norway to see King Óláfr.

'You will,' he says, 'be highly regarded wherever you come among high-ranking men, but I know the characters of you both, yours and the jarl's, that you will before long come to blows.'

Then Þorkell set out and went in the autumn to Norway and so to see King Óláfr, and stayed there the winter with the king on very friendly terms. He involved Þorkell very much in his affairs. It seemed to him, as was true, that Þorkell was a wise man, very outstanding. The king could see from what he said that he gave very different accounts of the jarls, and was a great friend of Þorfinnr, but was very critical of Jarl Einarr. And early in the spring the king sent a ship west over the sea to see Jarl Þorfinnr with this message, that the jarl was to come east to see the king. But the jarl did not forget this journey, for words of friendship accompanied the message.

[165] CHAPTER NINETY-NINE

Jarl Þorfinnr went east to Norway and came to see King Óláfr and was received there very well, and he stayed there for a large part of the summer. And when he was setting out to go to the west, King Óláfr gave him a fine large longship fully fitted out. Þorkell fóstri then undertook to accompany the jarl on this journey, and the jarl gave him the ship on which he had sailed from the west that summer. The king and the jarl parted on very friendly terms. Jarl Þorfinnr got to Orkney in the autumn. And when Jarl Einarr heard of this, then he kept a large number of men with him and stayed on board ship. Jarl Brúsi then went to see both the brothers and conveyed terms of settlement between them. It came about again that they reached terms and confirmed them with oaths. Þorkell fóstri was to be reconciled and friends with Jarl Einarr, and it was stipulated that each of them was to entertain the other to a banquet, and Jarl Einarr was to start by visiting Þorkell in Sandvík. And while the jarl was at the banquet there, then the hospitality was most liberal. The jarl was not merry. There was a large hall there with entrances at both ends.

The day that the jarl was supposed to be leaving, Þorkell was supposed to be going with him to his banquet. Þorkell sent men on ahead to get intelligence about the route on that day. And when the observers got back, then they told Þorkell that they had found three ambushes with armed men.

'And we think,' they said, 'that it must be a plot.'

And when Þorkell learned this, then he delayed his preparations and gathered his men around him. The jarl told him to get ready, saying that it was time to start riding. Þorkell says he had a lot to see to. He went now in, now out. There were fires in the middle of the hall. Then he went in through one entrance and following him a man who is named as Hallvarðr. He was an Icelandic man and from the Eastern Fiords. He closed the door behind him. Þorkell went on in between the fire and where the jarl was sitting. [166] The jarl asked:

'Are you still not ready?'

Þorkell replies: 'Now I am ready.'

Then he struck at the jarl a blow on his head. The jarl plunged down onto the floor. Then said the Icelander:

'Here I see there is the most complete lack of initiative, when you do not pull the jarl out of the fire.'

He thrust an Irish axe[187] at him and hooked it under the jarl's neck-bone and hauled him up onto the raised floor.[188] Both Þorkell and his companion went out quickly through the opposite entrance to that they had gone in by. There outside Þorkell's men were standing fully armed. But the jarl's men took him up, and he was now dead, and all their hands failed them as far as vengeance was concerned. It was also the case that it had happened quickly, and no one expected this deed from Þorkell, for they all thought that things must be as had previously been arranged, and there was friendship between the jarl and Þorkell. The men inside were also mostly unarmed, and many of them previously good friends of Þorkell's. It also happened that by good luck Þorkell was fated to go on living. Þorkell now had, when he came out, a following no smaller than the jarl's men.

Þorkell then went to his ship, and the jarl's men went away. Þorkell sailed away immediately that day and east out to sea, and it was now after the winter nights,[189] and he reached Norway safely and went as fast as he could to see King Óláfr, and was well received there. The king was pleased at what had been done. Þorkell stayed with him over the winter.

CHAPTER ONE HUNDRED

After the fall of Jarl Einarr, Jarl Brúsi took that part of the lands that Jarl Einarr had previously had, because it was known to many people on what terms the brothers Einarr and Brúsi had made their compact. But Þorfinnr thought it fairest that each of them should have half the islands, and yet [167] Brúsi held two shares of the lands that winter. The following spring Þorfinnr put his claim to the lands to Brúsi, that he wanted to have half shares with Brúsi, but Brúsi did not give his agreement to this. They held assemblies and meetings on these matters. Then their friends came forward to settle this affair, and the result was that Þorfinnr would not accept anything else but having half the islands, adding that Brúsi did not need to have more than a third, considering the character that he had. Brúsi says:

[187] Presumably one with a long point underneath the blade.

[188] The raised floors in a Norse hall ran down both long sides of the building, leaving the earth floor between them for the fire(s). They were used for sitting on during the day and sleeping on at night. Tables for eating and drinking at would be erected in front of each raised floor, between it and the fire, at each mealtime.

[189] The last three nights before the beginning of winter (late October).

'I was content with that,' he says, 'having a third of the lands that I took as inheritance after my father. Moreover, no one disputed this with me. And now I have taken another third as inheritance after my brother according to lawful agreements. And though I may be incapable of contending with you, brother, yet I shall try anything else but agree to giving up my power as things stand.'

They thus ended this conference.

But when Brúsi saw that he would not be capable of standing on an equal footing with Þorfinnr, since Þorfinnr had much more power and support from his mother's father, the king of the Scots, then Brúsi made up his mind to go from the country east to see King Óláfr, taking with him his son Rǫgnvaldr. He was now ten years old. And when the jarl met the king, he was well received. And when the jarl had presented his business to the king, telling the king the whole state of affairs that existed between the brothers, he asked the king to give him support in holding on to his power, offering in exchange his absolute friendship. The king speaks and began his story first of all with how Haraldr inn hárfagri had taken possession of all patrimonies in Orkney, so that the jarls ever since had held those lands in fief, but never in freehold.

'And this is proof,' he says, 'that when Eiríkr blóðøx and his sons were in Orkney, the jarls were subject to them, and when my kinsman Óláfr Tryggvason came there, then your father Jarl Sigurðr became his man. Now I have inherited everything from King Óláfr. I will make you this offer, that you [168] become my man. I will then grant you the islands in fief. We shall then see, if I give you my support, whether it will be of more avail than the backing of the king of the Scots to your brother. But if you do not want these terms, then I shall try to get hold of the possessions and patrimonies that our kinsmen and forefathers have held there in the west.'

The jarl fixed these statements in his mind and consulted his friends about them, asking for their advice as to what he should agree to, whether he should come to an agreement with King Óláfr and become his man.

'But this is less clear to me, how my fate will turn out at our parting if I say no to it, for the king has made explicit the claim he is making to Orkney, and what with his ambition and the fact that we are come here, it will be a small matter for him to do what he pleases with us.'

And although the jarl felt there were disadvantages in both courses, he chose the alternative of submitting everything to the king's authority, both himself and his rule. Then King Óláfr took over from the jarl his rule and control over all the jarl's inherited lands. The jarl then became his man and confirmed it with oaths.

CHAPTER ONE HUNDRED AND ONE

Jarl Þorfinnr learned this, that his brother Brúsi had gone east to see King Óláfr and look for support from him. But because Þorfinnr had earlier been to see King Óláfr and got himself onto friendly terms with him, he felt he had prepared the ground well there, and was sure that there would be many there to put in a word for his interests, and yet he expected that there would be even more if he went there in person. Þorfinnr acts on this plan, getting ready as soon as he could and going east to Norway, thinking that he would not be very far behind Brúsi, and that his business would not have been concluded before Þorfinnr got to see the king. But it [169] turned out differently from what the jarl had planned, because by the time Jarl Þorfinnr got to see King Óláfr, the whole agreement between the king and Jarl Brúsi was concluded and finished. Jarl Þorfinnr also did not realise that Brúsi had given up his rule before he himself got to King Óláfr. And as soon as they met, Jarl Þorfinnr and King Óláfr, then King Óláfr raised the same claim to power in Orkney as he had done with Jarl Brúsi, and he demanded from Þorfinnr the same thing, that he should grant the king that part of the lands that he had previously held. The jarl replies to the king's words courteously and calmly, and says this, that he felt friendship with the king was very important.

'And if you, lord, feel you need my help against other rulers, then you will already have done plenty to deserve it, but it is not suitable for me to grant submission to you, since I am already a jarl of the king of the Scots and subject to him.'

And when the king saw the reluctance in the jarl's replies to the case he had just put to him, then the king said:

'If you, jarl, are not willing to become my man, then there is this alternative, that I set a man over Orkney whom I want. And I desire that you give me oaths to make no claim to those lands and let whomever I set over the lands be in peace on your part. But if you accept neither of these choices, then it will be regarded by whomever is ruling the land, that hostilities are to be expected from you. You will then not find it strange if valley meets hill.'[190]

The jarl replies, asking him to give him time to consider the matter. The king did so, giving the jarl a while to discuss this choice with his men. Then the jarl requested this, that the king should allow him to delay until the next summer, and to first go west over the sea, since his counsellors were back at home, and he was but a youth in regard to his years. The king told him to make his choice then. Þorkell fóstri was then with King Óláfr. He sent someone to Jarl Þorfinnr privately telling him not to think, whatever his

---

[190] Literally, if harshness meets harshness, i.e. conflict is unavoidable (*ONP*), or if high meets low, if the high one has a fall? Cf. Halldórr Halldórsson 1954, 146–47.

[170] intentions were, of parting just now with King Óláfr without reaching an agreement, seeing that he was now come into the king's hands. As a result of such reminders, the jarl realised that the only option was to let the king now have his way, feeling that the other was not advisable, to have no expectation himself of his patrimony, but having to give oaths that they should hold the realm in peace who were not born to it. And because he felt his getting away was uncertain, his choice was to submit to the king and become his man, as Brúsi had done. The king perceived that Þorfinnr was much more proud-minded than Brúsi, and took this bullying much worse. The king trusted Þorfinnr worse than Brúsi. The king saw that Þorfinnr would be thinking that he might expect the backing of the king of the Scots if he broke this agreement. The king understood from his insight that Brúsi entered into all compacts reluctantly, but only spoke in them what he intended to stand by. But as for Þorfinnr, when he had decided what he was going to accept, then he cheerfully took on all the terms, and did not make any objection to whatever the king was the first to put forward. But the king suspected that the jarl would go back on some of the agreements.

CHAPTER ONE HUNDRED AND TWO

When King Óláfr had considered in his mind all this affair, he had a horn blown to summon a large assembly, having the jarls called there. Then the king said:

'The settlement between me and the jarls of Orkney I shall now announce to the general public. They have now agreed to my possession of Orkney and Shetland and both become my men and confirmed it all with oaths, and [171] I will now give it to them in fief, to Brúsi a third of the lands, to Þorfinnr another third, just as they have previously had. But the third that Einarr rangmuðr had, that I shall take into my keeping because he slew my follower and partner and dear friend Eyvindr úrarhorn. I shall look after that part of the lands that I deem appropriate. I will also stipulate with you, my jarls, that I wish you to accept a settlement from Þorkell Ámundason for the slaying of your brother Einarr. I want the judgment to be up to me, if you are both willing to accept this.'

And it was like other things, the jarls agreed to everything the king said. Then Þorkell went forward and confirmed that the case should be up to the king's judgment, and so the assembly broke up. King Óláfr adjudged compensation for Jarl Einarr equal to that for three landed men, but because there was guilt on his side, a third of the payment was to be waived. Jarl Þorfinnr then asked the king for leave to depart, and as soon as that was granted, the jarl got ready in great haste. And when he was quite ready, it happened one day, while the jarl was drinking on board ship, that there came before him suddenly Þorkell Ámundason and laid his head on the jarl's lap and bade him do whatever he liked with it. The jarl asked why he was behaving like this.

'We are already men who are reconciled by the king's judgment, so stand up, Þorkell.'

He did so. Þorkell said:

'The settlement that the king made I will abide by as regards what was between me and Brúsi, but the part that relates to you is for you to decide. Though the king has assigned to me possessions or residence in Orkney, I know your character, that I will not be able to go to the islands unless I go with your goodwill, jarl. I am willing,' he says, 'to pledge to you never to come to Orkney, whatever the king has to say about it.'

The jarl was silent and was slow to reply. He said:

'If you would rather, Þorkell, that I give a judgment on our case, rather than abide by the king's judgment, then I shall make the beginning of our settlement that you shall go with me to Orkney and stay with me [172] and not part from me except with my permission or leave, be obliged to defend my land and to carry out all the actions that I wish to have done as long as we are both alive.'

Þorkell says: 'This shall all be at your command, jarl, like everything else over which I have control.'

Þorkell then approached and confirmed to the jarl all this that the jarl had stated. The jarl said that he would later decide about the payments, but he now received oaths from Þorkell. Þorkell now straightway set out with the jarl. The jarl left as soon as he was ready, and he and King Óláfr never saw each other again. Jarl Brúsi stayed behind there and got ready more at leisure. And before he went away, then King Óláfr had meetings with him and said as follows:

'It seems to me, jarl, that I shall have you as my trusted representative there across the sea to the west. What I intend is that you shall have two parts of the lands to govern, those that you have had previously. I want you to be no less a man and no less powerful now you are subject to me, than you were before. I shall secure your trustworthiness in this way, that I want your son Rǫgnvaldr to stay behind here with me. I can see that then, when you have my support and two parts of the lands, you will be well able to hold your own properly against your brother Þorfinnr.'

Brúsi accepted this with thanks, having two parts of the lands. After this Brúsi stayed a short while before he went away, and came in the autumn west to Orkney. Brúsi's son Rǫgnvaldr stayed behind in the east with King Óláfr. He was of all men the handsomest, his hair long and gold like silk.

He was at an early age big and strong. He was the most accomplished of men both as regards intelligence and courtesy. He was with King Óláfr for a long time after this. Óttarr svarti speaks of all this in the *drápa*[191] that he composed about King Óláfr:

82. Good folk-kings' power *Hǫfuðlausn* 20
fittingly you hold, trusty one; *Fsk* 181
[173] inhabitants of Hjaltland are *Orkn* 41
held to be your subjects. *Skald* I 766
There has been no battle- *Skáldsk* 105
brisk ruler in the land eastward
who forced rule on western islands,
before your arrival.

CHAPTER ONE HUNDRED AND THREE

When the brothers came west to Orkney, Þorfinnr and Brúsi, then Brúsi took two parts of the lands to govern, and Þorfinnr a third. He was mainly on Katanes and in Scotland, setting his men over the islands. Brúsi then was solely in charge of the defence of the islands, but at that time there was a good deal of raiding, because Norwegians and Danes were raiding a lot on viking expeditions to the west and often came in to Orkney on their way to and from the west and raided the outlying coast. Brúsi complained to his brother Þorfinnr that he put out no warships off Orkney and Shetland, but had his full share of the taxes and dues. Then Þorfinnr offered him this choice, that Brúsi should have a third of the lands, and Þorfinnr two parts and be solely responsible for defence of the land on behalf of them both. And although this change did not take place immediately at that time, yet it is said in Jarlasǫgur (*Orkneyinga saga*) that this change, so that Þorfinnr had two parts, and Brúsi a third, had been put into effect by the time that [174] Knútr inn ríki (the Great) had subjected Norway to himself, but King Óláfr had left the country. Jarl Þorfinnr Sigurðarson was the most distinguished there has been in the Islands, and had the greatest power of any of the jarls of Orkney. He gained possession of Shetland and Orkney, the Hebrides; he had also great power in Scotland and Ireland. On this Arnórr jarlaskáld said:

83. The harmer of rings[192] folk had to *Þorfinnsdrápa* 23
heed—I tell men truly, *Orkn* 81
all were thought to be Þorfinnr's— *Skald* II 257–58
from Þursasker to Dublin.

[191] An elaborate poem of some length with refrains (*stef*); distinct from a *flokkr*, a poem of simpler structure consisting of a series of stanzas (*vísur*) without refrains.
[192] *hringstríðir*: 'enemy of rings', generous man.

Þorfinnr was the greatest warrior. He received the jarldom at the age of five and ruled more than sixty winters and died of sickness in the latter days of Haraldr Sigurðarson. But Brúsi died in the days of Knútr inn ríki, shortly after the fall of King Óláfr inn helgi (the Saint).

CHAPTER ONE HUNDRED AND FOUR

Now two stories are running parallel, and we shall now take it up there where we left off, where it was told about how Óláfr Haraldsson had made peace with King Óláfr of the Svíar, and about how King Óláfr went that summer north to Þrándheimr. He had now been king for five years. That autumn he set up his winter quarters in Niðaróss and stayed there the winter. That winter there was with King Óláfr Þorkell fóstri Ámundason, as was written above. King Óláfr then made extensive enquiries about the observance of Christianity, how it was in the country then, and he learned that there was hardly any observance of Christianity [175] when one made one's way north into Hálogaland, and that it was a long way short of being satisfactory even over Naumudalr and in over Þrándheimr.

There is a man named Hárekr, son of Eyvindr skáldaspillir (Poet-Spoiler). He lived on the island that is called Þjótta. This is in Hálogaland. Eyvindr had been not too wealthy a man, of high lineage and a very outstanding person. On Þjótta there lived at that time small farmers and not so very few. Hárekr first bought a farm there, not so very large, and moved there. And in a few seasons he had cleared away all the farmers that had lived there before, so that he was now sole owner of the whole island, and then built a large manor there. Hárekr soon became immensely rich. He was a man of great wisdom and an enterprising man. He had long been held in high esteem by leading men. He had kinship with kings of Norway. For these reasons Hárekr was highly regarded by the rulers of the land. Hárekr's paternal grandmother Gunnhildr was daughter of Jarl Hálfdan and Haraldr inn hárfagri's daughter Ingibjǫrg. Hárekr was now rather getting on in years when these events took place. Hárekr was the most distinguished man in Hálogaland. He had now for a long time been official trader with the Lapps and was king's agent in the Mǫrk (Finnmǫrk). He had sometimes held these offices alone, but sometimes some others had acted with him. He had never been to see King Óláfr, but yet communications and messengers had often passed between them, and it had all been friendly, and that winter, when King Óláfr was staying in Niðaróss, men again went between him and Hárekr from Þjótta. Then the king announced this, that the following summer he planned to go north to Hálogaland and all the way to the land's end, though the Háleygir had very various opinions about this expedition.

[176] CHAPTER ONE HUNDRED AND FIVE

King Óláfr made preparations now in the spring with five ships taking nearly three hundred men. And when he was ready, then he set out north along the coast, and when he got to Naumdœlafylki, he called assemblies with the farmers. He was then accepted as king at every meeting. He also had there as elsewhere the laws proclaimed in which he was commanding people in that country to observe Christianity, and declared the penalty of life and limbs or total confiscation of property on any person who would not submit to Christian laws. The king imposed heavy punishments on many people there and made this affect both the powerful and the humble. In every district he ended up with all people agreeing to observe the holy faith. And most men of the ruling class and many great landowners provided banquets to entertain the king. So he went on all the way to Hálogaland. Hárekr on Þjótta gave a banquet for the king, and there was a very large number of people at it and a most splendid banquet. Hárekr then became King Óláfr's landed man.[193] The king then granted him revenues, the same as he had received from previous rulers of the land.

CHAPTER ONE HUNDRED AND SIX

There is a man named Grankell or Granketill, a wealthy farmer and now rather getting on in years. But when he was at a youthful age he had been on viking expeditions and then a great warrior. He was a very accomplished man in most respects as far as physical skills were concerned. His son was called Ásmundr, and he was in everything like his father or somewhat superior. It was said by many that in respect of good looks, strength and physical skills, he has been the third best endowed in Norway, after mentioning Hákon [177] Aðalsteinsfóstri and Óláfr Tryggvason. Grankell invited Óláfr to a banquet, there was the most liberal entertainment there. Grankell sent him away with huge gifts of friendship. The king invited Ásmundr to go with him, and used much persuasion, but Ásmundr felt he could not turn down such an honour, and agreed to go with the king and afterwards became his man and got to be on very close terms with the king. King Óláfr stayed the greater part of the summer in Hálogaland and went to all the assembly districts and converted all the people there to Christianity.

There lived then on Bjarkey Þórir hundr (Dog). He was the most powerful man there in the north. He then became King Óláfr's landed man.[194] Many powerful landowners' sons then joined King Óláfr on his travels. When the summer drew to a close, the king came from the north and then turned in

---

[193] See note 52 above.
[194] See note 52 above.

along Þrandheimr to Niðaróss and stayed the following winter there. And that winter Þorkell fóstri came from the west from Orkney after he had killed Jarl Einarr rangmuðr. That autumn there was a great shortage of corn in Þrándheimr, whereas previously there had for a long time been good seasons, but there was famine over the whole of the north of the land, and the worse the further north, while corn was plentiful in the east of the country and also across Upplǫnd. But it helped greatly in Þrándheimr that people there had much corn left over from previous seasons.

CHAPTER ONE HUNDRED AND SEVEN

That autumn King Óláfr was told the news from inland Þrándheimr that the farmers there had held well attended banquets at the winter nights.[195] There were great drinking feasts there. The king was told that at them all the toasts were dedicated to the Æsir in accordance with the ancient custom. It was also a part of this tale, that at them cattle and horses were slaughtered and altars stained with blood and worship performed and the prayer offered that it was to be for better harvests. It was added that everyone thought it obvious that [178] the gods had been angry that the Háleygir had turned to Christianity. And when the king learned of these events, then he sent men inland into Þrándheimr summoning to himself the farmers that he chose to name.

There is a man named Ǫlvir at Egg. He was called that from the farm he lived on. He was a powerful man and of noble family. He was the leader of this group of men travelling to the king on behalf of the farmers. And when they met the king, then the king challenged the farmers with these accusations. But Ǫlvir replies on behalf of the farmers, saying that they had had no banquets that autumn except their neighbourhood feasts or social drinking feasts, and in some cases gatherings of friends.

'But what you have been told,' he says, 'about what is said by us Þrœndir when we drink, all sensible men know how to take care not to make such speeches, but I cannot speak for foolish and drunken men, what they may have said.'

Ǫlvir was a skilful and bold speaker. He rebutted these accusations against the farmers. But in the end the king says that the Innþrændir must give their testimony for themselves about what their beliefs are. The farmers were given leave to return home. They went, too, as soon as they were ready.

CHAPTER ONE HUNDRED AND EIGHT

Later that winter the king was told that the Innþrœndir were gathering in large numbers at Mærin and there were great sacrificial banquets there at

---

[195] See note 189.

midwinter. They were worshipping now for peace and a good winter. So when the king felt convinced of the accuracy of these reports, then the king sends men with a message inland into Þrándheimr summoning the farmers out to the town, naming for this those men he thought were most sensible. The farmers then held talks together and [179] discussed this message among themselves. Those were all least eager to make this journey who had been before that winter, but at the entreaty of all the farmers, Ǫlvir undertook the journey. And when he got out to the town, he went straightway to see the king, and they began to talk. The king accused the farmers of having held midwinter sacrificial feasts. Ǫlvir replies saying that the farmers were not guilty of this offence.

'We held,' he says, 'Yule[196] banquets and in many places in the districts drinking parties. The farmers do not make such scant provision for their Yule banquets that there is not a lot left over, and that was what they were drinking, lord, for a long time afterwards. At Mærin there is a large centre and huge buildings, and extensive settlements round about. People find it good to drink together there for enjoyment in large numbers.'

The king answers little and looked rather displeased, feeling he knew something more accurate than what now was being reported. The king told the farmers to go back.

'And I shall,' he says, 'find out the truth, so that you will not conceal and will not contradict. But whatever has been going on here, do not let it happen again.'

The farmers then went home and reported their mission, and this, that the king was rather angry.

CHAPTER ONE HUNDRED AND NINE

King Óláfr held a great banquet at Easter and had many townspeople as his guests as well as farmers. But after Easter the king had his ships launched and the tackle and oars shipped, had the decks and awnings installed, and let the ships thus prepared ride by the jetties. After Easter, King Óláfr sent men into Veradalr.

There is a man named Þóraldi, the king's steward. He was in charge of the king's residence at Haugr. And the king sent him word that he was to come to him as quickly as possible. Þóraldi did not neglect this journey and went immediately out to the town with the messengers. [180] The king called him to a private talk and enquired what truth there was 'in what I am told about the practices of the Innþrœndir, whether it is so that they are turning to pagan worship. I want you,' says the king, 'to tell me how it is and what

---

[196] See note 125 above.

you know to be closest to the truth. You have an obligation to do this, since you are my man.'

Þóraldi replies: 'Lord, I want to tell you first that I moved my two sons and wife and all the movable property that I was able to bring with me to this farm. So if you want to have an account of this from me, that shall be as you wish. But if I tell you how it is, then you must look after me.'

The king says: 'Tell the truth about what I ask you, and I shall look after you so that you will come to no harm.'

'To tell you the truth, king, if I am to say how it is, inland over Þrándheimr nearly all the folk are completely heathen in their beliefs, though some people there are baptised. And it is their custom to hold a sacrificial feast in the autumn to welcome the winter, another at midwinter, and a third in the summer, to welcome the summer. Involved in this are some Eynir and Sparbyggvar, Verdœlir, Skeynir. There are twelve of them that are leaders in the sacrificial feasts, and now this spring Ǫlvir has to conduct the feast. He is now hard at work at Mærin, and all the supplies that are needed for the feast are being brought there.'

So when the king found out the truth, then he had his troops summoned together by horn and had people told that they were to make for the ships. The king named men to captain the ships and lead the detachments and where each detachment was to board ship. They were soon off. The king had five ships and three hundred men and made his way in along the fiord. There was a favourable wind and the warships went well before the wind, and no one expected that the king would come inland there so quickly. The king came during the night inland to Mærin. Then [181] a house there was straightway surrounded. Ǫlvir was captured in it, and the king had him and many other men killed. But the king confiscated all the provisions for the feast and had them carried off to his ships, and all the property there too, both house furnishings and clothes and valuables that people had brought there, and shared it out among his men like spoils of war. The king also had the homes of the farmers that he thought had been most involved in these doings attacked in their homes. Some were captured and put in irons, though some managed to run away, and the property of many was confiscated.

Then the king called an assembly of the farmers. But because he had taken prisoner many of the leading men and had them in his power, then their relatives and friends decided to yield submission to the king, and there was no resistance made against the king at that time. He converted all the people there to the true faith and established clergy there and had churches built and consecrated. The king declared no compensation to be due for Ǫlvir's death, and took possession of all the property he had owned. But as for the other men that seemed to him to be most guilty, he had some killed, some maimed, and some he exiled from the land, appropriating the property of some. Then the king returned to Niðaróss.

CHAPTER ONE HUNDRED AND TEN

There is a man named Árni Armóðsson. He was married to Þorsteinn gálgi's (Gallows's) daughter Þóra. These were their children: Kálfr, Finnr, Þorbergr, Ámundi, Kolbjǫrn, Arnbjǫrn, Árni, Ragnhildr. She was married to Hárekr from Þjótta. Árni was a landed man,[197] powerful and excellent, a great friend of King Óláfr. At this time his sons Kálfr and Fiðr were with King Óláfr, held there in high esteem. The woman who had been married to Ǫlvir at Egg was young and beautiful, of noble family and wealthy. This match was considered excellently good, but the king was now her guardian. She and Ǫlvir [182] had two young sons. Kálfr Árnason asked of the king that he should give him this woman, who had been married to Ǫlvir, in marriage, and for friendship's sake the king granted him this, and with her all the possessions that Ǫlvir had had. Then the king made him a landed man, giving him stewardship over inland Þrándheimr. Kálfr then became a great chieftain and was a very intelligent person.

CHAPTER ONE HUNDRED AND ELEVEN

King Óláfr had now been in Norway for seven years. That summer Jarls Þorfinnr and Brúsi came to him from Orkney. King Óláfr had taken possession of those lands, as was written above. That summer King Óláfr travelled round both Mœrrs and into Raumsdalr in the autumn. There he left his ships and went on to Upplǫnd and came out in Lesjar. There he had all the best men in both Lesjar and Dofrar rounded up and they had to accept Christianity or suffer death or run away, those who managed to do so. But those who accepted Christianity handed over their sons to the king as hostages for their good faith. The king stayed the night at a place called Bœjar in Lesjar and established priests over it. Then he went across Lorudalr and on across Ljárdalr and ended up in a place called Stafabrekka. Now this river flows along the valley that is called Ótta, and there is a fine settlement on both sides of the river, and it is called Lóar, and the king could see right along the settlement.

'It is a pity,' says the king, 'that such a fine settlement has to be burned.'

And he made his way down into the valley with his troops, and they stayed the night at the farm [183] that is called Nes, and the king took himself a lodging in an upper room, in which he slept himself, and that still stands there today, and nothing has been done to it since. And the king was there

[197] See note 52 above.

five nights and sent out an assembly summons calling people to meet him from both Vági and Lóar, and from Hedalr, making this order accompany the summons, that they must either fight a battle with him or suffer burning at his hands or accept Christianity and give him their sons as hostages. After that they came to see the king and submitted to him. Some fled south into Dalar.

CHAPTER ONE HUNDRED AND TWELVE

There was a man called Dala-Guðbrandr (of the Dales) who was as if he were king over the Dales, and he had the title of Hersir (Lord). Sigvatr skáld (Poet) compared him in power and extent of his lands with Erlingr Skjálgsson. Sigvatr said about Erlingr:

84. Other Jalkr's plank-destroyer[198]   Poem about Erlingr Skjálgss.1
like you only one I knew;   *Skald* I 628
the guardian of men[199] governed—
Guðbrandr his name—lands widely.
I declare you are thought equal,
country-of-worm's hater,[200]
both; the snake's land lessener[201]
lies, who thinks himself better.

[184] Guðbrandr had one son who is mentioned here. When Guðbrandr learned this news, that King Óláfr was come to Lóar and was forcing people to accept Christianity, then he sent out a war summons and called all the Dœlir to the farm that is called Hundþorp, to a meeting with him. And when they had all come, then there was a countless multitude of people, for nearby there lies the lake that is called Lǫgr, and they were equally well able to get there by ship as by land. And Guðbrandr had a meeting with them there, saying that the man was come to Lóar 'who is called Óláfr, and he wants to preach us a different faith from what we have had previously, and to break all our gods to bits, saying this, that he has a much greater god and a mightier, and it is amazing that the earth does not burst apart under him when he dares to speak such things, or that our gods let him go any further. And I expect, if we carry Þórr out from our temple where he stands in this place, and who has always served us well, and he sees Óláfr and his men, then his God will melt away, and he himself and his men too, and come to nothing.'

[198] *Jalks bríktǫpuðr*: 'destroyer of Jálkr's (Óðinn's) plank (shield)', warrior.
[199] *gumna gætir*: 'guardian of men', lord.
[200] *ormláðs hati*: 'hater of the serpent's land (gold)', one who gives away treasure, generous man; here, Erlingr.
[201] *linnsetrs lægir*: 'diminisher of the snake's resting place', generous man.

Then they shouted out all together, saying that Óláfr should never get away from there, if he came to see them.

'And he will not dare to go any further south along the Dales,' they say.

After that they gave seven hundred (840)[202] men instructions to go on the watch north to Breiða, and the leader in charge of this troop was Guðbrandr's eighteen-year-old son, and many other excellent men with him, and they came to the farm that is called Hof, staying there three nights, and many forces came there to them that had fled from Lesjar and Lóar and Vági, and who did not want to submit to Christianity. But King Óláfr and Bishop Sigurðr left behind clergy at Lóar and at Vági. After that they went [185] across over Vágarǫst and came down at Sil and stayed there for the night and learned the news that a great force lay in front of them. The farmers that were on the Breiða also discovered this, and prepared for battle against the king. And when the king got up, then he armed himself and went southwards along Silvellir and did not stop before they got on to the Breiða and saw a large army in front of them there, ready for battle. Then the king drew up his troops and rode ahead himself and addressed the farmers and invited them to accept Christianity. They replied:

'You shall achieve something other than mockery of us.'

And they shouted war cries and beat their weapons on their shields. The king's men then ran forward shooting their spears, but the farmers immediately turned in flight, so that only a few remained standing. Guðbrandr's son was captured, and King Óláfr gave him quarter and kept him with him. The king stayed there four nights. Then the king said to Guðbrandr's son:

'Go back to your father and tell him that I shall soon be coming there.'

After that he went back home and tells his father the harsh news, that they had met the king and held a battle with him.

'But all our troops fled right at the start, but I was captured,' he says. 'The king gave me quarter and told me to go and tell you that he would be coming here soon. Now we have here no more than two hundred (240?) men of all the troops that we had then against him. Now I give you this advice, father, not to fight with this man.'

'One can hear this,' says Guðbrandr, 'that all the grit has been knocked out of you. And you went from home with little luck, and this expedition will be long remembered for you, and you now believe in the wild fancies that this man is going around with, and he [186] has caused shameful disgrace to you and your men.'

And the next night Guðbrandr dreamed that a man came to him, shining, inspiring great fear, and said to him:

[202] It is uncertain whether the duodecimal hundred would still be applicable at this date.

'Your son had no victorious trip meeting King Óláfr, and yours will be even less so, if you are planning to fight a battle with the king, and you yourself will fall and all your troops, and wolves will drag you and all the rest off and ravens will tear you.'

He was very much afraid of this threat and tells Þórðr ístrumagi (Fat Belly), who was chieftain over the Dœlir. He says:

'The same thing appeared to me.'

And in the morning they had a horn blown for an assembly and said that it seemed advisable to have a conference with this man who has come from the north with a new teaching, and find out with what proofs he comes. Then Guðbrandr spoke to his son:

'You shall now go to meet this king, who has given you quarter, and twelve men with you.'

And so was done. And they came and met the king and tell him their errand, that the farmers wanted to hold a conference with him and establish a truce between the king and the farmers. The king expressed himself well pleased at this, and they confirmed it by personal agreements between them as long as the conference lasted. And with this they went back and tell Guðbrandr and Þórðr that truce was agreed. The king then went to the farm that is called Liðsstaðir, and stayed there five nights. Then the king went to meet the farmers and held a conference with them. But it was very wet during the day. When the conference was in session, then the king stood up and says that the Læsir and those at Lóar, at Vági have accepted Christianity and broken down their heathen temples, 'and believe now in the true God who created heaven and earth and knows all things.'

After that the king sits down. And Guðbrandr replies:

'We do not know whom you are talking about. You call him God whom neither you nor anyone else can see. But we have a god who can be seen every day [187] and is not out today only because the weather is wet, and you will find him terrifying and mighty. I expect you will get in a panic if he comes to the conference. But since you say that your God can do so much, let him now bring it about that the weather is cloudy tomorrow, but no rain, and we shall meet here then.'

Then the king went back to his lodging, and Guðbrandr's son went with him as hostage, while the king gave them another man in exchange. Then in the evening the king asks Guðbrandr's son how their god was constructed. He says that he was patterned on Þórr.

'And he has a hammer in his hand and is of great size and hollow inside, and under him there is made something like a scaffold, and he stands up on top of it when he is outside. There is no lack of gold and silver on him. Four loaves of bread are brought him every day and meat with it.'

Then they went to bed, but the king was awake that night and was at his prayers. But when it was day, the king went to Mass and afterwards to a meal and then to the conference. And the weather was of such a kind as Guðbrandr had requested. Then the bishop stood up in a cope and had his mitre on his head and crozier in his hand and expounded the faith before the farmers and related many miracles that God had performed, and concluded his speech well. Then Þórðr ístrumagi replied:

'A great deal says this horned chap,[203] who has a staff in his hand and up on top has as if it were a curved ram's horn. But since you fellows claim your God performs so many miracles, speak to him then, so that tomorrow before sunrise he may make it be bright and sunny, and let us meet then and then do one of [188] two things, be in agreement on this matter or fight a battle.'

And they parted now for the time being.

CHAPTER ONE HUNDRED AND THIRTEEN

There was a man called Kolbeinn sterki (the Strong), who was with the king. His family was from Firðir. He always carried this equipment, that he was girded with a sword and had a great cudgel in his hand, that people call a club (klubba). The king spoke with Kolbeinn, saying that he was to stay next to him in the morning. Then he said to his men:

'You are to go down in the night to where the farmers' ships are, and bore holes in them all, but ride off with their horses from the farms where they are kept.'

And this was done. But the king spent all that night in prayer, and prayed God for this, that he should provide a solution to their difficulty by means of his grace and mercy. And when the king had finished prayers, and that was almost at dawn, after that he went to the assembly.

And when he got to the assembly, then some of the farmers had arrived. Then they saw a great multitude of farmers coming to the assembly and carrying between them a huge image of a person, adorned with gold and silver. And when the farmers that were at the assembly saw that, then they all leapt up and bowed down to this monstrosity. After that it was placed in the middle of the assembly field. On one side sat the farmers, on the other the king and his men. After that Dala-Guðbrandr stood up and said:

'Where is your God now, king? I think that now that he is carrying the beard on his chin rather low, and it looks to me as if your bragging and that of the horned chap that you call bishop and sits there next to you is less than

---

[203] The mitre was supposed to represent the horns of Moses (Exodus 34:29, Vulgate *cornuta esset facies sua*). Cf. http://en.wikipedia.org/wiki/Moses (Michelangelo's statue of Moses in the Church of San Pietro in Vincoli, Rome).

yesterday, for now our god is come, who rules all things, and is looking at you with keen eyes, and I see that you are now frightened and scarcely dare raise your eyes. Now put aside [189] your superstition and believe in our god, who has you entirely at his mercy.'

And he ended his speech.

The king spoke with Kolbeinn so that the farmers did not notice:

'If it happens during my speech that they look away from their god, then strike him a blow the hardest you can with your cudgel.'

After that the king stood up and spoke:

'Much have you spoken to us this morning. You express yourself strangely about your not being able to see our God, but we are expecting that he will soon come to us. You threaten us with your god, who is blind and deaf and can neither save himself nor anyone else and cannot get away anywhere from where he is unless he is carried, and I am thinking that now he is not far from disaster. So see now there, and look to the east, there comes our God now with a great light.'

Then the sun rose, and all the farmers looked towards the sun. And at that moment Kolbeinn struck their god so that it broke all to pieces, and out of it ran mice, as big as if they were cats, and adders and snakes. But the farmers got so frightened that they fled, some to ships, but when they pushed out their ships, then water ran in and filled them up, and they could not board them, while those that ran to horses, found none. After this the king had the farmers called, saying that he wishes to have a discussion with them, and the farmers turn back and the assembly went into session. And the king stood up and spoke:

'I do not know,' he says, 'what is the reason for this noise and dashing about that you are carrying on. But now you can see what power your god had, on whom you lavished gold and silver, food and provisions, and you have seen now what creatures have consumed it, mice and snakes, adders and toads. And they are worse off who believe in such and will not put aside their folly. Take your gold and jewels, that is scattered here now across the field, and take it home to your wives and never again put it on stocks or stones. But now there are two alternatives here before us, the one, that you now accept Christianity, otherwise fight a battle with me today, and let [190] whoever the God in whom we believe wills be victorious over the others today.'

Then Guðbrandr stood up and said: 'Great harm have we suffered for our god. And yet since he was unable to help us, we will now believe in the God in whom you believe.'

And then they all accepted Christianity. Then the bishop baptised Guðbrandr and his son and put in place clergy and they parted friends, who before had been enemies. And Guðbrandr had a church built there in the Dales.

CHAPTER ONE HUNDRED AND FOURTEEN

King Óláfr went after this out into Heiðmǫrk and made it Christian there, for when he had captured the kings, he did not have the confidence to travel widely over the land with a small force after such a great deed. At that time Christianity had not been introduced in many parts of Heiðmǫrk. But in this expedition the king did not stop until Heiðmǫrk was fully Christianised and churches were consecrated there and clergy provided. Then he went out to Þótn and Haðaland and made people's religion orthodox, and when he had finished, it was completely Christian there. From there he went to Hringaríki, and people adopted Christianity entirely. The Raumar learned that King Óláfr was setting out to go up there, and they gathered together a great force and said among themselves that they would never be able to forget the visitation that Óláfr had carried out there the previous time, saying that he was never going to act like that again. So when King Óláfr came up through Raumaríki with his troops, then a large gathering of farmers came against him by the river that is called Nitja. The farmers had a host of men. And when they met, the farmers straightway set about attacking, but it soon got too hot for them, and they immediately gave way and were taught a lesson, because they accepted Christianity. The king travelled over that district and did not leave off until [191] everyone there had accepted Christianity. From there he went east to Sóleyjar and made that settlement Christian. Then Óttarr svarti came to him and asked to become his man. Earlier that winter King Óláfr of the Svíar had died. Now Ǫnundr Óláfsson was king in Svíþjóð. King Óláfr then turned back to Raumaríki. The winter was now nearly past. Then King Óláfr called a well attended assembly in the place that afterwards came to be Heiðsævisþing. He then made it law that Upplendingar should attend this assembly and the Heiðsævislǫg should apply over all districts in Upplǫnd and also in many other places where it has since applied. And when spring comes, he made his way out to the sea, then had his ships made ready and in the spring went out to Túnsberg and stayed there during the spring while it was most crowded there and cargoes were being transported to the town from other countries. There was then a good season all over the Vík and fairly good right north to Stað, but great famine all the way north from there.

CHAPTER ONE HUNDRED AND FIFTEEN

King Óláfr sent orders in the spring west over Agðir and all the way north over Rogaland and over Hǫrðaland, that he wants to have neither corn nor malt nor meal sold from there to other districts, announcing at the same time that he would be coming there with his forces and travelling round and receiving hospitality, as the custom was. These orders went round all these districts, but the king stayed in the Vík over the summer and travelled all the way east to the land's end. Einarr þambarskelfir had been with King Óláfr of the Svíar since his brother-in-law Jarl Sveinn died, and had become the king of the Svíar's man, receiving from him many revenues. But when the king was dead, then Einarr became keen to get himself a truce with Óláfr digri, and during the spring messages had passed between them. So while King Óláfr was lying in the Elfr, then Einarr þambarskelfir came there [192] with a few men. He and the king then discussed their settlement, and it was agreed between them that Einarr should go north to Þrándheimr and keep all his possessions and also the properties that had come to him with Bergljót as her dowry. Einarr then went his way north, while the king stayed in the Vík and was for a long time in Borg in the autumn and the first part of the winter.

CHAPTER ONE HUNDRED AND SIXTEEN

Erlingr Skjálgsson had kept his dominion, so that all the way north from Sognsær and east to Líðandisnes he could have his own way with the farmers in everything, but he had many fewer royal revenues than previously. Now he was held in such awe that everyone put the weights on the scales as he wished. The king thought Erlingr's power was getting too great.

There was a man called Áslákr Fitjaskalli (Baldy of Fitjar), of noble kin and powerful. Erlingr's father Skjálgr and Áslákr's father Áskell were cousins. Áslákr was a great friend of King Óláfr, and the king appointed him to Sunn-Hǫrðaland, granting him there a great fief and many royal revenues, and the king told him to stand up to Erlingr. But it did not turn out thus when the king was not around. Then Erling had his own way, just as he wanted, in their dealings together. He was not any the milder when Áslákr tried to increase his own power at Erlingr's expense. Their dealings took such a turn that Áslákr could not continue in the district. He went to see the king and tells him of his dealings with Erlingr. The king told Áslákr to stay with him 'until Erlingr and I meet.'

The king sent word to Erlingr that he was to come to Túnsberg in the spring to see the king. And when they met, then they appointed meetings, and the king said:

'I am told this about your power, Erlingr, that there is no one to the north of Sognsær as far as Líðandisnes who can maintain his freedom because of you. There are many people that feel they [193] have an inherited right to have fair treatment from people of equal birth to them. Now here is your kinsman Áslákr, and he feels he has noticed a certain coldness from you in your dealings together. Now I am not sure which is more the case, that he has given cause for this, or whether he suffers because I have placed him there in charge of my interests. But although I have mentioned him in connection with this, yet many others make the same complaint to us, both those who occupy offices, and also agents who look after residences and are obliged to provide hospitality for me and my troops.'

Erlingr replies: 'This can soon be answered,' he says, 'I deny that I am blaming Áslákr or anyone else for being in your service. But I acknowledge that it is the case now, as it has been for a long time, that every one of our family wants to excel the others in power. I also acknowledge too, that I am very willing to bend my neck to you, King Óláfr, but I shall find it hard to bow down to Sel-Þórir (Seal-Þórir), who is descended from slaves on all sides, even if he is now your steward, or to any others who are his like in kinship, even if you hold them in high regard.'

Then those who were friends of both intervened and begged that they should be reconciled, saying that no one would be of such great support to the king as Erlingr 'if he can be your absolute friend.' On the other side they put it to Erlingr that he should give way to the king, saying that if he kept in friendship with the king, he would then find it all easy to do whatever he liked with everyone else. This meeting ended with Erlingr having the same revenues as he had had before, and all the charges that the king had against Erlingr were dropped. Also his son Skjálgr was to come to the king and stay with him. Then Áslákr returned to his estates and they were then nominally reconciled. Erlingr also went back home to his estates and kept up his established custom in his rule.

[194] CHAPTER ONE HUNDRED AND SEVENTEEN

There was a man called Sigurðr Þórisson, brother to Þórir hundr in Bjarkey. Sigurðr was married to Skjálgr's daughter Sigríðr, Erlingr's sister. Their son was called Ásbjǫrn. He was considered a very promising man in his youth. Sigurðr lived on Þrándarnes in Ǫmð. He was a very wealthy man, a man highly esteemed. He had not entered the king's service, and Þórir was the more highly esteemed of the brothers, since he was a landed man[204] of the king's, but at home, Sigurðr was in no way inferior in the magnificence of his housekeeping. During the pagan period, he was accustomed to hold three sacrificial banquets every year, one at the winter nights, the second at midwinter, the third in the summer. And when he accepted Christianity, he still kept up his established custom with the banquets. Then, in the autumn he held a great party for his friends, and also a Yule feast in the winter and then again invited many people; a third banquet he held at Easter, and then too it was well attended. He kept this up as long as he lived. Sigurðr died

[204] See note 52 above.

of sickness. Ásbjǫrn was then eighteen years old. He then came into his inheritance from his father. He kept up the established custom and held three banquets every year, as his father had done. There was a very short interval between Ásbjǫrn coming into his patrimony and when the seasons began to worsen and people's crops failed. Ásbjǫrn kept the same practice with his banquets, and he was helped by the fact that there was corn and the supplies that were needed left over from previous years. But when the first two seasons[205] had passed and others came in, then the corn was no better than in the previous ones. Then Sigríðr wanted the banquets to be discontinued, some or all of them. Ásbjǫrn did not wish to do that. He went that autumn to see his friends and bought corn wherever he could, and then got it from some. This carried on for that winter, Ásbjǫrn keeping up all his banquets. But the next spring there were few crops planted, [195] for no one managed to buy seed corn. Sigríðr talked about reducing the number of servants. Ásbjǫrn did not want to do that, and he carried on the same with everything that summer. The corn harvest looked rather like being a bad one. There was also the fact that King Óláfr had banned transportation of corn and malt and meal from the south and to the north of the country.

Now Ásbjǫrn felt the supplying of his household was getting problematical. So this was what he decided to do, he had a cargo ship of his launched. It was constructed for ocean-going. It was a good ship and the rigging was carefully done. It had a sail with coloured stripes. Ásbjǫrn set out and with him twenty men; they went southwards in the summer, and there is nothing to tell of their journey until they got to Karmtsund one evening and came to land by Ǫgvaldsnes. A large farmstead stands there up on the island of Kǫrmt, which is known as at Ǫgvaldsnes. This was a royal residence, a splendid farmstead. Þórir selr (Seal) was there in charge of it. He was steward there. Þórir was a man of lowly birth and had turned out a fine person, a hard worker, eloquent of speech, showy in his dresss, pushy and unyielding. He could afford to be like this, since he had the king's backing. He was a man hasty of speech and outspoken.

Ásbjǫrn and his men lay there that night. And in the morning, when it had got light, Þórir went down to the ship and some men with him. He asked who was in charge of this magnificent ship. Ásbjǫrn says who he is and gave his father's name. Þórir asks what was the furthest he was making for and what his business was. Ásbjǫrn says he wants to buy himself corn and malt. He says, as was true, that there was great famine in the north of the country.

'But we are told that here you have had a good season. Will you, farmer, sell us corn? I see that you have large ricks. [196] It would be a solution to us not to have to travel further.'

---

[205] *þau misseri* i.e. the first summer and winter of the famine.

Þórir replies: 'I shall provide you with a solution, so that you will not need to travel further for the purchase of corn, or to any other places here round Rogaland. I can tell you this, that you may as well turn back and go no further, for you will get no corn here nor anywhere else, for the king has forbidden corn to be sold from here to the north of the country, so go back, Háleygr. That is your best course.'

Ásbjǫrn says: 'If it is so, farmer, as you say, that we shall make no purchase of corn, then my business will take me at least as far as to pay a visit to my kin at Sóli and to see where my kinsman Erlingr lives.'

Þórir says: 'How close is your relationship to Erlingr?'

He says: 'My mother is his sister.'

Þórir says: 'Then it may be that I have not spoken advisedly, if you are nephew to the king of the Rygir.'

Then Ásbjǫrn and his men threw off their awnings[206] and turned the ship out to sea.

Þórir shouted to them: 'Farewell, and call in here on your return.'

Ásbjǫrn says they would do so. They now travel on their way and in the evening arrive at Jaðarr. Ásbjǫrn went ashore with ten men, while another ten guarded the ship. And when Ásbjǫrn came to the farm, he was welcomed there, and Erlingr was most merry with him. Erlingr made him sit next to him and asked him about many of the things that had happened in the north of the country. Ásbjǫrn told as plainly as he could about his errand. Erlingr says it was very unfortunate then, that the king had banned the sale of corn.

'I know,' he says, 'no likelihood of any man daring to break the king's command. I have to be very careful about the king's attitude, for there are many wanting to spoil our good relationship.'

Ásbjǫrn says: 'The truth is slow to come out. I was taught when I was young that my mother was of free birth in all sides of her descent, and this also, that Erlingr at Sóli was now the noblest of her kinsmen, but now I hear you say that because of the king's slaves you are not free enough [197] to do with your corn whatever you like.'

Erlingr looked at him and grinned and said: 'You know less about the king's power, you Háleygir, than we Rygir. But you must be outspoken at home, and where you inherit this from is not far to seek. Let us now drink for the time being, kinsman; let us see tomorrow how things stand with your errand.'

They did so and were merry during the evening. The next day they talk together, Erlingr and Ásbjǫrn, and Erlingr said:

'I have given some thought to your purchase of corn, Ásbjǫrn. So how fussy will you be about whom you do business with?'

[206] Awnings were hung over the ship at night for the crew to sleep under.

He says that he does not care about whom he buys corn from as long as it is sold freely.

Erlingr said: 'I think it more than likely that my slaves will have corn so that you can buy as much as you want. They are not subject to the same laws or local regulations as other men.'[207]

Ásbjǫrn says that he will accept this offer.

Then the slaves were told about this bargain. They made corn available, and also malt, and sold it to Ásbjǫrn. He loaded his ship with as much as he wanted. And when he was ready to leave, Erlingr sent him off with friendly gifts and they parted on affectionate terms.

Ásbjǫrn got a favourable wind and came to land in the evening in Karmtsund by Ǫgvaldsnes and stayed there the night. Þórir selr soon got intelligence of Ásbjǫrn's travels, and also that his ship was heavily laden. Þórir summoned troops to himself during the night, so that by dawn he had sixty men. He went to see Ásbjǫrn when it was just scarcely light. They went straight out onto the ship. By then Ásbjǫrn and his men were dressed, and Ásbjǫrn greeted Þórir. Þórir asks what cargo Ásbjǫrn had on his ship. He says that it was corn and malt. Þórir says:

'Then Erlingr must be doing as usual, treating all the king's commands as rubbish, and he still does not weary of being his opponent in everything, and it is [198] amazing that the king lets him get away with everything.'

Þórir ranted away for a while, and when he stopped, then Ásbjǫrn says that the corn had belonged to Erlingr's slaves. Þórir snapped in reply, that he was not interested in his and Erlingr's tricks.

'The only thing for you to do now, Ásbjǫrn, is for you to go ashore, otherwise we shall throw you overboard, because we want no crowding by you while we clear out the ship.'

Ásbjǫrn saw that he had no forces to match Þórir, and Ásbjǫrn and his men went ashore, but Þórir had all the cargo removed from the ship. And when the ship was cleared, then Þórir walked along the ship. He said:

'It is a very fine sail that you Háleygir have. Get our old cargo-ship sail and give it them. That is plenty good enough for them, sailing as they are with an empty ship.'

This was done, the exchange of sails. Ásbjǫrn and his men went off on their way with things as they were, and he made his way north along the coast and did not stop until he got home in the beginning of winter, and this expedition got widely known about. Now Ásbjǫrn had no work to do in preparation for banquets that winter. Þórir[208] invited Ásbjǫrn to a Yule

---

[207] This statement about the legal status of slaves has no support in the earliest extant law codes.

[208] sc. *hundr*, as stated in manuscripts of *ÓH*.

banquet with his mother and any people they wanted to bring with them. Ásbjǫrn refused to go and stayed at home. It was felt that Þórir thought Ásbjǫrn had acted slightingly over the invitation. Þórir made a joke out of Ásbjǫrn's expedition.

'Both things are true,' he says, 'that there is a great difference in the esteem in which we kinsmen of Ásbjǫrn are held, and also he has behaved accordingly, such trouble as he took in the summer in visiting his kinsman Erlingr in Jaðarr, while he will not come here next door to see me. I am not sure whether he thinks that Sel-Þórir will be lying in wait for him on every little island.'

Ásbjǫrn heard about these words of Þórir's and others like them. Ásbjǫrn was greatly dissatisfied with his expedition and even more so when he heard these things made into jokes and mockery. He stayed at home during the winter and went to no parties.

[199] CHAPTER ONE HUNDRED AND EIGHTEEN

Ásbjǫrn had a longship. It was a cruiser (*snekkja*), with twenty rowing benches,[209] kept in a great boatshed. After Candlemas[210] he had this ship launched and the tackle brought and had the ship rigged. Then he summoned his friends to him and had nearly ninety men all well armed. And when he was ready and there was a favourable wind, then he sailed south down the coast, and they continued their journey and the winds gave them rather slow progress, but as they made their way to the south of the country, then they travelled by the outer route more than the common one[211] when it was possible. Nothing much happened on their journey until they came on the evening of the fifth day of Easter[212] in to Kǫrmt. This place is situated as follows, it is a large island, long and for most of its length not broad, lying by the main sea route on its outside. There is a large settlement there, and many parts of the island are uninhabited, where it lies open to the sea. Ásbjǫrn and his men came to land on the outside of the island, where it is uninhabited. And when they had put up their awnings, then Ásbjǫrn said:

'Now you are to stay behind here and wait for me, but I shall go up onto the island to look around and see what is going on on the island, for we did not find out anything about it before.'

Ásbjǫrn had on wretched clothes and a hood that hid his face, a staff in his hand, a sword girded on underneath his clothes. He went up ashore and over

---

[209] i.e. 40 oars.

[210] 2nd February.

[211] i.e. past the islands on the seaward side where there would be less traffic and they would be less noticed, rather than the normal more public and protected route between the islands and the mainland.

[212] i.e. the Thursday after Easter Sunday.

on the island. And as he got to a certain height, when he could see over to the farm at Ǫgvaldsnes and so on to Karmtsund, then he saw a lot of movement of people both by sea and on land, and these people were all making for the farm at Ǫgvaldsnes. He thought this strange. After that he went up to the farm and towards where servants were preparing food. He could soon hear them and understand what they were saying, which was that King Óláfr was come there to a banquet, and also that the king had sat down to the table. Ásbjǫrn turned then into the reception room, and when he came into the anteroom, there was one man coming out and another going in, and no one took any notice of him. The reception room door was open. [200] He saw that Þórir selr was standing in front of the high seat table. It was now late in the evening. Ásbjǫrn listened to how Þórir was asked about his dealings with Ásbjǫrn and also how Þórir told a long story about it, and Ásbjǫrn thought he gave an obviously unfair account. Then he heard someone say:

'How did Ásbjǫrn respond when you were clearing out his ship?'

Þórir says: 'He bore it fairly well, and yet not really well when we cleared the ship, but when we took the sail from him, then he wept.'

And when Ásbjǫrn heard this, then he drew his sword determinedly and swiftly and leapt into the room, immediately striking at Þórir. The blow got him in the back of his neck, his head fell on the table in front of the king, and his body at his feet. The tablecloths were soaked in blood both on the top and underneath. The king spoke, commanding him to be taken hold of, and this was done, Ásbjǫrn was taken prisoner and led out of the room, and then the tableware and cloths were removed and taken away; also Þórir's body was carried out and everything cleaned up that was bloody. The king was very angry and controlled his words well, as he was always accustomed to do.

Skjálgr Erlingsson stood up and went before the king and said this:

'Now it will be as on other occasions, king, that things will have to be put right when you are involved. I will offer money on behalf of this man so that he may keep life and limb, but you, king, must decide and settle everything else.'

The king says: 'Is it not a capital offence, Skjálgr, if a man break the Easter peace, and another, that he killed a man in the king's chamber; a third, that you and your father will think of little account, that he used my feet as his chopping block?'

Skjálgr replies: 'It is a shame, king, that you are displeased, but otherwise this deed is of the finest. But if you find this deed, king, obnoxious and of great significance, then I trust that I may receive much from you on account of my [201] service. There are many who will say that this would be very appropriate for you to do.'

The king says: 'Although you are very deserving, Skjálgr, yet I am not for your sake going to break the law and lower my royal dignity.'

Skjálgr then turned away and out of the room. Twelve men had been there with Skjálgr, and they all went with him, and many others went away with him. Skjálgr said to Þórarinn Nefjólfsson:

'If you wish to have my friendship, then make every effort possible to prevent the man being killed before Sunday.'

Then Skjálgr and his men went and got a rowing boat that he had and row south as hard as they could and by dawn reached Jaðarr, went straight up to the farm and to the upper room that Erlingr slept in. Skjálgr ran at the door so that the nails sprang out. At this Erlingr and others that were in there awoke. He was soonest up on his feet and snatched up his shield and sword and ran to the entrance and asked who was going there so impetuously. Skjálgr said who he was and told him to open the door. Erlingr says:

'I might have known that it would be you if someone was going on so foolishly, but are some men after you?'

Then the door was opened. Then Skjálgr said:

'I expect, though you think I am going on impetuously, that your kinsman Ásbjǫrn will not think it too fast, as he sits north on Ǫgvaldsnes in irons, and it is more like a man to be going there and helping him.'

Then the father and son had some words together. Skjálgr then tells Erlingr all the circumstances surrounding the killing of Sel-Þórir.

CHAPTER ONE HUNDRED AND NINETEEN

King Óláfr sat down in his seat when everything was put to rights in the room, and he was very angry. He asked what had been done with the killer. He was told that he [202] was kept out on the balcony under guard. The king says:

'Why is he not killed?'

Þórarinn Nefjólfsson says:

'Lord, don't you call it murder to kill men by night?'

Then the king said: 'Put him in irons and kill him tomorrow.'

Then Ásbjǫrn was fettered and shut up alone in a building for the night. The next day, the king heard morning prayers. Then he went to meetings and sat there until High Mass. Then he went to Mass, and as he was leaving the service, he said to Þórarinn:

'Will the sun now be high enough for your friend Ásbjǫrn to be able to be hanged?'

Þórarinn said, bowing to the king: 'Lord, last Friday the bishop said that the king who has power over all things put up with trials of his spirit, and he is blessed, who can rather follow his example than that of those who then sentenced him to death, or that of him who caused his killing. Now it is not long until morning, and then it will be a working day.'

The king looked at him and said: 'You shall have your way so far, that he shall not be killed today. You shall now take charge of him and guard him, and be sure of this, that you will pay with your life if he gets away by whatever means.'

The king then continued on his way, and Þórarinn went to where Ásbjǫrn was sitting in irons. Þórarinn then had the fetters taken off him and took him to a small room and had him given drink and food, telling him what the king had laid down if Ásbjǫrn ran away. Ásbjǫrn says that Þórarinn need not fear that. Þórarinn stayed there with him for a long time during the day, and he also slept there during the night. On Saturday the king got up and went to morning prayers. Then he went to meetings, and there were large numbers of farmers come there, and they had many cases to bring. The king stayed there for a large part of the day, and High Mass was held rather late. After that the king went to eat, and when he had eaten, he drank for a while, with the tables still standing.[213] Þórarinn went to [203] the priest who was in charge of the church and gave him two ounces of silver to ring for the Sabbath as soon as the king's tables were taken away. So when the king had been drinking for as long as he thought fit, then the tables were taken away. Then the king spoke, saying that now it was a good idea for slaves to take the slayer and kill him. At that moment the bell rang for the Sabbath. Then Þórarinn went before the king, saying:

'The man must be spared over the Sabbath, even though he has ill deserved it.'

The king says: 'You guard him, Þórarinn, so that he doesn't get away.'

Then the king went to church and attended nones,[214] but Þórarinn again stayed by Ásbjǫrn during the day. On Sunday the bishop went to Ásbjǫrn and heard his confession and gave him permission to hear High Mass. Þórarinn then went to the king and asked him to get men to guard the slayer.

'I now wish,' he said, 'to give up responsibility for his case.'

The king gave him thanks for having taken it. Then he got men to guard Ásbjǫrn. Then he was chained up. And when High Mass was held, then Ásbjǫrn was taken to the church. He stood outside in front of the church together with those who were guarding him. The king and all the people attended Mass.

---

[213] The tables were erected for each meal and taken away the rest of the time.

[214] Nones was the monastic service for the ninth hour, usually held at about three p.m. In Norwegian law the Sabbath began on Saturday at nones.

CHAPTER ONE HUNDRED AND TWENTY

Now the story must be taken up where earlier we left off, where Erlingr and his son Skjálgr made their plans about this problem, and it was agreed at the urging of Skjálgr and his other sons that they should gather troops and send out a war summons. Then a large troop was soon mustered and took ship, and their number were then counted, and they were nearly fifteen hundred (or 1800) men.[215] They went with these [204] troops and came on the Sunday to Ǫgvaldsnes on Kǫrmt and went up to the farm with their whole troop and arrived just when the Gospel was finished, went straight up to the church and took Ásbjǫrn, breaking off his fetters. And at the sound of this clattering and clashing of weapons then everyone that was previously outside ran into the church, while those who were in the church then looked out, except the king. He stood and did not look round. Erlingr and his men ranged their troops on both sides of the paved road that led from the church to the banqueting hall. Erlingr and his sons stood nearest the hall. And when the whole service had been sung, then the king went straight out of the church. He walked on in front between the ranks of men, and then one after another of his men. When he got back to the doorway of the building, then Erlingr went before the doorway and bowed to the king and greeted him. In reply the king bade God help him. Then Erlingr began his address:

'I have been told that my kinsman Ásbjǫrn has fallen into a great misdemeanour, and that is bad, king, if it has come about that you are displeased at it. Now I am come in order to offer on his behalf atonement and compensation, as much as you yourself wish to have awarded, and to have in return his life and limbs and right to remain in the country.'

The king replies: 'It seems to me, Erlingr, as though you must now think you have power over Ásbjǫrn's fate. I do not know why you pretend that you have to offer compensation for him. I believe that you have brought here an army of men because you intend to have your own way in our dealings.'

Erlingr says: 'You shall have your way, and make your decision so that we can part in agreement.'

The king said: 'Are you trying to cow me, Erlingr? Is that why you have a large troop?'

'No,' he says.

'But if you have something else in mind, I am not going to flee.'

Erlingr says: 'You have no need to remind me that in our meetings up to now, I have had little military strength against you. But now I shall not conceal from you what I have in [205] mind, that I want us to part in peace, otherwise I expect I shall not risk further meetings between us.'

[215] Cf. note 202 above.

Erlingr was now red as blood in the face. Then Bishop Sigurðr came forward and spoke to the king:

'Lord, I bid you under submission for God's sake, that you settle with Erlingr, in accordance with his offer, so that this man may have safety for life and limb, but you alone shall determine all the terms.'

The king replies: 'You shall have your way.'

Then said the bishop: 'Erlingr, give the king such assurances as he wants, and then let Ásbjǫrn accept quarter and be at the king's mercy.'

Erlingr gave assurances, and the king accepted. Then Ásbjǫrn accepted quarter and put himself at the king's mercy and kissed the king's hand. Then Erlingr turned away with his troop. There were no farewells. Then the king went into the hall and Ásbjǫrn with him. Then the king pronounced the terms of atonement, saying as follows:

'This shall be the beginning of our agreement, Ásbjǫrn, that you shall submit to the law of the land, that a man who kills one in the king's service shall undertake the same service, if the king wishes. So I wish you to take up the stewardship that Sel-Þórir has had, and be in charge of my residence at Ǫgvaldsnes.'

Ásbjǫrn says that it should be as the king wished.

'But first I have to go to my home and make arrangements there.'

The king was pleased to accept this. He went on from there to another banquet that had been arranged for him, but Ásbjǫrn set out for home with his companions. They had lain in hidden creeks all the time that Ásbjǫrn was away. They had had intelligence of how things had been going for him, and they did not want to leave before they knew what the outcome was going to be. Then Ásbjǫrn set off and did not stop before the spring and he arrives home to his dwelling in the north. He came to be known as Ásbjǫrn Selsbani (Seal-Slayer). And when Ásbjǫrn had been not long at home, then the kinsmen, he and Þórir [hundr], met and speak together. Þórir asks [206] Ásbjǫrn in detail about his journey and all the circumstances surrounding the events there, and Ásbjǫrn told the story of what had happened. Then Þórir says:

'Then you will be thinking that you have wiped out the disgrace of having been robbed last autumn.'

'That is so,' said Ásbjǫrn. 'So how does it seem to you, kinsman?'

'I can soon tell you,' said Þórir. 'The earlier journey that you took to the south of the country was quite disgraceful, and that took some putting right, but this journey has brought shame upon both you and your kinsmen, if it results in you becoming the king's slave and the equal of the worst of men, Þórir selr. Now behave like a man, and stay rather on your property here. We your kinsmen shall give you support so that you never again get into such a fix.'

Ásbjǫrn thought this looked good, and before he and Þórir parted, this idea was confirmed, that he was to stay at his home and not again go to see the king or into his service, and he did this and stayed at home on his property.

CHAPTER ONE HUNDRED AND TWENTY-ONE

After King Óláfr and Erlingr Skjálgsson had met on Ǫgvaldsnes, the dissension between them arose anew, and increased until it resulted in open hostility between them. In the spring King Óláfr travelled around Hǫrðaland to banquets, and then he went up into Vǫrs, since he had heard that the people there were were not strong in their faith. He held a meeting with farmers at a place called at Vangr. The farmers came there in great numbers and fully armed. The king invited them to accept Christianity, but the farmers invited him to battle in return, and it came to this, that both sides drew up their troops. What happened with the farmers then was that they panicked, and no one would stand in the frontline, and what happened in the end, which was much the best thing for them, was that they submitted to the king [207] and accepted Christianity. The king did not leave the place until it had become fully Christian.

It happened one day that the king was riding on his way singing his psalms, and when he came to face these mounds,[216] he stopped and said:

'These words of mine shall pass from man to man, that I declare it advisable that never again should a king of Norway pass between these mounds.'

It is moreover reported that most kings have avoided this since.

Then King Óláfr went out into Ostrarfjǫrðr and came to his ships there, then went north into Sogn and there received banquets during the summer. And when autumn came, he turned inland into the fiord, travelling from there up into Valdres. It had up to this been heathen there. The king rushed as fast as he could up to the lake,[217] taking the farmers by surprise and capturing their ships there, going on board himself with all his troops. Then he sent round a summons to an assembly, and set up the assembly so close to the lake that the king had easy access to ships if he felt he needed them. The farmers attended the assembly with a host of men fully armed. The king preached Christianity to them, but the farmers shouted against it and bade him be silent, immediately making a great racket and clashing of weapons. So when the king saw that they did not want to listen to what he was teaching them, and that besides, that they had a great crowd of men that it was impossible to withstand, then he changed tack, asking them about whether there were any people at the assembly who had suits against each

---

[216] It is not specified what mounds these were.
[217] Probably Mjǫrs.

other that they wanted him to settle between them. It soon became apparent in the words of the farmers, that many were in dispute with each other who now had banded together to oppose Christianity. And as soon as the farmers began to put forward their problems, then each of them gathered supporters on their side to push their cases forward. This went on all day. In the evening the assembly broke up. As soon as the farmers had heard that King Óláfr had travelled round Valdres and had reached their area, then they had [208] sent round a war summons and called together freemen and thralls, going with this host against the king, though at that time it was in many places completely uninhabited in the area. The farmers kept together when the assembly broke up. The king knew about this. And when he got to his ships, then he had them rowed across the lake during the night. There he got his men to go up into the settlement, having everything there burned and plundered. Later on that day they rowed from one ness to another. The king had the whole settlement burned. And the farmers that were gathered together, when they saw the smoke and flames from their farms, then they scattered from their assemblage. Then everyone set off and made for home to see if they could find their households. And when the host started to break up, then one after another left until they were all scattered into small groups. But the king rowed across the lake and then burned on the shore both sides. The farmers then came to him and begged for mercy, offering their submission. He gave every man quarter who came to him and asked it, and their property. Then no one spoke against Christianity. The king then had the people baptised and took hostages from the farmers. The king stayed there a long time during the autumn, having had the ships dragged across the isthmus between the lakes. The king travelled little through the land higher up from the lakes, for he did not trust the farmers. He had churches built and consecrated there and installed clergy. But when the king thought frosts were likely, then he made his way up inland, coming out then in Þótn. Arnórr jarlaskáld speaks of this, how King Óláfr carried out burnings in Upplǫnd, when he composed about his brother Haraldr:

85.	Following his family's fashion,[218] the king burnt houses of Upplendingar; that people paid for the prince's wrath, of men foremost.	*Haraldsdrápa* 5 *Skald* II 265–67
[209]	Mighty men were not willing to mind the glorious victor—	

[218] *Gengr í ætt* seems to mean 'it runs in the family', as in Modern Icelandic; this is confirmed by the citation here in support of the account of Óláfr's actions of a poem about the later deeds of his brother-in-law, Haraldr Sigurðarson. The *yngvi* 'king' in the verse is Haraldr, but he is said to be following the example of his half-brother Óláfr.

the king's foes gained the gallows—
they had got into trouble before this.

Afterwards King Óláfr travelled north through the Dales all the way to the mountain and did not stop until he got to Þrándheimr and right to Niðaróss, living there for his winter quarters and staying there throughout the winter. This was the tenth winter of his reign as king. The previous summer Einarr þambarskelfir travelled out of the country, going first west to England, meeting there his father-in-law Jarl Hákon, staying there with him for a while. Then Einarr went to see King Knútr and received great gifts from him. After that Einarr travelled south over the sea and right to the City of Rome, returning the next summer, going then to his estates. He and King Óláfr did not meet at this time.

CHAPTER ONE HUNDRED AND TWENTY-TWO

There was a woman called Álfhildr, who was referred to as the king's concubine. She was, however, descended from good families. She was the most beautiful of women. She was in the king's household. And that spring it came about that Álfhildr was with child, and people in the king's confidence knew that he must be the father of the child. It happened one night that Álfhildr was taken ill. There were few people present there, some women and a priest and Sigvatr skáld and a few others. Álfhildr was very poorly, and she came to be close to death. She gave birth to a boy child, and for a while it was the case that they did not know for certain (210) whether there was any life in the child. But when the child began to breathe, and very weakly, then the priest told Sigvatr to tell the king. He replies:

'I dare on no account to wake the king up, for he has forbidden anyone to interrupt his sleep for him until he wakes of his own accord.'

The priest replies: 'It is now essential for this child to receive baptism. It seems to me to be very unlikely to live.'

Sigvatr said: 'I would rather dare to take it upon myself, that you baptise the child, than that I should wake the king, and I will bear the blame and give it a name.'

They did so, baptising the child and calling him Magnús. The next morning, when the king was awake and dressed, he was told all that had happened. Then the king had Sigvatr called to him. The king said:

'Why were you so bold as to have my child baptised before I knew about it?'

Sigvatr replies: 'For this reason, that I had rather give God two people than one to the devil.'

The king said: 'How should that have been involved?'

Sigvatr replies: 'The child was at the point of death, and it would have been the devil's man if it died a heathen, but now it would be God's man. Moreover, I knew that although you would be angry with me, it would involve no more than my life, but if you desire that I lose that for this offence, then I trust that I would be God's man.'

The king said: 'Why did you have the boy called Magnús? That is not the name of any in our family.'

Sigvatr replies: 'I called him after King Karla-Magnús.[219] I knew that he was the best man in the world.'

Then the king said: 'You are a very lucky man, Sigvatr. It is not surprising when luck goes with wisdom. The opposite is unusual, which can sometimes happen, that such luck is found in unwise people, so that unwise [211] undertakings turn out fortunately.'

The king was then very pleased. The boy grew up and soon became promising as he increased in age.

CHAPTER ONE HUNDRED AND TWENTY-THREE

That same spring King Óláfr transferred to Ásmundr Grankelsson stewardship in Hálogaland in half shares with Hárekr on Þjótta, though the latter had previously held it all, partly as a grant, and partly as a fief. Ásmundr had a light ship with nearly thirty men on it well armed. And when Ásmundr came north, then he and Hárekr met. Ásmundr tells him how the king had organised the stewardship, showing the king's authorisation. Hárekr says this, that it was up to the king who should have the stewardship.

'And yet previous rulers have not acted thus, diminishing our rights, who have a hereditary claim on power, to receive it from kings, but handing it over to sons of farmers who have not previously had control of it.'

But though it was apparent in Hárekr that he found this against his inclination, still he let Ásmundr take over the stewardship, in accordance with the king's message. Then Ásmundr went back home to his father's, staying there a short time, after that going to his stewardship north in Hálogaland. But when he got north to Langey, then there were two brothers living there. One was called Gunnsteinn, the other Karli. They were wealthy men and highly respected. Gunnsteinn was active in managing the farm and the elder of the brothers; Karli was handsome in appearance and a very showy man, but both of them were accomplished men in various ways. Ásmundr was received well there and stayed there a while, collecting from the district whatever was available. Karli spoke of this with Ásmundr, that he wanted to

---

[219] Charlemagne (Carolus Magnus, Charles the Great).

travel south with him to see King Óláfr [212] and ask to join his following. Ásmundr encouraged this idea and promised his support with the king, so that Karli might achieve the boon he was seeking. Karli then joined company with Ásmundr. Ásmundr heard that Ásbjǫrn Selsbani had gone south to Vágastefna and had a cargo ship that he owned, with nearly twenty men on it and he was now expected back from the south. Ásmundr and Karli made their way south along the coast and met headwinds, though they were not strong. Ships sailed towards them on their way from Vágafloti. They made confidential enquiries about Ásbjǫrn's movements. They were told that he must be on his way from the south. Ásmundr and Karli were bedfellows, and they were very close friends.

It happened one day, when Ásmundr and Karli were rowing on through a certain sound, then a cargo ship sailed towards them. This ship was easily recognisable. It had brightly coloured bows, painted with white paint and red. They had a sail with coloured stripes. Then Karli said to Ásmundr:

'You are often saying that you are very curious to see this Ásbjǫrn Selsbani. I am no good at recognising ships if it is not he sailing there.'

Ásmundr replies: 'Be so kind, comrade, as to tell me if you recognise him.'

Then the ships passed each other, and Karli said: 'There is Selsbani, sitting by the helm in a dark tunic.'

Ásmundr replies: 'I shall give him a red tunic.'

Ásmundr shot a spear at Ásbjǫrn Selsbani and it hit him in the middle of his body, flew through him so that it stuck fast on into the headboard. Ásbjǫrn fell dead from the tiller. After that each ship continued on its course. They took Ásbjǫrn's body north to Þrándarnes. Sigríðr had Þórir hundr sent for from Bjarkey. He arrived when Ásbjǫrn's body had been laid out in accordance with their custom. And when they were leaving, Sigríðr chose her friends [213] presents. She accompanied Þórir to his ship, but before they parted, she said:

'This is how it is now, Þórir, that my son Ásbjǫrn used to follow your kindly counsels. Now his life has not lasted long enough for him to repay that as it deserved. Now although I be less able to do so than he would have been, yet I shall do my best. Now here is a gift that I am going to give you, and I would like it to be of some service to you.'

It was a spear.

'Here is now the spear that was stuck through my son Ásbjǫrn, and there is still blood on it. You will therefore be well able to remember that it will match the wound that you have seen in your brother's son Ásbjǫrn. It would now be a fine thing for you if you were only to let this spear go from your grasp when it sticks in Óláfr digri's breast. Now I make this pronouncement,' she says, 'that everyone may judge you base if you fail to avenge Ásbjǫrn.'

Then she turned to go. Þórir was so angry at her words that he could make no reply, and he did not think to let go of the spear, and he did not notice the gangplank, and he would have walked into the water if his men had not taken hold of him and steadied him as he went aboard his ship. It was an inlaid spear, not all that big, and the socket was inlaid with gold. Þórir and his men then rowed away and back to Bjarkey. Ásmundr and his companion continued on their way until they came south to Þrándheimr and got to see King Óláfr. Then Ásmundr told the king what had happened during his travels. Karli became a member of the king's following. He and Ásmundr continued good friends. But the exchange of words that had taken place between Ásmundr and Karli before the slaying of Ásbjǫrn came about, this did not remain a secret, because they themselves told the king about it. But in this it proved, as they say, that everyone has a friend among his enemies. There were some there who kept these things alive in their memory, and as a result they came to the ears of Þórir hundr.

[214] CHAPTER ONE HUNDRED AND TWENTY-FOUR

King Óláfr got ready in the spring, towards its end, and prepared his ships. After that in the summer he went south along the coast, having meetings with the farmers, settling people's disputes and reforming the religion of the country, also receiving royal dues wherever he went. In the autumn the king got all the way east to the land's end. King Óláfr had now Christianised the country, wherever there were large settlements. He had also now drawn up laws all over the country. He had now also made Orkney subject to himself, as was told above. He had also had contact and made himself many friends in both Iceland and Greenland and also in the Faeroes. King Óláfr had sent to Iceland timber for a church, and this church was built at Þingvǫllr, where the Alþingi is. At the same time he sent a great bell, which is still there. This was after the Icelanders had altered their laws, and established Christian law in accordance with what King Óláfr had prescribed for them. After this many men of note left Iceland who entered the service of King Óláfr. Among them were Þorkell Eyjólfsson, Þorleikr Bollason, Þórðr Kolbeinsson, Þórðr Barkarson, Þorgeirr Hávararson, Þormóðr Kolbrúnarskáld (Kolbrún's poet). King Óláfr had sent friendly gifts to many leading men in Iceland, and they sent him such things as were available there and they hoped that he would most like to have sent him. But beneath these tokens of friendship that the king gave to Iceland there lay other things that later became apparent.

[215] CHAPTER ONE HUNDRED AND TWENTY-FIVE

That summer King Óláfr sent Þórarinn Nefjólfsson to Iceland on business of his, and Þórarinn took his ship out from Þrándheimr at the same time as the king left, and accompanied him south to Mœrr. Then Þórarinn sailed out to sea and got such a fast favourable wind that in eight sailing shifts[220] he sailed as far as reaching Eyrar in Iceland, went straight to the Alþingi and got there when people were at the Law Rock, going straight to the Law Rock. And when people had delivered their legal proceedings there, then Þórarinn Nefjólfsson began to speak:

'Four nights since I parted from King Óláfr Haraldsson. He sent greetings to this land to all the leading men and rulers of the country and as well to all the population of men and women, young and old, rich and poor, from God and himself, adding that he wishes to be your lord, if you are willing to be his subjects, and each to be friends of the other and supporters in all good enterprises.'

People responded well to his speech. Everyone said they would gladly be friends of the king, if he would be a friend of the people of this country. Then Þórarinn began to speak:

'This comes with the king's greeting, that he would like to request in friendship from the people of the north of the country, that they give him an island or outlying skerry that lies off Eyjafjǫrðr, that is known as Grímsey, wishing to offer in return whatever goods from his own country people may want to tell him about, and sent word to Guðmundr of Mǫðruvellir to facilitate this business, since he has heard that Guðmundr has most say there.'

Guðmundr replies: 'I am keen to have King Óláfr's friendship, and I consider that much more to my advantage than the outlying skerry that he asks for. But yet the king has not been correctly informed that I have more power over it than others, for it has now been made public land. We shall now have a meeting about it between ourselves, the people who have most [216] profit from the island.'

Afterwards people went to their booths.[221] After this the people of Northern Iceland hold a meeting among themselves and discuss this business. Everyone put forward whatever their views were. Guðmundr was a supporter of the proposal, and many others sided with him. Then people asked why his brother Einarr had nothing to say about it.

'We feel he,' they say, 'can see most clearly about most things.'

Then Einarr replies: 'The reason I have had little to say about this business is that no one has called upon me to speak about it. But if I am to give my opinion, then I think that the course for us dwellers in this land is not to submit here to the taxes paid to King Óláfr and all the burdens such as he

---

[220] *dœgr* is a period of 12 hours; 8 *dœgr* = 4 days and nights.
[221] *búð* is a temporary shelter used during the summer assembly in Iceland (and elsewhere), consisting of turf and stone walls over which an awning would be spread when it was in use.

has imposed on people in Norway. And we shall be causing this deprivation of freedom not only to ourselves, rather both to ourselves and our sons and all our families that inhabit this land, and this bondage will never go away or disappear from this land. So though this king may be a good man, as I firmly trust that he is, yet it will happen from now on as it has before now, when there is a change of ruler, that they turn out differently, some well, some badly. But if the people of this country wish to keep their freedom, which they have had since this land was settled, then it will be best to grant the king no foothold on it, either in possession of land here or by payment from here of specific taxes which may be interpreted as acknowledgement of allegiance. But this I declare to be quite proper, that people should send the king friendly gifts, those who wish to, hawks or horses, hangings or sails or other such things that are suitable to send. It is making good use of these things, if they are rewarded by friendship. But as for Grímsey, there is this to say, if nothing is transported from there that can be used as food, then a host of men could be maintained there. And if a foreign army is there and they come from there with longships, then I think many a cottager would feel that oppression was at hand.'

And when Einarr had said this and mentioned all the possible outcomes, then [217] all the people were converted to the one opinion, that this must not be granted. Þórarinn saw then what the outcome of his errand on this business would be.

CHAPTER ONE HUNDRED AND TWENTY-SIX

The next day Þórarinn went to the Law Rock and then gave another speech, beginning thus:

'King Óláfr sent word to his friends here in this country, mentioning particularly Guðmundr Eyjólfsson, Snorri goði, Þorkell Eyjólfsson, Lawspeaker Skapti, Þorsteinn Hallsson. He sent you a message about this, that you were to go to see him and get there offers of friendship. He said this, that you were not to fail to carry out this journey if you were concerned about his friendship.'

They replied to this speech, thanking the king for his offer, saying that they would inform Þórarinn later about their journeys when they had thought about it themselves and consulted with their friends. So when these prominent men started to discuss it between themselves, then each put forward his views about this journey. Snorri goði and and Skapti spoke against running the risk with the Norwegians of all those who had most power in the country leaving Iceland together to go there. They said that they felt that what seemed most suspicious in this message was, as Einarr had said, that the king might be planning some extortion on the Icelanders if he had his way. Guðmundr and Þorkell Eyjólfsson were very keen to act in accordance with the king's message, declaring that it would be a very honourable undertaking. And as they debated this matter between themselves, then the main decision they came to was that they should not go themselves, but each of them should appoint a person that he thought most suitable on his behalf, and they parted at that assembly leaving matters thus, and there were no journeys abroad that summer. But Þórarinn travelled out and back the same summer and came in the autumn [218] to see King Óláfr and told him the result of his mission, such as it was, saying also that the leaders would come from Iceland, in accordance with the message he had sent, or else their sons.

CHAPTER ONE HUNDRED AND TWENTY-SEVEN

That same summer there came in from the Faeroes to Norway in response to a message from King Óláfr Lawspeaker Gilli, Leifr Qzurarson, Þórálfr of Dímon and many other farmers' sons. But Þrándr in Gata got ready to go, and when he was nearly ready, then he suffered a stroke, so that he was unable to go anywhere, and he had to stay behind. And when the Faeroese people came to see King Óláfr, then he called them to have a talk and held a meeting with them.Then he brought up the business that lay behind their travels, telling them that he wished to receive taxes from the Faeroes, and also that the Faeroese were to have the laws that King Óláfr instituted for them. And at this meeting it was clear from what the king said that he was going to take assurances for these matters from the Faeroese people that were come there about whether they were willing to confirm this agreement with oaths, inviting the men whom he thought were most distinguished to become his men and receive from him honours and friendship. But the Faeroese felt suspicious about the king's words, as to how their affairs would turn out if they were unwilling to agree to everything that the king asked of them. But although there had to be further meetings arranged [219] about this business before it was concluded, still everything was put into effect that the king asked. They became subject to the king and became his men, Leifr and Gilli and Þórálfr, while the whole party gave sworn promises to King Óláfr to uphold in the Faeroes the laws and regulations that he established for them, and payment of the taxes that he determined. After that these Faeroese got ready to return home. And at parting the king gave friendly gifts to those who had become his men. They went on their way when they were ready. And the king had a ship fitted out and got a crew for it and sent men to the Faeroes to collect the taxes there that the Faeroese were to pay him. They took some time to get ready, and of their journey there is this to say, that they do not return nor do any taxes either the summer next following, because they never reached the Faeroes. No one there had collected any taxes.

CHAPTER ONE HUNDRED AND TWENTY-EIGHT

In the autumn King Óláfr went in to the Vík and sent word on his behalf to Upplǫnd, to have banquets ordered, and he made plans to travel round Upplǫnd during the winter. Then he set out on the journey and went to Upplǫnd. King Óláfr stayed the winter in Upplǫnd, going to banquets there and putting right those things that he thought in need of improvement, then reforming Christianity again there where he thought it necessary. It came about, when the king was in Heiðmǫrk, that Ketill kálfr of Hringunes made a proposal of marriage. He asked for Sigurðr sýr's and Ásta's daughter Gunnhildr. Gunnhildr was King Óláfr's sister.[222] The king was responsible for replying to this proposal and the arrangements for the match. He received it welcomingly. This was because he knew about Ketill, that he was of noble family [220] and wealthy, a sensible man, a great leader. He had also for a long time before this been a great friend of King Óláfr, as has been told above.[223] All this resulted in the king granting this match to Ketill. It was brought about that Ketill married Gunnhildr. King Óláfr was present at the banquet. King Óláfr travelled north to Guðbrandsdalar, receiving banquets there. A man lived there who was called Þórðr Gothormsson, at the farm called at Steig. Þórðr was the most powerful person in the northern part of Dalar. And when he and the king met, then Þórðr made a proposal of marriage, asking for King Óláfr's mother's sister Ísríðr Guðbrandsdóttir. The king was responsible for replying to this proposal. And when they had sat considering this matter, then it was decided that the match should be agreed, and Þórðr married Ísríðr. He afterwards became a sincere friend of King Óláfr and so did many other kinsmen and friends of Þórðr who followed his example. King Óláfr then went back south over Þótn and Haðaland, then to Hringaríki and from there out to the Vík. In the spring he went to Túnsberg and stayed there for a long time while the market and import of goods was busiest. He then had his ships fitted out and kept with him a large number of men.

CHAPTER ONE HUNDRED AND TWENTY-NINE

That summer there came from Iceland in response to King Óláfr's message Lawspeaker Skapti's son Steinn, Snorri goði's son Þóroddr, Þorkell's son Gellir, Síðu-Hallr's son and Þorsteinn's brother Egill. Guðmundr Eyjólfsson had died the winter before. These Icelandic men went to see King Óláfr as

---

[222] Actually his half-sister. Ásta was his mother, but his father was Haraldr grenski.
[223] Ch. 75 above.

soon as they could manage it. And when they met the king, they got a good reception there and they all stayed with him. That same summer King Óláfr learned that the ship had disappeared, the one he had sent to the Faeroes for taxes the previous summer, and it had nowhere [221] reached land, as far as was known. The king provided another ship and men with it and sent it to the Faeroes for taxes. These men went and set out to sea, but after that nothing was heard of them any more than of the previous ones. And there were many theories about what must have happened to these ships.

CHAPTER ONE HUNDRED AND THIRTY

Knútr inn ríki, whom some people call the old Knútr, he was king at this time over England and over the Danish realm. Knútr ríki was Sveinn tjúguskegg Haraldsson's son. They and their forebears had long ruled over Denmark. Knútr's grandfather Haraldr Gormsson had got Norway after the fall of Haraldr Gunnhildarson and taken taxes from it, placing Jarl Hákon inn ríki (the Great) in charge of it. Haraldr's son King Sveinn of the Danes also ruled over Norway and put in charge over it Jarl Eiríkr Hákonarson. He and his brother Sveinn Hákonarson then ruled the country until Jarl Eiríkr went west to England in response to a message from his brother-in-law Knútr inn ríki, leaving behind to rule in Norway his son and Knútr inn ríki's sister's son Jarl Hákon. But after Óláfr digri came to Norway, then he first captured Jarl Hákon and deposed him from rule, as is written above. Then Hákon went to his mother's brother Knútr, and had afterwards been staying with him all the time until this point in the story. Knútr inn ríki had won England through battles and fought to gain it and had a long struggle before the people of the country had submitted to him. But when he felt he had got to be in control of that country, then he called to mind what he felt he possessed in the country that he himself had no control of, that was in Norway. He felt he had a hereditary right to the whole of Norway, but his sister's son Hákon thought it was partly his, and moreover he felt he had [222] lost it disgracefully. One reason why Knútr and Hákon had made no move to lay claim to Norway was primarily that when Óláfr Haraldsson came to the country, all the common people and multitudes rose up and would hear of nothing other than that Óláfr should be king over the whole land. But then afterwards, when people felt they had lost their freedom through his rule, then some decided to leave the country. Very many of the powerful men went to see King Knútr, and also powerful farmers' sons, under various pretexts. But each of them that came to see King Knútr wanting to join with him, they all got from him their hands full of money. Much more splendour was to be seen there too than in other places, both in the large numbers that were there daily and the other appointments that were there in the apartments that he possessed and occupied himself. Knútr inn ríki took taxes and dues from the countries that were richest in the Northern lands, and to the whole extent that he had the right to take more than other kings, he also gave all the more than every other king. In his whole realm there was such stable peace that no one dared to disturb it, and the people of the countries had peace and the ancient laws of their country. From all this he gained great renown throughout all lands. But those who came from Norway many of them complained of their lack of freedom and spoke of it to Jarl Hákon, and some of them to the king himself, saying that the people of Norway would now be ready to return to allegiance to King Knútr and the jarl and receive from them their freedom. Such talk was much to the jarl's liking, and he put it before the king, asking him to try and find out whether King Óláfr would be willing to give up his rule to them or to share it under some agreement. In this many supporters sided with the jarl.

[223] CHAPTER ONE HUNDRED AND THIRTY-ONE

Knútr inn ríki sent men from the west from England to Norway, and their journey was equipped very splendidly. They had a letter and the seal of King Knútr of the English. They came to see King Óláfr Haraldsson of Norway in the spring in Túnsberg. And when the king was told that an embassy of Knútr inn ríki was come, then he was annoyed at it, saying that Knútr could send no men there with such messages as would be advantageous to him or his men, and for a few days the embassy did not get to see the king. But when they got leave to speak with him, then they went before the king and brought out King Knútr's letters and announce the message that came with it, that King Knútr declares his possession of all Norway, and claims that his forebears have held that realm before him. But because King Knútr wants to bring peace to all lands, he does not want to invade Norway with an army if there is an alternative. But if King Óláfr Haraldsson wants to be king over Norway, then let him come to see King Knútr and receive the land from him as a fief and become his man and pay him taxes, such as jarls have done in the past. Then they presented letters, and they said all the same thing. Then King Óláfr replies:

'I have heard it said in ancient accounts, that King Gormr of the Danes was considered to be a worthy national king, and he ruled over just Denmark. But these kings of the Danes that we have had since find that is not enough. It has now come about that Knútr rules over Denmark and over England, and he has now even made subject to himself a large part of Scotland. Now he is laying claim to my patrimony from me. He must in the end learn moderation for his greed. Or can it be his intention to become sole ruler over all the Northern lands? [224] Or does he plan to eat all the cabbage in England on his own? He will be able to achieve that sooner than I will offer him my head or any sort of homage. You shall now tell him what I say, that I will defend Norway with point and edge, as long as my life lasts, and moreover pay no man taxes from my realm.'

After this decisive answer King Knútr's embassy began to set off for home, and were not pleased with the result of their errand.

The poet Sigvatr had been with King Knútr, and King Knútr gave him a gold ring that weighed half a mark. Also there at that time with King Knútr was Bersi Skáld-Torfuson (son of the poet(ess) Torfa), and King Knútr gave him two gold rings, each one weighing half a mark, and an ornamented sword as well. So said Sigvatr:

> 86. Knútr the fine, most famous *Vestrfararvísur* 5
> for feats, has splendidly *Skald* I 622
> embellished the arms of both of us,
> Bear-cub,[224] when we met the ruler.
> In many ways wise, a mark or
> more of gold he gave you,
> and a sharp sword; God himself
> decides all; to me a half-mark.

Sigvatr had a talk with King Knútr's embassy and asked them about all kinds of news. They told him whatever he asked, about their interview with King Óláfr and also about the conclusion of their mission. They say that he received their business with great hostility.

'And we do not know,' they say, [225] 'why he dares to refuse to become King Knútr's man and go to see him. And that would be his best course, for King Knútr is so kindly that men of rank never offend him so greatly that he does not forgive it all when they go to see him and pay homage to him. It happened a little while ago that two kings came to him from the north, from Fife in Scotland, and he gave up his anger with them, and gave up to them all the lands that they had had earlier, and great friendly gifts as well.'

Then said Sigvatr:

> 87. To Knútr outstanding kings have *Skald* I 714
> carried their heads out of
> the north, from Fife's centre,
> the forfeit of peace paying.
> Óleifr never yielded—
> he often won victory—
> the Stout, his skull to any
> soul in this world in that way.

[224] *Húnn* 'bear', punning on the name Bersi, meaning 'bear, bear-cub'.

King Knútr's embassy went on their way home, and they had a good journey across the sea. After that they went to see King Knútr and told him the outcome of their mission, and also the final words that King Óláfr spoke to them last. King Knútr replies:

'King Óláfr is mistaken if he thinks that I would want to eat all the cabbage in England on my own. I [226] would rather wish him to discover that I have more beneath my ribs than just cabbage, for from now on shall cold counsels issue for him from under every rib.'

That same summer there came from Norway to King Knútr Erlingr of Jaðarr's sons Áslákr and Skjálgr, and they got a good welcome there, for Áslákr was married to Jarl Sveinn Hákonarson's daughter Sigríðr. She and Jarl Hákon Eiríksson were cousins.[225] King Knútr gave the brothers great banquets there with him.

CHAPTER ONE HUNDRED AND THIRTY-TWO

King Óláfr summoned to him his landed men[226] and mustered a large number of men in the summer, for the word was going around that Knútr inn ríki would be travelling from the west[227] in the summer. People thought they had understood from trading ships that were coming from the west that Knútr must be collecting together a large army in England. But as the summer drew to a close, then one person would assert, while another denied, that an army would come. But King Óláfr spent the summer in the Vík and had men on the lookout for King Knútr coming to Denmark. King Óláfr sent men in the autumn east to Svíþjóð to see his brother-in-law King Ǫnundr, and had him told about King Knútr's embassy and the claim that he had made against King Óláfr about Norway, saying also that he thought that if Knútr subjected Norway to himself, Ǫnundr would not possess the Swedish realm in peace for long after that, and maintained it was advisable for them to join forces and rise against him, saying that they did not lack the power to contend with King Knútr. King Ǫnundr welcomed King Óláfr's communication, and sent these words in reply, that he is willing to make an alliance on his part with King Óláfr so that each may give support to the other from his own kingdom, whichever is the first to need it. This was also in messages between them, that they [227] were to meet and make their plans. King Ǫnundr was planning to go the following winter over Vestra-Gautland, but King Óláfr was preparing himself winter quarters in Sarpsborg. Knútr inn ríki came

---

[225] *brœðraborn*: children of brothers (actually half-brothers: Sveinn and Eiríkr were sons of Hákon by different mothers).
[226] See note 52 above.
[227] *vestan*, i.e. from the British Isles (cf. Vestrlǫnd).

that autumn to Denmark and stayed there over the winter with very large numbers of men. He was told that men and messages had passed between the king of Norway and the king of the Svíar, and that plans for some great undertaking must underlie them. King Knútr sent men during the winter to Svíþjóð to see King Ǫnundr, sending him great gifts and words of friendship, saying this, that he might as well not get involved in the disputes between himself and Óláfr digri.

'For King Ǫnundr,' he says, 'and his realm shall be in peace as far as I am concerned.'

But when the messengers came to see King Ǫnundr, then they brought out the gifts that King Knútr was sending him together with his friendship. King Ǫnundr received these speeches with no alacrity, and the messengers felt they could see by this that King Ǫnundr must be very inclined to friendship with King Óláfr. They went back and tell King Knútr the outcome of their errand and this too, that they told him to expect no friendship from King Ǫnundr.

CHAPTER ONE HUNDRED AND THIRTY-THREE

King Óláfr stayed that winter in Sarpsborg and had large numbers of men with him. Then he sent Karli the Hálogalander to the north of the country on his business. Karli went first to Upplǫnd, then north over the mountain, coming out in Niðaróss, receiving there the king's money, as much as he had sent a request for, and a fine ship, that he thought would be very suitable for the journey that the king had planned, and that was to go north to Bjarmaland. What was planned was that Karli should be in partnership with the king and they each should have a half share of the money. Karli took the ship north to Hálogaland early [228] in the spring. His brother Gunnsteinn joined with him on the journey, and took with him goods for trading. They were nearly twenty-five men on the ship, setting out straight away early in the spring north to the Mǫrk. Þórir hundr heard about this. He then sent men with a message to the brothers, saying this, that he was planning to go to Bjarmaland in the summer, and he wished them to sail together and share equally what they got in the way of gains. Karli and Gunnsteinn sent word in reply that Þórir should take twenty-five men, the same as they had. They then wished that of the wealth that came their way, an equal division should be made between the ships, apart from the trading goods that individuals possessed. But when Þórir's messengers returned, he had now launched a huge cargo-carrying longship that he owned, and had had it fitted out. He manned this ship with his house servants, and there were on the ship nearly eighty men. Þórir was solely in charge of this troop, and thus of all the proceeds that came of this expedition. And when Þórir was ready he took his ship north along the coast and met Karli's party north in Sandver. After that they all travelled together, and the winds were favourable. Gunnsteinn spoke to his brother Karli, when they met Þórir, that he felt Þórir had far too many men.

'And I think,' he says, 'that it would be more advisable for us to turn back, and not travel in such a way that Þórir could do what he likes with us, for I greatly mistrust him.'

Karli says: 'I don't want to turn back, though it is true that if I had known, when we were back on Langey, that Þórir hundr was going to join us on the expedition with such a large troop as he has, we would have brought more men with us.'

The brothers discussed this with Þórir, asking what it [229] meant, him having many more men with him than had been specified between them. He answers thus:

'We have a large ship that needs a large crew. It seems to me that on such dangerous expeditions one can't have too many good fellows.'

They sailed in the summer mostly on well frequented routes. When the wind was light, the ship with Karli's party sailed faster, and they then got away, but when it was windier, Þórir's party caught up. They were seldom all together, and yet each always knew where the other was. And when they got to Bjarmaland, then they made their way to a market town. Then trading began. All the men who had money to spend got full value for their money. Þórir got a huge number of grey furs and beaver and sable skins. Karli also had a very great deal of money, with which he bought many fur goods. And when the market there was over, then they made out along the River Dvina. Then the truce with the natives was declared at an end. So when they get out to the open sea, then they hold a meeting of the crews. Þórir asks if people are minded at all to go up ashore and get themselves some wealth. People replied that they were keen on this if there were easy pickings to be got. Þórir says that wealth was to be got if their venture turned out well.

'But it is not unlikely that there will be danger to life in the trip.'

They all said that they would have a go if there was a prospect of wealth. Þórir says that the arrangements were, when wealthy men died, that the movable goods should be divided between the dead man and his heirs. He should have half or a third, but sometimes less. That wealth was to be carried out into the forests, sometimes into a mound, and covered with earth. Sometimes buildings were built over it. He says that they should be ready for the expedition in the evening of that day. This was agreed, that no one was to run away from the others, and no one was to be left behind when the captains said that they were to leave. They left men behind to guard the ships while they [230] went up ashore. First there were flat fields, after that a great forest. Þórir went ahead of the brothers Karli and Gunnsteinn. Þórir told the men to go silently.

'And strip bark off trees, so that each tree can be seen from the next.'

They came out into a large clearing, and in the clearing there was a high fence, with an entrance to it that was locked. There were six men of the local people that had to watch over the enclosure every night, each pair for a third of the night at a time. When Þórir and his men got to the fence, the watchmen were gone home, and those who were supposed to be on the watch next were not come to their post. Þórir went to the fence and hooked his axe up onto it, hauling himself up after it, thus getting in over the fence on one side of the entrance. Karli had now also got over the fence the other side of the entrance. They reached the entrance at the same time, then took away the bar and opened the gate. Then men went in to the enclosure. Þórir said:

'Inside this enclosure is a mound, with gold, silver and earth all mixed together in it. Men are to attack it. But inside the enclosure stands the god of the Bjarmar, who is called Jómali. Let no one be so bold as to plunder him.'

After that they went to the mound and took the wealth, as much as they could, carrying it in their clothes. There was a great deal of earth with it, as was to be expected. Then Þórir said that the men should depart. He says this:

'Now you two brothers, Karli and Gunnsteinn, are to go in front, and I will follow last.'

They all then turned to go out to the gate. Þórir went back to Jómali and took a silver bowl that was standing on his lap. It was full of silver coins. He poured the silver into the skirts of his tunic and drew the handle that was on top of the bowl onto his arm, going then [231] out to the gate. The whole company were then come out of the enclosure, then realised that Þórir had stayed behind. Karli turned back to look for him, and they met inside the gate. Karli saw that Þórir had the silver bowl there. Then Karli ran to the Jómali. He saw there was a thick necklace on his neck. Karli swung his axe and struck the band that the necklace was fastened with on the back of his neck in two. The blow was so heavy that Jómali's head flew off. There was then such a loud crash they were all amazed at it. Karli took the necklace. Then they went away. But as soon as the crash had happened, the watchmen came out into the enclosure and immediately blew their horns. Next they heard the sound of horns coming from all directions. Then they made their way forward to the forest and into the forest, hearing from behind in the clearing shouting and calling. The Bjarmar were come there. Þórir hundr was going in the rear of all the men of his troop. Two men went in front of him holding a sack in front of him. In it was what looked most like ashes. Þórir put his hand into it and scattered it behind in their tracks, sometimes throwing it forward over the troops, carrying on like that on out of the forest onto the fields. They could hear the army of Bjarmar coming after them with shouting and horrible bellowing. Then they rushed out of the forest after them and so on both sides of them, but neither the Bjarmar nor their weapons ever got so close to them as to do them any injury. But they discovered that the Bjarmar could not see them. And when they got to the ships, then Karli and his men went on board first, for they were ahead before, while Þórir was furthest inland. As soon as Karli and his party got onto their ship, they threw off the awnings and and cast off the cables. After that they hoisted their sail. The ship soon went out into the open sea. But Þórir's party got on slower with everything. Their ship was less easy to manage. And when they started [232] on their sail, by then Karli and his party had got far away from land.They then both sailed across Gandvík. It was still light by night. They then sailed both nights and days, right on until Karli and his party late one day came to land on some islands, lowered the sail and cast anchors and waited there for the tide to ebb, as there was a great tide race before them. Then Þórir and his party come up behind them. They also cast anchor. Then they launched a boat. Þórir went aboard it and some men with him, and they rowed then to Karli's party's ship. Þórir went aboard the ship. The brothers welcomed him. Þórir asked Karli to give him the necklace.

'I think I am the most proper person to have the valuable items that were taken there, because I felt you all benefited from my help so that our escape took place without any danger to our lives. But I thought you, Karli, were taking us towards the greatest disaster.'

Then says Karli: 'King Óláfr owns a half share in everything I gain on this expedition. Now I intend the necklace for him. Go and see him, if you wish, it may then be that he will give you the necklace, if he does not want to keep it on account of the fact that it was I that took it from the Jómali.'

Then Þórir replies and says that he wants them to go up on the island and share out their booty. Gunnsteinn says that now the tide was turning and it must be time to sail. After that they haul up their anchor cables. And when Þórir saw that, he went down into his boat. They rowed to their ship. Karli and his party had by then hoisted their sail and were well on their way before Þórir's party had got their sail up. They then continued thus, with Karli's party sailing always ahead, and both parties making every effort they could. Thus they went on until they got to Geirsver. There one finds the landing stage first when approaching from the north. Both of them arrived not before late in the day and sailed into harbour there at the landing stage. Þórir's party lay in the inner part of the harbour, while Karli's party were in the outer part of the harbour. And when Þórir's party had spread their awnings, then he went up ashore and a very large number of men with him. They went to [233] Karli's ship. They had by then settled in. Þórir called out to the ship and told the captains to go ashore. The brothers went ashore and some men with them. Then Þórir started raising the same matters as before, asking them to go ashore and bring the wealth that they had taken as spoils of war to be shared out. The brothers said that there was no need for that until they got back home. Þórir says that it was not the custom not to share out the spoils of war before they were at home and thus be at the mercy of people's honesty. They spoke some words about this, each stuck to his own opinion. Then Þórir went off. And when he had got a short distance, then he turned round and told his men to wait there. He calls to Karli:

'I want to speak with you in private,' he says.

Karli walked towards him. And when they met, Þórir thrust his spear at him in the middle of his body so that it stuck through him. Then Þórir said:

'Here you can find out, Karli, what one Bjarkey man is like. I thought, too, that you should find out about the spear Seal's Avenger.'

Karli died immediately, but Þórir and his men went back to their ship. Gunnsteinn and his men saw Karli fall. They ran up straight away and took the body, carried it to their ship, took down their awnings and gangplanks and made out away from land. Then they hoisted sail and went on their way. Þórir and his men saw this, then they threw off their awnings and set off as hastily as they could. But while they were hoisting their sail, then the mainstay snapped. The sail went down athwart the ship. This greatly delayed Þórir and his men until they managed to get the sail up a second time. Gunnsteinn and his party had now got a long way by the time Þórir's ship got under weigh. Þórir's party did both, sailed and rowed under sail. Gunnsteinn's party did the same. They both then went as furiously as they could day and night. They drew together slowly, since as soon as they got to the straits between the islands, then it [234] was easier to manoeuvre Gunnsteinn's ship. And yet Þórir's party gained on them, so that by the time Gunnsteinn's party came off Lengjuvík, turning into the shore there and leaping off the ship and up inland, it was only a little later that Þórir's party got there, leaping up after them and chasing them. A certain woman managed to help Gunnsteinn and hide him, and they say that she was very skilled in magic. And Þórir and his party went back to their ship, took all the wealth that was on Gunnsteinn's ship, put stones in its place, took the ship out into the fiord, struck holes in it and sank it. After that Þórir's party went back to Bjarkey. Gunnsteinn's party went at first very much under cover, travelling on small boats, moving by night but lying low during the day, going on until they got past Bjarkey and right on until they got out of

Þórir's stewardship area. Gunnsteinn first went home to Langey and stayed there a short while. Then he went straight away right the way south. He did not stop until he got south to Þrándheimr and there got to see King Óláfr, telling him the news of what had happened on the Bjarmaland expedition. The king was displeased about their expedition, but invited Gunnsteinn to stay with him, saying that he would redress Gunnsteinn's position as soon as he could manage it. Gunnsteinn accepted this invitation, and he stayed with King Óláfr.

CHAPTER ONE HUNDRED AND THIRTY-FOUR

It was said above that King Óláfr was east in Sarpsborg the winter that Knútr inn ríki was in Denmark. King Ǫnundr of the Svíar was that winter riding over Vestra-Gautland with more than three thousand (3600?) men. Then men and messages passed between him and King Óláfr. They arranged a conference between themselves, that they should meet in the spring by Konungahella. They put off the meeting because they wanted to know, before they met, what [235] action King Knútr was going to take. But when the spring drew to a close, King Knútr made ready to go with his army west to England. He left his son Hǫrða-Knútr behind in Denmark, and with him Þorgils sprakaleggr's (Break-Leg's) son Jarl Úlfr. Úlfr was married to King Sveinn's daughter Ástríðr, sister of Knútr inn ríki. Sveinn, who was later king in Denmark, was their son. Jarl Úlfr was a most notable man. Knútr ríki went west to England. So when the kings Óláfr and Ǫnundr leaned this then they went to their conference and met by Konungahella on the Elfr. There was a joyful meeting there and with a great display of friendship, so that it was manifest to all the people, and yet they discussed many things between themselves which were known to only the two of them, and some of this was later put into effect and made known to everyone. And at the parting of the kings they exchanged gifts with each other and parted friends. Then King Ǫnundr went up into Gautland, while King Óláfr then went north into the Vík and after that out into Agðir and from there north along the coast, lying for a very long time in Eikundasund waiting for a wind. He learned that Erlingr Skjálgsson and the inhabitants of Jaðarr with him were lying gathered together with a host of men. It happened one day that the king's men were discussing the wind among themselves, whether it was a southerly or a southwesterly, and whether the wind was fit for sailing past Jaðarr or not. Most considered that it was not possible to sail. Then Halldórr Brynjólfsson replies:

'I would have thought,' he says, 'that this wind would have been thought fit for sailing past Jaðarr if Erlingr Skjálgsson had prepared a banquet for us at Sóli.'

Then said King Óláfr that they were to take down the awnings and turn round the ships. This was done. They sailed past Jaðarr that day, and the wind served splendidly, they came to land at Hvítingsey in the evening. The king then travelled north to Hǫrðaland and attended banquets there.

[236] CHAPTER ONE HUNDRED AND THIRTY-FIVE

That spring a ship had travelled from Norway out to the Faeroes. On this ship went messages from King Óláfr to this effect, that there was to come back in from the Faeroes one or other of his followers, Leifr Ǫzurarson or Lawspeaker Gilli or Þórálfr of Dímun. So when this message came to the Faeroes and they themselves had been told about it, then they discuss between themselves what could underlie the message, and they were united in concluding that the king must want to enquire about the events that some people believed had truly taken place in the islands, relating to the fate of the king's messengers, the crews of the two ships from which not a man had survived. They resolved that Þórálfr should go. He set about going, preparing a cargo ship that he owned, and got men for it. They were on the ship ten or twelve. And when they were ready and were waiting for a wind, then it came about on Austrey at Gata at Þrándr's, that one fine day Þrándr went into his living room, but his brother's two sons Sigurðr and Þórðr were lying on the raised floor. They were sons of Þórlákr. The third one was called Gautr inn rauði (the Red). He was also a relation of theirs. All the lads brought up at Þrándr's were accomplished young men. Sigurðr was the eldest of them and most superior to them in every way. Þórðr had a nickname: he was called Þórðr inn lági (the Short). Yet he was the tallest of men, and what was more, he was a well built man and had great strength.

Then Þrándr spoke: 'There are many changes in the life of man. It was uncommon then, when we were young, for people to be sitting or lying down on fine days, [237] those who were young and well capable of doing anything. People of former times would not have thought it likely that Þórálfr of Dímun would be a more manly person than any of you. Now the cargo ship that I have owned and that stands here in the boat-house is, it seems to me, now getting so old that it will be rotting under the tar. Here every building is full of wool and it is not being offered for sale. It would not be so if I were a few years younger.'

Sigurðr leapt up and called to Gautr and Þórðr, saying he could not endure Þrándr's taunting. They go out and over to where the house servants were, go to the cargo ship and launch it. They then had cargo brought and loaded the ship. There was no lack of goods for this in the house, likewise all the rigging for the ship. They got it ready in a few days. They were ten or twelve men on the ship. They and Þórálfr's party all sailed out on the same wind, each knowing where the other was all the time out at sea. They came to land at Hern late one day. Sigurðr's party lay further out by the shore, and yet there was only a short distance between them. It happened in the evening when it was dark and Þórálfr's party were about to get ready for bed, that then Þórálfr went up ashore and another man with him. They sought a place to relieve themselves. And when they were ready to go down, then the man accompanying him, so he says, had a cloth thrown over his head, was lifted up off the ground. At that moment he heard a crash. After that he was taken and swung down, but beneath was the sea, and he was plunged under the water, though he managed to get ashore. He went to where he and Þórálfr had parted. He found Þórálfr there, and he was cloven down to the shoulders, and he was now dead. And when the crew realised this, then they carried his body out onto the ship and laid it down to watch over it during the night. King Óláfr was then attending a banquet on Lygra. Word was sent there. [238] Then an assembly was called with an arrow summons,[228] and the king attended the assembly. He had had summoned to it the Faeroese men from both ships, and they were come to the assembly. And when the assembly was in session, then the king stood up and said:

'The events that have taken place here—it were better that such were seldom heard of. Here is a fine man deprived of life, and we believe he was guiltless. So is there anyone at this assembly who is able to say who is responsible for this deed?'

But no one owned up. Then the king said:

'I will make no secret of what my opinion is about this deed, it is that I believe the men from the Faeroes are responsible. It seems to me the most likely way that it was done is that Sigurðr Þorláksson will have killed the man, while Þórðr inn lági will have flung the other one into the water. And this follows, that I would guess this, that the reason for it will turn out to have been that they would not want Þórálfr to report those criminal acts that he must have known they were truly guilty of, and we had suspected, in relation to the murders and evil deeds whereby my embassies have been murdered there.'

So when the king had finished his speech, then Sigurðr Þorláksson stood up. He said:

'I have not spoken at assemblies before. I expect I will not be thought eloquent. And yet I feel there is sufficient need for some reply to be made.

[228] The manuscript has *ǫrvarboð eða þing*. This is a characteristic way for a scribe to make a correction without crossing out an error. He was probably intending to write *ǫrvarþing* (which is the reading of *ÓH*). Assemblies could be called by sending a symbolic arrow round a district.

I will hazard a guess that this speech that the king has publicly made here will have originated in the mouths of people who have much less common sense and are far worse than he is, and there is no concealment of the fact that they want to be our absolute enemies. The idea that I should wish to do any harm to Þórálfr is absurd, for he was my foster-brother and good friend. But if there had been any other reason for it and there had been grounds for a quarrel between me and Þórálfr, then I have got sufficient sense to have ventured on this deed back in the Faeroes rather than here where I am at your mercy, [239] king. Now I shall reject this accusation as regards me and all of us ship's company. I will offer to swear oaths upon it, in accordance with what your laws prescribe. Or if you feel it in any way more satisfactory, then I am willing to undergo the ordeal of carrying hot iron. I want you yourself to be present at the ordeal.'

So when Sigurðr had finished his speech, then there were many that supported him, begging the king that Sigurðr might be granted a chance to clear himself, thinking that Sigurðr had spoken well and declaring that he would be found not guilty of what he was charged with. The king says:

'There are two strongly opposed possibilities about this man. And if he is falsely accused of this matter, then he must be a good man, but otherwise he must be rather bolder than there can be precedents for, and my feeling about this is no less strong than before. But I guess that he himself will provide the evidence for this.'

So at people's request the king now took assurances from Sigurðr about the ordeal of carrying iron. He was to come the next day to Lygra. The bishop was to organise the ordeal. And so the assembly broke up. The king went back to Lygra, and Sigurðr and his companions to their ship. It then soon began to get dark as night fell.

Then Sigurðr said to his companions:

'To tell the truth, however, we have got into a great difficulty. and have been subjected to great calumny, and this king is crafty and cunning, and it is obvious what will happen to us if he has his way, for first of all he had Þórálfr killed, and now he wants to make us all into criminals. He will have no difficulty in falsifying the result of this ordeal. I now think anyone will have the worst of it who tries this with him. Moreover, there is now something of a light breeze blowing off the mountains out along the sound. My advice is that we hoist our sail and make out to sea. Let Þrándr go next summer with his wool if he wants to sell it, but if I get away, then I think it likely that I shall never again come to Norway.'

His companions thought this [240] an excellent plan. They begin to hoist their sail and make out to sea during the night as fast as they can. They do not stop until they get to the Faeroes and back to Gata. Þrándr was displeased with their journey. Their replies were not pleasant and yet they stayed at home with Þrándr.

CHAPTER ONE HUNDRED AND THIRTY-SIX

King Óláfr soon learned that Sigurðr and his companions were gone away, and then nasty reports spread about their doings. There were many who now declared it likely that Sigurðr and his men must have been truly accused who previously had rejected the accusations against him and spoken in his defence. King Óláfr said very little about this affair, but he felt sure he knew the truth of the matter was as he had previously suspected. The king them went on his way and attended banquets where they had been prepared for him. King Óláfr called to talk with him the men that had come from Iceland, Þóroddr Snorrason, Gellir Þorkelsson, Steinn Skaptason, Egill Hallsson. Then the king began to speak:

'This summer you have raised with me this matter, that you wished to set out for Iceland, but I have up to now made no decision on this matter. I will now tell you what I propose to do. Gellir, I am planning that you should go to Iceland, if you are willing to take a message there for me. But as for the other Icelandic men that are now here, none are to travel to Iceland until I hear how those matters are being received that you, Gellir, are to take there.'

So when the king had made this announcement, then those that were eager to go and had been banned felt that they had been treated in a beastly way and felt that their having to stay and lack of freedom were hard. But Gellir got ready for his journey and went in the summer [241] to Iceland, taking there with him the messages, which he presented at the assembly the next summer. And this was the king's message, that he asked the Icelanders this, that they should accept the laws that he had laid down in Norway, and pay weregilds and a poll-tax from their country to him, a penny for every nose, equivalent to one tenth of an ell of standard cloth. With this came his promise to the people of his friendship, if they were minded to accept all this, but otherwise harsh treatment, as much as he was able to inflict. In discussion of this people sat a long time, talking it over among themselves, and finally came to the conclusion with the agreement of everybody to refuse the payment of taxes and all the imposts that had been demanded. So Gellir travelled abroad that summer and to see King Óláfr and met him that autumn east in Vík, when he had come down from Gautland, as I expect will be narrated further later in the saga of King Óláfr.[229] When autumn drew to a close, King Óláfr made his way north into Þrándheimr and took his following to Niðaróss, having winter quarters arranged there for himself. King Óláfr stayed the following winter in Kaupangr. This was the thirteenth winter of his reign.

---

[229] Cf. ch. 159 below.

CHAPTER ONE HUNDRED AND THIRTY-SEVEN

There was a man called Ketill Jamti (of Jamtaland), Jarl Ǫnundr from Sparabú in Þrándheimr's son. He had fled east over Kjǫlr before King Eysteinn illráði (the Evil-Doer).[230] He cleared forests and settled there where it is now called Jamtaland. Numbers of men also fled to the east there from Þrándheimr before this hostility, for King Eysteinn imposed taxes on the Prœndir and established his dog, called Saurr, as king there. Þórir Helsingr (of Helsingjaland) was Ketill's grandson. Helsingjaland is named after him. He lived there. [242] And when Haraldr inn hárfagri was clearing his way to power, then again men fled the land before him, Prœndir and Naumdœlir, and settlements then came into being eastwards across Jamtaland, and some went all the way from the east, away from the sea, into Helsingjaland, and they were subject to the king of the Svíar. But when Hákon Aðalsteinsfóstri was over Norway, then peace was established, and trading journeys from Þrándheimr to Jamtaland, and because of the king's popularity, the Jamtr now made their way from the east to see him and agreed to be his subjects and paid him tax. He laid down laws and regulations for them. They preferred to be subject to his rule than to be under the king of the Svíar, since they were descended from Norwegian stock, and so did all the Helsingjar, whose kin were from the north across Kjǫlr. And this continued for a long time after, right on until Óláfr digri and the Swedish King Óláfr of the Svíar had a dispute about the boundaries; then the Jamtr and the Helsingjar changed back to being under the king of the Svíar, and then the boundary was formed by Eiðaskógr on the eastern side, and then by Kilir all the way north to Finnmǫrk. Then the king of the Svíar began to receive taxes from Helsingjaland and also from Jamtaland. But King Óláfr believed that it had been included in the agreement with the king of the Sviar that tax from Jamtaland was to go in a different direction from how it had been in former times. And yet the position had been for a long time that the Jamtr had then paid tax to the king of the Svíar, and that by him stewards had been appointed over the land. Then the Svíar also would hear of nothing but that the whole country that lay on the eastern side of Kjǫlr should go back to being under the king of the Svíar. It was just as often happens, that although there was relationship by marriage and friendship between the kings, even so each one wanted to have all the power to which he felt he had some claim. King Óláfr had had word sent round to Jamtaland that it was his desire that the Jamtr should pay him homage, threatening them with harsh treatment otherwise. But the Jamtr had made their decision, that they wanted to be subjects of the king of the Svíar.

[230] Cf. vol. I 164, *Hákonar saga góða* ch. 12.

[243] CHAPTER ONE HUNDRED AND THIRTY-EIGHT

Þóroddr Snorrason and Steinn Skaptason were annoyed that they could not depart in freedom. Steinn Skaptason was the most handsome of men and most accomplished in skills, a good poet and a very ostentatious man in dress and full of ambition. His father, Skapti, had composed a *drápa*[231] about King Óláfr and had taught it to Steinn. It was intended that he should present the poem to the king. Steinn did not hold back from talking to the king and criticising him, both in ordinary speech and in verse. Both he and Þóroddr were careless in speaking, saying that the king would be judged more harshly than those who had sent their sons to him in good faith, and the king had made them prisoners. The king got angry. It happened one day that Steinn Skaptason was in the presence of the king and asked to speak with him, if he wished to hear the *drápa* that his father Skapti had composed about the king. He says:

'That must come first, Steinn, that you recite what you have composed about me.'

Steinn says that it is nothing that he has composed.

'I am no poet, king,' he says, 'but even if I were able to compose, then you would find that, like everything else about me, of rather little worth.'

Steinn then went away, and thought he could see what his words would lead to.

The king's steward, who was in charge of his residence in Orkadalr, was called Þorgeirr. He was at this time staying with the king, and heard the conversation between him and Steinn. Þorgeirr returned home shortly afterwards. One night Steinn ran away from the town and his servant with him. They went up over Gaularáss and so towards the sea until they got to Orkadalr, and in the evening they came to the king's residence that Þorgeirr was in charge of. Þorgeirr invited Steinn to stay there the night and asked what was the purpose of his journey. Steinn asked him to give him a horse and a sledge[232] with it. He saw that corn was being driven home. Þorgeirr says:

'I am not sure what is the position as regards your journey, [244] whether you are going with the king's leave. It seemed to me the other day the conversation between you and the king was not going smoothly.'

Steinn said: 'Although I am not a free agent in my relationship with the king, I will be so with his slaves.'

He drew his sword and then killed the steward, but took the horse and told his boy to jump on its back, while Steinn sat in the sledge, travelling then on the road, driving all night. They went on their way until they came

---

[231] See note 191 above.

[232] In medieval Scandinavia sledges drawn by horses were used that were dragged along even when the ground was not covered with snow.

down in Súrnadalr in Mœrr. Then they got themselves a passage across the fiord. He travelled as fast as he could. They did not tell people about this killing, wherever they came, but claimed they were the king's men. They were well provided for wherever they came. They came one evening to Þorbergr Árnason's dwelling in Gizki. He was not at home, but his wife, Erlingr Skjálgsson's daughter Ragnhildr, was at home. Steinn got a very good welcome there, for they had before this been on very good terms. The following incident had previously taken place, when Steinn had been leaving Iceland—he owned the ship himself at that time, when he came in from the open sea at Gizki and lay there off the island—then Ragnhildr was at her lying-in and was about to give birth and was in a very bad state, but there was no priest on the island nor anywhere near. Then someone was sent to the trading ship to ask if there was any priest there. There was a priest on board called Bárðr, a man from Vestfirðir, young and with rather little learning. The messengers asked the priest to go with them to the house. He felt that this would be a matter of some difficulty, knowing his ignorance, and would not go. Then Steinn put in a word to the priest, bidding him go. The priest answers:

'I will go if you go with me. I shall feel more confident with your guidance.'

Steinn says that he will certainly do that to aid matters. After that they go to the farm and to where Ragnhildr was. Soon after she gave birth to a child, it was a girl, and she seemed rather weak. Then the priest baptised [245] the child, and Steinn stood godfather to it, and the girl was called Þóra. Steinn gave the girl a finger-ring. Ragnhildr promised Steinn her complete friendship, and he was to come there to see her if he felt in need of her help. Steinn says this, that he would not be standing godfather to any more female children, and they parted on these terms. But now it had come about that Steinn was come to call on Ragnhildr for the fulfilment of this kind offer, saying what had befallen him and also that he must have become subject to the king's anger. She says this, that she would do the utmost in her power to help, telling him to wait now for Þorbergr, placing him in the seat next to her son Eysteinn orri (Black Grouse). He was then twelve years old. Steinn gave presents to Ragnhildr and Eysteinn.

Þorbergr had heard all about Steinn's adventures before he got home, and he was rather cross. Ragnhildr went to talk to him and tells him about Steinn's adventures and asked him to welcome Steinn and see to his affairs. Þorbergr says:

'I have heard,' he says, 'that the king has had an assembly called by arrow summons[233] about Þorgeirr and Steinn has been made an outlaw, also that the king is extremely angry. And I have more sense than to take on my hands a

---

[233] See note 228 above.

foreigner and as a result incur the king's anger. Make Steinn go away from here as soon as possible.'

Ragnhildr answers, saying that either they would both go away or both of them stay. Þorbergr told her to go wherever she wanted.

'I expect,' he says, 'that even if you go, you will soon come back, for here you will find you are most highly regarded.'

Then their son Eysteinn orri went forward. He spoke, saying that he will not stay behind if Ragnhildr went away. Þorbergr says that they were displaying great obstinacy and impetuousness in this affair.

'And the best thing now,' he says, 'is that you have your way [246] in this, though you are giving it excessive importance. But you are following too much in your family's footsteps, Ragnhildr, in paying such little regard to the words of King Óláfr.'

Ragnhildr says: 'If you find it such an impossible undertaking to keep Steinn, then go with him yourself to see my father Erlingr, or provide him with sufficient following for him to get there in safety.'

Þorbergr says that he is not going to send Steinn there.

'And Erlingr will still have plenty on his hands that that will not be to the king's liking.'

Steinn stayed there for the winter. But after Yule the king's messengers came to Þorbergr with this message, that Þorbergr was to come to see him by the middle of Lent, and this summons was made very imperative. Þorbergr put this to his friends and sought their advice whether he should take the risk of going to see the king when the affair had gone thus far, but more of them were against it and declared it was advisable to get Steinn off his hands before putting himself at the king's mercy. Þorbergr on the other hand was more keen not to delay this journey. A little later Þorbergr went to see his brother Finnr, and put this matter to him and asked him to make the journey with him. Finnr replies, saying that he thought such female dominance was bad, not to dare because of one's wife to stay loyal to one's liege lord.

'You can choose,' says Þorbergr, 'not to go, but yet I think that your reluctance is more for the sake of fear than loyalty to the king.'

They parted in anger. After that Þorbergr went to see his brother Árni Árnason, and tells him about the stage this affair had reached, and asked him to go with him to the king. Árni says:

'I find it strange in you, such a sensible man and having such forethought, that you should have stumbled into such misfortune and have incurred the anger of the king when there was no necessity for it. There would be some excuse for protecting a kinsman of yours or a foster-brother, but none at all for having taken on your hands the protection of an Icelander, [247] an outlaw of the king's, putting at risk yourself and all your kinsmen.'

Þorbergr says: 'It is as they say: There is always a degenerate in every family. This misfortune of our father's is to me the most obvious, how much his getting of sons went downhill, that he should have that one last who has none of the characteristics of our family and is worthless. It would seem most suitable, if I did not feel it was to speak shame of my mother, for me never to call you a brother of ours.'

Þorbergr then set off and went home and was rather gloomy. After that he sent word north to Þrándheimr to his brother Kálfr, asking him to come to Agðanes to meet him. And when the messengers met Kálfr, then he promised to go and made no comment about it. Ragnhildr sent men east to Jaðarr to her father Erlingr, and asked him to send her men. There set out from there Erlingr's sons Sigurðr and Þórir, and each of them had a ship with twenty benches[234] with ninety men on them. And when they came north to Þorbergr's, then he welcomed them most warmly and gladly. He prepared then for the journey, and Þorbergr had a twenty-benched ship. Then they took their course north. And when they came . . .[235] then there lay ahead of them Þorbergr's brothers Finnr and Árni with two twenty-benched ships. Þorbergr welcomed his brothers warmly, saying that now his provocation had borne fruit. Finnr said this had seldom been necessary with him. After that they went with all these forces north to Þrándheimr, and Steinn went along there with them. And when they got to Agðanes, then in front of them they found Kálfr Árnason and he had a well manned twenty-benched ship. They went with these forces in to Niðarhólmr and lay there during the night. The next morning they held a conference. Kálfr, and Erlingr's sons too, wanted them to take their whole force in to the town and let fate take its course, but Þorbergr wanted them first to proceed with moderation [248] and allow offers to be made. Finnr agreed with this, and also Árni. It was then decided that Finnr and Árni were to go first to see King Óláfr, in a party of a few men. The king had now heard about the large number of men that they had, and looked rather annoyed during their speeches. Fiðr made offers on behalf of Þorbergr and also on behalf of Steinn. He offered that the king should assess damages as highly as he wished, but Þorbergr was to retain the right of residence in the country and his revenues, Steinn safety to life and limb. The king says:

'It seems to me that this expedition is such that you will now be thinking that you have halfway or more control over me. But the last thing I would have expected from you brothers is that you should go against me with an army. I can see through this plan, which those people of Jaðarr must have cooked up. But there is no point in offering me money.'

---

[234] See note 209 above.
[235] The manuscript has a gap here, filled in some manuscripts of *ÓH* by 'north' or 'near Finnr Árnason's dwelling'.

Then says Finnr: 'We brothers have not mustered troops for the purpose of threatening you with hostilities, king, the reason is rather, king, that we want first of all to offer you our services, but if you refuse us and intend any harsh terms for Þorbergr, then we shall all go, taking with us the forces that we have, to see Knútr inn ríki.'

Then the king looked at him and said: 'If you brothers are willing to swear me oaths to follow me within this country and abroad and not part from me without my leave and permission—you are not to conceal it from me, if you know of any treachery being plotted against me—then I will accept atonement from you brothers.'

After that Finnr went back to his troops and announces these terms that the king had offered them. They now have a discussion together. Þorbergr says that he is in favour of this option for his own part.

'I am not keen,' he says, 'to flee from my properties and seek out foreign rulers. I hold that it will always be to my honour to follow King Óláfr and to be wherever he is.'

Then says Kálfr: 'I shall swear no oaths to the king, but be with the king only as long [249] as I keep my revenues and other marks of my status and the king will be my friend, and it is my wish that we should all do the same.'

Finnr answers: 'My advice is to let King Óláfr decide the terms between us.'

Árni Árnason says as follows: 'If I am determined to follow you, brother Þorbergr, even if you want to fight with the king, then I shall not part from you if you take a better course, and I shall follow you and Finnr and accept the option that you see as most advantageous.'

Then the three brothers went aboard one ship, Þorbergr, Finnr, Árni, and rowed in to the town, and after that they went to see the king. Then this agreement was adopted, that the brothers swore oaths to the king. Then Þorbergr sought atonement with the king for Steinn. And the king says that Steinn should go in safety as far as he was concerned wherever he wished.

'But he shall not stay with me again,' he says.

Then Þorbergr and the others went out to their troops. Then Kálfr went in to Egg, while Finnr went to the king, but Þorbergr and their other troops went back south. Steinn went south with Erlingr's sons, and early in the spring he went west to England, and after that became subject to Knútr inn ríki and stayed with him for a long time in high favour.

CHAPTER ONE HUNDRED AND THIRTY-NINE

After Finnr Árnason had been staying with King Óláfr for a little while, it happened one day that the king calls Finnr to speak with him and some other men as well who he was accustomed to have at his plan making. Then the king began to speak and says as follows:

'This plan has become fixed in my mind that I intend in the spring to call out a levy from the whole country, both of men and ships, and after that to take all the forces I can muster against Knútr inn ríki, for I know about the claim that he has raised against me to rule, [250] which he will not be intending to drop as wasted speech. Now I have this to say to you, Finnr Árnason, that I wish you to go on a mission for me north to Hálogaland and carry out a levy there, call upon the people for troops and ships and summon this force to meet me at Agðanes.'

After that the king appointed other men, sending some inland in Þrándheimr, and some to the south, thus letting this summons go all over the country. This is to be told of Finnr's journey, that he had a small ship with nearly thirty men on it, and when he was ready he went his way until he got to Hálogaland. Then he called an assembly with the farmers, announcing his business and demanding a levy. The farmers had in the area large ships suitable for a levy. They responded to the king's message and fitted out their ships.

So when Finnr made his way north in Hálogaland, then he held assemblies and sent some of his men to demand the levy wherever he thought fit. Finnr sent men to Bjarkey to Þórir hundr, having the levy demanded there as elsewhere. And when the king's orders came to Þórir, then he made preparations for the journey and manned with his workmen the ship that he had earlier in the summer taken to Bjarmaland, fitting it out at his own expense. Finnr called the Háleygir together in Vágar, all those that lived north of there. There gathered there in the spring a great force, and they all waited there until Finnr returned from the north. Þórir hundr was also come there then. So when Finnr arrived, then he had the call sounded to summon the whole levy to a brigade meeting. And at this assembly men showed their weapons, and then also an inspection was made of the men conscripted in every levied ship. And when this had been carried out, then Finnr said:

'I want you to give thought to this, Þórir hundr. What restitution will you offer King Óláfr for the killing of his follower Karli, and for the robbery in which you appropriated the king's wealth north in Lengjuvík? I am charged by the king to see to this matter now, and I wish to know your response now.'

Þórir looked [251] around and saw on both sides of him many fully armed men, recognising there Gunnsteinn and a large number of Karli's kinsmen. Then Þórir said:

'My offer is soon made, Finnr, it is that I wish to submit to the king's judgment whatever wrong he thinks I have done.'

Finnr replies: 'It is most likely that you will be granted less honour now, for it is to my judgment that you now have to commit yourself if there is to be a settlement.'

Þórir says: 'Then I think the matter will still be in good hands, and there shall be no holding back from that.'

Then Þórir went forward to pledge himself, and Finnr dictated everything. After that Finnr announced the terms of the agreement, that Þórir was to pay the king ten marks of gold, and to Gunnsteinn and his kinsmen another ten marks, and for the theft and loss of property a third ten marks.

'And to be paid up straight away now,' he says.

Þórir says: 'That is a great deal of money to pay.'

'The alternative is that the whole agreement is void,' says Finnr.

Þórir says that Finnr must allow him time to seek loans from his comrades. Finnr told him to pay there on the spot, and moreover in addition that Þórir must hand over the great necklace that he took from Karli's dead body. Þórir said he had taken no necklace. Then Gunnsteinn went forward and says that Karli had had a necklace on his neck when they parted.

'But then it was gone when we took up his body.'

Þórir says he had not taken any notice of that necklace.

'But if we had had any necklace, then it would be lying at home on Bjarkey.'

Then Finnr put the point of his spear against Þórir's breast, saying that he must hand over the necklace now. Then Þórir took the necklace from his neck and gave it to Finnr. After that Þórir turned away and went out on board his ship. Finnr went after him out on board the ship and many men with him. Finnr walked along the ship and they took up the boards. And by the mast they saw down under the decking two barrels so large that they were amazed at them. Finnr asked what was in these barrels. [252] Þórir says that his drink was lying in them. Finnr said:

'Why do you not give us something to drink, comrade, when you have got so much drink?'

Þórir told one of his men to pour from the barrel into a bowl. After that Finnr and his men were given drinks, and it was the finest drink. Then Finnr told Þórir to pay the money. Þórir walked along the ship up and down and spoke with various men. Finnr called out, telling him to hand over the money. Þórir told him to go up ashore and said he would pay it out there. Then Finnr went ashore and his men. Then Þórir came there and paid out silver. It was poured there from a purse, ten marks by weight.[236] Then he put out many knotted cloths. In some was a mark by weight, in some half a mark or a few ounces. Then said Þórir:

'This is borrowed money that various men have let me have, since I think most of the ready money that I have is finished.'

After that Þórir went out on board his ship, and when he came back, he paid out silver bit by bit. Then the day was drawing to a close. So when the

---

[236] A mark was eight ounces.

assembly broke up, then people went to their ships and got ready to depart. People began to sail as soon as they were ready. So it came about that most men had sailed. Then Finnr realised that the men round him had thinned out. Men now called out to him and told him to get ready. There was by then still one third of the money not yet paid. Then said Finnr:

'It is, however, going slowly, Þórir, the payment. I can see that you are very reluctant to pay the money. So we shall now let it be for the time being. You shall now pay what remains to the king.'

Then Finnr got up. Þórir says:

'I am well pleased, Finnr, that we shall part, and I shall be willing to find enough to pay this debt in such a way that the king will not find it underpaid, or you either.'

Then Finnr went to his ship and sailed on after his troops. Þórir takes a long time to get ready to leave the harbour. And when their sail was hoisted, then they made their way out across Vestfjǫrðr and after that out to sea and so south [253] parallel to the coast so that the sea rose halfway up the mountainsides or sometimes the land disappeared below the horizon, so taking a course southwards right on until he sailed into Englandshaf and ended up in England, going after that to see King Knútr, and he welcomed him. Then it got round that Þórir had there a huge amount of cash, having there all the money that they had taken in Bjarmaland, both he and Karli. And then in the great barrels there was a false bottom a little way from the true one, and between these was drink, but each of the barrels themselves was full of grey furs and beaver and sable. Þórir then stayed with King Knútr. Finnr Árnason went with the forces to King Óláfr, telling him all about his journey, and saying also that he thought that Þórir was gone from the land and west to England to see Knútr inn ríki.

'And I feel he will be doing us no good.'

The king says: 'I believe that Þórir will be an enemy to us, and it seems to me better always to have him further away from me rather than closer.'

CHAPTER ONE HUNDRED AND FORTY

Ásmundr Grankelsson had that winter been in his stewardship area in Hálogaland staying at home with his father Grankell. There is a fishing place out in the sea there, where both seals and birds, eggs and fish can be got, and this had from ancient times belonged to the farm that Grankell owned. But Hárekr from Þjótta laid claim to it. It had reached the point that he had taken from this place all the produce for several seasons. But at that time Ásmundr and his father had the support of the king for all just suits. Father and son both went then in the spring to see Hárekr and tell him what King Óláfr had said and the proofs of it, that Hárekr was to relinquish his claim on the fishing place. Hárekr responded roughly, saying that Ásmundr had gone to the king with lies about this and other things.

'I have all the evidence [254] to support my case. You, Ásmundr, should learn to act with some discretion, though you now think yourself so powerful, having the support of the king. It is also the case, even if you can get away with killing some leading men and arrange it so as not to have to pay compensation for them, and rob us, who have still felt ourselves from far back in time well able to stand up to such as you, even when they were of equal birth to us, that now you are very far from being my equals as regards descent.'

Ásmundr replies: 'Many find out about you, Hárekr, that you have powerful relatives and are a bully. Many have to put up with getting the worst of it from you. And yet it is now most likely that you, Hárekr, will on another occasion find yourself trying to impose your unfairness on someone other than us and have to suffer as much injustice as this is.'

After this they parted. Hárekr sent ten or twelve of his workmen with a kind of large rowing boat. They went to the fishing place, took there all sorts of produce and loaded the boat. But as they were setting off, then Ásmundr Grankelsson came upon them there with thirty men and ordered them to hand over all they had taken. Hárekr's men showed some reluctance. Then Ásmundr's party attacked them. The difference in numbers then began to tell. Hárekr's men were some of them beaten up, some wounded, some thrown into the water and all they had taken was taken off their ship, and Ásmundr's party took it with them. With that, Hárekr's men came back home and tell Hárekr about their trip. He replies:

'Every fresh event is taken to be news. This has not been done before, beating up my men.'

This affair remained dormant, and Hárekr said nothing about it and was as cheerful as anything. In the spring Hárekr had a light warship fitted out, a twenty-benched one, and manned it with his workmen, and this was very well fitted out both with men and all its rigging. In the spring Hárekr joined the levy. So when he met King Óláfr, then Ásmundr Grankelsson was also there. Then the king arranged a meeting between Ásmundr and Hárekr and [255] and brought about a settlement between them. It was determined that it should be put to the king to arbitrate. After that Ásmundr brought forward testimony that Grankell had owned the fishing place. The king gave judgment accordingly. Then the case became one-sided. Hárekr's workmen were deemed not to be subject to compensation, and the fishing place was awarded to Grankell. Hárekr says that there was no disgrace to him in submitting to the king's judgment, however the case might turn out afterwards.

CHAPTER ONE HUNDRED AND FORTY-ONE

Þóroddr Snorrason had stayed in Norway in accordance with the king's command, while Gellir Þorkelsson got leave to go to Iceland, as was written above,[237] and he now stayed with King Óláfr, very dissatisfied with the lack of freedom in not being able to go on his way wherever he wished. At the beginning of the winter that King Óláfr stayed in Niðaróss, the king announced that he wishes to send men to Jamtaland to collect tax. But people were not keen to undertake this journey, since those messengers of King Óláfr that he had sent previously, Þrándr hvíti and his party of twelve, had been deprived of life, as has been written above, and the Jamtr had subsequently continued to be subject to the king of the Svíar. Þóroddr Snorrason volunteered for this journey, because he now cared very little what befell him as long as he could go of his own free will. The king agreed to this and Þóroddr went in a party of twelve. They proceeded eastwards to Jamtaland and called at the home of a man whose name is given as Þórarr. He was lawman[238] there and a man of the highest status. They were well received there. So when they had been staying there a little while, then they presented their business before Þórarr. He says that other people of the country and leading ones had no whit less responsibility than he for dealing with this matter, and declared that an assembly should be called about it. This was done, an assembly summons was sent out and a large assembly was arranged. Þórarr went to the assembly, but the messengers stayed meanwhile at his house. Þórarr [256] presented this matter to the people, and it was agreed by everyone that they were not willing to pay any tax to the king of Norway, and some wanted to have the messengers hanged, and some to have them used as heathen sacrifices. But the final decision was that they should be kept there until the king of the Svíar's stewards got there—they would then deal with them in whatever way they wished, with the consent of the people of the country—and giving the impression that the messengers were being well treated and that they were being kept there to await the tax payments, and they were to be sent to various lodgings in pairs. Þóroddr stayed with one other man at Þórarr's. There was a great Yule feast and drinking party held there. There were many farmers there in the village, and they were all drinking together over Yule. There was another village a short way away. A kinsman of Þórarr's by marriage lived there, powerful and wealthy. He had a grown-up son. The brothers-in-law were to hold half the Yule feast at each of their houses, to start with at Þórarr's. The brothers-in-law were drinking together, and Þóroddr with the farmer's son, and there was competition in drinking and

[237] p. 240.
[238] The word *lǫgmaðr*, though in early Iceland it could occasionally mean 'lawyer, one skilled in the law' (e.g. Njáll Þorgeirsson in *Njáls saga*, *ÍF* XII 57), in Norway and Sweden usually means 'president of a legislative assembly' (= *lǫgsǫgumaðr*).

in the evening disputes and comparison of persons[239] between the Norwegians and Svíar, and next it was about their kings, both those who had been in the past and these that there were now, and also about the conflicts that there had been between their countries in the slaughter and plundering that had taken place across their borders. Then said the farmer's son:

'If our kings have lost more men, then the king of the Svíar's stewards will even it up with the lives of twelve men when they arrive from the south after Yule, and you do not fully realise, you wretched men, why you are being kept here.'

Þóroddr considered his position, and many sneered at them and used scornful words about them and their king. What Þóroddr had previously not suspected now came out into the open, when the ale spoke through the Jamtr. The next day Þóroddr and his companion got together all their clothes and weapons and kept them ready by them. The [257] following night, when people were asleep, they ran away to the forest. The next morning, when people became aware of their running away, men went after them with bloodhounds and came across them in the forest where they had hidden themselves, and took them back to the house and into a storehouse. It had a deep pit inside. They were put in there and the door locked on them. They had little food and no clothes but what they stood in. And when the middle of the Yule period came, Þórarr and all the free men with him went to his brother-in-law's. He was to feast there the latter part of Yule. Þórarr's slaves were to guard the pit. But they had now been apportioned plenty of drink, and they did not hold back much on the drinking and already that evening they were drunk. So as they felt quite drunk, then they talked among themselves, those that were to bring food to the men in the pit, that they must not go short. Þóroddr recited a poem and entertained the slaves, so they said he was surely a kind fellow and gave him a very large candle, with a flame on it. Then the slaves that were already in there came out and called importunately that the rest must go in, and both lots were drunk silly so that they shut neither the pit nor the storehouse. Then Þóroddr and his companion cut their cloaks into strips and tied these together and made a knot at the end and threw it up onto the storehouse floor. It wrapped itself round the leg of a chest and held fast. They tried then to find a way to get up. Þóroddr lifted his companion up until he was standing on his shoulders. After that he hauled himself up through the opening. There was no lack of rope in the storehouse and he let it down to Þóroddr, but when he tried to pull Þóroddr up, then he could not

---

[239] *Mannjafnaðr* was an entertainment in which each would choose his favourite person (usually from those of high status) and compare their qualities to see whose choice was most popular. It was an entertainment that would characteristically end in trouble.

move him at all. Then Þóroddr said that he should throw the rope over the cross-beam that was in the building, and make a loop in the end, put timber and stones in it so that it was more than equal to him in weight. He did so. Then the counterweight went [258] down into the pit, and Þóroddr went up. They took themselves whatever clothing they needed from the storehouse. There were in there some reindeer skins and they cut off the foot pieces and tied them facing backwards under their feet. But before they left they set fire to a great barn of corn that was there, and after that ran away in the pitch darkness. The barn burned and many of the other buildings in the village. Þóroddr and his companion travelled all night through uninhabited areas and hid during the day. In the morning they were missed. Bloodhounds were then used to search for them along all the paths leading from the farm. But the dogs traced the tracks back to the farm, because they recognised them from the reindeer's foot pieces and they followed the track in the direction the hooves had pointed from the reindeer's foot pieces, so the search was called off. Þóroddr and his companion travelled a long time through uninhabited areas and arrived one evening at a small farmstead and went into it. There inside sat a man and a woman by the fire. He gave his name as Þórir and said it was his wife sitting there, and also that the cottage was theirs. The husband invited them to stay there, and they accepted. He tells them that he had come there because he had fled from the settlement on account of some killings. Þóroddr and his companion were given hospitable entertainment. They all ate by the fire. After that beds were made for Þóroddr and his companion on the raised floor, and they lay down to sleep. But the fire was still alight there. Then Þóroddr saw a man come in there from another building, and he had never seen a man so big. This man had scarlet clothes[240] on, with gold thread in the borders, and was of most imposing appearance. Þóroddr heard him telling the couple off for receiving guests when they hardly had sufficient food to stay alive. The housewife replied:

'Don't be angry, brother, rarely has this come about. Rather do you give them something to help them, for you are better able than we.'

Þóroddr heard this big man addressed as Arnljótr gellini (from Gellin in Jamtaland), and also that the housewife was his sister. Þóroddr [259] had heard tell of Arnljótr, and this too, that he was a very great highwayman and evil-doer. Þóroddr and his companion slept through the night, as they had been tired from the walking. But when it must have been a third of the night still to go, then Arnljótr came over to them, telling them to get up and be on their way. Þóroddr and his companion immediately got up and dressed. They were given breakfast. After that Þórir gave skis to each of the two of them. Arnljótr joined them on their journey. He put on skis. They were

[240] *Skarlatsklæði* was an expensive type of foreign clothing, often coloured bright red.

both broad and long. And when Arnljótr pushed with his ski poles, then he was far, far ahead of them. So he waited for them and said they would get nowhere like that, telling them to step onto his skis with him. They did so. Þóroddr went close to him and held under Arnljótr's belt, while Þóroddr's companion held onto him. Arnljótr then slid along as fast as if he were travelling unencumbered. They came to a certain shelter for travellers when about a third of the night had passed, made a fire there and prepared their food. But while they were eating, then Arnljótr spoke, telling them not to throw away any of the food, neither bones nor scraps. Arnljótr took from his shirt a silver dish and ate from it. And when they had finished eating, then Arnljótr picked up what was left of the food. After that they got ready for bed. At one end of the building there was a loft up on the crossbeams. Arnljótr and his companions went up into this loft and lay down there to sleep. Arnljótr had a great halberd, and the socket of its head was inlaid with gold, but the shaft was so long that one could just reach the socket with upstretched arm, and he was girded with a sword. They took both their weapons and their clothes up into the loft with them. Arnljótr told them to keep quiet. He lay nearest the entrance to the loft. A little later twelve men came there into the building. It was merchants who were going to Jamtaland with their goods. But when they got into the house, they made a lot of cheerful noise around themselves and were merry, making themselves large fires. And while they [260] were eating, then they threw away all the bones. Afterwards they got ready for bed and lay down there on the raised floor by the fire. But when they had been sleeping a little while, then there came there to the building a great trollwife. And when she came in, she gathered everything up fast, taking the bones and everything that she thought edible, and thrust it in her mouth. After that she snatched up the man that was nearest to her, tearing and breaking him all up and throwing him on the fire. Then the others woke up, and to a bad dream, and leapt up, and she put them to death one after another, so that one was left alive. He ran in under the loft and shouted for help, if there should be anything in the loft such as might help him. Arnljótr reached down to him and took hold of his shoulders and pulled him up into the loft. Then she dashed forward to the fire and began to eat the men who were roasted. Then Arnljótr stood up and grabbed his halberd and thrust it between her shoulders so that the point ran out through her breast. She flinched violently and gave a horrible cry at this and ran out. Arnljótr lost his grip on the spear, and she took it away with her. Arnljótr went up and cleared out the men's corpses, putting in place the door of the building and the door frame, for she had broken it all away when she ran out. They then slept through what remained of the night. So when it got light, they got up, first of all taking their breakfast, and when they had eaten, Arnljótr said:

'Now here we shall part. You must now travel along the tracks made by the merchants when they travelled here yesterday, while I shall go and find my spear. I shall have as payment for my labour whatever seems to me worth anything of the goods that these men had with them. You, Þóroddr, are to convey my greeting to King Óláfr, and tell him this, that he is such a man as I have the greatest desire to meet. But he will think my greeting of no value.'

He picked up his silver dish and wiped it with his cloth, saying: 'Take the king [261] this dish, say that this is my greeting.'

Then they both got ready to go and with that they parted.

Þóroddr and his companion, and also the one man who had got away out of the party of merchants, set off. Þóroddr travelled on until he found King Óláfr in Kaupangr, and tells him all about his travels, delivering to him Arnljótr's greeting and giving him the silver dish. The king says it was a pity that Arnljótr had not come to see him.

'And it is a great shame that such a fate should have afflicted such a fine fellow and remarkable man.'

Þóroddr stayed after this with King Óláfr for the remains of the winter, and then got leave from him to go to Iceland the following summer. He and King Óláfr parted then in friendship.

CHAPTER ONE HUNDRED AND FORTY-TWO

King Óláfr prepared in the spring to leave Niðaróss, and large numbers of troops joined him both from Þrándheimr there, and also from further north in the country. And when he was ready to set out, then he first went with his troops south to Mœrr and gathered together an army levied from there and also from Raumsdalr. After that he went to Sunn-Mœrr. He lay for a long time in Hereyjar and waited for his troops, holding then assemblies of his men frequently. Much came there to his ears that he felt needed discussion. It was at one assembly that he held that he happened to be speaking, talking about the loss of men that he had suffered from the Faeroes.

'And the tax that they have promised me,' he says, 'is now not materialising. I am now planning to send men there again for the tax.'

The king put this matter to various people, whether they would undertake this journey, but the answers he got in reply were that everyone declined to go on the trip. Then a man stood up at the assembly, tall and of imposing build. He had on a red tunic, a helmet on his head, [262] girded with a sword, a great halberd in his hand. He began to speak:

'It is true to say,' he said, 'that there are here men of very different kinds. You have a good king, and he has bad men. You say no to a mission that he offers you, when you have already received from him friendly gifts and many honourable favours. But I have been up to now no friend of this king. He has also been my enemy, believing that there are reasons for this. I will now offer you, king, to go on this trip if there is no better alternative available.'

The king says: 'Who is this manly-looking person who is replying to what I have said? You are behaving very differently from other men who are here, in volunteering for the journey, when those have declined whom I would have expected to have responded well. But I know nothing about you, and I do not know your name.'

He replies as follows: 'There is no difficulty about my name, king. I expect you will have heard it mentioned. I am known as Karl mœrski (of Mœrr).'

The king says: 'It is indeed so, Karl, I have heard tell of you before, and to tell the truth, there have been times when, if we had happened to meet, you would not have been able to report the outcome. But now I shall not act worse than you, since you are offering me your help, by not responding with thanks and pleasure. You, Karl, shall come to me and be my guest today. We shall then discuss this matter.'

Karl says that so it should be.

CHAPTER ONE HUNDRED AND FORTY-THREE

Karl inn mœrski had been a viking and a very great robber, and the king had very often sent men for him and wanted to deprive him of life. Yet Karl was a man of good family and a very enterprising man, an able man and a man of accomplishments in many ways. So since Karl was determined on this journey, [263] the king agreed to be reconciled with him and then became fond of him, having his journey set up as well as possible. They were nearly twenty men on the ship. The king sent messages to his friends on the Faeroes, commending Karl to their support and protection in the case of Leifr Ǫzurarson and lawspeaker Gilli, sending his tokens to back this up. Karl went as soon as he was ready. They made good progress and reached the Faeroes and put into Þórshǫfn on Straumey. After that an assembly was called there, and it was well attended. Þrándr from Gata came to it with a large crowd of men. Leifr and Gilli also came to it. They also had large numbers of men. And when they had covered their booths[241] and put them to rights, then they went to see Karl mœrski. There were kindly greetings. After that Karl presented King Óláfr's messages and tokens and friendly words to Gilli and Leifr. They received these happily and invited Karl to stay with them and offered to back his business and to provide him with such protection as was within their power. He accepted this gratefully. A little later Þrándr came there and welcomed Karl.

[241] See note 221 above.

'I am,' he says, 'pleased that such a good fellow has come here to our country on our king's business, which we are all duty bound to assist. I will agree to nothing else, Karl, but that you go to my house for winter lodging and all those of your men with you that will make your standing higher than it was before.'

Karl says that he was already engaged to go to Leifr's.

'But I would otherwise,' he says, 'gladly accept this invitation.'

Þrándr says: 'Then Leifr will gain great honour by this. But are there any other things then that I can do so as to be of assistance to you?'

Karl answers that he thought it would be a great help if Þrándr collected the tax from all over Austrey and also from all over the whole of Norðreyjar. Þrándr says that this was his duty and pleasure that he should provide this furtherance to the king's business. Þrándr then goes back to his booth. There was nothing else of importance that happened at this assembly. Karl went to stay with Leifr Qzurarson and he was [264] there the following winter. Leifr collected tax over Straumey and all the islands south of there. The next spring Þrándr from Gata got sick, having trouble with his eyes and was poorly in still other ways, and yet he got ready to go to the assembly, as was his custom. So when he got to the assembly and his booth was being covered, he had it covered inside at the back with black covering, so that it would then let less light in.

So when a few days of the assembly had passed, then Leifr and Karl came to Þrándr's booth and had a lot of men with them. And when they got to the booth, then there were a few men standing outside. Leifr asked whether Þrándr was inside in the booth. They say that he was there. Leifr said that they were to ask Þrándr to come out.

'Karl and I have business with him,' he says.

But when the men came back, then they say that Þrándr had such a pain in his eyes that he could not come out.

'And he asked you, Leifr, to go in.'

Leifr told his companions that they should go warily when they got into the booth, not to crowd each other.

'The one who goes in last must be the first to go out.'

Leifr went in first, and next Karl, then his companions, and all went fully armed, as if they were getting ready for battle. Leifr passed further inside to where the black awnings were, asking then where Þrándr was. Þrándr says, and greets Leifr. Leifr responded to his greeting, asking afterwards whether he had collected any tax across Norðreyjar, and whether the payment of the silver could now be discharged. Þrándr replies, saying that he had not forgotten what he and Karl had discussed, and also that the payment of the tax would be discharged.

'Here is a purse, Leifr, which you are to take charge of, and it is full of silver.'

[265] Leifr looked around and saw few men in the booth. There were men lying on the raised floor, but few were sitting up. After that Leifr went up to Þrándr and took the purse and carried it to the outer part of the booth, where it was light, and poured the silver down onto his shield, stirring it round with his hand and saying that Karl should look at the silver. They examined it for a while. Then Karl asked how the silver looked to Leifr. He says:

'This is what I think, that every false coin there is in Norðreyjar must have ended up here.'

Þrándr heard this and said: 'Do you think the silver looks no good, Leifr?'

'That's right,' he says.

Þrándr said: 'Our kinsmen are not half scoundrels though, since one cannot trust them in anything. I have sent them this spring to collect tax in the islands in the north, since I was not able to do anything this spring, and they have taken bribes from farmers to accept such forgeries that are not considered legal tender. And the best thing, Leifr, is to examine this silver, that has been paid for my land dues.'

Leifr then took the silver back, and picked up another purse and took it to Karl. They examined this money. Karl asked how this money looked to Leifr. He says that he thought this money bad and not such as could be accepted for these dues, which had been claimed carelessly.

'And I am not going to accept this money on the king's behalf.'

A man that was sitting on the raised floor threw his cloak off his head and said:

'It is true what was said in olden times: Everyone gets more of a coward as he gets older. So it is with you, Þrándr, letting Karl inn mœrski heap up money at your expense all the time.'

This was Gautr inn rauði. Þrándr leapt up at Gautr's words and started to rant madly, telling his kinsmen off in strong terms. But finally he said that Leifr was to give him that silver.

'But take this purse here, that my tenants have brought in to me this spring. And though my eyesight is not good, nevertheless one's hand itself is the most reliable.'

A man rose up on his elbow who was lying on the [266] raised floor. This was Þórðr inn lági. He said:

'We are not half getting taught a lesson by this Mœra-Karl, and he deserves to have some recompense.'

Leifr took this purse and again took it to Karl. They look at this money. Leifr said:

'We don't need to spend long examining this silver. Here every coin is better than any other, and we shall accept this money. Get someone, Þrándr, to see to the weighing.'

Þrándr says that he thought the best thing was to get Leifr to see to it himself. Leifr and Karl then go out and a short way from the booth. They then sat down and weighed the silver. Karl took his helmet off his head and poured into it the silver that had been weighed. They saw a man walking by them and he had a mace in his hand and a hood low over his head and a green cape, bare-footed, with linen breeches tied close to his legs. He put down the mace on the ground and left it there and said: 'Be careful, Mœra-Karl, that you are not harmed by my mace.'

Shortly after this a man came running there and shouted excitedly at Leifr Qzurarson, telling him to go as soon as he could to Lawman Gilli's booth.

'Sigurðr Þorláksson ran in through the end of the awning there and has given a mortal wound to one of the inmates.'

Leifr immediately leapt up and went off to see Gilli. With him went all the men of his booth, but Karl remained behind. The Norwegians stood round him in a circle. Gautr rauði ran at them and struck with a hand-axe over the men's shoulders, and this blow struck Karl on the head, and the wound was not very serious. Þórðr lági snatched up the mace that was standing in the ground and struck down on the back of the [hand-]axe so that the axe stuck in the brains. A lot of men then rushed out of Þrándr's booth. Karl was carried away dead. Þrándr expressed his regret about this deed, and yet offered money in atonement on behalf of his kinsmen. Leifr and Gilli took up a prosecution, and there was no monetary compensation. Sigurðr was outlawed for his injuring [267] of Gilli's booth-mate, and Þórðr and Gautr for the killing of Karl. Norwegians got the ship ready that Karl had brought there, and went east to see King Óláfr . . .[242] but there was no chance of this because of the war that had now started in Norway and has yet to be told about. And now we have finished telling about the events that resulted from King Óláfr's claiming tax from the Faeroes. And yet conflicts took place afterwards in the Faeroes arising from the killing of Karl mœrski, and Leifr Qzurarson and kinsmen of Þrándr from Gata were involved in them then, and about this there are substantial accounts.[243]

CHAPTER ONE HUNDRED AND FORTY-FOUR

But now the account must be continued which was begun earlier, where King Óláfr was travelling with his troops and had a levy out off the coast.

---

[242] There is a gap in the manuscript here, and clearly something is missing. Various attempts have been made to fill it in manuscripts of *ÓH*, e.g. 'the king was very displeased about their journey and said he would take vengeance for it as soon as he could manage it', but they are clearly scribal rather than authorial.

[243] See *Færeyinga saga* chs 48–58.

All the landed men[244] from the north of the country were following him except Einarr þambarskelfir. He had stayed quiet at home at his estates since he came into the country, and was not in the service of the king. Einarr had very extensive possessions and kept himself in fine style even though he had no royal revenues. King Óláfr took this army south past Staðr. Large numbers of troops still joined him from the local areas. King Óláfr now had the ship that he had had built the previous winter, which was called Visundr (the Bison), the largest of all ships. On the prow there was a bison's head, decorated with gold. The poet Sigvatr mentions this:

88. The heather-fish[245] of the fearful-   *Erfidrápa Óláfs helga* 3
of-flight son of Tryggvi[246]   *Skald* I 668
[268]   bore gills[247] with ground gold reddened—
God so wished—for booty.
Óleifr the Stout set a
second, finely fitted,
a bison, to tread the billows,
the beast's horns[248] sea washed constantly.

The king then travelled south to Hǫrðaland. He heard the news that Erlingr Skjálgsson was gone out of the country taking a large force, four or five ships. He himself had a large longship, while his sons had three twenty-benched ships, and they had sailed west to England to join Knútr inn ríki. Then King Óláfr travelled eastwards along the coast, and he had a very large army. He made enquiries about whether anyone knew anything of the movements of Knútr inn ríki. And everyone was able to tell him that he was in England, and it was also said as well that he had a levy out and was planning to go to Norway. But because King Óláfr had a large force and could not find out for certain where he should make for to meet with Knútr, and people thought it was no good staying in one place with such a large army, then he decided to sail with his army south to Denmark, taking with him all the men he thought were the best fighters and were best equipped, and gave the rest leave to go home, as is said here:

89. Under oars word-keen Óleifr   *Skald* I 1087
urges Visundr southwards;

[244] See note 52 above.
[245] *lyngs fiskr*: 'fish of the heather', snake; a pun on the name of Óláfr Tryggvason's famous ship, *Ormr inn langi* ('the Long Serpent').
[246] Óláfr Tryggvason.
[247] *gjǫlnar* 'gills': extends the metaphor of the ship as a fish, and may refer to the decorations on the bows (Jesch 2001, 147).
[248] i.e. the pointed stem and stern of the ship.

[269]   out at sea a second king's *dreki*[249]
          splits the wave-world[250] northwards.

Now the troops went home that he thought would be least help. King Óláfr had there a large and splendid force. In it there were most of the landed men of Norway except those that were earlier said to have left the country or to have remained behind at home.

CHAPTER ONE HUNDRED AND FORTY-FIVE

When King Óláfr had sailed to Denmark he laid his course to Sjóland, and when he got there he started to make raids, making sallies ashore. So the inhabitants were both robbed and some of them killed, some were captured and bound and taken like that to the ships, but everyone fled who could manage it, and there was no resistance. King Óláfr caused there very great damage. And while King Óláfr was in Sjóland, he heard the news that King Ǫnundr Óláfsson had got a levy out and had gone with a great army to the eastern side of Skáni and was making raids there. Then the plan that King Óláfr and King Ǫnundr had made by the Elfr, when they formed their alliance and friendship, became known, that both were going to offer resistance to King Knútr. King Ǫnundr travelled until he found his brother-in-law King Óláfr. And when they met, then they announced, both to their troops and the people of the country, that they were planning to subject Denmark to themselves and request acceptance by the people of the country. And it came about, examples of which are to be found in various places, that when the people of a country are faced with warfare and have not the power available to resist, then most agree to all the impositions that will buy them peace. So it happened that many people submit to the kings and agreed [270] to be subject to them. They subjected many parts of the country to themselves wherever they went, and otherwise harried. The poet Sigvatr speaks of this harrying in the *drápa*[251] that he composed about King Knútr inn ríki:[252]

---

[249] *dreki* 'dragon', 'dragon-ship': warship, possibly particularly large, with carved dragon head on the prow (Jesch 2001, 127). The 'second king' presumably means Ǫnundr (see next chapter).

[250] *unnheimr*: 'wave-world', sea.

[251] See note 191 above.

[252] Sigvatr's *Knútsdrápa* is in a variant of the verse form Snorri calls *tøgdrápuháttr* or *tøglag* 'journey(-poem) form' (*Háttatal* 68–70). This form basically has four syllables in each line, but 'it is not wrong if there are five syllables in the line when some of them are short and quick [i.e. have resolution or contraction or other extra light unstressed syllables]. For *tøgdrápa* form there must be a *stef* (refrain) for the first line and its sense is completed in the last line [or section] of the poem' (Snorri Sturluson 1987, 207). The beginning of this 'split refrain' (*klofastef*) appears in sts 90/1 and 96/1; it is completed in sts 98/8 and 99/8.

90. Knútr was, under heavens . . . *Knútsdrápa* 3
    Haraldr's son,[253] from reports *Fsk* 184
    I hear, in warfare *Legendary saga* 142–43
    was brave enough. *Skald* I 653
    South from the Nið sent
    the season-blessed
    prince, Óleifr, on the pollack's
    path,[254] his fleet

91. From the north swept, *Knútsdrápa* 4
    known it's become, *Fsk* 184
    with the king, cool *Legendary saga* 142–43
    keels to flat Silund. *Skald* I 655
    So with a second,
    Swedish, army
    at the oars, Ǫnundr
    after the Danes goes.

[271] CHAPTER ONE HUNDRED AND FORTY-SIX

King Knútr had heard west in England that King Óláfr of Norway had a levy out, and also that he was taking this force to Denmark and there was warfare in his kingdom. Then Knútr began to muster troops. Soon a great army and a large number of ships were gathered there. Jarl Hákon was a second leader of these troops. The poet Sigvatr came to England that summer from Rúða in Valland in the west, and with him a man called Bergr. They had gone there on a trading voyage the previous summer. Sigvatr composed the *flokkr*[255] that was called *Vestrfararvísur*, and this is the beginning of it:

92. Bergr, we've remembered that many *Vestrfararvísur* 1
    mornings I had the stem[256] *Skald* I 617
    roped to the western rampart
    of Rouen's walls, with men's escort.

So when Sigvatr got to England, then he went straight to see King Knútr, wanting to ask for leave for himself to go to Norway. King Knútr had put a ban on all merchant ships before he got his army ready. But when Sigvatr came to him, then he went to the apartment that the king was in. The apartment

[253] King Óláfr.
[254] *lýs gata*: 'road of the pollack (fish)', sea.
[255] See note 191 above.
[256] *barð*: prow of a ship; here plural, which may mean the ship was moored at both ends.

was locked at the time, and he stood outside for a long time. And when he got to see the king, then he got leave, as he had requested. Then he spoke:

[272]

93. I'd to ask outside the entrance —   *Vestrfararvísur* 2
I found the building barred to men —   *Skald* I 618
in order to get audience
with the Jótar's ruler.[257]
But our business — I
bear on my arm often
iron sleeves[258] — Gormr's descendant[259]
settled well in the hall.

And when Sigvatr realised that King Knútr was preparing an invasion against King Óláfr, and he found out what a great force King Knútr had, then Sigvatr spoke:

94. Eager Knútr, all claws open —[260]   *Vestrfararvísur* 3
the king's death I'll be dreading —   *Fsk* 190–91
and Hǫ́kon prove themselves primed to   *Skald* I 619
put Óleifr's life in danger.
Let the king[261] keep, though the jarls and
Knútr hardly wished it, to the
mountains for the moment; easier
a meeting, if he himself escapes.

[273] Sigvatr composed many other verses about Knútr and Hákon's expedition. Then he also said:

95. The most excellent jarl must[262]   *Vestrfararvísur* 4
make peace between Óleifr   *Skald* I 621
and old farmers, who most often
opened this matter.

---

[257] *Jóta stillir*: 'ruler of the Jótar', king of Denmark.
[258] Presumably this means that the poet often wears armour, i.e. takes part in battle.
[259] *Gorms ǫ́ttungr*: 'descendant of Gormr', Danish king, i.e. Knútr.
[260] *allt hefr sás úti*: 'who has all (forces) out'. The word order of this clause is problematic; see Jesch in *Skald* I (620) for alternative interpretations. The translation here renders a modern Icelandic idiom (cited in *ÍF* XXVII), *að hafa úti allar klær* 'to have all claws out', i.e. to have all one's resources (perhaps more literally 'all spears)' ready, presumably here: be ready to attack.
[261] *vǫrðr*: 'guardian'. This is a common element in kennings meaning 'king' but here lacks a determinant.
[262] *átti* (past tense).

Before, they have, in greater fury—
foremost is the kin of Eiríkr—[263]
dealt in heads[264] too much for Hǫkon
hatred to make even.

CHAPTER ONE HUNDRED AND FORTY-SEVEN

Knútr inn ríki had fitted out his army to leave the country. He had a huge number of men and amazingly large ships. He himself had a dragon ship that was so large that it had sixty rowing benches.[265] There were also gold-adorned figureheads on it. Jarl Hákon had another dragon ship. This had forty rowing benches. There were also gilded figureheads on this, and the sails of both were all striped with blue and red and green. These ships were all painted above the waterline. All the equipment of these ships was most splendid. They had many other [274] ships, large and well equipped. This is what the poet Sigvatr says in *Knútsdrápa*:

96. Knútr was, under heavens . . .[266] *Knútsdrápa* 7
 He heard from the east, *Fsk* 183
 fair, keen-eyed *Legendary saga* 140–41
 king of Danes' son. *Skald* I 658
 From the west the wood[267] slid—
 it was splendid—which bore
 out Aðalráðr's
 enemy[268] from there.

97. And they bore in the breeze *Knútsdrápa* 8
 black sails on the yard— *Fsk* 183–84
 proud was the lord's passage— *Legendary saga* 142–43
 the prince's dragons.[269] *Skald* I 659
 And the keels that
 came from the west,
 sailed over the sea,
 the surf, to Limafjǫrðr.

It is said that King Knútr took this great army from England in the west and brought his whole troop safely to Denmark and made for Limafjǫrðr. There was already there a large assembly of people of that country.

[263] the jarl, Hákon Eiríksson.
[264] i.e. exchanged killings.
[265] i.e. 120 oars.
[266] The first line of the refrain which is completed in st. 98 and 99/8. See note 312 below.
[267] i.e. ship.
[268] i.e. Knútr.
[269] *drekar*: warships with carved dragons on the prows.

[275] CHAPTER ONE HUNDRED AND FORTY-EIGHT
Jarl Úlfr Sprakaleggsson had been installed as defender of the country in Denmark when King Knútr went to England. He had put his son, who was called Hǫrða-Knútr, into Jarl Úlfr's charge. It was the previous summer, as has been said above.[270] But the jarl immediately announced that King Knútr had entrusted him with this undertaking at their parting, that he wanted them to take King Knútr's son Hǫrða-Knútr as king over the Danish realm.

'It was for that reason that he gave him into our charge. I,' he says, 'and many other people of this country and those in high positions have often complained to King Knútr about this, that people find it very difficult to stay here without a king, when previous kings of the Danes thought it plenty to do to hold the position of king over just the Danish realm on its own. But in former times there were many kings ruling over this kingdom. And yet there is now a much greater problem than there has been before, for we have up to now managed to remain in peace from foreign rulers, but now what we have heard is that the king of Norway is planning to make war against us, and moreover people have a suspicion that the king of the Svíar may also be going to join in the expedition. But King Knútr is now in England.'

Then the jarl brought out letters with seals that confirmed all this that the jarl was putting forward. This undertaking was supported by many other leading men. And at their combined persuasion the people decided to take Hǫrða-Knútr as king, and this was done at the same assembly. But it was Queen Emma who had been the instigator of this plot. She had had these letters written and had them sealed. She had got hold of the king's seal by trickery, but this was all concealed from him himself.

So when Hǫrða-Knútr and Jarl Úlfr realised that King Óláfr was come from Norway in the north with a great army, [276] then they went to Jótland, because it is there that the greatest power of the Danish realm lies. They then raised a war arrow[271] and mustered a large army. But when they heard that the king of the Svíar was also come there with his army, then they felt they did not have the resources to engage in battle with them both. Then they kept their host in Jótland, intending to defend that land from the kings, and the naval force they gathered all together in Limafjǫrðr, and waited thus for King Knútr. And when they heard that King Knútr was come from the west to Limafjǫrðr, then they sent messengers to him and to Queen Emma, asking her to find out whether the king was angry with them or not, and keep them in the picture. The queen discussed this matter with the king, saying that their son Hǫrða-Knútr was willing to atone for everything the king wanted, if he had done anything that the king felt was not to his liking. He replies, saying that Hǫrða-Knútr had not carried out his instructions.

[270] Ch. 84.   [269] See note 180 above.

'It has so turned out,' he said, 'as was to be expected, since he was a child and a fool, that he wanted to be called king and got a problem on his hands, that the whole country was about to be invaded and subjected to foreign rulers if our help did not come. If he now wants to make some amends to me, then let him come to see me and lay aside this silly name of having himself called king.'

After this the queen passed on these same words to Hǫrða-Knútr and this too, that she bade him not to neglect making this visit, saying, as was true, that he would not have the power to stand against his father. And when this message came to Hǫrða-Knútr, then he sought the advice of the jarl and other leading men who were with him. But it was soon found, when the people of the country heard that Knútr inn gamli had arrived, that then all the common people thronged to him, feeling that in him lay all their hope. Jarl Úlfr and his other [277] comrades realised that they had two choices available, either to go to see the king and put all at his mercy, or else to head away abroad. But everyone urged Hǫrða-Knútr to go to see his father. He did so. And when they met, then he fell at the feet of his father and laid the seal that belonged to the king's name in his lap. King Knútr took Hǫrða-Knútr by the hand and sat him in a seat as high as he had sat before. Jarl Úlfr sent his son Sveinn to see King Knútr. Sveinn was King Knútr's sister's son. He sought for pardon for his father and atonement with the king and offered to stay as hostage on behalf of the jarl. Sveinn and Hǫrða-Knútr were of the same age. King Knútr ordered these words to be told to the jarl, that he was to muster an army and ships and thus come to meet the king, but he would talk later about his atonement. The jarl did so.

CHAPTER ONE HUNDRED AND FORTY-NINE

So when King Óláfr and King Ǫnundr learned that King Knútr was come from the west, and also that he now had an invincible army, then they sail east round Skáni, beginning now to harry and burn settlements, so making their way east along the coast towards the realm of the king of the Svíar. So when the people of the country heard that King Knútr was come from the west, then there was no more becoming subject to the king. The poet Sigvatr mentions this:

98.	The keen rulers	*Knútsdrápa* 6
	could not attract	*Fsk* 185
	Denmark under them	*Legendary saga* 144–45
	by dint of warfare.	*Skald* I 657

[278] Then fiercely
the feller of Danes[272]
had Skáney harried;
. . . the outstanding prince.

Then the kings made their way east along the coast and came to land at a place called Áin helga, and stayed there for a while. Then they learn that King Knútr was travelling with his army eastwards after them. Then they take counsel together and decided that King Óláfr with some of his troops should go up ashore and all the way through the forests to the lake that Áin helga flows from, making there at the river mouth a dam with timber and turf, so damming up the lake, and also they cut great dikes, making several lakes flow into each other, forming huge swamps, and felling trees into the river bed. They were at this labour many days, and King Óláfr took the management of these schemes, while King Ǫnundr now had command of the naval force. King Knútr learned about the movements of the kings and also about all the damage they had done in his realm, making his way to meet them where they were lying in Áin helga, and he had a great army and one twice as big as their two put together. Sigvatr mentions this:

99.	Once in his land the lord of Jótland[273] would not be deprived; people were pleased. Very little plundering of land the protecting shield of Danes[274] permitted, . . . the outstanding prince.	*Knútsdrápa* 9 *Fsk* 186 *Legendary saga* 146–47 *Skald* I 660

[279] CHAPTER ONE HUNDRED AND FIFTY

It happened one day in the evening that some of King Ǫnundr's men on the lookout saw where King Knútr was sailing, and he was not far away. Then King Ǫnundr had horns blown as a summons to war. The men then threw off the awnings and armed themselves, rowed out of the harbour and eastwards along the coast, brought their ships alongside each other and tied them together and prepared for battle. King Ǫnundr rushed the lookout men up inland. They went to see King Óláfr and told him what had been going on. Then King Óláfr had the dams demolished and let the river flow back in its bed, while

---

[272] Presumably Óláfr.
[273] *Jótlands jǫfurr*: 'lord of Jutland (i.e. of Denmark)', Knútr.
[274] Knútr.

he went during the night down to his ships. King Knútr came level with the harbour. Then he saw where the kings' army was lying ready for battle. He felt that now it would be late in the day to engage in battle by the time his army was completely ready, as his fleet required a lot of space in the sea in order to sail. There was a great distance between the first of his ships and the last, and also between the one that was travelling furthest out to sea, and the other that was travelling closest to the land. There was little wind. So when King Knútr saw that the Svíar and the Norwegians had quit the harbour, then he made into the harbour, together with the ships there was room for, though the main part of his naval force lay out in the open sea. In the morning, when it was almost light, then many of their troops were up ashore, some chatting, some enjoying themselves. Then the next thing they know is that water is rushing down at them in a torrent. With it came huge pieces of timber which drove against their ships. Their ships were damaged by them, while the water flooded across the whole area. The people that were ashore and many of those that were on board the ships perished, while all those who could manage it cut their cables and got [280] clear, and the ships were tossed all over the place. The great dragon ship that the king himself was aboard was driven out with the current. It could not easily be turned round by the oars. It was driven out to where King Ǫnundr's fleet was. So when they recognised the ship, then they immediately attacked it from all sides. But because the ship stood high out of the water like a stronghold and had a lot of men on board and a crew selected from the finest men, who were also armed in the most dependable way possible, so the ship was not easy to overcome. It was not a long time before Jarl Úlfr attacked with his troop, and then a battle began. Next King Knútr's army drew close on all sides. Then the kings Óláfr and Ǫnundr saw that now they must have for the moment won as much of a victory as was going to be allotted them; they pulled their ships astern with the oars and got clear of King Knútr's army and the fleet scattered. And because this attack had not worked out as King Knútr had arranged for it to, the ships not having gone forward in the way that had been ordered, so the engagement came to nothing, and Knútr and his men inspected their troops and began to line up their troops and put them in order. So when they had parted and each fleet was sailing separately, then the kings inspected their forces and found that they had suffered no loss of life. They also saw that if they were to wait there until King Knútr had got the whole army that he had there ready, and after that attacked them, the difference in numbers was so great that there was little hope that they would be victorious, and it was obvious that if battle was engaged, there would be a very great loss of men there. Now the decision was made to row the whole army eastwards along the coast. But when they saw King Knútr's fleet was not pursuing them, then they put up masts and hoisted their sails. Óttarr svarti discusses this engagement in the *drápa*[275] that he composed about Knútr inn ríki:

[281]
100. Swedes you stayed, ruler
unstinting of gems;[276] plenty
of wolf-food[277] the she-wolf
won at Ó en helga.
You held, where no raven hungered,
(unhesitant you are, towards men)
the territory against two princes,
terror-staff[278] (ferocious).

Knútsdrápa 11
Fsk 186 (1st half)
Legendary saga 146
Skald I 781
Skáldsk 66

The poet Þórðr Sjáreksson composed a memorial *drápa* about King Óláfr, it is called *Róðadrápa*, and there this engagement is mentioned:[279]

101. A clash of arms[280] Óleifr,
Egðir's lord,[281] engaged in
against the excellent king of
Jótar,[282] who cleaves ring-mail.
Shot quite keenly at him
the king of the Skónungar;[283]
Sveinn's son was no weaking;
the wolf howled over carrion.

Róðudrápa 1
Fsk 187
Skald I 243
Legendary saga 146

[282] CHAPTER ONE HUNDRED AND FIFTY-ONE

King Óláfr and King Ǫnundr sailed eastwards along the coast of the king of the Svíar's realm, and in the evening of that day they came to land at a place called Barvík. The kings lay there that night. And then it became apparent about the Svíar, that they were now keen to go home. There was a large part of the army of Svíar that sailed during the night east along the coast, and they did not stop their travelling until each one had reached his home. So when King Ǫnundr realised this and it was now daylight, then he

[275] See note 191 above.
[276] *siklingr søkkva ǫrr*: 'king generous with jewels': the sense of 'jewel, gold' for *søkk* was proposed by Kock (*NN* §1783).
[277] *ulfs beita*: 'wolf's fodder', corpses.
[278] *ógnar stafr*: 'staff of terror (battle)', warrior.
[279] For Þórðr Sjáreksson, see *Heimskringla* I, note 249. This is the only surviving stanza of his *Róðudrápa* (Rood Poem?) in memory of St Óláfr.
[280] *stála þrima*: 'clash of weapons', battle.
[281] *Egða dróttinn*: 'lord of people of Agðir', a district of Norway; i.e. king of Norway.
[282] *Jóta ǫðlingr*: 'ruler of the Jótar', people of Jutland, i.e. king of Denmark (Knútr).
[283] *Skónunga gramr*: 'king of people of Skáni', i.e. king of Denmark.

had an assembly of his troops summoned by horns. Then all the troops went ashore, and the assembly was inaugurated. King Ǫnundr began to speak:

'It is the case,' he says, 'as you, King Óláfr, know, that we have this summer raided far and wide round Denmark. We have gained a great deal of wealth, though not of land. I did have this summer three hundred and fifty ships, but now there remain no more than a hundred ships. Now it seems to me as though we shall not gain honour by fighting with no larger army than we now have, even though you have fifty ships, as you did have in the summer. Now I feel it will be best to go back into my kingdom, and it is good to get back home safe and sound. We have gained on this expedition, and lost nothing. Now I wish, brother-in-law Óláfr, to invite you to go with me, and let us be together the whole winter. Have such of my realm as will enable you to maintain yourself and the troops that are following you. Then when spring comes we can make such plans as seem good to us. But if you prefer as an alternative to use our land to travel over, and wish to travel by land to your realm in Norway, then you shall be free to do so.'

King Óláfr thanked King Ǫnundr for the kind invitation that he had given him.

'And yet, if I have my way,' he says, 'then another plan will be adopted, and we shall [283] keep this army that now remains together here. I did have, at the beginning of summer, before I left Norway, three hundred and fifty ships; but when I left the country, then I chose out of all that army that troop that I thought was best. I manned these sixty ships that I have now. Now it seems to me the same with your troops, that they will have run away who had least spirit and provided the worst support, but I can see here all your leading men and captains of royal troops, and I know that this troop, which is a royal troop, is all better off for weapons. We still have a large army and such a fine naval force, that we may well stay out on the ships all winter, as kings used to do in the past. But King Knútr will only stay a short while in Áin helga, for there is no harbour there for the number of ships he has got. He will travel east after us. Then we shall move away, and then troops will soon join us. But if he turns back there to where the harbours are where he can lie with his fleet, then there will be there by no means fewer troops eager to be home than here. I expect that we have so managed things here this summer that the villager will know what he will be doing both in Skáni and in Sjóland. Knútr's army will soon scatter all over the place, and there is no knowing then who will be victorious. Let us first have a lookout kept as to what course he takes.'

King Óláfr ended his speech with everyone applauding enthusiastically, and the plan was adopted that he wished to have followed. Then lookouts were posted for King Knútr's forces, while both kings lay there.

CHAPTER ONE HUNDRED AND FIFTY-TWO

King Knútr saw this, that the king of Norway and the king of the Svíar took their troops eastwards along the coast. He immediately put a troop up ashore, having his men ride by the inland route [284] day and night, as the kings' troops travelled along by sea. One party of lookout men rode out when the others came back. Knútr knew every day about what happened in their travels. There were also spies of his in the kings' army. And when he (Knútr) found out that a large part of their forces had left them, then he took his army back to Sjáland and put into Eyrarsund with his whole army. Some of the force lay off Sjáland, and some off Skáni.

King Knútr rode up to Hróiskelda the next day before Michaelmas,[284] and a large company of men with him. And there his brother-in-law Jarl Úlfr had prepared a banquet for him. The jarl's provision was very liberal and he was very merry. The king said little and looked in rather a bad temper. The jarl kept speaking to him, trying to find the topics that he thought would most please the king. The king made little response. Then the jarl asked if he wanted to play a board game.[285] He agreed. They got a set of pieces and played. Jarl Úlfr was a man ready of speech and unyielding both in words and in all other things, and one eager for action in regard to his rule and a great warrior, and there are many things told about him.[286] Jarl Úlfr was the most powerful man in Denmark, apart from the king. Gyða, whom Jarl Guðini Úlfnaðrsson married, was Jarl Úlfr's sister, and their sons were King Haraldr of the English, Jarl Tósti, Jarl Valþjófr, Jarl Morukári, Jarl Sveinn. Their daughter was called Gyða, whom King Eatvarðr inn góði of the English married.

[285] CHAPTER ONE HUNDRED AND FIFTY-THREE

So while they were playing this board game, King Knútr and Jarl Úlfr, then the king made a very bad move. Then the jarl checked one of his knights. The king took back his piece, saying that he would make a different move. The jarl grew angry and threw down the board, got up and went away. The king said:

'Are you running away now, Úlfr the Cowardly?'

The jarl turned round by the doorway and said:

[284] Michaelmas is 29th September.

[285] *Skáktafl* actually means chess, but it is thought that the game as we now know it was not played in northern Europe until much later than this. It may be that here an earlier version of chess is meant, but it is perhaps more likely that if Knútr and Úlfr played anything at all, they played the viking game of *hneftafl*.

[286] Literally 'there is a great saga told about him'. This probably refers to written accounts of Úlfr, but *Knýtlinga saga* was not written until after *Heimskringla*. There is unlikely to have been any extensive oral narrative about him.

'You would have run further in Áin helga, if you could have managed it. You did not call me Úlfr the Cowardly when I sailed up to help you when the Svíar were beating you like dogs.'

The jarl then went out and went to bed. A little later the king went to bed. The next morning, when the king was getting dressed, then he said to his servant:

'Go,' he says, 'to Jarl Úlfr and kill him.'

The lad went and was away a short while and came back. Then the king said:

'Did you kill the jarl?'

He replies: 'I did not kill him, for he was gone to Lucius's Church.'[287]

There was a man called Ívarr hvíti (the White), Norwegian by origin. He was at this time a follower of King Knútr and his chamberlain. The king spoke to Ívarr:

'You go and kill the jarl.'

Ívarr went to the church and on into the choir and there stabbed his sword through the jarl. Jarl Úlfr got his death there. Ívarr went to the king, taking the bloody sword in his hand. The king asked:

'Did you kill the jarl?'

Ívarr replies: 'Now I have killed him.'

'You have done well, then,' he said.

But afterwards, when the jarl had been killed, the monks had the church locked. The king was then told of this. He sent a man to the monks, telling them to open the church and sing the service. They did as the king asked. [286] So when the king came to the church, then he conveyed extensive lands to the church, so that it formed a large domain, and the establishment became much more important afterwards. The consequence was that these lands have remained attached to it ever since.

Afterwards King Knútr rode out to his ships and stayed there for a long time in the autumn with a very large army.

CHAPTER ONE HUNDRED AND FIFTY-FOUR

When King Óláfr and King Ǫnundr learned that King Knútr had made for Eyrarsund and that he was lying there with his army, then the kings held a meeting of the troops. King Óláfr spoke, saying that this had gone as he had supposed, so that King Knútr had not stayed long in Áin helga.

'I expect that now other things will go in accordance with what I had supposed about our dealings. He now has small numbers compared with what he had in the summer, and he will have even fewer later on, for it will

---

[287] This church was dedicated to St Lucius (Pope Lucius I, AD 253–54), feast day 5th March.

be no less unpleasant for them than for us to be lying out on board ships for this coming autumn, and we shall be granted victory if we do not lack determination and daring. He has so fared this summer, that we have had fewer troops, but they have lost both men and wealth by us.'

Then the Svíar began to speak, saying that it was not a good idea to wait there for winter and freeze, 'even though the Norwegians are urging this. They do not fully realise how icy it can get here, and the whole sea often freezes in the winter. We want to go home and not stay here any longer.'

Then the Svíar all started grumbling, and one after another added their voices. It was decided in the end that King Qnundr was to leave now with all his forces, and King Óláfr was to stay on behind.

[287] CHAPTER ONE HUNDRED AND FIFTY-FIVE

So as King Óláfr lay there, he had frequent discussions and councils of his men. It happened one night that they were set to keep watch for the king's ship, Egill Hallsson and the man who was called Tófi Valgautsson. His origin was from Vestra-Gautland, a man of good family. And while they sat there on watch, then they heard weeping and wailing from where captured warriors were sitting tied up. They had been tied up overnight up on shore. Tófi says that he found it unpleasant to listen to their howling, and told Egill that they should go and free the people and let them run away. They carried out this same plan, went up and cut their bonds and made all these people run away, and this deed was very unpopular. The king, too, was so angry that they were on the brink of the utmost peril. And afterwards, when Egill was ill, then it was for a long time that the king would not come to see him though many people begged him. Then Egill repented greatly of having acted so that the king was displeased, and asked his forgiveness. In the end the king granted him this. King Óláfr laid his hands over Egill's side under which the pain lay, and said his prayers, and immediately all the pain went away. After that Egill got better. And Tófi later managed to make atonement. It is said that as a condition of this he had to get his father to come to see King Óláfr. Valgautr was a man heathen as a dog, and he accepted Christianity by the king's persuasion and died as soon as he was baptised.

CHAPTER ONE HUNDRED AND FIFTY-SIX

Now when King Óláfr was having a discussion with his men, then he sought advice from leading men, what they wanted to do. But there was little agreement among people about this. One person declared that [288] a bad thing to do that another thought promising, and they pondered among themselves what they should do for a very long time. King Knútr's spies were continually in the midst of their army and got to talk to many people, and they made offers of money and friendship on behalf of King Knútr, and many people let themselves be persuaded and pledged their troth that they would become King Knútr's men and bring the country into his hands if he came to Norway. Many were found to be guilty of this later, though it remained secret for a while. Some received gifts of money straight away, and some were promised money later. But those were very numerous who had already received large friendly gifts from him, for it was true to say of King Knútr that everyone that came to see him, of those that he thought had any sign of manhood in them and wanted to attach themselves to him, then they all got their hands full of money from him. As a result he became enormously popular. And the most remarkable was his generosity to foreigners, especially those that had come from furthest off.

CHAPTER ONE HUNDRED AND FIFTY-SEVEN

King Óláfr often had discussions and meetings with his men and asked about plans. And when he found that each one made different suggestions, then he suspected that there were some that must be saying something different about it from what must seem to them most advisable, and so it could not be decided whether everyone could be carrying out their true duty to him as regards loyalty. There were many who urged that they should use a favourable wind and sail to Eyrarsund and so north to Norway. They said that the Danes would not dare to attack them, even though they were lying there in front of them with a large force. But the king was sensible enough to see that this was an impossible plan. He also knew that it had worked out differently for Óláfr Tryggvason, when he had a small force and he engaged in battle where there was a great army facing him, from the Danes not daring to fight then. [289] The king also knew that in King Knútr's army there was a large number of Norwegians. The king suspected that those who had given him this advice must be more loyal to King Knútr than to him. King Óláfr now made his decision, saying this, that men were to get ready, those who were willing to follow him, to travel by land across inland Gautland and so to Norway.

'And our ships,' he says, 'and all the cargo that we cannot carry with us, I will send east into the realm of the king of the Svíar and have it kept there on our behalf.'

CHAPTER ONE HUNDRED AND FIFTY-EIGHT

Hárekr from Þjótta replied to King Óláfr's speech, saying this:
 'It is obvious that I cannot go to Norway on foot. I am an old man and heavy and little used to walking. I feel reluctant to part from my ship. I have

taken such trouble over my ship and its equipment that I should be loath to let my enemies get hold of this ship.'

The king replies: 'Go with us, Hárekr. We shall carry you along with us if you are unable to walk.'

Hárekr then uttered a verse:

> 102. I've resolved to straddle   *Fsk* 188
> my steed, long, resounding,   *Legendary saga* 148
> of Rhine-flame's land,[288] from here,   *Skald* I 808
> rather than on my way walking,
> though out in Eyrarsund
> the arm-fetter's grove[289] is lying—
> all men know my courage—
> Knútr, out with his warships.

[290] Then King Óláfr prepared to set out. The men had the clothes they had on and their weapons, and whatever they could get in the way of horses was loaded with clothes and money. But he sent men and had them convey his ships east to Kalmarnir. They got the ships beached there and all the gear and other goods put into store. Hárekr did as he had said he would, he waited for a wind and then sailed from the east past Skáni until he got from the east to Halarnir, and by then it was evening. But there was a good wind blowing. Then he had the sail lowered and also the masts, the weathervane taken down and all the ship above the water line wrapped in grey awnings, and had rowers on a few benches fore and aft and made most of the men sit low down in the ship. So King Knútr's watchmen saw the ship and discussed among themselves what kind of ship that might be, and guessed that it must be salt or herring that was being transported, since they saw few men and not much rowing, while the ship looked grey to them and unpitched and as if the ship must have been bleached by the sun, and they could see that the ship was heavily laden. But when Hárekr got on into the sound and past the army, then he had the masts raised and the sail hoisted, had a gilded weathervane put up. The sail was as white as snow and coloured with red and blue stripes. Then King Knútr's men saw and tell the king that it was more than likely that King Óláfr had sailed by there. But King Knútr says this, that King Óláfr was a sensible enough man not to have travelled with a single ship through King Knútr's army, and said he thought it more likely that it must have been Hárekr from Þjótta there or his like. People take the truth to be that King Knútr knew about Hárekr's travels and that he would [291]

[288] *Rínleygs láðs dynmarr*: 'noisy horse of the land (sea) of the Rhine's fire (gold)', ship.

[289] *leggfjǫturs lundr*: 'grove (tree) of the fetter of the limb (bracelet, ring)', man.

not have got by like that if there had not previously passed friendly overtures between him and King Knútr, and this seemed to be manifest afterwards, when the friendship of King Knútr and Hárekr became universally known. Hárekr composed this verse as he sailed north past Veðrey:

103. I will not let ladies[290]   *Fsk* 189
of Lund, or Danish maidens   *Legendary saga* 150
jeer—beyond the island   *Skald* I 810
the oak of the sea-ring[291] we drive on—
that in autumn I dared not,
Jǫrð of the hawk's vessel,[292]
on the flat paths of Fróði[293]
fare back in the bollard-steed.[294]

CHAPTER ONE HUNDRED AND FIFTY-NINE

King Óláfr set out on his journey, going first up through Smálǫnd and coming out in Vestra-Gautland, travelling quietly and peacefully, and the people of the country gave them hospitable treatment. The king went on until he came down in the Vík, and so north along the Vík until he got to Sarpsborg. He then stopped there and then had [292] winter quarters got ready there. The king then gave leave to go home to the greater part of his force, but kept with him such of the landed men as he thought fit. There with him were all the sons of Árni Armóðsson. They were the most highly valued by the king. Then Gellir Þorkelsson came to King Óláfr, having arrived from Iceland earlier that summer, as was written above.[295]

CHAPTER ONE HUNDRED AND SIXTY

The poet Sigvatr had been with King Óláfr for a long time, as has been written here, and the king had made him his marshal. Sigvatr was not a man quick of speech in prose, but he had such facility in verse that he spoke it

[290] *ekkja*: 'widow'; in poetry, often means 'woman' in general.

[291] *læbaugs eik*: 'oak of the ring of the sea (= the encircling sea)', ship. *Læ* is a poetical term for the sea. Elsewhere *læ* means 'deceit, harm, poison'. In *ÍF* 27, *læbaugr* is interpreted as 'poison-ring', i.e. dragon, a reference to the carved dragon's heads on the prows of warships; the 'oak of the dragon' is the ship.

[292] *ifla flausts Jǫrð*: 'Jǫrð (goddess) of the hawk's ship (hand, on which the hawk perches)', woman.

[293] *Fróða flatslóðir*: 'level paths of Fróði (a sea-king)', the sea.

[294] *krapta valr*: 'horse of the bollard', ship. The *krapti* was 'the wooden protuberance on the hull of a ship (or boat) to which the mooring-rope could be attached' (Jesch 2001, 170).

[295] p. 241 above.

extempore, just as if he was saying something in the ordinary way. He had been on trading expeditions in Valland, and on that journey he had come to England and met Knútr inn ríki and got leave from him to go to Norway, as was written above.[296] And when he got to Norway, then he straight away went to see King Óláfr and met up with him in Borg, going into the king's presence while he was sitting at table. Sigvatr greeted him. The king looked at him and said nothing. Sigvatr said:

104.	We are come home hither—	*Vestrfararvísur* 6
	heed this, prince of people—	*Skald* I 623
	your marshal; my words let men	
	mark, as I utter them.	
	Say where you have assigned a	
	seat for men, great ruler,	
	among pines of gold;[297] to me all places	
	are pleasant within your hall.	

[293] Then the old saying proved true, that many are the king's ears. King Óláfr had heard all about Sigvatr's travels, how he had seen King Knútr. King Óláfr said to Sigvatr:

'I am not sure whether you now plan to stay as my marshal. But have you now become a follower of King Knútr?'

Sigvatr said:

105.	Knútr asked me, with assets	*Vestrfararvísur* 7
	open-handed, if I wanted	*Skald* I 625
	to be useful to him as to	
	Óleifr, the glad-hearted.	
	One lord at a time—honestly	
	I thought that I answered—	
	I said suited me; good examples	
	are set for every man.	

Then King Óláfr said that Sigvatr was to go to the seat that he was accustomed to have before. Sigvatr soon got himself again onto the same close terms as he had been on earlier.

CHAPTER ONE HUNDRED AND SIXTY-ONE

Erlingr Skjálgsson and all his sons had during the summer been in King Knútr's army and in Jarl Hákon's troop. Þórir hundr was also in it then and was held in great honour. And when King Knútr learned that King Óláfr

---

[296] p. 271.
[297] *seims þollr*: 'tree of gold', man.

[294] had gone to Norway by land, then King Knútr broke up the levy and gave everyone leave to get themselves winter quarters. There was then in Denmark a great host of foreigners, both Englishmen and Norwegians and come from various lands when troops had joined the army in the summer. Erlingr Skjálgsson went to Norway with his men in the autumn, and received from King Knútr great gifts at their parting. Þórir hundr stayed behind with King Knútr.With Erlingr there travelled north to Norway King Knútr's embassy, taking with them a huge amount of money. They travelled widely round the country during the winter handing out the money that King Knútr had promised people in the autumn for their support, and gave it to many others too whose friendship to King Knútr they were able to purchase with money. And they had Erlingr's protection for their travels round.Then it came about thus, that a large number of men turned to friendship with King Knútr, promising him their service, and this also, to offer resistance to King Óláfr. Some did this openly, but those were much more numerous that kept this secret from the ordinary people. King Óláfr heard about all these doings. Many were able to tell him about these doings, and there was much talk of it there among the king's men. The poet Sigvatr said this:

> 106. The prince's foes prowl there, with Skald I 715
> purses open; often
> people offer, for the prince's
> priceless skull, solid metal.
>
> [295] Each man who for gold gives up
> his gracious lord knows his
> home will be in black hell;
> he has deserved it.

And again Sigvatr said this:

> 107. A bad bargain, when those who Skald I 716
> base treason dealt their lord
> in heaven, the deep home of
> high fire[298] went seeking.

The opinion was often expressed there, how ill it beseemed Jarl Hákon to bring an army against King Óláfr, when he had granted him life when the jarl had fallen into his power. But Sigvatr was a very great friend of the jarl, and then, when Sigvatr heard the jarl criticised again, he said:

---

[298] *heimr hás elds*: 'the home, world of high fire', hell. This interpretation follows *ÍF* 27, which takes the quatrain as an allusion to the Fall of the Angels. R. D. Fulk in *Skald* I (717) takes it to mean 'There is sorrow in the heavens over the treachery [against Óláfr]'.

108. Those who, of the king of Hǫrðar's²⁹⁹ *Skald* I 718
housecarls, accept money
for Óleifr's life, would then be acting
even worse than the jarl.
[296] It taints his retinue,
talked of in this fashion;
for us it would be easier
if all were clear of treachery.

CHAPTER ONE HUNDRED AND SIXTY-TWO

King Óláfr held a great Yule feast, and there came to him then many men of rank. It was the seventh day of Yule that the king was walking and few men with him. Sigvatr was with the king day and night. He was with him now. They went into a building. In this the king's treasures were kept. He had at this time been making great preparations, as was his custom, gathering together his treasures to give friendly gifts on the eighth evening of Yule. Standing there in this building there was no very small number of gold-adorned swords Then Sigvatr said:³⁰⁰

109. Swords stand there—oars of *Legendary saga* 132
straits of wounds³⁰¹ we honour— *Skald* I 796
for us the war-leader's favour
is finest—gold-decorated.
I would accept, if you wanted—
I was with you once, spreader
of gulf's fire,³⁰² great ruler—
to give the poet something.

[297] The king took one of the swords and gave it him. Its haft was wrapped in gold and the hilt guard and boss were decorated with gold. This was a very fine treasure, though the gift was not unenvied, and this will be heard about later. Immediately after Yule, King Óláfr set out on his way to Upplǫnd, for he had a large following and no revenues had come to him that autumn from the north of the country, and because the levy had been out in the summer and the king had devoted all the payments that were available to that. There were also no ships now in which to take his troops to the north of the country. Moreover the reports he had from the north were only ones

---

²⁹⁹ *Hǫrða hilmir*: 'king of the Hǫrðalanders', king of Norway, Óláfr.
³⁰⁰ In Styrmir's fragmentary Life of St Óláfr, this verse is attributed to Bersi Skáld-Torfuson; in the *Oldest saga of St Óláfr* and the *Legendary saga* it is attributed to Óttarr svarti.
³⁰¹ *sárs sunda ár*: 'oar of the channels of the wound (blood)', sword.
³⁰² *víka elds sendir*: 'sender of the fire of bays (gold)', generous man.

that he thought did not bode peace if he did not go with a large force. The king therefore decided to travel over Upplǫnd. But it was not so very long since he had gone round attending banquets there under the provisions of the law and as the custom of kings had been. But as the king made his way up through the country, then landed men and powerful farmers invited him to their homes and thus lightened his expenses.

CHAPTER ONE HUNDRED AND SIXTY-THREE

There is a man called Bjǫrn, Gautish by origin. He was a friend and acquaintance of Queen Ástríðr and somewhat related in kinship, and she had granted him a bailiwick and stewardship in the upper part of Heiðmǫrk. He was also overseer in Eystri-Dalir. Bjǫrn was not beloved of the king, and he was not a popular man with the farmers. It had moreover happened in the area that Bjǫrn was in charge of, that [298] a large number of cattle and swine had gone missing there. Bjǫrn had an assembly called there about it and enquired into the disappearances. He declared the men most likely to be responsible for such things and evil tricks were those who resided in forest areas far from other people. He pointed the finger at those who lived in Eystri-Dalir. This settlement was very scattered, in habitations by lakes or in clearings in the forest, and in only a few places were there large settlements close together.

CHAPTER ONE HUNDRED AND SIXTY-FOUR[303]

There was a man called Rauðr who lived there in Eystri-Dalir. His wife was named Ragnhildr, his sons Dagr and Sigurðr. They were very promising men. They were present at this assembly and made answers on behalf of the people of Dalir, and defended them from these accusations. Bjǫrn thought they were acting arrogantly, and that they were very ostentatious with their weapons and clothes. Bjǫrn turned the accusations against the brothers, declaring them not unlikely to have done these things. They denied their own guilt, and so this assembly broke up. A little later King Óláfr came to Bjǫrn the Steward's with his retinue and received a banquet there. Then this business that had previously been made public at the assembly was brought before the king. Bjǫrn said that he thought Rauðr's sons were most likely to be the cause of these losses. Then Rauðr's sons were sent for. But when they came before the king, then he considered they did not look like thieves and he acquitted them of these charges. They invited the king to their father's to receive there a banquet of three nights with all his retinue. Bjǫrn spoke against the

---

[303] A longer version of the story in this chapter is found in some manuscripts of *ÓH*, and it must once have existed as an independent *þáttr*, which was probably the source of Snorri's summary version here. See Faulkes 1966.

trip. The king went nevertheless. At Rauðr's there was the most splendid banquet. Then the king asked what manner of man Rauðr was and his wife. Rauðr says that he was a Swedish man, wealthy [299] and of good family. 'But I eloped from there,' he says, 'with this woman, to whom I have remained married ever since. She is King Hringr Dagsson's sister.'

Then the king recollected both of their descents. He found that the father and his sons were very intelligent, and asked them about their accomplishments. Sigurðr says that he can interpret dreams and distinguish the time of day even when no heavenly bodies can be seen. The king tested this accomplishment, and it was as Sigurðr had said. Dagr chose as his accomplishment that he could discern the good and bad qualities of any person that came before his eyes, if he was to pay attention to them and consider them. The king told him to tell him what vice he saw in him. Dagr chose the one that the king thought correct.[304] Then the king asked about Bjǫrn the Steward, what vice he had. Dagr says that Bjǫrn was a thief, and moreover he says where Bjǫrn had hidden on his farm both bones and horns and hides of the cattle that he had stolen that autumn.

'He is responsible,' he says, 'for all the thefts of what has disappeared this autumn, which he has imputed to other people.'

Dagr tells the king all the clues to where the king must look. So when the king left Rauðr's, then he was sent off with fine friendly gifts. Rauðr's sons stayed with the king. The king went first to Bjǫrn's, and everything proved to him to be just as Dagr had said. Then the king made Bjǫrn leave the country, and he had the queen to thank for the fact that he kept life and limb.

[300] CHAPTER ONE HUNDRED AND SIXTY-FIVE

Ǫlvir at Egg's son Þórir, Kálfr Árnason's stepson and Þórir hundr's sister's son,[305] was the handsomest of men, a big man and strong. He was now eighteen years old. He had made a good match in Heiðmǫrk and gained a wealth of money with it. He was a most popular man and was thought likely to make a good leader. He invited the king to a banquet at his home with his retinue. The king accepted this invitation and went to Þórir's, receiving there very good hospitality. There was the most splendid banquet, the entertainment was very liberal, and all the provisions were of the finest. The king and his men discussed among themselves how it seemed to them very much in the balance, and they were uncertain which they found most outstanding, Þórir's accommodation or his table furnishings or the drink or the man who was providing it all. Dagr made little comment.

[304] In *Rauðúlfs þáttr*, the king's vice is *kvennanna ást* 'love of women'.
[305] Cf. chs 110, 183, 219 above.

King Óláfr was accustomed to have frequent talks with Dagr and asked him various things. The king found everything to be accurate that Dagr said, whether it was in the past or not yet happened. The king attached great confidence to his assertions. Now the king called Dagr to a private conversation and spoke then of many things to him. The conclusion of the king's remarks was that he set forth before Dagr, what an outstanding person Þórir was, who had provided for them this splendid banquet. Dagr made little comment and agreed it was all true, what the king said. Then the king asked Dagr what faults of character he saw in Þórir. Dagr said he thought Þórir must be of a very good disposition if he was so endowed as appeared to ordinary people's sight. Then the king told him to tell him what he asked, saying that it was his duty to do so. Dagr replies:

'Then, king, you must grant me that I may determine the punishment if I am going to discover his vice.'

The king [301] says that he is unwilling to hand over his judgments to other people, but bade Dagr tell him what he asked. Dagr replies:

'The ruler's word is supreme. This is what I shall suggest as Þórir's vice, which many can be subject to: he is too greedy for money.'

The king replies: 'Is he a thief or a robber?'

Dagr replies: 'It is not that,' he says.

'What is it then?' says the king.

Dagr replies: 'He did this for money: he became a traitor to his lord. He has accepted money from Knútr inn ríki for your head.'

The king replies: 'How can you prove that?'

'He wears on his right arm above the elbow a thick gold ring, which King Knútr has given him, and he lets no one see it.'

After that he and the king break off their conversation, and the king was very angry.

When the king was sitting at table and people had been drinking for a while and the men were very merry—Þórir was waiting on them—then the king had Þórir called to him. He approached the table from in front and raised his arms to grasp the edge of the table.[306]

The king asked: 'How old are you, Þórir?'

'I am eighteen years old,' he says.

The king said: 'You are a big man, Þórir, for your age, and noble-looking.'

Then the king felt round Þórir's right arm and stroked it up round the elbow. Þórir said:

---

[306] *tok hǫndum up á borðit*: In a large hall there would have been two lines of tables down the length of the hall on either side of the central fires, and guests would sit on the edge of the raised floor behind each table. Food and drink would have been served from the front of the tables, which may well have been quite high for someone standing on the central earth floor.

'Touch it gently there. I have a boil on my arm.'
The king held his arm and felt that there was something hard underneath. The king said: 'Have you not heard that I am a physician? So let me see the boil.' Þórir realised that it would do no good to conceal it, then took off the ring and delivered it up. The king asks whether it was the gift of King Knútr. Þórir says that it could not be denied. The king had Þórir taken prisoner and put in irons. Then Kálfr went up and begged for mercy for Þórir and offered money on his behalf. Many people supported this request and offered their own money too. The king was so angry that he would not listen to anything. He says that Þórir must [302] have the very judgment that he had intended for him. Then the king had Þórir killed, and this act gave rise to the greatest resentment both there over Upplǫnd and just as much north over Þrándheimr, where his kin was most numerous. Kálfr took much to heart the execution of this man, for Þórir had been his foster-son in his youth.

CHAPTER ONE HUNDRED AND SIXTY-SIX

Grjótgarðr, Ǫlvir's son and Þórir's brother, he was the elder of the brothers. He was the most noble-looking man and kept a retinue with him. He was also now located in Heiðmǫrk. Now when he heard of the execution of Þórir, then he made attacks wherever he found the king's men or property, living now in forests, now in other hiding places. So when the king heard about these hostilities, then he had watch kept on Grjótgarðr's movements. The king becomes aware of his movements. Grjótgarðr had got a night's lodging not far from where the king was. King Óláfr set out that very night, arriving there at dawn, surrounded the apartment that Grjótgarðr and his men were in. Grjótgarðr and his men awoke at the noise of men and clashing of weapons. They then straight away ran to their weapons. Grjótgarðr ran out into the entrance hall. Grjótgarðr asked who was in charge of the troop. He was told that King Óláfr was come there. Grjótgarðr asked if the king was able to hear what he was saying. The king was standing at the entrance. He says that Grjótgarðr could say whatever he wished.

'I hear what you are saying,' says the king.

Grjótgarðr said:'I will not ask for mercy.'

Then Grjótgarðr ran out, holding a shield above his head and a drawn sword in his hand. It was not very light, and he could not see clearly. He thrust his sword at the king, but Arnbjǫrn Árnason was in line for it. The blow went under [303] his coat of mail and passed into his belly. Arnbjǫrn got his death from it. Grjótgarðr was immediately killed too, and nearly all his troop. After these events the king returned to his journey south to the Vík.

CHAPTER ONE HUNDRED AND SIXTY-SEVEN

Now when King Óláfr got to Túnsberg, then he sent men into all areas, and the king requested men and a levy for himself. His naval strength was now meagre. There were now no ships except farmers' transport boats. But troops gathered to him satisfactorily from the areas round about, but few came from a long distance, and it soon became apparent that the people of the country must now have turned from loyalty to the king. King Óláfr made his troops go east to Gautland, sending now for his ships and the goods that they had left behind in the autumn. But the progress of these men was slow, for it was no easier to travel through Denmark now than in the autumn, since King Knútr had an army out in the spring all over the Danish realm, and had no fewer than twelve hundred ships.

CHAPTER ONE HUNDRED AND SIXTY-EIGHT

The news became known in Norway that Knútr inn ríki was mustering an invincible army in Denmark, and this too, that he was planning to take the whole force to Norway and subject the country there to himself. And when this became known, then the men became the more difficult for King Óláfr to get hold of, and after this he got little from farmers. His men often spoke of this among themselves. Then Sigvatr spoke this:

> 110. England's great king calls out *Skald* I 719
> cohorts, while we gather—
> [304] scant fear I see in our ruler—
> scarce troops and smaller vessels.
> The prospects are poor if his country's
> people leave this king lacking
> troops; money is removing
> men from their constancy.

The king held meetings of his followers, and occasionally an assembly of his whole force, asking men for ideas as to what now seemed best to do.

'There is no point in concealing the fact,' he says, 'that King Knútr is going to come and pay us a visit this summer, and he has a large army, as you will have heard, and we have small forces as things are now to oppose his army, and the people of the country are now not reliable.'

But people responded in various ways to the king's speech, those whom he was addressing. And this is spoken of here, where Sigvatr says:

> 111. One can flee—but jibes will *Skald* I 720
> on our hands be laid—the foes of

the mighty ruler, and pay money;
murmurs of fear come at us.
Each follower must, though the fortune
of friends of the king dwindles,
take care of himself—overturned
treason shall be—far the longest.

[305] CHAPTER ONE HUNDRED AND SIXTY-NINE

That same spring these events took place in Hálogaland, that Hárekr from Þjótta called to mind that Áskell Grankelsson had robbed and beaten his servants. The ship that Hárekr had, of twenty rowing benches, was afloat in front of his farm, with awnings up and the decking in place.[307] He sent round word that he was planning to go south to Þrándheimr. One evening, Hárekr went to his ship with his troop of servants, and had nearly eighty men. They rowed through the night and came, at dawn, to Grankell's farm, surrounded the buildings there, then made an attack on them, afterwards setting fire to the buildings. Grankell was burned inside there and some men with him, though some were killed outside. Altogether thirty men died there. Hárekr went back home after this deed and remained on his farm. Ásmundr was staying with King Óláfr. It was the case with the men that were in Hálogaland, both that no one demanded compensation of Hárekr for this deed, and indeed he never offered any.

CHAPTER ONE HUNDRED AND SEVENTY

Knútr inn ríki mustered his army and made for Limafjǫrðr. And when he was ready, then he sailed from there with his whole force for Norway, travelling fast and not lying near the land on the eastern side of the fiord, then sailed across Foldin and came to land at Agðir, demanding assemblies there. Farmers came down and held assemblies with King Knútr. Knútr was accepted as king across the whole country there. Then he appointed men to stewardships there, and [306] took hostages from farmers. No one spoke in opposition to him. King Óláfr was now in Túnsberg while Knútr's army was travelling round the shore of Foldin. King Knútr travelled north along the coast. Men came to him from the local areas there, and all agreed to be subject to him. King Knútr lay in Eikundasund for some time. There Erlingr Skjálgsson came to him with a large troop. Then he and King Knútr confirmed their friendship again anew. It was among the promises to Erlingr on the part of King Knútr that he was to have all the land to be in charge of between Staðr and Rýgjarbit. After that King Knútr went on his way, and this, in the fewest possible words, is to be told about his journey,

[307] Cf. ch. 108 above.

that he did not stop until he got north to Þrándheimr and made for Niðaróss. He then called an assembly of the eight districts in Þrándheimr. At this assembly Knútr was accepted as king over all Norway. Þórir hundr had left Denmark with King Knútr, and he was present. Hárekr from Þjótta was also come there then. Then he and Þórir were made King Knútr's landed men[308] and confirmed it with oaths. King Knútr gave them great revenues and granted them the trade with Lapps, giving them on top of that great gifts. All landed men who were willing to transfer to him he endowed both with revenues and with money, letting them all have more power than they had had previously.

CHAPTER ONE HUNDRED AND SEVENTY-ONE

King Knútr had now subjected all the land in Norway to himself. Then he had a large assembly of both his own men and the people of the country. Then King Knútr announced this, that he was going to give his kinsman Jarl Hákon all the land that he had won in this expedition to oversee, and at the same time, that he was installing in the high seat beside himself his son Hǫrða-Knútr, and giving him the title of king and with it the realm of Denmark. King Knútr took hostages from all the landed men and [307] important farmers, taking their sons or brothers or other close relatives or the men whom they were most fond of and he thought most suitable. Thus the king strengthened the loyalty of people to him in the ways that have just been stated. As soon as Jarl Hákon had taken over rule in Norway, then his kinsman Einarr þambarskelfir joined fellowship with him. Then he took up all the revenues that he had had previously when jarls ruled the land. King Knútr gave Einarr great gifts and entered into close friendship with him, promising this, that Einarr should be the greatest and noblest of untitled men in Norway as long as the land lay under his sway. But he said as well that he thought Einarr best suited to bear a title of nobility in Norway, if there was no jarl available, or his son Eindriði, because of his descent. Einarr valued these promises greatly, and promised in return his loyalty. Then began anew Einarr's career as leader.

CHAPTER ONE HUNDRED AND SEVENTY-TWO

There was a man called Þórarinn loftunga (Praise-Tongue). He was an Icelandic man by descent, a great poet, and he had been very much among kings and other rulers.[309] He was staying with King Knútr and had composed a

---

[308] See note 52 above.

[309] Little other than this is known of Þórarinn. Verses survive from his poems for Knútr and his son Sveinn. Only these two lines survive of the poem mentioned in this anecdote, called *Hǫfuðlausn* 'Head-Ransom' because of the threat to the poet's life unless he expands it (to at least thirty stanzas, according to the fuller version of the story in *Knýtlinga saga* (*ÍF* XXXV 125)). For other head-ransom stories, see Finlay 2011.

flokkr[310] about him. But when the king found out that Þórarinn had composed a *flokkr* about him, then he got angry and told him to present him with a *drápa*[308] the next day, when the king was sitting at table. If he did not do so, then the king said that Þórarinn would be hanged aloft for his insolence in having composed a runt of a *drápa* about King Knútr. Þórarinn then composed a refrain and inserted it into the poem and added a few stanzas or strophes. This is the refrain:

112. Knútr guards the land as the guardian   *Hǫfuðlausn* 1
of Greece[311] the kingdom of heaven.   *Skald* I 850

[308] King Knútr gave a reward for the poem of fifty marks of silver. This *drápa* is called *Hǫfuðlausn* (Head Ransom). Þórarinn composed another *drápa* about King Knútr, which is called *Tøgdrápa* (Journey Poem (?)). In this *drápa* we are told of these expeditions of King Knútr, when he went from Denmark in the south to Norway, and this is one refrain section:[312]

113. Knútr is, 'neath sun's . . .   *Tøgdrápa* 1
Custom-versed,[313] went   *Fsk* 191–92
my friend, with mighty   *Legendary saga* 168
forces, thither.[314]   *Skald* I 852
The skilful king
steered out from Limafjǫrðr
a fleet, not little,
of land of the otter.[315]

114. Agðir dwellers,   *Tøgdrápa* 2
doughty in battle,   *Fsk* 192
feared the journey   *Legendary saga* 168
of the feeder of the war-swan.[316]   *Skald* I 854
The king's ship was garnished
with gold all over.
Such a sight to me was
more splendid than telling.

[310] See note 191 above.
[311] *Grikklands gætir*: 'guardian of Greece', Christ.
[312] A section of a *drápa* in which the refrain (*stef*) begins in line 1 of the first verse and would have been completed with the last line of the concluding stanza of the section. A full *drápa* would have several such sections. What is quoted here is not a complete refrain section, however, for the second line of the refrain does not appear. Cf. sts 96 and 98–99 above.
[313] *siðnæmr*: 'quick to learn conduct, religious observances'.
[314] *þinnig*: to Norway.
[315] *otrheimr*: 'home of the otter', sea; *otrheims flota* 'a fleet of ocean-going vessels'.
[316] *ǫrbeiðir sigrlana svans*: 'insistent caller out of the swan (raven, eagle) of battle-heaps (corpses)', warrior.

[309] 115. And past Listi
        on the sea by Hádýr
        quickly passed forwards
        coal-black vessels;
        On the side landward
        of the surf-boar,[317] to the south,
        all covered with sea-skis[318]
        was the sound of Eikund.

        Tøgdrápa 3
        Fsk 192
        Legendary saga 168
        Skald I 855

116. And men truce-trusting[319]
        travelled keenly
        by the ancient hill
        of Hjǫrnagli.
        Where sped past Staðr the
        stud of the prow-cliff,[320]
        the arrow-asker's[321]
        journey was not wasted.

        Tøgdrápa 4
        Fsk 309
        Legendary saga 168–70
        Skald I 857

117. Surf-beasts[322] succeeded,
        strong in wind, in
        hauling the slimmed
        hulls,[323] very long, past Stimr.
        So sailed from the south the
        steeds of the cool region[324]
        that north into Nið came
        the needful army-speeder.

        Tøgdrápa 5
        Legendary saga 170
        Skald I 858

[310] 118. Then he bestowed,
        resourceful, the whole of
        Norway on his nephew,[325]
        enabler of glory-Jótar.[326]

        Tøgdrápa 6
        Legendary saga 170
        Skald I 860

[317] *brimgǫltr*: 'sea-boar', kenning for ship; here, by *ofljóst* 'wordplay', a reference to the mountain Hádýr (whose name can be interpreted to mean 'rowlock-animal', i.e. ship).

[318] *sæskíð*: 'sea-ski', ship.

[319] *griðfastir friðmenn*: 'men of peace, secure in truce': retainers who enjoy peace and protection from the king (Knútr).

[320] *stafnklifs stóð*: 'stud of the prow-cliff (wave)', fleet of ships.

[321] *ǫrbeiðir*: 'one who demands arrows', warrior. Contrast note 316 above.

[322] *brimdýr*: 'surf-animals', ships.

[323] *svangs súðir*: 'planks of the empty belly', i.e. the streamlined hulls.

[324] *svalheims valr*: 'horse of the cool world (sea)', ship.

[325] Knútr's sister's son, Hákon Eiríksson.

[326] *njótr veg-Jóta*: 'user, employer of glory-Jótar (glorious inhabitants of Jutland)', king of Denmark, Knútr.

Then he bestowed—
so I declare—on his son[327]
Denmark, the dark halls of
the dale of swans.[328]

Here it says that sight was better than story as regards King Knútr's expedition for him who composed this, for Þórarinn boasts of having been in company with King Knútr when he came to Norway.

CHAPTER ONE HUNDRED AND SEVENTY-THREE

The men that King Óláfr had sent east to Gautland for his ships afterwards took the ships that they thought best, and burned the rest, carrying with them the tackle and the other goods that belonged to the king and his men. They sailed from the east when they learned that King Knútr was gone to the north of Norway, sailing after that from the east through Eyrarsund, so north to the Vík to meet King Óláfr, bringing him his ships. He was now in Túnsberg. So when King Óláfr learned that King Knútr had gone with his troops north along the coast, then King Óláfr made his way [311] into Óslóarfjǫrðr and up into the water that is called Drafn, and he stayed there until King Knútr's army was gone past to the south. And on this journey, by which King Knútr travelled from the north along the coast, he held an assembly in every district, and at every assembly the land was made over to him by oath and hostages were given. He went eastwards over Foldin to Borg and held an assembly there. The land was made over to him by oath there as elsewhere. After that King Knútr went south to Denmark, having got possession of Norway without a battle. He now ruled over three great countries. So says Hallvarðr Háreksblesi when composing about King Knútr:[329]

119. The king bold in battle,	*Knútsdrápa* 6
bark-reddener of the prayer-ship,[330]	
rules alone—peace grows easier—	
over England and Denmark.	

---

[327] Probably Knútr's son Hǫrða-Knútr.
[328] *svana dals dǫkksalar*: 'dark halls of swans' valley (sea)', description of Denmark. This interpretation, which requires emendation of manuscript *-sala* to *-sali*, was proposed by Kock (*NN* §1792). For other possibilities, see *ÍF* 27.
[329] Little is known of Hallvarðr beyond the surviving eight part-stanzas of his poem for Knútr. He is recorded as a poet of Knútr in *Skáldatal*. On his nickname see index.
[330] *bœna nǫkkva barkrjóðr*: 'reddener of the bark, covering (mailcoat) of the ship of prayer (breast)', warrior.

And the noise-Freyr of armour[331]
under him has forced Norway;
he, war-keen, quells the hunger
of hawks of the Leikn of spear-points.[332]

[312] CHAPTER ONE HUNDRED AND SEVENTY-FOUR

King Óláfr took his ships out to Túnsberg as soon as he heard that King Knútr was gone south to Denmark. Then he got ready to set out with those troops who were willing to follow him, and he now had thirteen ships. After that he sailed out along the Vík, and he got little of money and similarly of men, except for those who followed him who lived on islands or outlying headlands. The king did not now go inland, taking only whatever of money or men that lay in his path. He found that the land was now defected from him. He now travelled according to what wind there was. It was the beginning of winter. Their progress was rather slow. They lay in Sóleyjar for a very long time and there heard news from merchants coming from the north of the country. The king was now told that Erlingr Skjálgsson had a great gathering of troops at Jaðarr, his warship was lying all ready off the coast together with a large number of other ships owned by farmers. These were cruisers and fishing boats and large rowing boats. The king made his way from the east with his troops and lay for a while in Eikundarsund. Then each got wind of the other. Erlingr was now gathering men as quickly as he could.

CHAPTER ONE HUNDRED AND SEVENTY-FIVE

Thomas's day[333] before Yule immediately at dawn the king sailed out of the harbour. There was then a very favourable wind, rather a keen one. He then sailed north along the coast of Jaðarr. The weather was rather wet and there was some drifting fog. Immediately intelligence travelled overland across Jaðarr, as the king sailed along the coast. So when Erlingr realised this, that the king was sailing from the east, then he had all his troops summoned [313] to the ships by horn call. Then all the people rushed to the ships and prepared for battle. So the king's ship was quickly carried up north past Jaðarr. Then he made his way in close to the shore, intending to lay his course into the fiords and get himself men and money there. Erlingr sailed after him and had a host of men and a large number of ships. Their ships were swift-gliding, as they had nothing on board but men and weapons. Now Erlingr's warship travelled much faster than his other ships. Now he had the sail furled and

[331] *malma jalm-Freyr*: 'Freyr (a god) of the noise of weapons (battle)', warrior.

[332] *odda Leiknar haukr*: 'hawk of the Leikn (giantess) of spear-points (valkyrie)', raven, eagle.

[333] The Feast of St Thomas the Apostle, 21st December.

waited for his troops. Now King Óláfr saw that Erlingr and his followers were gaining on him fast, for the king's ships were very heavy laden and waterlogged, since they had been afloat on the sea the whole summer and the autumn and the winter up until then. He saw that he was bound to be very much outnumbered if he met Erlingr's troops all at once. Then he had the message passed from ship to ship that men were to let the sails down and rather slowly, but to take off the reefing strings, and this was done. Erlingr and his men noticed this. Then Erlingr called out and gave orders to his troops, telling them to sail faster.

'Do you see,' he says, 'that now their sails are being lowered, and they are getting away from us.'

He then had the sail unfurled on his warship. It soon moved forward.

CHAPTER ONE HUNDRED AND SEVENTY-SIX

King Óláfr made his way into Bókn. Then they lost sight of each other. After that the king ordered them to lower their sails and row forward into a narrow sound that lay there. Then they brought their ships together there. A rocky headland lay round them. His men were now all armed. Erlingr now sailed up to the sound and the first thing they knew was that an army was lying before them, and they [314] could see that the king's men were rowing all their ships at once at them. Erlingr and his men rushed down their sail and snatched up their weapons. But the king's army was lying on all sides round his ship. A battle was joined there and it was of the keenest. Now the slaughter soon affected Erlingr's troops. Erlingr stood on the raised deck of his ship. He had a helmet on his head and a shield before him, sword in hand.

The poet Sigvatr had stayed behind in the Vík and heard the news of these events there. But Sigvatr was a very great friend of Erlingr and had received gifts from him and stayed with him. Sigvatr composed a *flokkr* about the fall of Erlingr, and it contains this stanza:

| 120. | Erlingr ordered the launching of the oak ship, he who reddened the eagle's pale foot, it is beyond doubt, against the ruler. Thus then among the monarch's mighty host his warship lay alongside others; lusty men fought with swords there. | *Flokkr on Erlingr Skjálgss.* 1 *Skald* I 631 |

Now Erlingr's troops began to fall, and when this started and a way became clear to board the warship, then each man fell at his station. The king himself pressed forward hard. So says Sigvatr:

121. The fierce lord cut down fighters;   *Flokkr on Erlingr Skjálgss.* 2
furious, he walked over warships.   *Skald* I 632
Planks were piled tight with corpses;
the campaign off Tungur was heavy.
The prince bloodied the planks'
plain[334] north of broad Jaðarr.
Blood flowed—the famous ruler
fought—warm into the ocean.

Erlingr's men fell so completely that not a single man was standing up on the warship except him alone. It was the case both that men made little appeal for quarter, and also they got none, even if they did appeal; and they could not turn in flight, because ships were lying all round the warship. It is truly said that no man sought to flee. Sigvatr says further:

122. All fallen was Erlingr's—   *Flokkr on Erlingr Skjálgss.* 3
young, to the north of Tungur   *Skald* I 633
the king cleared the warship—
crew off Bókn's shoreline.
Alone the son of Skjálgr
stood for long, friendless,
hardy, on the afterdeck
of his empty ship, sinless.

Now an attack was made upon Erlingr both from the forward position[335] and from other ships. There was a lot of space on the raised deck, and it rose very high up above the other ships, and it could not be reached by anything except missiles and to some extent by spear thrusts, and he struck all that away from himself. Erlingr defended himself so nobly that no man [316] had seen anything to match it, one man having stood so long in the face of attack from so many men, never seeking to escape or asking for quarter. So says Sigvatr:

123. From king's men no quarter   *Flokkr on Erlingr Skjálgss.* 4
he claimed, tough-minded avenger   *Skald* I 634
of Skjálgr, though the storms of
the skerry of the axe[336] did not slacken.
And after will come no greater
over-bold spear-respecter[337]

---

[334] *borðvǫllr*: 'plain of (ships') planks', i.e. the sea.

[335] The *fyrirrúm* was the position immediately in front of the raised deck at the stern of a longship (where the steersman or captain normally stood).

[336] *gýgjar skers skúr*: 'shower of the skerry of the axe (shield)', battle.

[337] *geirs virðir*: 'one who evaluates the spear', warrior.

to the sea-washed wide base of
the warding vessel of the tempest.[338]

King Óláfr then made his way aft to the forward position and saw what Erlingr was doing. The king then addressed him, saying this:
'Forward are you facing today, Erlingr.'
He replies: 'Face to face shall eagles claw each other.'
Sigvatr quotes these words:

[317]
124. Face to face, said Erlingr, who   *Flokkr on Erlingr Skjálgsson* 5
for long well kept the country,   *Skald* I 636
eager—his land-watch not faltering—
eagles must claw each other,
when Ǫleifr there at Útsteinn—
earlier he was ready
to do battle—during the fighting
he addressed with true words.

Then said the king: 'Will you submit, Erlingr?'
'I will,' he says.

Then he took the helmet off his head and laid down his sword and shield and went forward into the forward position. The king thrust with the point of his axe at his cheek, saying:
'The traitor to his lord must be marked.'

Then Áslákr Fitjaskalli leapt at him and struck with his axe at Erlingr's head so that it stuck down in the brain. This was an immediate death wound. Erlingr lost his life by it. Then spoke King Óláfr to Áslákr:
'You are the most wretched of men in your striking![339] Now you have struck Norway from my hand.'

Áslákr says: 'It is bad, then, king, if you are harmed by this blow. I thought I was striking Norway into your hand. But if I have done you harm, king, and you feel annoyed at this deed, then I shall be in a bad way, for I shall have so many men's resentment and hatred for this deed that then I shall rather need to have your support and friendship.'

The king says that he should have it.

Afterwards the king told every man to go on board his ship and prepare for departure as quickly as possible.

'We shall,' he says, 'not plunder these dead bodies. Both sides are to keep [318] what they have got.'

Men then went back to their ships and got ready as quickly as they could. So when they were ready, then ships glided into the sound from the south, the

---

[338] *glyggs varðkeri víðbotn*: 'wide base of the guarding vessel (sky) of the storm', earth.
[339] *Hǫgg þú allra manna armastr!*, literally 'Strike thou [as] the most miserable of all men', perhaps equivalent to 'Damn you for striking that blow!'

troops of farmers. Then it was as it frequently turns out, that though a great host gathers, when men receive a great reverse and lose their leader, men lose all their courage, and are then without leadership. None of Erlingr's sons were there. Nothing came of the farmers' attacking, and the king sailed north on his way, while the farmers took Erlingr's body and laid it out and carried it home to Sóli, likewise all the dead that had fallen there. And Erlingr was very greatly mourned, and it has been men's judgment that Erlingr Skjálgsson has been the noblest and most powerful man in Norway, of those that did not bear a higher title of rank. The poet Sigvatr also composed this:

125. Erlingr fell, and the heir of rulers,   *Flokkr on Erlingr Skjálgss.* 6
all-powerful, brought this   *Skald* I 637
about—no better man will
abide death—through his victory.
I know of no other
able to maintain his
standing life-long, though he lost his
life so very early.

Then he also says that Áslákr had given rise to kin-slaying and quite senselessly:

126. Crime against kindred   *Flokkr on Erlingr Skjálgss.* 7
is increased by Áslákr;   *Skald* I 639

[319]   the Hǫrðar's land's guard is laid
low; few should rouse such conflict.
One cannot deny killings
of kin; let them look to—
families must refrain from
fury—the old sayings.

CHAPTER ONE HUNDRED AND SEVENTY-SEVEN

Erlingr's sons were some of them north in Þrándheimr with Jarl Hákon, and some of them north in Hǫrðaland, some in the inland fiords, and they were in these places mustering troops. But when the fall of Erlingr became known, then with the story came a demand for a levy from the east over Agðir and over Rogaland and Hǫrðaland. An army was there called out and it was a very great host, and this army travelled to the north with Erlingr's sons in pursuit of King Óláfr. When King Óláfr went from the battle between him and Erlingr, he sailed north through the sounds, and the day was now far spent. People say that then he composed this verse:[340]

---

[340] This is the only stanza in *Hkr* attributed to Óláfr helgi, and the attribution here ('people say . . .') and in other sources may indicate scepticism of his authorship. Finnur Jónsson ascribes 11 verses altogether to Óláfr; *Skald* credits him with nine.

127. Hardly will the pale fellow[341]   *Fsk* 196
    be pleased tonight in Jaðarr;   *Legendary saga* 158–59
    raven eats corpse acquired;[342]   *Skald* I 527
    we caused Gunnr's clamour.[343]
[320]   Robbing me thus wrought for him—
    enraged, I walked over warships—[344]
    land causes men's killing—
    a quite evil outcome.

Afterwards the king travelled north along the coast with his troops. He heard the whole truth about the gathering of farmers. There were now with King Óláfr many landed men. All the sons of Árni were there. Bjarni Gullbrárskáld (Gullbrá's poet) speaks of these things in the poem that he composed about Kálfr Árnason:[345]

128. You were east, where Haraldr's   *Kálfsflokkr* 1
    heir, weapon-bold, commanded   *Fsk* 195 (1st half)
    conflict—Kálfr, men learn of   *Skald* I 879
    your courage—off Bókn itself.
[321]   For Gríðr's mount[346] you gathered
    goodly Yule provisions;
    You were seen at the slate stones'
    and spears' meeting[347] foremost.

129. Men fared ill in the onslaughts;   *Kálfsflokkr* 2
    Erlingr there was taken.   *Fsk* 196 (ll. 3–6)

---

[341] *halr enn hvíti*: a stereotyped allusion to a coward. The future tense may suggest that it refers to one of Erlingr's sons.

[342] *hrafn etr af ná getnum*: cf. *Hkr* I, st. 143, attributed to Þorleifr jarlsskáld: *etr hrafn af ná getnum*.

[343] *gný Gunnar*: 'noise of Gunnr (a valkyrie)', battle.

[344] *ek gekk reiðr of skeiðar*: cf. Sigvatr's stanza, 121 above: *reiðr gekk hann of skeiðar*.

[345] Bjarni gullbrárskáld is known only as the poet of *Kálfsflokkr*, of which seven stanzas survive in *Hkr* and other Kings' sagas and one in *Orkneyinga saga*. The poem is named in *Hkr* III (*Magnúss saga ins góða*, ch. 14). It is unusual as a poem in honour not of a king, but of his opponent, Kálfr Árnason; and also in covering events over a span of many years, from Erlingr's death in 1027–28 to the Battle of Rauðabjǫrg in 1045, while still being addressed to the poem's subject. Bjarni is identified with the Bjarni Hallbjarnarson from Laxárdalr in Skagafjǫrðr, northern Iceland, named in *Þorgríms þáttr Hallasonar* (Hulda-Hrokkinskinna), which refers to his poem for Kálfr.

[346] *Gríðar sóti*: 'the mount of Gríðr (giantesses ride on wolves)' wolf (cf. *Gylf* 46/26); 'provisions for the Yule feast' refers to the wolf's food, carrion.

[347] *flettugrjóts ok spjóta fundr*: 'meeting of split stones (i.e. probably pieces of slate or flint, used as missiles) and spears', battle.

> Black boards advanced through *Skald* I 880
> blood to the north of Útsteinn.
> It is clear: of his country
> the king lost possession,
> lands relinquished to the Egðir;
> larger I heard their force was.

King Óláfr went on until he came north past Staðr, and he made for Hereyjar and learned there this news, that Jarl Hákon had a large force in Þrándheimr. After this the king sought the views of his men. Kálfr Árnason was strongly in favour of making for Þrándheimr and fighting Jarl Hákon, even though the odds were great. Many others supported this plan, but some were against it. Then it was put to the king's decision.

[322] CHAPTER ONE HUNDRED AND SEVENTY-EIGHT

Afterwards King Óláfr sailed in to Steinavágr and lay there during the night. But Áslákr Fitjaskalli took his ship in to Borgund. He stayed there for the night. Vígleikr Árnason was already there. So in the morning, when Áslákr was about to go to his ship, then Vígleikr made an attack on him, wanting to avenge Erlingr. Áslákr fell there. Then men came to the king from Frekeyjarsund in the north, followers of his who had been staying at home during the summer, and told the king the news that Jarl Hákon and many landed men with him were come the evening before to Frekeyjarsund with large numbers of men.

'And they want to take your life, king, and those of your followers, if it is within their power.'

So the king sent some of his men up onto a mountain that lies there. And when they got up onto the mountain, then they saw to the north towards Bjarney that a large troop was travelling from the north with many ships, and they went back down and tell the king that the army was travelling from the north. But the king was lying there with twelve ships. After this he had a horn blown and the awnings came down off his ships, and they took to the oars. And when they were all ready and they were moving out of the harbour, then the farmers' host travelled from the north round Þrjótshverfi and they had twenty-five ships. Then the king made his way round the inside of Nyrfi and in past Hundsver. But when King Óláfr came level with Borgund, then a ship went out towards him that had been Áslákr's. And when they met King Óláfr, then they told their news, that Vígleikr Árnason had taken the life of Áslákr Fitjaskalli for his having killed Erlingr Skjálgsson. The king was displeased at this news, and yet could not delay his journey because of the hostilities, and he travelled in then past Vegsund and past Skot. Then troops left him. [323] Kálfr Árnason parted from him and many other landed men and masters of ships too, and they made their way towards the jarl. But King Óláfr continued his journey and did not stop until he came into Toðarfjǫrðr, and he came to land in Valldalr and disembarked from his ships, having there five ships, and beached them and put into store sails and tackle. After that he put up his land tent on the spit of land that is called Sult, and there are there fine fields, and he raised a cross nearby on the spit. Now a farmer lived on Mœrin called Brúsi, and he was the head man over the valley. After this Brúsi came down and many other farmers too to see King Óláfr and welcomed him, as was proper, and he responded kindly to their welcome. Then the king asked if there was a possible route there up over land from the valley and to Lesjar. Brusi tells him that there was a heap of fallen stones in the valley that is called Skerfsurð.

'And there it is impassable both for men and horses.'

King Óláfr answered him: 'An attempt will have to be risked now, farmer. Let it turn out as God wills. So come here now in the morning with your draught animals and yourselves, and after that let us see how things are when we come to the heap of stones, whether we can see some scheme to get over with horses or men.'

CHAPTER ONE HUNDRED AND SEVENTY-NINE

So when day came, then the farmers went down with their draught animals, as the king had told them to. They transport them with the animals their goods and clothes, while all the men walked, as did the king himself. And he walked to where the place called Krossbrekka is and rested, when he got to the slope, and sat there [324] for a while and looked down into the fiord and said:

'It is a difficult journey they have imposed upon me, my landed men, who have now changed their allegiance, when they had for a while been my trusted friends.'

Two crosses now stand there on the slope where the king sat. The king then climbed on the back of one of the horses and rode up along the valley and did not stop until they got to the heap of stones. Then the king enquired of Brúsi whether there were sheds of any kind there that they could stay in. He said there were. So the king put up his land tent and stayed there the night. And then in the morning the king told them to go to the heap of stones and try whether they could find a way over the stones. They went up to it, while the king sat back at the tent. But in the evening they came back, the king's followers and the farmers, insisting that they had had a lot of difficulty and made no progress, and saying that never would a way over be found or constructed. And they were there another night, and the king was at his prayers all night. And when the king noticed that it was getting light, then he told men to go to the heap of stones and try again whether they could find a way over it. They went, but reluctantly, saying that they would achieve nothing. But when they were gone, then the man who was in charge of the provisions came to the king and says that there was no more food than two cattle carcases of meat.

'But you have four hundred of your followers and a hundred farmers.'

Then the king said that he was to bring out all the pots and put some of the meat into each pot, and this was done. So the king went up and made the sign of the cross over them and told them to cook the meal. But the king went to Skerfsurð, where they were supposed to be clearing the way. And when the king got there, then they were all sitting down and were tired from their toil. Then said Brúsi:

'I told you, king, and you would not believe me, [325] that it was not possible to achieve anything with this pile of stones.'

After this the king laid down his cloak, saying that they were all to go and try again, and they did so. And now twenty men moved stones where they wanted, which previously a hundred men could no way move, and the way was cleared by midday so that it was passable both by men and by horses with packs just as well as on smooth ground. Afterwards the king went back down to where their food was, where it is now known as Óláfr's Cave. There is also a spring there near the cave, and the king washed himself in it. And if people's livestock in the valley get sick and drink from the water in it then they recover from the sicknesses.

Afterwards the king went to eat, as did they all. And when the king had eaten, then he enquired whether there were any shielings in the valley up from the heap of stones and near the mountain, where they might stay the night. But Brúsi says:

'There are shielings, that are called Grœningar, and no one can stay in them at night because of the presence of trolls and noxious beings that are there near the shieling.'

After this the king told them that they must start off on their journey, saying that he wanted to stay the night there at the shieling. Then the man who was in charge of the provisions came to him and says that there is a huge amount of provisions.

'And I don't know where they are come from.'

The king thanks God for what He had sent, and he had loads of food packed for the farmers who were going down along the valley.

So the king stayed at the shieling overnight. But at midnight, when men were asleep, then from the milking pen outside came the sound of a hideous voice saying:

'King Óláfr's prayers are burning me so much,' said this creature, 'that I cannot now stay in my home, and I have now to flee and never come to this milking pen again.'

And in the morning, when men awoke, then the king went to the mountain and said to Brúsi:

'A farm [326] shall now be built here, and the farmer who lives here will always have means, and never shall corn here freeze though it freeze both above the farm and below.'

Then King Óláfr went over the mountain and came down in Einbúi and stayed there the night. King Óláfr had now been king in Norway fifteen winters including the winter when both he and Jarl Sveinn were in the country, and the one which now for a while has been told about and had now passed beyond Yule, when he left his ships and went up inland, as has just been told. This aspect of his kingship was first written down by the priest Ari Þorgilsson, who both was truthful, had a good memory, and lived to such an age that he remembered the people and had received accounts from them, who were old enough so that as far as their age was concerned they could remember these events, as he himself has said in his books, naming the people involved from whom he had got information. But this is common knowledge, that Óláfr was fifteen years king over Norway before he fell, and those who say this count Jarl Sveinn as having been ruler the winter that he was last in the country, for Óláfr was after that king fifteen winters while he was alive.

CHAPTER ONE HUNDRED AND EIGHTY

After King Óláfr had been overnight at Lesjar, then he travelled with his troops day after day, first to Guðbrandsdalar, and from there out to Heiðmǫrk. It then became apparent who his friends were, for they were now following him, while those now abandoned him who had served him with less devotion, and some switched to enmity and absolute hostility, as became clear. This applied [327] particularly to many people of Upplǫnd who had been ill-pleased by the execution of Þórir, as was said above. King Óláfr gave leave to go home to many people who had farms and children to be concerned about, for these people felt it was uncertain what mercy would be shown to the households of those men who left the country with the king. The king now revealed to his friends that it was his intention to leave the country, going first east into the realm of the Svíar, and then deciding where he planned to go or to turn to after that, but asking his friends to assume that he would be planning to try to get back to the country and to his kingship if God granted him long enough life, saying that it was his feeling that all the people in Norway would return to their allegiance to him.

'But I would think,' he says, 'that Jarl Hákon will have power over Norway for a short time, and many people will not find that strange, for Jarl Hákon has in the past had little luck against me. But this few people will believe, though I say what my feeling is will happen to Knútr inn ríki, that he will be dead after the space of a few years and all his power will be gone, and there will be no revival of his line if things go as my words indicate.'

So when the king concluded his speech, then men set out on their way. The king turned with the troops that were following him east to Eiðaskógr. There were now with him Queen Ástríðr, their daughter Úlfhildr, King Óláfr's son Magnús, Rǫgnvaldr Brúsason, Árni's sons Þorbergr, Finnr, Árni and still other landed men. He had choice troops. Bjǫrn the Marshal got leave to go home. He did go home too, to his estate, and many other friends of the king went back to their dwellings with his permission. The king requested that they should let him know if anything happened in the country which it would be important for him to know. Then the king went on his way.

[328] CHAPTER ONE HUNDRED AND EIGHTY-ONE

There is this to tell about King Óláfr's journey, that he travelled first out of Norway east through Eiðaskógr to Vermaland and then out to Vatsbú and from there through the forest as the road lies, and came out in Næríki. There he found a powerful and wealthy man called Sigtryggr. His son was called Ívarr, who later became a fine person. There King Óláfr stayed the spring with Sigtryggr. But when summer came, then the king set out on his journey and got himself a ship. He travelled through the summer and did not stop until he came east to Garðaríki to see King Jarizleifr and Queen Ingigerðr. Queen Ástríðr and the king's daughter Úlfhildr remained behind in Svíþjóð, but the king took east with him his son Magnús. King Jarizleifr welcomed King Óláfr and invited him to stay with him and to have land there to provide such maintenance as he needed to keep his troops on. King Óláfr accepted this and stayed there.

It is said that King Óláfr was of pure life and diligent in prayer to God during the whole of his life, but after he found that his power was diminishing, and his adversaries were getting more powerful, then he put all his effort into carrying out the service of God. It did not keep him then from other concerns or from the work that he had previously had in hand, for he had during the time that he held the kingdom laboured at what he felt was the most beneficial, first to bring peace to the country and free it from the oppression of foreign rulers, and after that to convert the people of the country to the true faith and as well to establish laws and regulations, and this part he did in the interest of justice in judgment to chastise those who wanted to do wrong. It had been a great custom in Norway for sons of landed men or powerful farmers to go on warships and so win wealth for themselves, and they would go freebooting both abroad and within the country. But after King Óláfr took over the kingdom, then he brought peace [329] to his land by abolishing all plundering in that country. And if it was possible to inflict punishment on them, then he insisted that no other should be inflicted but loss of life or limbs. Neither people's entreaties nor offerings of money would avail them. So says the poet Sigvatr:

130.	Those practising plunder proffered red gold often to the proud prince to buy off punishment; the king refused it. He had a sword used for haircuts—[348] that's how to guard robbed country— men were seen to suffer sanctions plain for robbery.	*Erfidrápa Óláfs helga* 4 *Skald* I 669
131.	The very fine king who crippled the clan of thieves and filchers— so he slashed thievery— succoured wolves chiefly. Kind, the king caused each quick thief to be lacking feet and—so peace improved in the prince's land—hands also.	*Erfidrápa Óláfs helga* 5 *Skald* I 671
[330] 132.	That he had the hair of hundredfold vikings, the country's guard, shorn with sharp weapons, showed his power clearly. He made many gains happen, Magnús's generous father; Most victories, I avow, furthered the advance of Óleifr inn digri.	*Erfidrápa Óláfs helga* 6 *Skald* I 672

He inflicted the same punishment on powerful and humble, though this seemed to landed men presumptuous, and they became filled with hostility in response, when they lost their kinsmen because of the king's righteous judgment, even though they were guilty of the charge. The cause of the rebellion that the people of the country raised against King Óláfr was that they could not put up with his justice, but he would rather lose his position than depart from righteous judgment. And the charge against him that he was mean with money towards his men was not well founded. He was most generous to his friends. But it did happen that when men started hostilities against him, people found him harsh and severe in his punishments, while King Knútr offered huge amounts

---

[348] A euphemism for beheading.

of money—though great leaders were deceived when he offered each of them honour and power—and there was this, too, that people were eager in Norway to welcome Jarl Hákon, for he had already been a most popular man with the people of the country before when he ruled the land.

[331] CHAPTER ONE HUNDRED AND EIGHTY-TWO

Jarl Hákon had taken his troops out of Þrándheimr and gone to meet King Óláfr south in Mœrr, as was written above. And when the king made his way into the fiords, then the jarl pursued him there. Then there came to meet him Kálfr Árnason and many others of those men who had parted from King Óláfr. Kálfr was welcomed there. After that the jarl made his way in to where King Óláfr had beached his ships, in Toðarfjǫrðr in Valldalr. The jarl took charge of the ships that had been the king's. The jarl had the ships launched and fitted out. Men were chosen by lot to command these ships. There was a man with the jarl who is named Jǫkull, an Icelandic man, son of Bárðr Jǫkulsson of Vatsdalr. Jǫkull got to command the Visundr, which King Óláfr had had. Jǫkull composed this verse:

133.	My lot was—the lady will hardly	*Fsk* 197
	learn that I am daunted—	*Skald* I 813
	to steer the ship from Sult—I expect a	
	storm on the bow-plain's reindeer,[349]	
	that owned by Ǫleifr, slopes of the flame of	
	the yew-bow's rest[350]—the monarch	
	himself this summer had victory	
	stolen from him—inn digri.	

To say here briefly what happened a long time afterwards, Jǫkull came up against King Óláfr's troops in Gotland and was captured, and the king had him taken to be executed, [332] and a twig was twisted in his hair and a man held it. Jǫkull sat on a sort of bank. Then a man tried to behead him. But when he heard the whistle of the axe, he straightened up, and the blow landed on his head, and it was a deep wound. The king saw that it was a death wound. The king then told them to leave him be. Jǫkull sat up and uttered a verse:

134.	Wounds smart with weariness;	*Skald* I 815
	I was often suited better.	
	An injury is on me that spurted	
	eager crimson liquid.	

[349] *hlýrvangs hreinn*: 'reindeer of the bow-plain (sea)', ship.

[350] *funa ýstéttar kleifar*: 'slopes (i.e. lands) of the flame (gold) of the yew-bow's stand (hand or arm)', women (vocative).

My gore gushed out of this
gash. I get used to endurance.
The honoured helm-noble ruler
hurls his anger at me.

Then Jǫkull died.

CHAPTER ONE HUNDRED AND EIGHTY-THREE

Kálfr Árnason went with Jarl Hákon north to Þrándheimr, and the jarl invited him to stay with him and enter his service. Kálfr says that he would first go in to Egg to his estate and after that make up his mind. Kálfr did so. But when he got home, then he soon realised that his wife Sigríðr was rather on her high horse and was reckoning up [333] her grievances that she claimed she had against King Óláfr, first of all, that he had had her husband Ǫlvir killed.

'And now on top of that,' she says, 'my two sons. And you, Kálfr, were present at their killing, and that is the last thing I should have expected of you.'

Kálfr says that it was much against his will that Þórir was deprived of life. 'I offered,' he says, 'money on his behalf. And when Grjótgarðr was killed, I lost my brother Arnbjǫrn.'

She says: 'That is good, that you got that from the king, since it may be that you will avenge him, though you will not avenge my grievances. You saw, when your foster-son Þórir was killed, how highly the king regarded you then.'

She continually brought up these grievances before Kálfr. Kálfr often replied crossly, and yet in the end it came about that he was persuaded by her arguments and then promised to submit to the jarl if the jarl would increase his revenues. Sigríðr sent word to the jarl and had him told what stage had been reached in Kálfr's position. So when the jarl realised this, then he sent word to Kálfr that he was to come out to the town to see the jarl. Kálfr did not neglect to make this journey, and went a little later out to Niðaróss and met Jarl Hákon there, was well received there, and he and the jarl had a talk together. Everything was agreed between them, and they decided that Kálfr was to enter the jarl's service and received great revenues from him. Afterwards Kálfr returned home to his estate. He had now most of the oversight everywhere within Þrándheimr. So as soon as spring came, Kálfr got ready a ship that he had, and as soon as he had finished, then he sailed out to sea and took the ship west to England, for he had heard this of King Knútr, that he was sailing early in the spring from Denmark west to England. By now King Knútr had given the jarldom in Denmark to Þorkell hávi's (the Tall's) son Haraldr. Kálfr Árnason went to see King Knútr as soon as he got to England. So says Bjarni Gullbrárskáld:

[334] 135. The great ruler set unswervingly   *Kálfsflokkr* 3
his stem[351] to carve the sea eastwards;   *Skald* I 882

[351] *stál*: 'stem-post', the top part of the ship's prow.

> Haraldr's battle-keen brother[352]
> was bound to seek out Garðar.
> But of men's actions   *Fsk* 198
> I am not prone to gather
> false stories; after your severance
> straight to Knútr you headed.

So when Kálfr met King Knútr then the king gave him an extraordinarily warm welcome and took him aside to talk to him. Part of what King Knútr said to him was that he asked Kálfr to commit himself to raising a rebellion against Óláfr inn digri, if he tried to return to the country.

'And I shall,' says the king, 'then give you a jarldom and let you then rule Norway. But my kinsman Hákon shall come to me, and that is the most suitable thing for him, for he is such a sincere person that I do not think he would shoot a single shaft against King Óláfr if they met.'

Kálfr listened to what King Knútr said, and he became eager for the honour. This plan was settled between the king and Kálfr. Kálfr then prepared to return home, and at parting King Knútr gave him splendid gifts. The poet Bjarni mentions this:

[335]

> 136. You owe the lord of England,   *Kálfsflokkr* 4
> jarl's offspring bold in battle,   *Skald* I 883
> thanks for gifts; you got your case to
> progress well forthwith.
> Before you left the west, land was—   *Fsk* 199
> delay happened—found for you,
> said the lord of London;
> your life is not meagre.

After this Kálfr went back to Norway and came home to his estate.

CHAPTER ONE HUNDRED AND EIGHTY-FOUR

Jarl Hákon that summer went out of the country and west to England, and when he got there, then King Knútr welcomed him. The jarl had a fiancée there in England, and he was going to conclude this match and was planning to hold his wedding in Norway, but was procuring the provisions for it in England that he thought most difficult to obtain in Norway. The jarl prepared for his journey home in the autumn, and was ready rather late. He sailed out to sea when he was ready, and of his journey there is this to relate, that the ship was lost and not a soul survived. But it is reported by some that the ship

---

[352] Óláfr, (half-)brother of Haraldr Sigurðsson, who may have been king when the poem was composed.

was seen north off Katanes one evening in a great storm, and the wind stood out into Péttlandsfjǫrðr. They say this, those who are willing to stand by this account, that the ship must have been carried into the whirlpool. But what is known for certain is that Jarl Hákon was lost at sea and nothing reached land that was on that ship. That same autumn [336] merchants carried the report that was circulating round the country, that it was thought that the jarl was lost. But what everyone knew was that he did not get to Norway that autumn, and the country was now without a ruler.

CHAPTER ONE HUNDRED AND EIGHTY-FIVE

Bjǫrn the Marshal remained at home on his estate after he had parted from King Óláfr. Bjǫrn was famous, and it became widely known that he was keeping out of things. Jarl Hákon heard this and so did others of the ruling class. After this they sent men and messages to Bjǫrn. And when the messengers fulfilled their errand, then Bjǫrn welcomed them. Afterwards he called the messengers to a private talk with him and asked them about their business, and the one that was their leader spoke, bringing King Knútr's and Jarl Hákon's greeting, and that of still other rulers.

'And this too,' he says, 'that King Knútr has heard great reports of you and also of how you have followed Óláfr digri for a long time and been a great enemy of King Knútr, and he thinks this is a shame, because he would like to be your friend as he is of all other worthy men, whenever you wish to change from being his enemy. And now the only thing for you to do is to turn there for security and friendship where it is most abundantly to be found, and which [337] everyone in the northern part of the world finds it an honour to have. You who have followed King Óláfr must consider this, how he has now abandoned you. You are all without protection from King Knútr and his men, and you harried his land last summer and killed his friends. Then there is this to take into account, that the king is offering his friendship, and it would be more fitting for you to be begging or offering money for it.'

So when he had finished his speech, then Bjǫrn answers, saying this:

'I want now to stay quietly at home on my estate and not serve rulers.'

The messenger replies: 'Men like you are men for kings. I can tell you this, that you have two choices available: the one is to leave your property as an outlaw, as your comrade Óláfr has now done. The other choice is this, which may now seem preferable, to accept King Knútr's and Jarl Hákon's friendship and become one of their men and give your word on this, and take here your pay.'

He poured out English silver from a great purse. Bjǫrn was a man with a great love of money, and he was very worried and stayed silent when he saw the money, wondering now to himself what to decide, thinking it a hard thing to lose his property, while considering it uncertain whether King Óláfr's recovery would ever take place in Norway. So when the messenger saw that Bjǫrn's mind was attracted by the money, then he threw down two thick gold rings, saying:

'Take this money now, Bjǫrn, and swear the oath. I promise you this, that this money is insignificant compared to what you will receive, if you go to King Knútr's and see him.'

And by the amount of the money and the fair promises and the great gifts he was now drawn to the love of money, took up the money and submitted after this to allegiance and oaths of fidelity to King Knútr and Jarl Hákon. Then the messengers went away.

[338] CHAPTER ONE HUNDRED AND EIGHTY-SIX

Bjǫrn the Marshal heard the reports which said that Jarl Hákon had perished. Then he changed his mind, regretting that he had broken faith with King Óláfr. He felt he was now free from the particular agreements which he had made in respect of homage to Jarl Hákon. Bjǫrn believed there was now arising some prospect of resurrecting King Óláfr's rule if he came to Norway, now that it was without a ruler there to oppose him. Bjǫrn then got ready to leave quickly, taking a few men with him, travelled on his way after that day and night, on horseback where it was possible, by ship where there was an opportunity, not stopping his journey until he came in the winter at Yule east into Garðaríki and found King Óláfr, and the king was very happy when Bjǫrn met him. The king then asked about all the news from the north from Norway. Bjǫrn says that the jarl had perished and the country was now without a ruler. People were pleased at this news, those who had accompanied King Óláfr out of Norway and had had possessions and kinsmen and friends there, and felt deeply homesick to go back. Bjǫrn told much other news from Norway that he was interested to hear. Then the king asked about his friends, how well they were keeping faith with him. Bjǫrn said it varied. After this Bjǫrn got up and fell at the feet of the king and embraced his legs and said:

'Everything at God's mercy and yours, king. I have taken money from Knútr's men and sworn oaths of loyalty to them, but now I want to follow you and not part from you as long as we both shall live.'

The king replies: 'Stand up quickly, Bjǫrn. You shall be reconciled with me. Atone for it to God. I realise this, that there must be few in Norway now who are keeping their loyalty to me, when such as you fail to. It is also true that many people are finding being there a great problem when [339] I am far away, and they have to face the hostility of my enemies.'

Bjǫrn tells the king about who were most prominent in undertaking to start a rebellion against the king and his men. He named in this context the sons of Erlingr at Jaðarr and others of their family, Einarr þambarskelfir, Kálfr Árnason, Þórir hundr, Hárekr from Þjótta.

CHAPTER ONE HUNDRED AND EIGHTY-SEVEN

After King Óláfr was come to Garðaríki, he had great anxiety and pondered what course he should take. King Jarizleifr and Queen Ingigerðr invited King Óláfr to stay with them and to take over the realm that is called Vúlgáríá, and this is one part of Garðaríki, and the people were heathen in that country. King Óláfr thought to himself about this offer, but when he put it to his men, then they were all against settling there and urged the king to aim north for Norway to get back his kingdom. The king still had in his mind his plan to renounce his kingly title and to travel out into the world to Jerusalem or to other holy places and enter a religious order. What weighed most in his mind for consideration was whether there might come to be any opportunity for him to get back his kingdom in Norway. But when he thought about this, then he called to mind that for the first ten winters of his rule everything was in his favour and worked out well, while after that all his plans were hard to get going and difficult to implement, and when he tried his luck, it all went wrong. Now he was doubtful for that reason whether it would be a sensible plan to trust so much to luck as to go with a small force into the hands of his enemies, when all the common people of the land [340] had joined with them to oppose King Óláfr. These concerns occupied him frequently and he referred his affairs to God, praying Him to let what He saw was best to do become apparent. He turned this over in his mind and was not sure what he should decide on, for trouble seemed to him obvious in whatever he proposed to himself.

CHAPTER ONE HUNDRED AND EIGHTY-EIGHT

It happened one night that Óláfr was lying in his bed and was awake a long time in the night and thinking about his plans, and had great anxiety in his mind. And when his brain became very tired, then he dozed into a sleep so light that he thought he was awake and could see everything that was going on in the building. He saw a man standing before the bed, tall and stately-looking, and he had splendid clothing. It mainly occurred to the king that it must be Óláfr Tryggvason come there. This man said to him:

'Are you very anxious about your plans, what you ought to decide to do? It seems to me strange that you ponder this in your mind, as it does if you are intending to renounce the kingly title that God has given you, likewise the intention to stay here and accept power from foreign kings, ones that are unknown to you. Rather return to your kingdom that you have received by inheritance and ruled for a long time with the strength that God gave you, and do not let your subjects frighten you. It is a king's glory to overcome his enemies, and a noble death to fall in battle with one's troops. Or do you have some doubt about this, whether you have a just cause in your dispute? You must not act in such a way as to hide the truth from yourself. It is for this reason that you can boldly fight for the country, that God will bear you witness that it is your property.'

And when the king awoke, then he thought he saw a fleeting glimpse of the man [341] as he went away. So from then on he took heart and affirmed to himself the intention to return to Norway, as he had previously been most keen to do, and had discovered that all his men wanted most to have done. He considered in his mind that the country would be easy to win, since it was without a ruler, as he had now learned. He believed that if he came there himself, many would then be ready to support him again. And when the king announced this plan to his men, then all received it gratefully.

CHAPTER ONE HUNDRED AND EIGHTY-NINE

It is said that this event took place in Garðaríki, while King Óláfr was there, that a high-born widow's son got an abscess in his throat and it got so bad that the boy could not get any food down, and he seemed like to die. The boy's mother went to Queen Ingigerðr, for she was an acquaintance of hers, and showed her the boy. The Queen says that she knew of no treatment to apply.

'Go,' she says, 'to King Óláfr, he is the best physician here, and ask him to pass his hands over the boy's hurt, and mention what I have said if he will not do it otherwise.'

She did as the queen said. But when she found the king, then she says that her son was like to die of an abscess in his throat, and bade him pass his hands over the abscess. The king says to her that he was no physician, telling her to go somewhere where there were doctors. She says that the queen had sent her to him.

'And she bade me mention what she said, that you were to apply the treatment you knew of, and she told me that you were the best physician in this place.'

Then the king set to work and passed his hands over the boy's abscess and handled the abscess for a very long time, until the boy [342] moved his mouth. Then the king took bread and broke it and laid it in a cross on his hand, then placed it in the boy's mouth, and he swallowed it down. And from that moment all the pain in his throat stopped. In a few days he was completely healed. His mother was very glad and so were the boy's other kinsmen and acquaintances. Then at first it was regarded in this way, that King Óláfr had such great healing hands as it is said of those people who are greatly gifted with this skill, that they have good hands, but afterwards when his miracle-working became universally known, then it was accepted as a true miracle.

CHAPTER ONE HUNDRED AND NINETY

This event took place one Sunday, that King Óláfr was sitting on his high seat at table and he was so deep in cares that he did not notice the time. He had a knife in his hand and was holding a small twig and whittling a few shavings off it. A serving boy saw what the king was doing and realised that he himself was thinking of other things. He said:

'It is Monday tomorrow, Lord.'

The king looked at him when he heard this, and it occurred to him then what he had been doing. After that the king asked for a lighted candle to be brought to him. He swept all the wood-shavings that he had cut into his hand. Then he set light to them and let the wood-shavings burn in his palm, and it could be deduced from this that he would observe the laws and commandments without deviation and not want to go beyond what he knew to be most correct.

[343] CHAPTER ONE HUNDRED AND NINETY-ONE

Afterwards, when King Óláfr had made his decision that he was going to turn back and go home, then he put this to King Jarizleifr and Queen Ingigerðr. They tried to persuade him not to make this journey, saying that he might have what power he felt was proper for himself in their realm, and begged him not to put himself at the mercy of his enemies with such a small force of men as he had there. Then King Óláfr tells them about his dream, saying this too, that he believed that this was God's providence. So when they realised that the king had made up his mind to go back to Norway, then they offer him all the help for his journey that he cared to have from them. The king thanks them in warm words for their kindness, saying that he will gladly accept from them what he needs for his journey.

CHAPTER ONE HUNDRED AND NINETY-TWO

Immediately after Yule, King Óláfr got busy with his preparations. He had nearly two hundred of his own men. King Jarizleifr provided all the transport animals with their gear that were necessary. So when he was ready, then he went. King Jarizleifr and Queen Ingigerðr set him splendidly on his way. But his son Magnús he left behind with the king.

So King Óláfr travelled from the east, first over the frosty ground all the way to the sea. But when spring came and the ice melted, then they prepared their ships, and when they were ready and a wind came, then they sail and their journey sped well. King Óláfr brought his ships to Gotland, getting news there from both the Swedish realm and Denmark and all the way from Norway. [344] Then it was learned for certain that Jarl Hákon had perished, and the country of Norway was without a ruler. The king and his men now felt the prospects looked good for their expedition, sailing on from there when they got a wind, and made for Svíþjóð. The king took his force into Lǫgrinn and made his way up inland to Áróss, after that sending men to see King Ǫnundr of the Svíar and arranged a meeting with him. King Ǫnundr responded well to his brother-in-law's embassy and went to meet with King Óláfr as his message had requested. Then Queen Ástríðr came to King Óláfr too with the men who had accompanied her. There was a joyful reunion between them all. The king of the Svíar welcomed his brother-in-law King Óláfr when they met.

CHAPTER ONE HUNDRED AND NINETY-THREE

Now it shall be told what they had been doing in Norway around this time. Þórir hundr had been engaged in trading with the Lapps for these two winters, and both winters he had spent a long time in the mountains and had made a lot of money. He did various kinds of trade [345] with the Lapps. He had prepared for himself there twelve reindeer-skin coats, using such powerful magic that no weapon could penetrate them, and much less than a coat of mail. So the second spring Þórir fitted out a longship that he owned and manned it with his servants. He summoned together the farmers and demanded a levy all over up to the northernmost assembly district, gathering together there a very large number of men, travelling north in the spring with this force. Hárekr from Þjótta also held a muster and got a large force. There took part in this journey many other distinguished men, though these were the most well known. They made an announcement that this gathering of troops was to go against King Óláfr and hold the land against him if he came from the east.

CHAPTER ONE HUNDRED AND NINETY-FOUR

Einarr þambarskelfir held most power out over Þrándheimr after the fall of Jarl Hákon became known. He and his son Eindriði were thought to be best entitled to the possessions that the jarl had had, and his wealth. Einarr then called to mind the promises and offers of friendship that King Knútr had made to him at parting. So Einarr had a fine ship that he owned fitted out, went on board himself with a large company. And when he was ready, he made his way south along the coast and then west across the sea and did not cease travelling until he came to England, going straight to see King Knútr. The king welcomed him. Then Einarr presented his mission to the king, saying that he was now come to take up the promises that the king had made, that Einarr should hold a title of high rank over Norway if Jarl Hákon was not available. King Knútr says that this business had taken quite a different turn. 'I have now,' he says, 'sent men with my tokens to my son Sveinn in Denmark, and moreover I have promised him power in Norway. But I [346] want to maintain my friendship towards you. You shall have the same rank from me as you are entitled to by birth and be a landed man,[353] and have great revenues and be the more senior to other landed men in that you have greater achievements than other landed men.'

Now as to his situation, Einarr saw what the result of his mission would be. He now prepares for his return home. And when he realised what the king's intention was, and also that there was a clear prospect, if King Óláfr came from the east, that there would be no peace in the land, it occurred to Einarr that it would not be worth hastening his journey more than very moderately, in case they should be fighting King Óláfr without gaining any advantage to his own power over what he had before. Einarr now sailed out to sea, when he was ready to do so, and got to Norway so that the events that were most important that summer had already taken place.

CHAPTER ONE HUNDRED AND NINETY-FIVE

Leading men in Norway had watch kept east in Svíþjóð and south in Denmark for if King Óláfr should come from Garðaríki in the east. They got immediate intelligence, as quickly as people could travel at their fastest, when King Óláfr was come to Svíþjóð. And as soon as this was known to be accurate, then a summons to war went round the whole country. The general public were called out as troops. Then a host was gathered together. And the landed men that were from Agðir and Rogaland and Hǫrðaland, they now split up, some turned north and some east, and it was felt necessary to have troops ready in both areas. Erlingr of Jaðarr's sons turned east, as did all the troops that were from the east of them, and they were leaders of this contingent, while to the north went Áslákr of Finney and Erlingr of Gerði and the landed men that were from north of them. These that have just been named were [347] all men who had sworn oaths to King Knútr to deprive King Óláfr of life if they found an opportunity.

CHAPTER ONE HUNDRED AND NINETY-SIX

So when it became known in Norway that King Óláfr was come to Svíþjóð from the east, then his friends gathered together, those that wanted to give him support. In that number the most high-born man was King Óláfr's

[353] See note 52 above.

brother Haraldr Sigurðarson. He was now fifteen winters old, a very tall man in stature and a grown-up man in appearance. There were many other distinguished men there. They had got altogether six hundred men when they left Upplǫnd, and with that troop they made their way east through Eiðaskógr to Vermaland. After that they made their way east through forests to Svíþjóð, then made enquiries about King Óláfr's movements.

CHAPTER ONE HUNDRED AND NINETY-SEVEN

King Óláfr was in Svíþjóð in the spring and from there got intelligence about the north of Norway, and heard from there only the one kind of report, that it would not be peaceful going there, and the men that came from the north advised him strongly not to enter the country. He was now resolved, just as before, to go. King Óláfr asked King Ǫnundr to say what support he would give him in invading his kingdom. King Ǫnundr replied, saying that the Svíar were not much for going to make war on Norway.

'We know,' he says, 'that Norwegians are tough and great warriors and hard to visit with warfare. I have no hesitation in telling you what I will contribute. I will give you four hundred men, and you can choose from my following fine warriors and ones well equipped for battle. After that I will give you leave to travel over my country and get yourself all the troops you can and that [348] are willing to follow you.'

King Óláfr accepted this offer, after that getting ready to depart. Queen Ástríðr remained behind in Svíþjóð, and the king's daughter Úlfhildr.

CHAPTER ONE HUNDRED AND NINETY-EIGHT

So when King Óláfr began his journey, then there came to him the troop that the king of the Svíar had given him, and these were four hundred men. The king travels by the route that the Svíar already knew. They made their way up inland to forests and came out there where it is called Járnberaland. There the troop came to meet the king that had been coming from Norway to join him, as has been told above.[354] There he met his brother Haraldr and many others of his kingdom, and this was the most joyful reunion. They had now altogether twelve hundred men.

CHAPTER ONE HUNDRED AND NINETY-NINE

There is a man named Dagr of whom it is said that he was son of King Hringr, who had fled the land before King Óláfr, but people say that Hringr was son of Dagr son of Haraldr inn hárfagri's son Hringr. Dagr was King Óláfr's

[354] Ch. 196.

kinsman. The father and son, Hringr and Dagr, had settled in the realm of the Svíar and had got a realm to rule over there. In the spring, when King Óláfr was come from the east to Svíþjóð, he had sent word to his kinsman Dagr that Dagr was to join him on his journey with all the support he had available, and if they gained possession of land in Norway, then Dagr should have no less power there than his forefathers had had. So when this message came to Dagr, then this was much to his liking. He was very homesick to go to Norway and receive there the power that his kinsmen [349] had held in the past. He responded to this business immediately and promised to go. Dagr was a man quick to speak and quick to make up his mind, a very impetuous man and a very valiant man, but not a man of great intelligence. After this he gathered troops to himself and got nearly twelve hundred men. He went with this troop to meet King Óláfr.

CHAPTER TWO HUNDRED

King Óláfr sent word out from himself into the settled areas with a message to the people who wanted to make money for themselves by getting a share of the gains and having the revenues that the king's enemies had appropriated, then they should come to him and follow him. King Óláfr now conveyed his army, travelling by way of forest settlements, and sometimes over wilderness areas and frequently over great lakes. They dragged or carried the ships with them between the lakes. Numbers of troops flocked to the king, forest people and some of them outlaws. Many places there have since been called Óláfsbúðir[355] where he stayed the night. He did not pause on his journey until he came out in Jamtaland, travelling north then after that to Kjǫlr. His troops split up in the inhabited areas and became very scattered as long as they knew no likelihood of hostility. But always when the troops split up, then the troop of Norwegians accompanied the king, while Dagr then travelled separately with his troop, and the Svíar in a third group with their men.

CHAPTER TWO HUNDRED AND ONE

Men are mentioned by name, of whom one was called Gauka-Þórir (Cuckoo-) and another Afra-Fasti (Buttermilk-). They were outlaws and the greatest robbers, having with them thirty men [350] like themselves. These brothers were taller and stronger than other men. They had no lack of daring and courage. They heard about this army that was travelling through the country there, and discussed among themselves that it might be a good plan to go to the king and follow him to his country and take part there in a great battle

---

[355] One of the meanings of *búð* is 'temporary shelter', such as might be used by travellers in uninhabited areas. Cf. note 221 above.

with him and thus put themselves to the test, for they had not before been in battles where troops were lined up in battle array. They were very interested to see the king's host lined up. Their companions liked this plan very much, they now set out to meet with the king. And when they come there, then they go with their band of men before the king, and their companions had their full armour. They greeted him. He asked what sort of men they were. They gave their names, saying that they were natives of the country. They presented their business and offered the king to go with him. The king says that it seemed to him that there would be good support in such men.

'I am keen,' he says, 'to take on such men. But are you Christian people?' he says.

Gauka-Þórir answers, saying he was neither Christian nor heathen.

'We comrades have no other faith than that we believe in ourselves, our strength and our luck in victory, and that does us all right.'

The king replies: 'A great pity that such useful-looking men should not believe in Christ, their creator.'

Þórir replies: 'Is there anyone in your company, king, a man of Christ, that has grown more a day than we brothers?'

The king told them to have themselves baptised and accept the true faith with it.

'And follow me then,' he says. 'I shall make you men of high rank. But if you do not wish to do that, then go back to your own occupations.'

Afra-Fasti replies, saying that he was [351] not willing to accept Christianity. After that they turn away. Then said Gauka-Þórir:

'It is very shameful that this king should reject us from his army. I have never experienced it before, that I was not found as good as other men. I shall never turn away leaving matters thus.'

After this they joined company with other forest people and went with their troop. Then King Óláfr made his way west to Kjǫlr.

CHAPTER TWO HUNDRED AND TWO

So when King Óláfr went from the east to Kjǫlr and made his way west from the mountain so that the land sloped down west from there to the sea, he could then see the landscape down there. Many troops were going ahead of the king, and many were behind him. He was riding where there was space round him. He was silent, not speaking to people. He rode for a large part of the day without looking about him. Then the bishop rode up to him and spoke, asking what he was thinking about, as he was so silent, for the king was always cheerful and talkative with his men on the journey, so cheering everyone up who was near him. Then the king replied with great anxiety:

'Strange things have been appearing to me for a while. Just now I could see over Norway, when I looked west from the mountain. It came into my mind then that I had been happy for many a day in that land. I then had a vision in which I could see over all Þrándheimr, and after that over all Norway, and as long as this vision was before my eyes, then I could see ever further, right on until I could see over all the world, both lands and sea. I recognised clearly the places I had been to and seen before. Just as clearly I saw places that I have not seen before, some that I have had reports of, and even those that I have not heard spoken of before, both inhabited and uninhabited, as widely as the world extends.'

The bishop says that this vision was holy and very remarkable.

[352] CHAPTER TWO HUNDRED AND THREE

Afterwards when the king made his way down off the mountain, then there was a farm before them that is called at Súl, at the beginning of the settled area of Verdœlafylki. And as they made their way down to the farm, then there lay cornfields by the wayside. The king told the men to go carefully and not spoil fields for the farmer. Men did this well while the king was near, but the groups that were coming behind now paid no heed to this, and men ran over the cornfield so that it was all flattened to the ground. The farmer that lived there, who was called Þorgeirr flekkr (Spot), saw. He had two sons just reached manhood. Þorgeirr welcomed the king and his men and offered him all the service that he had at his disposal. The king responded well to this, and then asked Þórgeirr for news, what was going on in that country and whether there was any gathering of forces being made against him. Þorgeirr says that a large force was being mustered there in Þrándheimr and landed men were come there both from the south of the country and from Hálogaland in the north.

'But I do not know,' he says, 'whether they are planning to direct this force against you or elsewhere.'

Then he complained to the king about his loss and the bad behaviour of the king's men when they had broken down and trampled all his cornfields. The king says that it was ill done if damage had been caused him. Afterwards the king rode to where the cornfield had stood and saw that the crop was all flattened to the ground. He rode around it and after that said:

'It is my expectation, farmer, that God will put right your loss, and this cornfield will be better after the space of a week.'

And this turned out to be the best crop, as the king had said.

The king stayed there overnight, and in the morning he set out. He says that farmer Þorgeirr was to go with him. But when he offered his two sons for the journey, then the king says [353] that they were not to go with him, but the boys, nevertheless, were willing to go. The king told them to stay behind, but since they would not be dissuaded, then the king's followers were going to tie them up. The king said, when he saw that:

'Let them go, they will come back.'

So it turned out for the boys as the king said.

CHAPTER TWO HUNDRED AND FOUR

Then they transported their army out to Stafr. So when he came to Stafamýrar, then he made a halt. Now he found out for certain that farmers were travelling with an army against him, and also that he would have a battle soon. Then the king inspected his troops, and a count was made of the numbers of men. Then there were found to be in the army nine hundred heathen men, and when the king realised that, then he told them to have themselves baptised, saying that he does not want to have heathen men in battle with him.

'We shall not,' he says, 'be able to rely on the numbers of our men. On God must we rely, for with [his] power and mercy shall we gain victory, and I do not wish to mix heathen folk with my men.'

So when the heathens heard this, then they took counsel together, and in the end four hundred men had themselves baptised, but five hundred refused Christianity, and this group returned to their own countries. Then the brothers Gauka-Þórir and Afra-Fasti come forward there with their troop, and again offer the king their support. He asks if they have now received baptism. Gauka-Þórir says that this was not so. The king told them to receive baptism and the true faith, and otherwise to go away. They then turned off aside and held a discussion between themselves and deliberated about what course to take up. Then said Afra-Fasti:

'This is to be said about my mood, that I am unwilling to turn back. I shall go into battle and give support to one side or the other, but it doesn't seem to me to matter which party I am in.'

Then Gauka-Þórir replies:

'If I am to go into battle, then I want to [354] give help to the king, for his need for help is greater. And if I must believe in any god, how is it worse for me to believe in the White-Christ than in another god? So this is my advice, that we have ourselves baptised, if the king thinks it so important, then afterwards go into battle with him.'

They all agree to this, going afterwards to the king and saying that they are now willing to accept baptism. Then they were baptised by clerics and were confirmed. The king then accepted them into the fellowship of his following, saying that they were to be under his banner in battle.

CHAPTER TWO HUNDRED AND FIVE

King Óláfr had now found out for certain that it would not be long before he must have a battle with the farmers. And after having inspected his troops and had a count made of the numbers of men, and he now had more than three thousand men, he thought this was a large army on one battlefield. After that the king spoke to his troops and said this:

'We have a great army and fine troops. I now wish to tell people what dispositions I want to have of my troops. I shall let my banner advance in the middle of the line, and my personal following and guests[356] are to accompany it, together with the troops that came to us from Upplǫnd as well as the troops that have come to us in Þrándheimr. And on the right hand side of my banner shall be Dagr Hringsson and with him all the troops that he brought into company with us. He shall have a different banner. And on the left hand side of my line shall be the troops that the king of the Svíar provided us with, and all the troops that came to us from the Swedish realm. They shall have the third banner. I want [355] men to be divided into companies and kinsmen and acquaintances to be grouped together, for then each will best look after the other and each one recognise the other. We shall mark all our troops, put signs on our helmets and shields, drawing on them in white the holy cross. And if we engage in battle, then we shall all have the one cry: "Forward, forward, Christ's men, cross's men, king's men!" We shall have to have thin lines if we have fewer troops, because I don't want them to surround us with their troops. Let men now divide themselves into companies, and afterwards we shall dispose the companies in battle formation, each must then know his station and take note of where he is in relation to the banner to which he is assigned. We shall now keep our formation, and men must be fully armed day and night until we know where our engagement with the farmers is to be.'

After the king had spoken, then they drew up their lines and disposed them in accordance with the king's orders. After that the king held a meeting with the leaders of companies. The men the king had sent round the local area to demand support from the inhabitants were now returned. They were able to report from the area that they had travelled over that in many places there was a complete dearth of men capable of bearing arms, and those people had joined the gathering of farmers, and wherever they had met men, then few would go with them, but most replied that they stayed at home because they did not want to follow either party, did not want to fight against the king nor against their own kinsmen. They had obtained few troops. Then the king asked men their advice, what course seemed best to take. Finnr replied to the king's question:

---

[356] *Gestir* ('guests') came to designate a member of the king's *hirð* ('personal following') of inferior rank.

'I shall say,' he says, 'what would be done if I had my way. Then we would ravage all the settlements, plunder all the property and burn all the habitations so thoroughly that not a hut remained standing, and thus repay the farmers for their treason against their lord. I think that many a one would then detach himself [356] from his company if he looks towards his home to see smoke or fire rising from the buildings, not knowing for sure what has happened to his children or womenfolk or old people, their fathers or mothers or other relations. I would expect,' he says, 'that if any of them were to suggest breaking up their gathering, then their battle lines would soon thin out, for that is the way farmers are, the most recent proposal is the one they all most approve.'

So when Finnr had finished his speech, then people applauded it. Many were well pleased to undertake plundering, and all thought the farmers deserved to suffer losses, and that what Finnr had said, that many farmers would detach themselves from the muster, was likely. Þormóðr Kolbrúnarskáld then uttered a verse:[357]

137. Let's kindle each kettle-crag[358]   *Fóstbrœðra saga* 260–61
we come upon within Inney;[359]   *Skald* I 829
with the sword folk are defending
from the king, the country.
Yew-grief[360]—let Innþrœndir have
all their houses made ashes
cold—shall be quickened, if I
can decide it, with brambles.[361]

But when King Óláfr heard the people's vehemence, then he demanded a hearing for himself, and after that said:

'The farmers deserve [357] that it should be done as you wish. They know that I have done this, burned dwellings for them and given them other great punishments. I did this, carrying out burnings for them, when they departed from their faith before and took up heathen sacrifices and would not do what I told them. We were then upholding the law of God. Now this treason against their lord is much less important, even though they do not keep faith with me,

[357] Þormóðr Bersason Kolbrúnarskáld was an Icelandic poet, one of the heroes of *Fóstbrœðra saga*, which tells of his love for Kolbrún and his vengeance, taken in Greenland, for his foster-brother Þorgeirr Hávarsson. Fifteen stanzas survive of his *Þorgeirsdrápa* for his friend, as well as many occasional verses, preserved in the saga and elsewhere, including a group on the battle of Stiklarstaðir.
[358] *hverbjarg*: 'kettle-crag', house; FJ takes Hverbjǫrg (pl.) to be a place name (*Skj* B I 264).
[359] FJ follows the alternative reading of some manuscripts, *inni* 'house'.
[360] *ýs angr*: 'sorrow of the yew', fire.
[361] *klungr*: 'thorn, bramble'.

and yet this will not be thought seemly for those who want to be decent men. Now I have here somewhat more right to treat them with some leniency when they are acting badly against me, than when they were displaying hatred of God. Now what I want is that men should go easy and do no plundering. I will first go to see the farmers. If we are reconciled, well and good, but if they engage in battle against us, then there will be two possibilities facing us, and if we fall in battle, then it will be a good idea not to go to it with proceeds of plunder, but if we are victorious, then we shall inherit the goods of those that are now fighting against us, because some of them will fall there, and some flee, and both will have forfeited all their property. And then it will be good to go to large dwellings and splendid farms, but these are of no use to anyone when they are burned. With plundering also a much greater part is spoiled than what can be benefited from. We shall now go in separate groups as we travel out through the settlement and take with us all men capable of bearing arms that we can get. Men shall also slaughter livestock or take other provisions, such as people need to feed themselves, but men must not cause any other damage. I will be quite happy for the farmers' spies to be killed if you capture them. Dagr shall go and his troops by the more northerly route down along the valley, while I shall travel out on the high road and we shall meet in the evening. We shall all share the same lodging for the night.'

[358] CHAPTER TWO HUNDRED AND SIX

So it is said, that when King Óláfr drew up his troops, then he placed some men so as to make a shield wall that was to be kept in front of him in battle, and chose the men for it that were strongest and most agile. Then he called his poets to him and told them to go inside the shield wall.

'You,' he says, 'shall be here and see the events that here take place. You will then not have to rely on verbal reports, for you will report them and compose about them later.'

There were now there Þormóðr Kolbrúnarskáld and Hofgarða-Refr's foster-father Gizurr gullbrá (Golden Eyelash), and thirdly Þorfinnr munnr (Mouth). Then Þormóðr said to Gizurr:

'Let us not stand so close together, comrade, that the poet Sigvatr shall not be able to get to his place when he comes. He will want to be in front of the king, and the king will not be pleased otherwise.'

The king heard this and replies:

'There is no need to deride Sigvatr, though he is not here. Often has he stood by me well. He will now be praying for us, and there will yet be very great need of that.'

Þormóðr says: 'That may be, king, that your greatest need now is for prayers, but thin would be the ranks around the banner pole if all your followers were now on the road to Rome. It was just, too, our complaint about no one finding room for Sigvatr, even if they wanted to speak to you.' Then they spoke among themselves, saying that it would be very fit to compose some memorial verses about the events that now would soon be upon them. Then spoke Gizurr:

[359]

138. News that I'm not cheerful
no thane's daughter will gather—
have this word heard; I prepare for
a host at Ífi's boards' meeting[362]—
although wise war-bushes[363]
warn of Heðinn's lady,[364]
Let's be, east in Áli's blizzard,[365]
a bulwark to the ruler.

Legendary saga 192
(attributed to Þormóðr)
Skald I 818

Then Þorfinnr munnr spoke another verse:

139. Twilight falls before the tempest
of the tough yard of the shield-rim;[366]
the Verdœlir force against the
valiant leader will battle.
Let's defend the free-handed ruler,
feed the cheerful gore-gull,[367]
bring down Þrœndr in Þundr's—
this we are urging—rainstorm.[368]

Legendary saga 188
Skald I 847

Then spoke Þormóðr:

[360]

140. Áli's mighty storm[369] masses,
missile projector;[370]
folk must not falter,
fearful—a sword-age[371] waxes.

Legendary saga 192–94
Fóstbrœðra saga 264
(1st half)
Skald I 831

[362] *Ífa borða þing*: 'assembly of boards of Ífi (sea-king) (shields)', battle.
[363] *sigrrunnar*: 'battle-bushes', warriors.
[364] *Heðins kona*: Hildr, daughter of Hǫgni, whose kidnap by Heðinn instigated the Hjaðningavíg, a legendary battle in which Hildr had the power to resuscitate dead warriors each day so that the battle continued indefinitely (*Skáldsk* 72). Her name is synonymous with battle.
[365] *Ála él*: 'storm of Áli (sea-king)', battle.
[366] *randar garðs regn*: 'rain of the enclosure of the shield (shield wall)', battle.
[367] *sveita mór*: 'gull of blood', raven or eagle.
[368] *Þundar hregg*: 'storm of Óðinn', battle.
[369] *Ála él*: 'storm of Áli', battle.
[370] *ǫrstiklandi*: 'arrow-shooter', warrior (vocative).
[371] *skálmǫld*: 'sword-age', battle.

> For the onslaught let's steel ourselves;
> slacker's speech a man war-happy
> must give up, as we go to
> the gathering of spears[372] with Óleifr.

People memorised these verses on the spot.

CHAPTER TWO HUNDRED AND SEVEN

After this the king set out and made his way out along the valleys. He got himself a lodging-place for the night, and then all his troops assembled together there, and lay that night outside under their shields. And as soon as it got light, the king got the army ready, then moved out along the valley when they were ready to do so. Then a large number of farmers came to the king and most joined forces with him and all had the same thing to say, that landed men had assembled an invincible army and they were planning to engage in battle with the king. Then the king took many marks of silver and handed it to one of the farmers and afterwards said:

'You are to look after this money and divide it up afterwards, paying some to churches, and giving some to clerics, some to almsmen, and give it for the life and soul of the men that fall in battle and are fighting against us.'

The farmer replies: [361] 'Shall this money be given for the salvation of the souls of your men, king?'

Then the king replies: 'This money is to be given for the souls of those men who are with the farmers in battle and fall before our men's weapons. But those men that follow us in battle and fall there, then we shall all be saved by this together.'

CHAPTER TWO HUNDRED AND EIGHT

That night, when King Óláfr lay among the gathering of men, as has already been told, he was awake for a long time and prayed to God for himself and his troops and slept little. A heaviness came over him towards dawn. And when he awoke, then the day rose up. The king thought it rather early to wake up the army. So he asked where the poet Þormóðr was. He was close by and replied, asking what the king wanted with him. The king says:

'Recite some poem for us.'

---

[372] *geirþing*: 'spear-assembly', battle.

Þormóðr sat up and spoke very loudly so that he could be heard over the whole army. He recited *Bjarkamál in fornu*, and this is the beginning of it:[373]

141. Daybreak has arisen: *Bjarkamál in fornu* 1
the cock's wings rustle: *Fóstbrœðra saga* 262–63
time for workers'
toil to begin.
Be wakeful, be wakeful,
best of friends,
all the noblest
of Aðils's followers!

142. Hár Hard-Gripping,   *Bjarkamál in fornu* 2
Hrólfr the Shooter,   *Fóstbrœðra saga* 263
[362] men of good family
who do not flee,
not for wine I wake you
nor woman's secrets,
but wake you for Hildr's
harsh exchanges.[374]

Then the troops awoke. And when the poem was finished, then men thanked him for the poem, and people were greatly affected and felt it was well chosen and called the poem *Húskarlahvǫt*.[375] The king thanked him for his performance. After that the king took a gold ring that weighed half a mark and gave it to Þormóðr. Þormóðr thanked the king for his gift, saying:

'We have a good king, though it is hard to see now how long-lived the king will be. This is my prayer, king, that you do not let us two be parted either alive or dead.'

The king replies: We shall all go together, as long as I am in charge, if you do not wish to part from me.'

Then said Þormóðr: 'I trust, king, that whether peace comes for better or for worse, that I may be somewhere close to you, as long as I have the opportunity, whatever we hear about where Sigvatr is going with his golden hilt.'

[373] Seven full or part-stanzas, in the Eddic *málaháttr* metre, survive of the poem *Bjarkamál*. Snorri's title *Bjarkamál in fornu* 'the Old' may imply that there were two poems of this name. A long paraphrase in Latin hexameters of what is assumed to have been the whole poem is preserved in the *Gesta Danorum* of Saxo Grammaticus. The speaker, Bjarki, referred to in the title, is identifiable as Saxo's Biarco and as the hero Bǫðvarr Bjarki of *Hrólfs saga kraka*. Bjarki and his companion Hjalti incite King Hrólfr´s followers before their last heroic batttle against King Aðils. In the poem *Aðils sinnar* 'the companions of Aðils' seem to be among those incited by the speaker, which may allude to events told earlier in the saga.

[374] *Hildar leikr*: 'game of Hildr (a valkyrie)', battle; cf. note 364 above.

[375] 'The Housecarls' Encouragement', see note 31 above.

Then spoke Þormóðr:

[363] 143. By your knee still I'll
stand, till you get other
poets—when do you expect them,
prince stalwart in battle?
We'll get away though we give the
greedy raven corpse-prey;
either that will be, wood of
the wave-steed,[376] or we'll lie here.

Legendary saga 194
Fóstbrœðra saga 265
(1st half)
Skald I 833

CHAPTER TWO HUNDRED AND NINE

King Óláfr took his army out along the valley. Then Dagr also went with his troops by a different route. The king did not cease his march until he came out in Stiklarstaðir. Then they saw the army of farmers, and that force was moving in a very disorderly manner, and was in such huge numbers that from every path the troops spread out, and especially where large groups were moving side by side. They saw where a company of men was going down out of Veradalr, and they had been on the watch and passed near to where the king's troops were, and they did not realise it before they were only a short distance off, so that people could recognise each other. Hrútr of Vigg was there with thirty men. After this the king said that the guests were to go against Hrútr and deprive him of life. Men were quick to take on this task. Then [364] the king spoke to the Icelanders:

'I am told that it is a custom in Iceland that the farmers are obliged to give their workmen a sheep for them to slaughter in the autumn. I am now going to give you a ram (*hrútr*) to slaughter.'

These Icelanders did not take much urging to this task and went straight up to Hrútr with some other men. Hrútr was killed together with the whole company that was with him. The king stopped and halted his army when he got to Stiklarstaðir. The king told men to dismount from their horses and make preparations there. Men did as the king ordered. After that the battle line was formed and the banners raised. Dagr was then not yet come with his troops, and that wing of the army was missing. Then the king said that the men of Upplǫnd were to advance there and take up the banners.

'I think it is advisable,' says the king, 'that my brother Haraldr should not be in the battle, for he is a child in age.'

Haraldr replies: 'I shall certainly be in the battle, but if I am so lacking in strength that I cannot wield a sword, then I know a good way of dealing with that, which is that my hand shall be tied to the haft. No one is going to have a greater desire than I to cause harm to the farmers. I shall go with my comrades.'

So men say, Haraldr then spoke this verse:

[376] *vága viggruðr*: 'bush of the steed of waves (ship)', sailor.

144. I'll dare to defend the flank—   *Fsk* 200
fulfilling the lady's wishes—   *Legendary saga* 188
in rage let us redden   (attributed to Þormóðr)
round shields—that I'm placed in.   *Skald* II 42–43
War-glad, the young poet will not,
where weapons swipe, take to
his heels before spears: men harden
hostile battle exchanges.

Haraldr had his way, so that he was in the battle.

CHAPTER TWO HUNDRED AND TEN

There is a man named Þorgils Hálmuson, a farmer who lived at Stiklarstaðir, father of Grímr góði (the Good). Þorgils offered the king his support and to be in battle with him. The king said he was grateful for his offer.

'But I want you, farmer,' says the king, 'not to be in the battle. Instead, grant us this, that you help our men after the battle, those that are wounded, and give them burial that fall in battle; similarly if it should come to pass, farmer, that I fall in this battle, then give such service to my corpse as arises from necessity, if it is not prohibited to you.'

Þorgils promised the king this that he asked.

CHAPTER TWO HUNDRED AND ELEVEN

So when King Óláfr had drawn up his troops, then he spoke before them, saying this, that men must take heart and advance boldly—

'If battle comes,' he says, 'we have fine troops and plenty of them, and though the farmers have somewhat larger forces, still fate will decide victory. There remains this for me to announce to you, that I am not going to flee from this battle. I shall either defeat the farmers or fall in battle. My prayer is this, that the outcome may be what God sees is right for me. We must place our confidence in this, that we have a much more just cause than the farmers, and also in this, that God will release our possessions for us after this battle, or otherwise grant us a much greater reward for the loss that we suffer here than we can ourselves desire for us. And if it is my lot to speak after the battle, then I shall enrich each of you according to your deserts and to how each goes forward into battle. There will then, if we have victory, be enough, both lands and money, to share with you, that have now been previously in the hands of our enemies. Let us make our first attack the hardest we can, for it will quickly go one way or the other if the odds are great. We have hope of victory from a swift attack, but on the other hand it will fall out worse for us

if we fight until we are exhausted so that men become as a result unable to fight. We will have fewer replacement troops than they, with whom different groups advance while some hold back and rest. But if we make such a hard attack that they turn back who are foremost, then they will fall over each other, and their difficulties will be the greater, the more there are of them.'
And when the king finished his speech, they applauded what he had said loudly and they encouraged each other.

CHAPTER TWO HUNDRED AND TWELVE

Þórðr Fólason was carrying King Óláfr's banner. The poet Sigvatr says this in the memorial poem that he composed about King Óláfr, and used material from the story of Creation for his parentheses:[377]

[367]

145. Þórðr, I heard, fought fiercely
the fight, then, beside Óleifr
with spears—the battle stiffened—
stout hearts trod there together.
He held high before the king of
Hringar,[378] war-bold, the finely-
gilded standard, strove fully,
the spirited brother of Ǫgmundr.

Erfidrápa Óláfs helga 7
Skald I 673

CHAPTER TWO HUNDRED AND THIRTEEN

King Óláfr was so equipped that he had a gilded helmet on his head and a shield white with the holy cross painted on it in red. In one hand he had the halberd that now stands in Christchurch by the altar. He was girded with the sword that was called Hneitir (Striker), a very sharp sword with the haft wound round with gold. He had a coat of mail. The poet Sigvatr speaks of this:

146. Óleifr the Fat felled soldiers;
forward he pressed in mailcoat,
the war-bold seigneur, seeking
a striking victory.
And the Svíar who wend westwards
waded with the gracious
lord the bright bloodstream;
battle waxed; much I say plainly.

Erfidrápa Óláfs helga 8
Skald I 674

[377] *Stál*, according to Snorri (*Hattatal* 12), were lines containing parenthetical statements. 'The Story of Creation' was probably the Book of Genesis, but of the 28 stanzas that survive, only the last seems possibly to have been one of these parentheses.
[378] *Hringa gramr*: 'king of the inhabitants of Hringaríki', i.e. of Norway.

[368] CHAPTER TWO HUNDRED AND FOURTEEN

So when King Óláfr had drawn up his troops, then the farmers were still come nowhere near. Then the king said that the troops should sit down and rest. The king then sat down himself and all his troops and they sat spread out. He leant over and laid his head on Finnr Árnason's knees. Then he fell asleep, and was so for a while. Then they saw the army of farmers, and these troops advanced to meet them, having raised their banner, and it was a very great host of men. Then Finnr woke the king, telling him that the farmers were now attacking them. And when the king woke up, he said:

'Why did you wake me, Finnr, and not let me dream my dream out?'

Finnr replied: 'Your dream would not have been such that it would not have been more important to wake up and prepare for the army that is coming against us. Or do you not see where now the rabble of farmers is come?'

The king replies: 'They are not yet come so near us that it would not have been better that I had slept on.'

Then said Finnr: 'What did you dream, king, that you think it such a great loss that you did not wake of your own accord?'

Then the king tells his dream, that he thought he saw a high ladder, and he was going aloft up it so far that heaven opened and it was there the ladder led.

'I was,' he says, 'just come to the last rung, when you woke me.'

Finnr replies: 'This dream does not seem as good to me as it must seem to you. I think it must portend your death if it is anything more than just dream phantasmagoria that appeared to you.'

[369] CHAPTER TWO HUNDRED AND FIFTEEN

Further, there happened something when King Óláfr was come to Stiklarstaðir, that a man came to him. Though this was not in itself marvellous, for many men came to the king from the local areas, but what seemed strange about this was that this man was not like others that had come to the king. He was a man so tall that no one else reached further than to his shoulders. He was a very handsome man in appearance and had beautiful hair. He was well armed, having a very fine helmet and a coat of mail, a red shield, and being girded with an ornamented sword, and had in his hand a great gold-inlaid spear with such a thick shaft that his hand could only just go round it. This man went before the king and greeted him and asked if the king would accept support from him. The king asked what his name was and his ancestry, and what country he came from. He replies:

'I have kinfolk in Jamtaland and Helsingjaland. I am known as Arnljótr gellini (from Gellin). The most I can tell you about myself is that I gave assistance to those men of yours that you sent to Jamtaland to collect tax there. I handed over to them a silver dish that I sent to you as a sign that I wanted to be your friend.'

Then the king asked whether Arnljótr was a Christian man or not. He says this about his faith, that he believed in his might and main.

'This faith has served me well enough up to now. But now I intend to believe in you, king.'

The king replies: 'If you want to believe in me, then you must believe in what I tell you. You must believe that Jesus Christ has created heaven and earth and all people, and all people shall go to him after death that are good and orthodox in belief.'

Arnljótr replies: 'I have heard tell of White-Christ, but I am not acquainted with what he does or where he rules over. I shall now believe in everything that you tell me. I wish to commit [370] the whole of my life into your hands.'

After that Arnljótr was baptised. The king taught him such of the faith as he deemed to be most important and assigned him to the van of his battle formation, in front of his banner. In this position he already had Gauka-Þórir and Afra-Fasti and their comrades.

CHAPTER TWO HUNDRED AND SIXTEEN

Now it must be told from where the story was broken off above, that landed men and farmers had assembled an invincible force as soon as they heard that the king had left Garðaríki and the east and that he had arrived in Svíþjóð. So when they learned that the king was come from the east to Jamtaland, and that he was planning to travel from the east over Kjǫlr to Veradalr, then they made their way with their army inland into Þrándheimr and then collected together all the population there, free and unfree, and so went inland to Veradalr, having there such a great force that there was not a person there that had seen such a great army assembled in Norway. It was the case with it, as it can often be in a great army, that its composition was very varied. There were a lot of landed men in it and a large number of powerful farmers, though the rest was all the rabble, who were peasants and labourers. And this was the whole of the main army that had gathered together there in Þrándheimr. These troops were very much inflamed with hostility to the king.

CHAPTER TWO HUNDRED AND SEVENTEEN

Knútr inn ríki had subjected all the land in Norway to himself, as was said above, and in addition that he appointed to rule it Jarl Hákon. He provided the jarl with a household bishop whose name was Sigurðr. He was Danish by origin and had been with King Knútr a long time. This bishop was a fiery man in temperament and a flowery man in his speech. He supported [371] King Knútr in what he said as much as he could, but was a very great enemy of King Óláfr. This bishop was in this army and spoke frequently before the troop of farmers and strongly urged rebellion against King Óláfr.

CHAPTER TWO HUNDRED AND EIGHTEEN

Bishop Sigurðr spoke at an assembly of the troops where there was now a huge host of men. He began his speech thus:

'Here is now assembled a great host, so that in this poor land there will be no opportunity to see a larger native army. This numerous force ought to come in very handy for you, for now there will be sufficient need for it if this Óláfr is again planning not to leave off harrying you. He became accustomed already at an early age to plundering and killing people and travelled through many countries for this purpose. But finally he turned to this country and began by making enemies most of all among those that were the best people and the most powerful: King Knútr, whom everyone has the highest duty to serve as well as they can, and he established himself on his dependent territory; similarly he supported King Óláfr of the Svíar, while driving out of their ancestral lands the Jarls Sveinn and Hákon. But he behaved most cruelly to his own kinsmen, when he drove all the kings out of Upplǫnd, though this was in some respects all right, since they had previously gone back on their words and oaths to King Knútr, and supported this Óláfr in every criminal design that he took up. Now their friendship has very properly been dissolved. He inflicted injuries on them and took over their realms, thus emptying the land of all high-born men. But after that you must know how he has treated landed men: the noblest are slain, and many have had to leave the country because of him. He has also travelled far and wide over this country with bands of plunderers, burning the local districts and [372] killing and robbing the people. But who is here of the ruling classes that will not have great wrongs to avenge on him? Now he is travelling with a foreign army, and it is mostly outlaws and robbers or other brigands. Do you imagine he is now going to be kind to you, when he goes with this scum, when he commited such ravages which all his followers tried to dissuade him from? I think a better course is for you to remember now the words of King Knútr, when he advised you, if Óláfr tried again to get back to the country, how you ought to defend the freedom that King Knútr promised you. He told you to resist and drive out of your way such rabble. The thing to do now is to go against them and cut down this scum for the eagle and wolf and let each one lie where he is struck down, unless you would rather drag their corpses into woods and rocky places. Let no one be so bold as to convey them to churches, for they are all vikings and evil-doers.'

And when he ended this addresss, then people gave it great applause, and all gave their consent to doing as he said.

CHAPTER TWO HUNDRED AND NINETEEN

The landed men, those who were assembled there, held a meeting and talk and discussion and made arrangements about how their lines should be drawn up and who should be leader over the troops. Then Kálfr Árnason said that Hárekr from Þjótta was best fitted to becoming chief over this army—
'For he is descended from the line of Haraldr inn hárfagri. The king bears him a very great grudge on account of the killing of Grankell, and he will face the severest punishment if Óláfr comes to power. Hárekr is well tried in battle and a man of high ambition.'

Hárekr answers that those men were better suited for this that were now at the most active [373] stage of their lives.

'But I am now,' he says, 'an old man and infirm and not very able to fight. There is also a family relationship between me and King Óláfr, and although he does not think much of that in respect of me, yet it is not seemly for me to be any further involved in this warfare against him than anyone else in our party. You, Þórir, are well suited to being the chief in engaging in battle with King Óláfr. There are also enough reasons for this. You have deaths of kinsmen to avenge on him, and also the fact that he drove you from all your possessions as an outlaw. You have also promised King Knútr and your kinsmen too to avenge Ásbjǫrn. Or do you think that there will be any better opportunity against Óláfr than such as is now to take vengeance for all these disgraces to your honour at once?'

Þórir replied to his speech: 'I do not have the confidence to carry a banner against King Óláfr or to become leader over these troops. The Þrœndir have the largest crowd of men here. I know their pride, that they will not want to listen to me or to any other man from Hálogaland. But there is no need to remind me of the injuries that I have to repay Óláfr for. I remember the loss of men in Óláfr having deprived four men of life and all of them distinguished in honour and kinship: my brother's son Ásbjǫrn, my sister's sons Þórir and Grjótgarðr, and their father Ǫlvir, and I have a duty to avenge each of them. Now this is to be said about me, that I have selected eleven of my men, that are the best fighters, and I believe that we shall not lose by comparison with others in exchanging blows with Óláfr if we get a chance of it.'

CHAPTER TWO HUNDRED AND TWENTY

Kálfr Árnason then began to speak: 'What is now necessary for us in regard to the course that we have started on, is that we should not make it turn out to be a mockery that the army has been mustered. We shall need to do something, if we are to engage in battle [374] with King Óláfr, other than each drawing back from taking the responsibility, for we can assume this, that although Óláfr does not have a great force compared to the army that we have, yet there is there a trusty leader, and all his troops will be faithful in following him. But if we who should most of all be leaders of our troops are now rather shaky and are not willing to encourage the army and exhort them and give them a lead, then straight away a large number of the army's hearts will fail them, and the next thing will be that each does what he thinks safest for himself. And although a great army is here assembled, yet we shall be put to such a test if we and King Óláfr with his army meet that defeat will be a certainty for us unless we, the organisers ourselves, are on the ball and the host rushes forward with one accord. But if that is not the case, then it will be better for us not to risk a battle, and then this course will seem obvious, to trust to Óláfr's mercy, if he seemed harsh then, when there were fewer charges against us than there will seem to him to be now.[379] And yet I know that there are men included in his troop such that there would be a chance for me of quarter if I wished to seek it. Now if you are minded as I am, then you, brother-in-law Þórir, and you, Hárekr, must go beneath the banner that we shall all raise up, and then follow it. Let us all make ourselves vigorous and active in these undertakings that we have engaged in, and support the army of farmers in such a way that they may not see in us any hesitation. And this will urge the common people forward, if we set about cheerfully drawing up and exhorting the troops.'

And when Kálfr had finished saying what he had to say, then everyone responded positively to his speech, saying that they wanted to have everything as Kálfr felt was right for them. Then everyone wanted Kálfr to be leader over the troops and assign everyone to the detachments that he wished.

[375] CHAPTER TWO HUNDRED AND TWENTY-ONE

Kálfr raised a banner and placed his men there underneath the banner, and with them Hárekr from Þjótta and his troop. Þórir hundr with his troop was in front of the leading part of their formation before the banners. Also there was a selected troop of farmers on both sides of Þórir, one that was most vigorous and best armed. This formation was made both long and thick, and in that part of the formation were the Þrœndir and Háleygir. And on the right hand side of this formation another formation was placed, and on the left side of the main formation the Rygir and Hǫrðar, Sygnir, Firðir had a formation, and they had a third banner there.

[379] If the text and translation are accurate, Kálfr is here speaking ironically.

CHAPTER TWO HUNDRED AND TWENTY-TWO

There is a man named Þorsteinn knarrarsmiðr (merchant ship builder). He was a merchant and a great craftsman, a tall and strong man, an energetic man in everything, a great warrior. He had fallen out with the king, and the king had taken from him a large and new trading ship that Þorsteinn had built. This was on account of Þorsteinn's unruly deeds and as compensation for a subject that the king was owed. Þorsteinn was there in the army. He went to the front of the formation and up to where Þórir hundr was standing. He spoke as follows:

'It is here I want to be in this detachment, Þórir, with you, since I intend, if I and Óláfr meet, to be the first to raise a weapon against him, if I can be positioned thus close, and to repay him for the confiscation of the ship when he robbed me of that ship that is the best one to be taken on trading voyages.'

Þórir and his men accepted Þorsteinn, and he joined their detachment.

[376] CHAPTER TWO HUNDRED AND TWENTY-THREE

So when the farmers had been assigned to detachments, then the landed men spoke, telling the men in the army to take note of their positions, where each was placed and under which banner each was now supposed to be and in which direction from the banner and how close he was placed to the banner. They told men to be alert now and quick to get into formation when the horns sounded and a war call rang out, and then to advance in formation, for they now still had a very long way to convey the army, and it was likely that the formations would break up on the march. After that they encouraged the troops. Kálfr said that all those men that had hateful treatment to repay King Óláfr for should now go forward under the banners that were to go against Óláfr's banner, bearing in mind now the injuries that he had inflicted on them, saying that they would not find a better opportunity to avenge their griefs and thus free themselves from the oppression and slavery that he had subjected them to.

'That person,' he says, 'is now a coward who does not bear himself as boldly as he can, for there is no lack of offences to charge those that are against you with. They will not spare you if they get a chance.'

There was very loud applause for his speech. There was now much shouting and egging on throughout the army.

CHAPTER TWO HUNDRED AND TWENTY-FOUR

After this the farmers conveyed their army to Stiklarstaðir. King Óláfr was already there with his troops. Kálfr and Hárekr advanced in the van with their banner. And when they met, then the onset did not take place very quickly, for the farmers delayed attacking because their forces were not anywhere near all advanced equally far, and they waited for the troops that were coming up behind. Þórir hundr had been going last with his company, since he [377] was supposed to take care that none of the troops were tempted to lag behind when the war cry rang out or the troops saw each other, and Kálfr's group were waiting for Þórir. The farmers were using this cry in their army to urge on their troops in battle: 'Forward, forward, farming men!' King Óláfr did not make an attack before because he was waiting for Dagr and the troop that was with him. Then the king's group saw Dagr's troop where it was on its way. It is said that the farmers had no fewer troops than ten thousand. And Sigvatr says this:

147.	My sorrow is savage, that the ruler scant help had from eastward; this king clasped the sword-grip covered with gold wire. The subjects were successful since they were twice as many; that snared the inciter of strife;[380] I reproach neither.	*Erfidrápa Óláfs helga* 9 *Skald* I 675

CHAPTER TWO HUNDRED AND TWENTY-FIVE

While both hosts were standing and the men were able to recognise each other, then the king said:

'Why are you there, Kálfr, since we parted as friends south in Mœrr? It ill befits you to fight against us or to shoot deadly shots into our troops, since four of your brothers are here.'

Kálfr replies: 'Much is now going differently, king, from what would be most fitting. You parted from us in such a way, that it was necessary to make peace with those that [378] had been left behind. Now each must stay where he stands, though we might still be reconciled if I had my way.'

Then Finnr replies: 'It is characteristic of Kálfr that if he speaks well, then he is determined to do ill.'

The king said: 'It may be, Kálfr, that you would like to be reconciled, but you do not look to me to be acting peacefully, you farmers.'

Then Þorgeirr of Kvistsstaðir answers: 'You shall now have such peace as many have had from you in the past, and you must pay for that now.'

The king replies: 'You do not need to be so eager for our engagement, for victory over us will not be granted to you today, for I have raised you to a position of power from being a little man.'

[380] *hildar hvǫtuðr*: 'inciter of battle', warrior.

CHAPTER TWO HUNDRED AND TWENTY-SIX

Þórir hundr now arrived and advanced in front of the banner with his company and called out:

'Forward, forward, farming men!'

Then they raised the war cry and shot both arrows and spears. Then the king's men shouted a war cry, and when that was done, then they urged each other on, as they had been told to do before, saying this:

'Forward, forward, Christ's men, cross's men, king's men!'

But when the farmers that were standing out in the wing heard this, then they said the same as they heard them say. And when other farmers heard this, then they thought these were king's men and raised weapons against them and fought them themselves, and many fell before they recognised each other. The weather was fine, and the sun was shining brightly. But when the battle began, then the sky reddened and the sun too, and before it was over, it became dark as night. King Óláfr had drawn up his troops where there was a sort of rise in the ground, and they threw themselves down on the farmers' troops and they delivered such a strong assault that the farmers' line gave way before it, so that the van of the king's formation now stood where before had been standing those that were most to the rear in the farmers' troop [379] and many of the farmers' troop were now on the point of fleeing, but the landed men and the landed men's men stood firm, and then there was a very fierce battle. So says Sigvatr:

> 148. Far and wide the field spread under   *Erfidrápa Óláfs helga* 10
> feet of men (peace was banned there);   Skald I 677
> then crashed into swift combat,
> clad in mailcoats, the army,
> when, in early morn, the envoys
> of the elm,[381] with bright helmets—
> a great steel-gust[382] set in at
> Stiklarstaðir—down came rushing.

The landed men exhorted their troops and pressed forward to advance. Sigvatr mentions this:

> 149. There went the Þrœndr's standard—   *Erfidrápa Óláfs helga* 11
> this deed is now regretted   Skald I 678
> by farmers—amid their formation
> forward; bold men met there.

---

[381] *alms ærir*: 'messengers of the elm (bow made of elm)', warriors.
[382] *stálgustr*: 'steel-gust', battle.

Then the farmers' troops attacked from all sides. Those that were standing furthest forward hewed, while those that were next thrust with spears, and all those that were further back shot spears or arrows or threw stones or hand axes or stone-headed shafts. It now soon became a bloody battle, and many fell from both sides. In the first assault Arnljótr gellini, Gauka-Þórir and Afra-Fasti fell and all their company, and [380] each of them took with them a man or two or in some cases more. Now the formation in front of the king's banner began to thin out. The king then told Þórðr to carry the banner forward, while the king himself went with the banner and that company of men that he had chosen to stay close to him in battle. These men in his troop were the bravest fighters of all and the best equipped. Sigvatr states this:

> 150. I heard my lord went hardest *Erfidrápa Óláfs helga* 12
> ahead, next to his banners; *Skald* I 678
> the standard preceded the ruler;
> strife there was ample.

When King Óláfr stepped forward out of the shield wall and into the van of the formation and the farmers saw into his face, then they became frightened, and their hands failed them. Sigvatr states this:

> 151. I guess it was ghastly *Erfidrápa Óláfs helga* 13
> for lagoon-flame spreaders[383] *Skald* I 679
> to catch the spear-keen gaze of
> combat-joyful Óleifr.
> Prœndish men were hesitant—
> the *hersar*'s lord seemed so
> awful—to look into
> his eyes, serpent-shining.

[381] Then there was a very fierce battle. The king went strongly forward himself into the hand-to-hand fighting. So says Sigvatr:

> 152. Scarlet with blood of soldiers *Erfidrápa Óláfs helga* 14
> were shields, men's hands also, *Skald* I 680
> and gory swords, where the troop assaulted
> the splendid mighty ruler.
> And the play of iron[384]
> the able king made Innprœndir
> enjoy, the keen sword he
> crimsoned in the parting's meadows.[385]

[383] *lóns loghreytandi*: 'spreader of flame of the lagoon (gold)', generous man.
[384] *ísarnleikr*: 'play of iron', battle.
[385] *reikar tún*: 'infield of the hair-parting', head.

CHAPTER TWO HUNDRED AND TWENTY-SEVEN

King Óláfr now fought very bravely. He struck at Þorgeirr of Kvistsstaðir, the landed man who was mentioned above, across his face and broke apart the nose-guard on his helmet, splitting his head underneath his eyes, so that it was nearly cut off. And as he fell, the king said:

'Is it true or not, what I told you, Þorgeirr, that you would not be victorious in our exchanges?'

At that moment Þórðr brought down the banner pole so hard that the pole stuck in the ground. Þórðr had just then received his death wound, and he fell there beneath the banner. Then Þorfiðr muðr and Gizurr gullbrá also fell there. And he had been attacking two men, and he killed [382] one of them and wounded the other before he fell. So says Hofgarða-Refr:[386]

153. On his own ash of battle[387]—
Óðinn's fire[388] yelled—bold in
steel-rain,[389] against two stalwart
soldiers waged Gunnr's clatter.[390]
The bow-spoiler[391] dealt the Draupnir's
dew-Freyr[392] his death-blow,
he reddened iron, and the other
envoy of currents[393] wounded.

*Poem about Gizurr
gullbrárskáld* 1

Then it came about, as was said above, that the sky was bright but the sun disappeared and it got dark. Sigvatr mentions this:

154. Men call it no minor
marvel that no warming
the cloudless sun could send to
steed-Njǫrðungar of the ship-pole.[394]

Erfidrápa Óláfs helga 15
SnE II 497 (1st half)
Skald I 682

[386] Hofgarða-Refr (Refr of Hofgarðar on Snæfellsnes or Skáld-Refr) Gestsson was an Icelandic poet, son of the poetess Steinunn Refsdóttir. This, thought to be from a poem in honour of his foster-father Gizurr gullbrá, is his only surviving full stanza; other fragmentary verses survive in versions of *Snorra Edda*.
[387] *rimmu askr*: 'ash-tree of battle', warrior.
[388] *Hóars bál*: 'Óðinn's fire', sword.
[389] *stála regn*: 'rain of steel (weapons)', battle.
[390] *Gunnar gnýr*: 'noise of Gunnr (a valkyrie)', battle.
[391] *dalsteypir*: 'bow-overthrower', warrior.
[392] *Draupnirs dǫgg-Freyr*: 'Freyr of the dew of Draupnir (Óðinn's mythical ring, from which eight new rings drip every ninth night) (gold)', man.
[393] *strauma ǫrr*: 'messenger of currents', sailor, man.
[394] *skorðu skæ-Njǫrðungar*: 'Njǫrðungar (gods) of the steed of the prop (ship), which was propped up with poles when on dry land)', sailors, men.

For the prince a great portent
appeared that day: day didn't
hold its bright hue; of the battle
I heard news from parts eastern.

[383] At this moment Dagr Hringsson arrived with the troop that he had had and he started then to draw up his line of battle and raised his banner, but because it was very dark, his attack could not take place quickly, since they could not see what was before them. And yet they turned to where the Rygir and Hǫrðar were facing them. Many of these events happened simultaneously or in some cases a little earlier or a little later.

CHAPTER TWO HUNDRED AND TWENTY-EIGHT

Kálfr and Óláfr were the names of two of Kálfr Árnason's kinsmen. They were standing on one side of him, tall men and valiant. Kálfr was son of Arnfinnr Armóðsson and nephew of Árni Armóðsson. On the other side of Kálfr Árnason Þórir hundr stepped forward. King Óláfr struck at Þórir hundr across the shoulders. The sword did not cut, and it looked as though dust flew up from the reindeer skin. Sigvatr mentions this:

155. Gracious, the king discovered   *Erfidrápa Óláfs helga* 16
       clearly how the mighty   *Skald* I 683
       spells of Finnish sorcerers
       saved most arrogant Þórir,
[384]   when the sender of sparks of mast-tops[395]
       struck with sword gold-decked—
       blunted, it bit little—
       about Hundr's shoulders.

Þórir struck at the king, and they then exchanged a few blows, and the king's sword did not cut where the reindeer skin was in front of it, and yet Þórir was wounded on his hand. Sigvatr also said:

156. The tree of gold[396] who blames Þórir   *Erfidrápa Óláfs helga* 17
       true courage obscures (I heard of   *Skald* I 685
       it at home); who from valiant
       Hundr has seen greater exploits?
       when the Óðinn of angled fences
       of the onset-hall's storm,[397] he who

[395] *húna hyrsendir*: 'sender of (i.e. one who gives away) fire of the (gilded) masttops (gold)', generous man, king.

[396] *seims þollr*: 'tree of gold', man.

[397] *gunnranns glyggs þvergarða Þróttr*: 'Óðinn of cross-fences (shields) of the storm (battle) of the war-hall (shield wall)', warrior.

surged forward, presumed to
strike at the king's person.

The king spoke to Bjǫrn the Marshal:
'You strike the dog that iron does not cut.'
Bjǫrn turned the axe in his hand and struck with the back of the blade. This blow fell on Þórir's shoulder and it was a very heavy blow, and it made Þórir stagger. And at that very moment the king turned towards Kálfr and his kinsmen and gave Kálfr's kinsman Óláfr his death wound. Then Þórir hundr thrust with his spear at Bjǫrn the Marshal in the middle of his body, giving him his death [385] wound. Then said Þórir:
'Thus we beat the bear.'

Þorsteinn knarrarsmiðr struck at King Óláfr with his axe, and this blow fell on his left leg just above the knee. Finnr Árnason immediately killed Þorsteinn. But at this wound the king leant up against a stone and threw down his sword and prayed God to help him. Then Þórir hundr thrust his spear at him. The thrust went up under his mail coat and passed up into his belly. Then Kálfr struck at him. This blow came on his left side in to his neck. People disagree about which Kálfr it was that gave the king this wound. King Óláfr received these three wounds that led to his death. And after his fall there now fell nearly all that company that had advanced with the king. Bjarni Gullbrárskáld composed this about Kálfr Árnason:

157.	Glad in war, you began with warfare	*Kálfsflokkr* 5
	to guard the land against Óleifr,	*Skald* I 885
	to the excellent king opened	
	enmity; I state I heard it.	
	At Stiklarstaðir, you strode sooner	
	than the standard surged; an exploit	
	true t'was, you kept attacking,	
	intrepid, till the king had fallen.	

[386] The poet Sigvatr composed this about Bjǫrn the Marshal:

158.	I've heard how Bjǫrn, with abundant	*Erfidrápa Óláfs helga* 18
	boldness, taught the marshals	*Skald* I 684
	at that time, too, how it was proper	
	to protect their lord; he pressed forward.	
	He fell in the force, amid the	
	faithful men of the retinue—	
	that loss of life—by the head of	
	the lord fame-rich—is lauded.	

CHAPTER TWO HUNDRED AND TWENTY-NINE

Dagr Hringsson now carried on the battle and made such a fierce first assault that the farmers gave way before it, and some turned in flight. Then numbers of the farmers' forces fell, and these landed men: Erlendr of Gerði, Áslákr of Finney. Then the banner that they had previously been carrying was cut down. Then there was the most furious battle. People have called it Dagr's storm.[398] Then Kálfr Árnason, Hárekr from Þjótta, Þórir hundr turned towards Dagr with the formation that belonged to them. Dagr was now overpowered, and he then turned in flight, as did all the forces that were left. And there happens to be a kind of valley leading up where the main body of those in flight went. Many troops fell there. People then dispersed in both directions. Many men were severely wounded, and many were so badly exhausted that they were fit [387] for nothing. Farmers pursued the fleeing men only a short way, for the leaders soon turned back and to where the slain were, for many had their friends and kinsmen to seek out there.

CHAPTER TWO HUNDRED AND THIRTY

Þórir hundr went to where King Óláfr's body was, and put it to rights, laying the body down and straightening it and spreading cloth over it. And when he was wiping the blood off his face, then he said this afterwards that the king's face was so beautiful, that there was a flush on his cheeks as if he was asleep, and much brighter than before when he was alive. Then the king's blood got onto Þórir's hand and ran up between his thumb and fingers, where he had previously been wounded, and he needed no bandage after that, it healed so quickly. Þórir himself bore witness to this incident when King Óláfr's sanctity became known, before the whole people. Þórir hundr was the first to uphold the king's sanctity of the men of the ruling class that had been there in the host opposing him.

CHAPTER TWO HUNDRED AND THIRTY-ONE

Kálfr Árnason sought his brothers that were fallen there. He came across Þorbergr and Finnr, and what people say is that Finnr threw a short sword at him and tried to kill him, speaking harsh words to him, calling him truce-breaker and traitor to his lord. Kálfr took no notice and had Finnr carried away from the fallen dead and Þorbergr as well. Then their wounds were looked into, and they had no life-threatening wounds. They had both fallen under the weight of weapons and from exhaustion. Then Kálfr sought to convey his brothers down to a ship and went with them himself. And as soon as

---

[398] *Dagshríð*: see verse 160 and note 404 below.

he turned away, then all the farmers' troops left whose homes were nearby, [388] except for those who were looking after their kinsmen and friends that were wounded, or the bodies of those that were fallen. Wounded men were conveyed back to the town, so that every building was full of them, while tents were put up outside over some. And so wonderfully many people as had gathered in the farmers' army, yet it seemed to people no less extraordinary how quickly the gathering dispersed once it had started, and the main reason for this was that the greatest number had gathered from country districts and were very keen to get home.

CHAPTER TWO HUNDRED AND THIRTY-TWO

The farmers that had dwellings in Veradalr went to see the leaders, Hárekr and Þórir, and complained to them of their problem, saying this:

'These men that are fleeing, when they have got away, will go up along Veradalr and will deal unfortunately with our homesteads, while we are unable to go home while they are here in the valley. Now please, go after them with a force and let not a child escape, for they would have intended the same treatment for us if they had got the better of it in our encounter, and so will they do again if we meet later on so that they have better luck than us. It may be that they will stay in the valley if they are not expecting they have anything to fear. They will straightway go through our settlements inconsiderately.'

The farmers spoke of this at great length and urged with great passion that the leaders should go and kill these people that had got away. So when the leaders discussed this among themselves, then they felt the farmers had said much that was true in their speech, then decided that Þórir hundr and his men should set out with the Verdœlir, and he took six hundred men of his own troops, then went. Then night began to fall. Þórir did not cease travelling until he got during the night to Súl, and he heard [389] there the news that during the evening Dagr Hringsson had come there and many others of King Óláfr's companies, had a pause for an evening meal and after that gone up onto the mountain. Then Þórir says that he was not going to wander over mountains after them, and he then turned back down into the valley, and then they got very few of the men killed. After that the farmers went to their homesteads, and Þórir went the next day, and his troops, out to their ships. But the king's men, those who were able to, escaped, hiding themselves in forests, some getting help from people.

CHAPTER TWO HUNDRED AND THIRTY-THREE

Þormóðr Kolbrúnarskáld was in the battle under the king's banner. And when the king was fallen and the onslaught was at its most furious, then the king's troops fell one after another, and most were wounded that were still standing. Þormóðr was badly wounded. He then did like the others, all retreated from there where there seemed the greatest danger to life, and some ran. Then began the battle that is known as Dagr's storm. Then all the king's troops, those that were still capable of bearing weapons, made their way there, but Þormóðr did not now come into the battle, as he was disabled both by wounds and by exhaustion, and he stood there by his comrades, though there was nothing else he could do. Then he was struck by an arrow in his left side. He broke the arrow shaft off himself and then went away from the battle and back to the houses and came to a kind of barn. It was a large building. Þormóðr had a naked sword in his hand. And when he went in, then a man came out towards him. This person said:

'There are terribly unpleasant noises inside here, wailing and bellowing; it is very shameful when valiant men cannot put up with their wounds. It may be that the king's men performed bravely, but very poorly do they endure their wounds.'

Þormóðr replies: 'What is your name?'

He said his name was Kimbi. Þormóðr replies:

'Were you in the battle?'

'I was,' [390] he says, 'with the farmers, where it was better.'

'Are you at all wounded?' says Þormóðr.

'Not much,' says Kimbi, 'but were you in the battle?'

Þormóðr says: 'I was with those who got the better of it.'

Kimbi saw that Þormóðr had a gold ring on his arm. He said:

'You must be a king's man. Give me the gold ring, and I will hide you. The farmers will kill you if you bump into them.'

Þormóðr says: 'You take the ring, if you can get it. I have now lost more than that.'

Kimbi stretched out his arm and was going to take the ring. Þormóðr swung his sword at him and cut off his hand, and it is said that Kimbi did not endure his wound one whit better than those whom he had criticised earlier. Kimbi went away, but Þormóðr sat down in the barn and stayed there for a while and listened to what people were saying. Most of their conversation was about each one saying what he claimed he had seen in the battle, and they discussed men's performance. Some praised most King Óláfr's valour, while some spoke of other men just as much. Then said Þormóðr:

159.	Óleifr's heart was active;	*Fóstbræðra saga* 271–72
	onwards in blood the king waded;	*Skald* I 838
	inlaid steel bit at Stiklar-	
	staðir; he urged troops to battle.	

I saw all the blizzard-trees
of Jalfaðr[399] but the ruler
himself shelter in the ceaseless
spear-storm;[400] most were tested.

[391] CHAPTER TWO HUNDRED AND THIRTY-FOUR

After this Þormóðr went off to a kind of storehouse and went in. There were already many men inside there badly wounded. There was a certain woman busy there bandaging men's wounds. There was a fire on the floor, and she was warming water to cleanse the wounds. So Þormóðr sat down out by the doorway. One man was going out there, and another in, who were busy attending to men's wounds. Then someone turned to Þormóðr and looked at him and after that said:

'Why are you so pale? Are you wounded, or why don't you ask for treatment for yourself?'

Then Þormóðr uttered a verse:

160.	I am not rosy, but rules a	*Legendary saga* 202–04
	red man[401] the white and	*Fóstbrœðra saga* 275
	slender hawks' seat Skǫgul;[402]	*Skald* I 840

scarce those who think of me, wounded.
The cause is that to me, thou accustomed
killer of flour of Fenja,[403]
deep tracks of Dagr's tempest[404]
and Danish weapons give pain.

After that Þormóðr stood up and went in to the fire and stood there for a while. Then the physician spoke to him:

[399] *Jalfaðs élþollr*; 'tree of the storm of Jalfaðr/Jǫlfuðr (Óðinn) (battle)', warrior.
[400] *fleindrífa*: 'spear-snowstorm', battle.
[401] The poet is pale, but reddened by blood
[402] *hauka setrs Skǫgul*: 'valkyrie of the seat of hawks (arm)', woman.
[403] *Fenja meldrar morðvenjandi* 'one accustomed to killing (i.e. lessening by giving away) Fenja's (a giantess's) flour (gold)', generous man (vocative). The poem *Grottasǫngr* relates how two giantesses, Fenja and Menja, ground gold from a magic mill for the Danish king Fróði (*Skáldsk* 52–58).
[404] *Dags hríð* (so most manuscripts): 'storm of Dagr (a legendary king)', battle. This seems to be the source for Snorri's account of the fiercest part of the fighting at Stiklarstaðir being known as *Dagshríð* after Dagr Hringsson; but if this verse is genuinely by Þormóðr, it is unlikely that he could have known of this description of the events of the battle. The manuscript K has *dals hríð* and Perg. 4to nr 2 has *dalhríð* 'bow-storm', 'storm of arrows' and the former is the reading followed in *ÍF* 27. (See R. D. Fulk in *Skald* I 840.) The tracks of battle are wounds.

'You, fellow, go out and get me the firewood that is lying out here in front of the entrance.'

He went out, carried in an armful of wood and threw it [392] down on the floor. Then the physician looked him in the face and said:

'Amazingly pale is this man. Why are you like that?'

Then spoke Þormóðr:

> 161. Why are we so pallid?   *Legendary saga* 202
> wonders the hawk's lands oak-tree.[405]   *Fóstbrœðra saga* 274
> Wounds make few fair, lady,   *Skald* I 843
> I faced a storm of arrows.
> Through me the dark[406] metal,
> mightily driven, came flying;
> the dangerous iron cut keenly
> close to my heart, as I reckon.

Then said the physician: 'Let me see your wounds and I shall give you some bandages.'

After that he sat down and threw off his clothes. And when the physician saw his wounds, then she examined the wound that he had in his side, felt that there was a piece of iron stuck in it, but could not tell for certain which way it had gone in. She had been cooking in a stone kettle there, ground garlic and other herbs and boiled it together and was giving it to wounded men and could find out like that whether they had intestinal wounds, for it smelt of garlic from out of the wound if it was intestinal. She brought this to Þormóðr, bidding him eat it. He replies:

'Take it away. I am not pining for gruel.'

Then she took some tongs and tried to pull the iron out, but it was stuck and would not move, there being only a little bit sticking out, for the wound was swollen. Then Þormóðr said:

'You cut in to where the iron is, so that it can easily be got at with the tongs, then give them to me and let me tug at it.'

[393] She did as he said. Then Þormóðr took a gold ring from his arm and gave it to the physician, telling her to do whatever she wanted with it:

'It was given by one who is good,' he says. 'King Óláfr gave me this ring this morning.'

After that Þormóðr took the tongs and pulled out the arrow head. But there were barbs on it, and there were fibres from his heart stuck on it, some of them red, some white, and when he saw this, he said:

---

[405] *ǫglis landa eik*: 'oak-tree of hawk's lands (arms)', woman.

[406] *døkkvi*: the reading of all manuscripts except K, which has *kløkkvi*, from *kløkkr* 'flexible'. This is less appropriate, but is accepted in *ÍF* 27.

'Well has the king nourished us. There is still fat around my heart strings.'
After that he sank back and was now dead. There ends the story of Þormóðr.

CHAPTER TWO HUNDRED AND THIRTY-FIVE

King Óláfr fell on the Wednesday, the fourth day before the kalends of the month of August.[407] It was nearly midday when they met, and the battle began before the mid-point between then and none,[408] while the king died before none, and the darkness lasted from that mid-point until none. The poet Sigvatr says this about the conclusion of the battle:

162. Harsh is the emptiness after   *Erfidrápa Óláfs helga* 19
 the Englishmen's foe, and painful,   *Skald* I 687
 since from the wounded king soldiers
 stripped life; the lord's shield shattered.
 Óleifr's life the war-keen army
 ended, where troops split shields;
 to the meeting of points[409] the commander
 marched, but Dagr departed.

[394] And again he spoke this:

163. No poles of war-skerry[410] expected   *Erfidrápa Óláfs helga* 20
 the power of the farmers—   *Skald* I 688
 the people caused the prince's
 passing—or of the *hersar*,[411]
 by which in war the trees of
 wound-fire[412] felled such a ruler—
 many fine forces in blood lay
 fallen—as Óleifr was considered.

The farmers did not plunder the slain, and what happened immediately after the battle was rather this, that many were seized with fear, those that had been against the king, and yet they retained their hostility and decided between themselves that all those men who had fallen with the king should not have the last rites or burial, that befitted good men, calling them all robbers and outlaws. But those men who were powerful and had kinsmen there among the slain took no notice of this, conveyed their kinsmen to churches and gave them last rites.

[407] 29th July. In fact Óláfr must have died on Monday 31st August.
[408] Half past one.
[409] *odda fundr*; 'meeting of (weapon-)points', battle.
[410] *ógnar skers meiðr*: 'pole of the skerry of battle (shield)', warrior.
[411] *hersar*: lords.
[412] *sárelds viðr*: 'tree of wound-fire (sword)', warrior.

CHAPTER TWO HUNDRED AND THIRTY-SIX

Þorgils Hálmuson and his son Grímr went to the slain in the evening when it had got dark. They took up King Óláfr's body and carried it away to where there was a kind of small, empty cottage on one side of the farmstead, taking [395] a light with them and water, then took the clothes off the body and washed the body and wiped it then with linen cloths, laid it down there in the building and covered it with pieces of wood so that no one could see it, even if people came into the building. After that they went away and back to the farmstead. Following both armies there had been a large number of beggars and those poor folk that used to beg for their food. Now that evening after the battle many of these folk had stayed there, and when it got dark, they sought lodgings for themselves through all the buildings both small and large. There was a blind man there, about whom there is a story. He was poor, and his boy went with him and guided him. They walked round the outside of the farmstead looking for a lodging for themselves. They got to this same deserted dwelling. The doorway was so low that one almost had to crawl in. And when the blind man got into the house, then he felt about on the floor, searching for whether he might be able to lie down. He had a hood on his head, and the hood fell down over his face when he bent down. He felt in front of him with his hands that there was a pool on the floor. He lifted up his wet hand and raised up his hood, and his fingers touched up by his eyes, and immediately he got such a great itching on his eyelids that he rubbed his eyes themselves with his wet fingers. After that he backed out of the building saying that it was impossible to lie inside, because it was all wet there. So when he got out of the building, then he could immediately to begin with make out his hands and everything that was near him that he could see in the darkness of night. He immediately went back to the farmstead and into the living room and there told everyone that he had got his sight and was now a seeing man. And there were many men there that knew that he had long been blind, for he had often been there and walked around the neighbourhood. He says that he first saw when he came out of a certain little wretched house.

'And it was all wet inside.' He says, 'I groped in it [396] with my hands and I rubbed my wet hands over my eyes.'

He also says where this house was. So the men who were there and saw all this were greatly amazed about what had happened and discussed among themselves what could be inside there in that house. But Farmer Þorgils and his son Grímr felt certain how this event must have arisen. They were very afraid that the king's enemies would go and search the house. After this they stole away and went to the building and took the body, carried it away out into the pasture and hid it there, went after that to the farmstead and slept through the night there.

CHAPTER TWO HUNDRED AND THIRTY-SEVEN

On the Thursday Þórir hundr came down from Veradalr out to Stiklarstaðir, accompanied by many troops. There were also many of the farmers' troops about. The slain were still being cleared away. People carried away the bodies of their kinsmen and friends and gave assistance to wounded men, those that people wanted to heal. But large numbers of men had now died since the battle had ended. Þórir hundr went to where the king had fallen and looked for the body, and when he could not find it, he made enquiries whether anyone could tell him what had become of the body, but no one could tell him. Then he asked Farmer Þorgils if he knew anything about where the king's body was. Þorgils replies as follows:

'I was not in the battle. I know little of what happened. There are now many stories going around. It is now said that King Óláfr has been met during the night up near Stafr and a company of men with him. But if he has fallen, then your comrades will have hidden his body in woods or rocky places.'

And though Þórir felt sure it was true that the king was fallen, yet many took up and spread the rumour that the king must have got away out of the battle and that it would not be long before he would get [397] an army and come back against them. Then Þórir went to his ships and after that out along the fiord. Then the whole troop of farmers began to scatter and moved away the wounded men, all those that could be moved.

CHAPTER TWO HUNDRED AND THIRTY-EIGHT

Þorgils Hálmuson and his son Grímr had King Óláfr's body in their keeping, and were very anxious about how they could manage to take care that the king's enemies were not able to get hold of it to mistreat the body, since they heard the farmers' talk of it being the best thing to do, if the king's body was found, to burn it or convey it out to sea and sink it down. The father and son had seen during the night as if it were a candle flame burning above where King Óláfr's body was among the slain, and similarly afterwards, when they had hidden the body, then they always saw at night a light from the direction where the king rested. They were afraid that the king's enemies would search for the body there where it was if they saw these signs. Þorgils and his son were keen to convey the body away to some place where it would be secure. Þorgils and his son made a coffin and took the greatest pains with it and laid the king's body in it, and afterwards they made another coffin and put in it straw and stones so that it weighed as much as a man, closing this coffin carefully. So when all the farmers' troops had gone from Stiklarstaðir, then Þorgils and his son got ready to leave. He got a kind of rowing boat. Altogether they were seven or eight men, and all kinsmen or friends of Þorgils. They secretly conveyed the king's body to the ship and put the coffin down under the decking. They also had with them the coffin that had stones in it, placed it in the ship so that everyone could see it, travelled after that out along the fiord, got a good tail wind, in the evening, when it began to get dark, came out to Niðaróss, landing at the king's jetty. After that [398] Þorgils sent men up into the town and had Bishop Sigurðr told that they were coming there with King Óláfr's body. So when the bishop hears this news, he immediately sent his men down to the jetties. They took there an oared ship and laid it alongside Þorgils's ship, demanding to be given the king's body. Þorgils and his men then took the coffin that was standing up on the deck and carried it into the oared ship. After that these men rowed out into the fiord and sank the coffin down there. The night was now dark. Þorgils and his men then rowed up along the river until the town was at an end, and landed at a place called Saurhlið. This was above the town. Then they carried the body up and into a certain empty storehouse that was standing there up above other buildings. They watched there all night over the body. Þorgils went down into the town. He got to speak with the men who had been most friends of the king there. He asked them if they would take charge of the king's body. No one dared do that. Afterwards Þorgils and his men conveyed the body up along the river and buried it there down in a sand dune that has formed there, cleared up there afterwards so that recent activity would not be apparent there. They had finished doing all this before day dawned, then went to their ship, made their way immediately out from the river, going after that on their way until they came back to Stiklarstaðir.

CHAPTER TWO HUNDRED AND THIRTY-NINE

Sveinn, son of King Knútr and Jarl Álfrimr's daughter Álfífa, he had been appointed to rule at Jómsborg in Vinðland, but now a message had come to him from his father King Knútr that he was to go to Denmark, and also that he was after that to go to Norway and take over the realm that was in Norway to govern, [399] and as well to have the title of king over Norway. After this Sveinn went to Denmark and got from there a large force. With him went Jarl Haraldr and many other men of the ruling class. Þórarinn loftunga mentions this in the poem that he composed about Sveinn Álfífuson that is called *Glælognskviða*:[413]

[413] *Glælognskviða* 'Calm Sea poem' is a poem in *kviðuháttr* of which 9 stanzas survive (see sts 166–174 below). It is the earliest text to assert Óláfr's sanctity, within the context of the rule of Sveinn Knútsson, to whom the poem is addressed. The title is preserved only here, and may allude to the journey of the Danes to Norway, mentioned in this stanza.

164. It is not hidden	*Glælognskviða* 1
how the Danes made	*Fsk* 201
a loyal journey	*Skald* I 865
with their leader.
There the jarl was first
and foremost,
and every man
after him following
each warrior
worthier than the next.

After this Sveinn went to Norway and with him his mother Álfífa, and he was accepted there as king at every legal assembly. He had then come from the east to the Vík when the battle took place at Stiklarstaðir and King Óláfr fell. Sveinn did not cease travelling until he came in the autumn north to Þrándheimr. He was accepted as king there as elsewhere. King Sveinn introduced new laws into the country in respect of many things, and these were set up after the pattern of how the laws were in Denmark, though some were much harsher. No one was to leave the country except with the leave of the king, but if he went, then his possessions fell to the king. And everyone that killed someone, he should forfeit land and movable property. If a man was convicted and an inheritance fell to him, then the king got this inheritance. At Yule every farmer was to give the king a measure of malt for every hearth[414] and a haunch of a three-winters-old ox — this [400] was known as *vinartoddi* ('wisp of meadow') — and a container[415] of butter, and each housewife a *rykkjartó* ('lady's tow'), this was cleaned flax, as much as could be grasped between the thumb and middle finger. Farmers were obliged to build all the houses that the king wished to have at his residences. Every seven men were to fit out one able-bodied one, and this applied to everyone that was five winters old, and would be responsible for a proportionate number of rowlocks.[416] Every man that rowed out fishing was to pay the king a landing string,[417] wherever he rowed out from, that is a bundle of five fish. Every ship that went away out of the country was to keep for the king a section across the hold. Every man that went to Iceland was to pay land dues, both natives and foreigners. Added to this was the rule that now

[414] *Mæli* (measure) must have varied from time to time and in different regions, but one medieval source indicates that in Norway it could be about 16.2 litres. 'For every hearth' means for each dwelling.

[415] *Spann* would also have varied, but could have been about 15 kg.

[416] *Hamla*, the loop into which the oar was fitted, was the unit of conscription to the levy, and represented one oarsman. For every oarsman the seven providers had to build and equip a proportionate part of the ship

[417] A string of fish for his landing place.

Danish men were to have this much standing in Norway, that the witness of one of them was to outweigh the witness of ten Norwegians. And when this legislation [401] was made public, then people immediately began to develop feelings of resistance and started grumbling among themselves. Those that had not taken part in the opposition to King Óláfr, spoke like this:

'Take up now, you Innþrœndir, the friendship and rewards from the Knýtlingar for which you fought against King Óláfr and removed him from the country. You were promised peace and improvement in your status, but now you have oppression and enslavement, and on top of that serious crimes and baseness.'

And it was not easy to contradict this. Now everyone realised that things had not been arranged for the best. People did not, however, have the confidence to start a rebellion against King Sveinn. The reason for this was that people had given their sons or other close kinsmen to King Knútr as hostages, and this too, that there was now no leader for a rebellion. People soon had much cause of complaint against King Sveinn, and yet people mostly blamed Álfífa for everything that they found contrary to their minds. And now the truth about King Óláfr was realised by many people.

CHAPTER TWO HUNDRED AND FORTY

That winter began the talk by many people there in Þrándheimr that King Óláfr was truly a saint, and many miracles took place supporting his sainthood. Now there came to be many invocations of King Óláfr about the things that people felt were important. Many people gained benefits from these invocations, some recovery from ailments, and some help on journeys or other things that were felt to present a need for this.

CHAPTER TWO HUNDRED AND FORTY-ONE

Einarr þambarskelfir was come back to his estates from the west, from England, and got the revenues that King Knútr had granted him when they met in Þrándheimr, and this almost amounted to a jarl's power. Einarr þambarskelfir [402] had not been in the rebellion against King Óláfr. He himself boasted of this. Einarr called to mind that Knútr had promised him jarldom over Norway, and also this, that the king had not fulfilled his promises. Einarr was the first of the ruling class to uphold the sainthood of King Óláfr.

CHAPTER TWO HUNDRED AND FORTY-TWO

Finnr Árnason only stayed for a short time at Egg with Kálfr, for he took it very badly that Kálfr had been in the battle against King Óláfr. Finnr constantly criticised Kálfr very severely on this account. Þorbergr Árnason was much more restrained in his speech than Finnr, and yet Þorbergr was very keen to go away and back to his estate. Kálfr provided these brothers of his with a fine longship with all its rigging and other equipment and a good party of men to go with them. They went back to their estates. Árni Árnason lay a long time with his wounds, and recovered and had no permanent injury. He went after that in the winter south to his estate. All the brothers accepted quarter from King Sveinn, and all the brothers settled down quietly at home.

CHAPTER TWO HUNDRED AND FORTY-THREE

The next summer there came to be much talk of King Óláfr's sainthood, and public opinion about the king all changed. There were now many that affirmed that the king must be saintly who previously had opposed him in absolute enmity and not let him in any respect get a fair report from them. People now began to turn to criticising the men that had most urged rebellion against the king. As a result Bishop Sigurðr was much blamed. People there became such great enemies of his that he saw his best course as to go away and west to England to see King Knútr. [403] After this the Þrœndir sent men and messages to Upplǫnd for Bishop Grímkell to come north to Þrándheimr. King Óláfr had sent Bishop Grímkell back to Norway when the king went east to Garðaríki. Bishop Grímkell had since then been in Upplǫnd. So when this message came to the bishop, then he immediately got ready for this journey. A large part of the reason why he went was that the bishop believed that it must be true what was said about the performing of miracles and the sainthood of King Óláfr.

CHAPTER TWO HUNDRED AND FORTY-FOUR

Bishop Grímkell went to see Einarr þambarskelfir. Einarr welcomed the bishop joyfully, they then discussed many things after that, including the fact that there had taken place in that country important events. They were of one mind between themselves in all their discussions. Then the bishop went inland to Kaupangr. There all the ordinary people welcomed him. He enquired in detail about the miracles that were related about King Óláfr. He received good information about this. After that the bishop sent messengers in to Stiklarstaðir to Þorgils and his son Grímr and summoned them out to the town to see him. The father and son did not neglect this journey. They went out to the town to see the bishop. They tell him all the signs that they had discovered, and also where they had taken the king's body. After that the bishop sent for Einarr þambarskelfir, and Einarr came to the town. Einarr and the bishop then held discussions with the king and Álfífa and asked the king to give permission for King Óláfr's body to be disinterred. The king gave his permission and told the bishop to do whatever he wished with it. There were now large crowds of people in the town. The bishop and Einarr and some people with them went to where the king's body was buried and had it dug for. [404] The coffin had now more or less come up out of the ground. It was then proposed by many people that the bishop should have the king interred at Clemenskirkja. So when twelve months and five nights had passed from the death of King Óláfr, then his holy relics were dug up. The coffin was now still nearly come up out of the ground, and King Óláfr's coffin was brand new as if it had been freshly planed. Bishop Grímkell then went up to where King Óláfr's coffin was being opened. There was a glorious sweet smell there. Then the bishop uncovered the king's face, and his countenance was in no way changed, such redness on his cheeks as would have been if he had just gone to sleep. In this people perceived a great difference, those who had seen King Óláfr when he fell, that since then his hair and nails had grown almost as much as they would have done if he had been alive here in the world all the time since he fell. Then there went up to see King Óláfr's body King Sveinn and all the leading people that were there. Then Álfífa spoke:

'Men rot amazingly slowly in the sand. It would not have been so if he had lain in earth.'

After that the bishop took shears and cut the king's hair, also clipping his moustaches. He had had long moustaches as was then the fashion among men. Then the bishop spoke to the king and Álfífa:

'Now the king's hair and moustaches are as long as when he died, but they had grown as much as you now see here cut off.'

Then Álfífa replies: 'Then this hair will seem to me a holy relic, if it does not burn in fire. For we have often seen people's hair complete and unharmed who have lain in the ground longer that this man.'

After that the bishop had fire brought in a fire-pan and blessed it and put incense on it. After that he put King Óláfr's hair in the fire, and when all the incense was burnt, then the bishop took the hair up out of the fire, and the hair was now unburnt. The bishop let the king and other leaders see it. Then Álfífa ordered the hair to be put into unconsecrated fire. Then Einarr [405] þambarskelfir replied, telling her to be silent and picked many harsh words for her. It was then decreed by the bishop with the king's agreement and the verdict of all the people that King Óláfr was truly saintly. Then the king's body was carried in into Clemenskirkja and set up before the high altar. The coffin was wrapped in precious cloth and all hung with velvet.[418]

---

[418] *Guðvefr* was a fine cloth, probably originally a kind of cotton from the east (the word is believed to be derived from the Arabian word for cotton), maybe often dark red in colour. Cf. I 126 and note 70 above.

There immediately took place many kinds of miracles at the holy relics of King Óláfr.

CHAPTER TWO HUNDRED AND FORTY-FIVE

There in the dune where King Óláfr had lain in the ground, a beautiful spring came up, and people got cures for their ailments from this water. A surround was built for it, and this water has ever since been looked after with care. First of all a chapel was built and an altar set up there where the king's grave had been, but now Christchurch stands in that place. Archbishop Eysteinn had a high altar set up there in the same place where the king's grave had been when he raised that great minster that still stands. There had also been in that place the high altar in the old Christchurch.[419] It is said that Óláfskirkja now stands there where at that time stood the disused storehouse that King Óláfr's body was put in for the night. It is now called Óláfr's gate where the king's holy remains were carried up from the ship, and this is now in the middle of the town. The bishop looked after King Óláfr's holy remains, cutting his hair and his nails, for both went on growing just like when he was a living person in this world. So says the poet Sigvatr:

[406] 165.   I lie unless Óleifr   *Erfidrápa Óláfs helga* 23
            like living bow-gods[420] has growing   *Skald* I 692
            hair; I praise in poetry
            principally the king's servants.
            The hair still holds that grew on
            his bright skull, who in Garðar
            gave sight to Valdamarr, bestowing
            succour for infirmity.[421]

Þórarinn loftunga composed the poem that is called *Glælognskviða* about Sveinn Álfífuson, and it includes these verses:

       166.   Now the prince   *Glælognskviða* 2
              has placed himself   *Skald* I 866
              on the throne
              at Þrándheimr.
              There will ever,
              all his life,

---

[419] i.e. the one built by Óláfr kyrri.
[420] *ýs tívar*: 'gods of (the bow made of) yew', men.
[421] This Valdamarr (Vladimir) is unknown, and the miracle referred to is not recorded elsewhere. Cf. Index of Names.

       the ring-breaker[422]
       rule the dwellings

167. where Óleifr   *Glælognskviða* 3
       earlier lived   *Skald* I 867
       before he left
       for heaven's realm
       and there was,
       as all are aware,
       enshrined alive,[423]
       latterly king.

168. Haraldr's son   *Glælognskviða* 4
       had betaken   *Skald* I 869
       himself firmly
       to heaven's kingdom,
       before the gold-breaker[424]
       became mediator . . .[425]

169, So that there, pure,   *Glælognskviða* 5
       the praise-blessed king   *Skald* I 870
       with his body
       unblemished lies
       and there, as
       on a living man,
       hair and nails
       on him do grow.

170. There in the belfry[426]   *Glælognskviða* 6
       bells can ring   *Skald* I 871
       over his bed
       of their own accord;
       and every day
       all people hear
       the sound of bells
       above the king.

[422] *bauga brjótr*: 'breaker of rings', generous man, who breaks up hoards of treasure by distributing them to his men; here, King Sveinn.

[423] That is, placed in a shrine, but still alive as a saint.

[424] *seimbrjótr*: 'breaker of gold', generous man (who would break off links of gold chain to give people).

[425] This assumes the emendation proposed in *LP*, of *setti* (most manuscripts) to *sætti* ('means of reconciliation'). Two lines of the stanza seem to be missing.

[426] *borðveggr*: 'wooden structure', bell-tower or choir?

[408] 171. And there up
over the altar,
pleasing to Christ,
candles burn.
So has Ǫleifr,
ere he died,
without sin
saved his soul.

Glælognskviða 7
Skald I 872

172. There comes a host
where the holy
king himself is,
creeping for help,
and people, the blind
and those who beg
for speech come there
and, cured, depart.

Glælognskviða 8
Skald I 873

173. Pray to Ǫleifr
to yield to you
his ground—
God's man he is—
he does get
from God himself
peace and plenty
for all people

Glælognskviða 9
Skald I 875

174. when you place
your prayers before
the sacred nail
of the speech of books.[427]

Glælognskviða 10
Skald I 875

[409] Þórarinn loftunga was with King Sveinn at this time and saw and heard these great signs of King Óláfr's sainthood, that through the power of heaven people could hear a sound above his holy relics like bells ringing and candles lighted themselves over the altar there by heavenly fire. And in that Þórarinn says that a host of people came to the holy King Óláfr, lame and blind or sick in other ways, and went away cured, he is saying or recording nothing other than that it must have been an innumerable multitude of people who gained health straightway then at the start from King Óláfr's miracle working. But King Óláfr's greatest miracles, they are written down and recorded, as are those that took place later.

[427] *bókmáls reginnagli*: 'mighty nail of the speech of books' or 'language of books, i.e. Latin', the saint, Óláfr.

CHAPTER TWO HUNDRED AND FORTY-SIX

People say, those that reckon in detail, that St Óláfr was king over Norway fifteen winters after Jarl Sveinn left the country, but the previous winter he received the title of king from the Upplendingar. The poet Sigvatr says this:

175.	Óleifr held, high-minded	*Erfidrápa Óláfs helga* 21
	head, the upper country	*Skald* I 689
	before he fell, for fifteen	
	full years—in that fiefdom.	
	Which greater people-governor	
	has gained the northern end of	
	the world? The leader lasted	
	less long than he should have.	

[410] King Óláfr the Saint was then thirty-five years of age when he fell according to the priest Ari inn fróði (the Learned). He had had twenty major battles. So says Sigvatr the poet:

176.	Some men in God trusted;	*Erfidrápa Óláfs helga* 22
	the troop was divided.	*Skald* I 691
	Twenty major battles	
	the ambitious king engaged in.	
	Celebrated, the Christian band he	
	bade stand at his right hand;	
	To fête the father of Magnús,	
	flight-shy, beg I Lord God.	

Now some part of the story of King Óláfr has been told, concerning some of those events that took place while he was ruling Norway, and also about his fall and about how his sainthood became known. And yet now it must not lie untold what his greatest glory resides in, to tell of his miracle working, even though it is written afterwards in this book.

CHAPTER TWO HUNDRED AND FORTY-SEVEN

King Sveinn Knútsson ruled over Norway for a few winters. He was childish both in age and discretion. His mother Álfífa had most of the government of the country in her hands, and the people of the country were great enemies of hers, both at that time and for ever after. Danish people had tyrannical power in Norway, and the people of the country greatly resented it. When discussion of these things took place, then other people of the country blamed it on the Þrœndir, [411] saying that it had been largely due to them that King Óláfr

the Saint had been removed from the country, and the people of Norway had been subjected to this evil rule, in which oppression and enslavement afflicted all the people, both high and low and all the whole population; they declared that the Prœndir had a duty to carry out an uprising—
'In order to rid us of this rule.'

It was also the opinion of the people of the country that the Prœndir had the most power now in Norway because of their leaders and the large population that there was there. So when the Prœndir realised that the people of the country were criticising them, then they acknowledged that it was justified and they had committed a very stupid act in depriving King Óláfr of life and land, and this too, that they had suffered very harshly for their unfortunate behaviour. The leaders had meetings and made plans among themselves. Einarr þambarskelfir took the lead in these discussions. It was also the same with Kálfr Árnason, that he now realised into what a snare he had walked as a result of King Knútr's urging. The promises that he had made or granted to Kálfr, these were now all broken, for King Knútr had promised Kálfr a jarldom and control of all Norway, so Kálfr had been the leader in holding a battle with King Óláfr and removing him from the land. Kálfr had no titles greater than before. He felt he had been greatly imposed upon, and messages now passed between the brothers Kálfr and Finnr, Þorbergr and Árni, and now their kinship was reaffirmed.

CHAPTER TWO HUNDRED AND FORTY-EIGHT

When Sveinn had been king in Norway for three years, the news reached Norway that west of the sea a great host was being gathered, and the one that was leader over it is named as Tryggvi. He claimed to be son of Óláfr Tryggvason and the English Gyða. So when King Sveinn heard this, that a foreign army would be entering the country, then he called out troops [412] from the north of the country, and most of the landed men left Þrándheimr with him. Einarr þambarskelfir stayed at home and would not go with King Sveinn. So when King Sveinn's message reached Kálfr inland at Egg to the effect that he was to take part in an expedition with the king, then Kálfr took a twenty-oared ship that he had. He went on board with his men and got ready in the greatest rush, made his way after that along the fiord, not waiting for King Sveinn. Kálfr after that made his way south to Mœrr, not ceasing travelling until he got south to his brother Þorbergr in Gizki. Then all the brothers, sons of Árni, arranged a meeting for themselves, and made plans between themselves. After that Kálfr went back north. But when he got into Frekeyjarsund, then they found before them in the sound King Sveinn with his army, and when Kálfr rowed into the sound from the south, then they called out to each other. The king's men told Kálfr to sail up and follow the king and defend his land. Kálfr replies:

'I have done enough of that, if not done too much, fighting against our countrymen to bring the Knýtlingar to power.'

Kálfr and his men then rowed north on their way. He now went on until he got home to Egg. None of the sons of Árni took part in this expedition with King Sveinn. King Sveinn took his force to the south of the country. But when he got no news of the army being come from the west, then he made his way south to Rogaland and right on to Agðir, for people were assuming that Tryggvi would want first to make for the Vík in the east, since it was there that his forefathers had been and had received the most support. He had a great deal of backing from kinsfolk there.

CHAPTER TWO HUNDRED AND FORTY-NINE

King Tryggvi, when he made his way from the west, brought his force in from the open sea at Hǫrðaland. Then he learned that King Sveinn had sailed south. Then King Tryggvi made his way south to [413] Rogaland. So when King Sveinn received intelligence about Tryggvi's movements after he had come from the west, then he turned back north with his army and the meeting between him and Tryggvi took place in Sóknarsund inside Bókn, close to where Erlingr Skjálgsson had fallen. There took place there a great and fierce battle. They say that Tryggvi threw javelins from both hands at once. He said:

'Thus my father taught me to say Mass.'[428]

His enemies had said that he must have been son of some priest, but he was boasting now that he took more after King Óláfr Tryggvason. Tryggvi was also a most accomplished man. In this battle King Tryggvi fell and much of his force, but some escaped in flight and some received quarter. Thus it says in *Tryggvaflokkr*:[429]

177.	Fame-whetted fared Tryggvi	*Tryggvaflokkr* 1
	from the north—killing resulted,	*ÓTM* II 339
	and King Sveinn with his soldiers	*Skald* I 644
	from the south to the battle.	
	I was close to their clamour;	
	quickly that led to a meeting.	
	The host suffered serious—	
	swords clanged then—loss of life there.	

[428] Cf. *Óláfs saga Tryggvasonar* ch. 109 (vol. I 363).

[429] This is the only stanza surviving of this poem, which is attributed to Sigvatr in one manuscript of the *Separate saga of St Óláfr*.

This battle is mentioned in the *flokkr* that was composed about King Sveinn:

178. That Sunday, Madam—that morning many men sank under blades—it was not like a maid bearing beer and leek to someone, when King Sveinn commanded his men to join together— raw flesh the raven was given to rend—the stems of warships.

[414]

Flokkr about Sveinn 1
ÓTM II 339
Skald I 1029

King Sveinn now still ruled the land after this battle. Then peace prevailed. The following winter King Sveinn stayed in the south of the country.

CHAPTER TWO HUNDRED AND FIFTY

Einarr þambarskelfir and Kálfr Árnason held meetings between themselves that winter, and were making plans and met in Kaupangr. Then King Knútr's messenger came to Kálfr Árnason there bringing him a message from King Knútr to the effect that Kálfr was to send him three dozen axes and to have them carefully made. Kálfr replies:

'I will send no axes to King Knútr. Tell him that I shall give his son Sveinn axes so that he shall find he has plenty.'

CHAPTER TWO HUNDRED AND FIFTY-ONE

Early in the spring Einarr þambarskelfir and Kálfr Árnason set out, taking a large company of men and the most select body of men available in Þrœndalǫg. They travelled in the spring east over Kjǫlr to Jamtaland, then to [415] Helsingjaland and came out into Svíþjóð, got ships there, travelling in the summer east to Garðaríki, arriving in the autumn at Aldeigjuborg. Then they sent messengers up to Hólmgarðr to see King Jarizleifr with this message, that they were offering King Óláfr the Saint's son Magnús that they would receive him and accompany him to Norway and give him support so that he might obtain his patrimony, and uphold him as king over the land. So when this message reached King Jarizleifr, then he took counsel with the queen and his other leading people. They reached agreement that the Norwegians should be sent word and summoned there to see King Jarizleifr and Magnús and his people. They were given safe conduct for this journey. So when they got to Hólmgarðr, then it was decided between them that the Northmen who had come there should pay homage to Magnús and become his men, and they confirmed this by oaths with Kálfr and all the men who had been against King Óláfr at Stiklarstaðir. Magnús granted assurances and complete atonement and confirmed it by oaths that he should be faithful and true to all of them, even if he gained power and kingship in Norway. He was to become foster-son to Kálfr Árnason, and Kálfr to be bound to do everything that Magnús felt would make his power greater and more independent than before.

Passages from Snorri's *Separate Óláfs saga helga* not in *Heimskringla*

[419] PROLOGUE

The priest Ari inn fróði (the Learned) Þorgilsson was the first person in this country to write down history, both ancient and recent, in the Norse language. He wrote in the beginning of his book first of all about the settlement of Iceland and the establishment of the laws, then about the lawspeakers, how long each had recited the law, and he used that reckoning of years first to the point when Christianity came to Iceland, and then all the way down to his own time. He also included much other material, both the lives of kings in Norway and in Denmark and in England, and the important events that had taken place in this country, and all his account seems to us most noteworthy. He was a very wise person, and so old that he was born in the year after the death of King Haraldr Sigurðarson. He wrote, as he himself says, the lives of kings of Norway according to the account of Oddr son of Kolr, son of Hallr of Síða, and Oddr learned them from Þorgeirr afráðskollr (Payment-Chap), a wise man and so aged that he was living on Niðarnes when Jarl Hákon inn ríki was killed. In [420] that same place Óláfr Tryggvason had a marketplace set up, though it was St Óláfr who built the market town.

At the age of seven Ari came to live with Hallr Þórarinsson in Haukadalr and stayed there for fourteen years. Hallr was a very intelligent man with a good memory. He remembered being baptised by the priest Þangbrandr at the age of three. That was a year before Christianity was adopted into the law of Iceland. Ari was twelve years old when Bishop Ísleifr died. Hallr travelled from country to country and had business dealings with King Óláfr the Saint, from which he gained great advancement. So he was knowledgeable about his reign. But when Bishop Ísleifr died, eighty years had passed since the death of King Óláfr Tryggvason, while Hallr died nine years after Bishop Ísleifr. He was then ninety-four years of age. He had set up his farm in Haukadalr when he was thirty, and lived there for sixty-four years. So wrote Ari.

Teitr, son of Bishop Ísleifr, was brought up by Hallr in Haukadalr and lived there afterwards. He taught Ari the priest and gave him much information which Ari afterwards wrote down. Ari also learned much information from Þuríðr, daughter of Snorri goði (the Priest/Chieftain). She had a highly intelligent [421] mind. She remembered her father Snorri. Snorri was nearly thirty-five when Christianity came to Iceland, and died one year after the death of King Óláfr. So it was not surprising that he was accurately informed about past events both here and abroad, since he had learned from old and wise people, and was himself retentive and eager to learn.

I have had written from the beginning the lives of the kings that have held rule in the Northern lands and have spoken the Scandinavian language, and also some of their genealogies in accordance with what we have found out from learned men and is still told in old poems or in records of paternal descent where kings have traced their pedigrees. The poet Þjóðólfr inn fróði (the Learned), who some say was of Hvinir, composed a poem in honour of King Rǫgnvaldr, son of King Óláfr of Vestfold. Óláfr was the brother of Hálfdan svarti (the Black), father of Haraldr inn hárfagri (the Fine-Haired). In that poem are listed thirty of Rǫgnvaldr's paternal ancestors, their names given and also details of each of their deaths, and the list goes right back to Ingunar-Freyr, whom heathen people reckoned was their god. There was another poem composed by Eyvindr skáldaspillir in honour of Jarl Hákon inn ríki Sigurðarson, and he listed paternal ancestors back to Sæmingr, who is said to have been son of Ingunar-Freyr, son of Njǫrðr. There also the death and burial place of each of them is told.

The first age was that in which all dead men had to be burned. And afterwards began the Age of Mounds. Then all men of the ruling class were laid in mounds, but all ordinary people buried in the ground when they were dead, and memorial stones were set up in their memory. But after Haraldr inn hárfagri was king in Norway, then people were able to tell much more accurately about the lives of the kings that had been in Norway. [422] In his time Iceland was settled, and then there was much travelling from Norway to Iceland. People then got news every summer between these countries, and this was later stored in their memory and used afterwards for stories. And yet that seems to me most noteworthy as far as accuracy is concerned which is said in plain words in poems or other verse that was composed about kings or other rulers so that they themselves heard them, or in memorial poems that the poets presented to their sons. The words that stand in verse will be the same as they were to begin with, if it is constructed correctly, though each person has later learned it from someone else, and it cannot be altered. But as for the stories that are told, with them there is the danger that they will not be understood by everyone in the same way. But some have no memory, when time has passed, of how they were told to them, and frequently they change a great deal in their memory, and the accounts become meaningless. It was more than two duodecimal hundred years[430] that Iceland had been settled before people began to write stories here, and this was a long period, and impossible for stories not to have changed in oral tradition if there had not been poems, both recent and old, from which people could obtain accurate

---

[430] 240 years.

history. It was the practice of historians in the past, when they wanted to find accurate information, to accept as true the words of those people who had themselves witnessed events and were then close by. And where the poets were in the battles, then their witness is acceptable, and also what he recited in the presence of the ruler himself, he would not then dare to recount deeds of his that both the ruler himself and everyone that heard knew that he had been nowhere near. It would then be mockery, and not praise.

Now we shall write of the events, with certain reservations, that took place during the life of King Óláfr the Saint, about both his travels and reign, and also something about the events leading up to the warfare in which the leading men of the country fought the battle against him in which he fell at Stiklarstaðir. I know that it will seem, if this account comes abroad, as though I have said a great deal about Icelandic people, but the reason for this is that Icelandic people who saw or heard about these events, carried these accounts here to this country, and people have afterwards learnt about them from them. And yet I write mostly according to what I find in the poems of the poets that were with King Óláfr.

[423] CHAPTER ONE

Haraldr inn hárfagri was king over all Norway for a long time, but previously there had been many kings in the country. Some had had one district to rule over, some rather more. But King Haraldr removed all these from power. Some fell in battle, some fled the land, and some gave up their kingdom, and no one managed to hold the title of king in that country then except him alone. He established a jarl in every district to rule the land and administer law.

King Haraldr had many wives and many children. He had twenty or more sons that were grown up, and they were all accomplished. They were nobly born on their mothers' side, and many of them were brought up with their mothers' families. These were the eldest: Guthormr and two Hálfdans, Eiríkr blóðøx. His mother was called Ragnhildr, daughter of King Eiríkr from Denmark. He was brought up in Firðir with Hersir Þórir Hróaldsson. These had the same mother: Guthormr, Hrœrekr, Gunnrøðr, whom some call Guðrøðr. Their mother was called Gyða, daughter of King Eiríkr of Hǫrðaland. They were brought up there in childhood. Hálfdan svarti and Hálfdan hvíti (the White) were twins, sons of Ása, daughter of Hákon Hlaðajarl Grjótgarðsson. Sigrøðr was the third. They were all brought up in Þrándheimr. Hálfdan svarti was foremost of the brothers. Óláfr, Bjǫrn, Sigtryggr, whom some call Tryggvi, Fróði, Þorgils; their mother was Hildr or Svanhildr, daughter of Jarl Eysteinn of Heiðmǫrk. King Haraldr put Jarl Eysteinn over Vestfold and gave him for fostering these five of his sons. Sigurðr hrísi (Brushwood), Hálfdan háleggr (Long-Leg), Guðrøðr ljómi

(Shiner), Rǫgnvaldr réttilbeini (Straight-Grown); these were sons of Snæfríðr the Lappish. Dagr, Hringr, Ragnarr ryk(k)ill (Snatcher); their mother was called Álfhildr, daughter of Hringr Dagsson of Hringaríki. They were brought up in Upplǫnd. Ingigerðr and Álof árbót (Improvement of Prosperity) were also their daughters. Ingibjǫrg was the name of a daughter of Haraldr inn hárfagri who was married to Jarl Hálfdan; their daughter Gunnhildr, who was married to Finnr inn Skjálgi (the Squinter); their children [424] Eyvindr skáldaspillir and Njáll, Sigurðr, Þóra. Njáll's daughter was Ástríðr, mother of King Steinkell of the Svíar. There were still more daughters of Haraldr inn hárfagri. Álof, King Haraldr's daughter, was married to Jarl Þórir þegjandi (Silent); their daughter Bergljót, mother of Hákon inn ríki. King Haraldr gave his daughters in marriage within the country to his jarls.

King Haraldr was the largest of all men in size, and the strongest, more handsome of face than any man, and better endowed with all skills. This became afterwards so characteristic of his family that it has remained in his family right down to within the memory of the people that are alive now. When King Haraldr raided land and fought battles, then he gained complete control both of all the land and all ancestral property—both settlements and pasture land and outlying islands he gained control of, also all forests and wastelands. All farmers were his tenants and landholders. Haraldr took the kingdom when he was ten years old, and ruled the country for seventy-three years. When he was sixty years of age, then many of his sons were full-grown, and some of them dead. Many of them became very overbearing men within the country and quarrelled among themselves. They drove the king's jarls from their possessions, and killed some of them. King Haraldr then called a large assembly in the east of the country and invited the people of Upplǫnd to it. Then he drew up laws. Then he gave all his sons the title of king, and set it down in the laws that his descendants were each to succeed to a kingdom after his father, and a jarldom any that were descended from him on the female side. He divided the country between them, letting be held Vingulmǫrk, Raumaríki, Vestfold, Þelamǫrk, these he gave to Óláfr, Bjǫrn, Sigtryggr, Fróði, Þorgils, and Heiðmǫrk and Guðbrandsdalar he gave to Dagr and Hringr and Ragnarr, to Snæfríðr's sons he gave Hringaríki, Haðaland, Þótn and what belonged to these districts. He put his son Guthormr in charge of the defence of the country at the frontier in the east and gave him control over Ranríki from the Elfr to Svínasund.

King Haraldr was himself mostly in the central part of the country. Hrœrekr and Guðrøðr were always within the household with the king and held great revenues in Hǫrðaland and Sogn. Eiríkr was with his father Haraldr. He loved him best of his sons and valued him most. He gave him Hálogaland and Norð-Mœrr and Raumsdalr. [425] North in Þrándheimr he put in charge Hálfdan svarti and Hálfdan hvíti and Sigrøðr. He granted his sons in each of these areas half-shares of all the revenues with himself, and this as well, that they were to occupy on a high-seat one step higher than jarls but one step lower than King Haraldr himself. But this seat after King Haraldr each of his sons intended to have for himself, but he intended it for Eiríkr, while the Þrœndir intended it for Hálfdan svarti, and the Víkverjar and the Upplendingar were best pleased for those to have power whom they had there under their control. From this there arose great disagreement all over again between the brothers. But since they felt they had small realms to rule over, they went on raids, as stories tell, Hálfdan hvíti falling in Estland, Hálfdan háleggr fell in Orkney, Fróði and Þorgils settled in Dublin in Ireland, Guthormr fell in Elfarkvíslar at the hands of Sǫlvi klofi (Cleaver). After that Óláfr took over the realm that he had had.

Eiríkr blóðøx intended himself to be supreme king over all his brothers. He was for long periods on raids. He was married to Gunnhildr konungamóðir (Mother of Kings). Rǫgnvaldr réttilbeini had Haðaland. He learned witchcraft and became a magician. King Haraldr thought magicians were evil. In Hǫrðaland there was a magician who was called Vitgeirr. The king sent him word and commanded him to cease casting spells. He replied and said:[431]

1.	It does little harm if we do magic, the children of churls and crones, if so does Rǫgnvaldr réttilbeini, great son of Haraldr, in Haðaland.	*Hkr* I 138–39

And then, when King Haraldr heard this said, on his instruction Eiríkr went to Upplǫnd and reached Haðaland. He burned Rǫgnvaldr in his house with eighty magicians, and this deed was greatly praised. Guðrøðr ljómi drowned off Jaðarr.

CHAPTER TWO

Bjǫrn was at that time ruling over Vestfold. There was at that time a market town there in Túnsberg. He was in residence there for long periods, but did not go raiding much. His brothers called him Bjǫrn kaupmaðr (Merchant). He was an intelligent person, and very moderate, and it was thought that he would make a good ruler. He had married well and suitably. He got a son

---

[431] Cf. vol. I, verse 57.

who was called Guðrøðr. Eiríkr blóðøx returned from the eastern Baltic with warships and a large force. He demanded [426] from his brother Bjǫrn that he should receive the taxes and revenues that were due to King Haraldr in Vestfold, but previously it had been the custom for Bjǫrn to take the tax to the king himself or to send men with it. He wanted to go on doing this and refused to hand it over. But Eiríkr felt he needed food supplies and tapestry and drink. The brothers disputed this obstinately, and Eiríkr still did not get his way and went away from the residence and came back during the night, then made an attack on Bjǫrn and slew him and many people with him. Eiríkr took a great deal of plunder there and went to the north of the country. This deed greatly displeased Víkverjar, and Eiríkr was very unpopular there. The word went around that King Óláfr would avenge Bjǫrn if he got an opportunity to do so.

CHAPTER THREE[432]

King Eiríkr went the following winter north into Þrándheimr and was receiving a banquet in Sǫlvi. And when Hálfdan svarti learned this, he went there with troops and surrounded the house they were in. Eiríkr was sleeping in an apartment outside the main building and managed to get out into the forest with four men, but Hálfdan and his men burned down the residence and all the troops that were in it. Eiríkr came to see King Haraldr with news of these events. The king became enormously angry at this and mustered an army and went northwards against the people of Þrándheimr. And when Hálfdan svarti hears about this, he calls out troops and ships and got together a very large number of men and sailed out to Staðr further in than Þorsbjǫrg. King Haraldr was lying with his troops out off Reinslétta. Then men went between them. There was a noble person called Guthormr sindri (Flint), and he was of a great family. He was now in Hálfdan svarti's troop, but he had previously been with King Haraldr and was a close friend of both of them. Guthormr was a great poet. He had composed poems about each of the two, father and son. They had offered him a reward, but he refused, and asked that they should grant him one request, and they had promised this. He then went and mediated for reconciliation between them and asked each of them to fulfil their promise and that they should be reconciled, and the kings held him in such great esteem that at his request they were reconciled. Many other noble persons supported this [427] plea with him. It was brought about on these terms, that Hálfdan was to keep all the realm that he had previously held, he was also not to subject his brother Eiríkr to any attacks. About these events Jórunn skáldmær (Poetess) composed some verses in *Sendibítr*:[433]

[432] Cf. *Haralds saga ins hárfagra* (vol. I), ch. 36.
[433] Cf vol. I, verse 59.

2. I learned, Hálfdan, that Haraldr   *Hkr* I 142
heard of harsh actions—
the blade-tester finds this poem
black-looking—the Fine-Haired.

CHAPTER FOUR[434]

Haraldr inn hárfagri got a son in his old age that was called Hákon. His mother is named as Þóra Morstǫng.[435] Her family was from Morstr in Sunn-Hǫrðaland. She was the finest of women and most beautiful. She was well born and was related to Hǫrða-Kári, and yet she was said to be the king's handmaid. At that time there were many in the king's service who were of good family, both men and women. Haraldr's sons thought this business of Hákon was disgraceful, and they called him Morstangarson (son of the Pole of Morstr). King Haraldr sent his son Hákon for fostering to King Aðalsteinn of the English, and Hákon was brought up there. He took after his father Haraldr most of all his sons and was the foremost of them in all accomplishments.

CHAPTER FIVE[436]

After the fall of Bjǫrn kaupmaðr, Óláfr took rule over Vestfold and adopted Bjǫrn's son Guðrøðr. Óláfr's son was called Tryggvi. He and Guðrøðr were foster-brothers and nearly the same age and both most promising and very able men. Tryggvi was bigger and stronger than anyone.

CHAPTER SIX[437]

When King Haraldr was eighty years of age, then he felt he was not in good enough health because of his age to travel by land or to manage the royal affairs. Then he took his son Eiríkr to his high seat and gave him rule over the whole country. But when news of this reached north in Þrándheimr, then Hálfdan sat himself on [428] a king's high seat. He then took the whole of Þrándheimr to rule over. All the Þrœndir backed him in this course of action. And when the Víkverir heard this, then they took Óláfr as supreme king over the whole of the Vík, and he kept that kingdom. Eiríkr was very displeased at this. Two years later Hálfdan svarti died suddenly inland in Þrándheimr at some banquet, and it was rumoured that Gunnhildr konungamóðir had bribed a woman skilled in magic to make him a poisoned drink. After that

---

[434] Cf. *Haralds saga ins hárfagra* (vol. I), chs 37 and 39.
[435] Probably a phonetic or orthographical variant of Morstrstǫng (Pole of Morstr).
[436] Cf. *Haralds saga ins hárfagra* (vol. I), ch. 41.
[437] Cf. *Haralds saga ins hárfagra* (vol. I), chs 41–43.

the Prœndir took Sigrøðr as king. One year later Haraldr inn hárfagri died in Rogaland, and he was buried in a mound by Haugasund. The following winter Eiríkr took all the revenues over the central part of the country.

CHAPTER SEVEN[438]

That same spring Eiríkr calls out a great army and ships and turns east to Vík, as there was a favourable wind. But both the Víkverir and the Prœndir had gathered together in hosts in many places. King Sigrøðr travelled east by land to meet up with his brother King Óláfr, and they were staying in Túnsberg. King Eiríkr got such a strong favourable wind that he sailed day and night and no intelligence went before him until he got to Túnsberg. Then Óláfr and Sigrøðr took their troops eastwards out of the town onto the slope and formed up there. Eiríkr had a much larger force, and he gained victory, but Sigrøðr and Óláfr both fell there, and the mounds of each of the two of them are there on the slope, where they had lain fallen. Eiríkr then went round the Vík and subjected it to himself and stayed there much of the summer. Tryggvi and Guðrøðr then fled to Upplǫnd.

CHAPTER EIGHT[439]

That same summer Hákon Aðalsteinsfóstri came from the west from England. He immediately went north to Prándheimr and to see Sigurðr Hlaðajarl, who was the most sensible of men in Norway, and was given a good reception there, and they entered into fellowship with each other. Hákon promised the jarl great power if he became king. Then they had a large assembly called, and at the assembly Jarl Sigurðr spoke on behalf of Hákon and proposed him to the farmers as king. After [429] that Hákon himself stood up and spoke. Then they said to each other, each to his neighbour, that now Haraldr inn hárfagri was come there and had become young a second time. Hákon made this the beginning of his speech, that he asked the farmers to give him the title of king and also to give him backing and support to hold on to the kingship, and in return he offered to make all farmers entitled to their patrimony and to give them their inherited land that they were then dwelling in. There was such great applause for this that the crowd of farmers shouted and called out that they wanted to accept him as king. And thus it was done, that the Prœndir took Hákon as king over the whole country. Then he got himself a following and travelled round the country. This news reached Upplǫnd, that the Prœndir had taken a king for themselves similar in every way to what Haraldr inn hárfagri had been, except for the fact that Haraldr had oppressed

---

[438] Cf. *Haralds saga ins hárfagra* (vol. I), ch. 43.
[439] Cf. *Hákonar saga góða* (vol. I), ch. 1.

all people in the land, while this Hákon wished everyone well and offered to return the farmers their patrimonies which King Haraldr had taken from them. At this news everyone became glad and everyone passed it on. It flew like wildfire all the way east to the land's end. Many travelled from Upplǫnd to see King Hákon, some sent him men, some sent messages and tokens, and all to the effect that they wanted to become his men.

CHAPTER NINE[440]

King Hákon went to Upplǫnd at the beginning of winter, summoned assemblies there, and everyone that was able thronged to see him. He was accepted as king at every assembly. Then he went east to Vík. His nephews Tryggvi and Gunnrøðr came there to him, and many others, reckoning up the troubles that they had been subject to at the hands of his brother Eiríkr. Eiríkr's unpopularity grew ever the more as everyone became fonder of Hákon and became more confident in speaking their minds. King Hákon gave Tryggvi and Gunnrøðr the title of king and the same rule as King Haraldr had given their fathers. To Tryggvi he gave Ranríki and Vingulmǫrk, and to Gunnrøðr Vestfold. But because they were young and still children, he set noble and wise men to rule the land with them. He gave them land on the same conditions [430] that had applied previously, that they should share half the dues and taxes with him. King Hákon went north to Þrándheimr when spring came.

In the spring King Hákon called out a great army from Þrándheimr, and the Víkverir [came] from the east also with a very great army. Eiríkr mustered an army in the centre of the country, and he found it difficult to get troops, since many of the ruling class forsook him and went over to Hákon. And when he saw he had no means of withstanding Hákon's army, he sailed west across the sea with those troops that were willing to go with him. He went first to Orkney and had a large force with him. Then he sailed south to England and made raids there. King Aðalsteinn of the English sent word to Eiríkr and invited him to accept rule from him in England, and was willing to do this to make peace between the brothers Eiríkr and Hákon, give him Northumberland, which is reckoned to be a fifth part of England. Eiríkr accepted this offer. He was king in Northumberland as long as he lived. Eiríkr fell while raiding in the west.

Eiríkr and Gunnhildr had many children. Their sons were Gamli, Haraldr gráfeldr (Grey-Cloak), Sigurðr slefa (Lisp), Erlingr, Guthormr, Ragnfrøðr, Guðrøðr. Ragnhildr was the name of their daughter, who was married to Jarl Þorfinnr's son Jarl Arnfinnr.

[440] Cf. *Hákonar saga góða* (vol. I), chs 2–4.

CHAPTER TEN[441]

King Hákon ruled over Norway twenty-seven years. His period was so good that ever since the people of that country have remembered it. There were then all kinds of plenty, both on sea and land. Both farmers and merchants were on good peaceful terms with each other, so that no one harmed anyone else's property and no one committed a breach of the peace against anyone else.

King Hákon was the most cheerful of all men and the most eloquent and most condescending. He was a man of great wisdom and devoted great energy to lawmaking in Norway. He set up Gulaþingslǫg and Frostaþingslǫg and Heiðsævislǫg straight away at the beginning, but previously the people of each district all had their own laws. King Hákon gave his kinsman by marriage[442] Sigurðr Hlaðajarl power over all of Þrándheimr, just as Hálfdan had had, and his father Hákon, in the days of Haraldr inn hárfagri. King Hákon was at a banquet with his kinsman by marriage Sigurðr. Then Sigurðr's wife Bergljót gave birth to a son [431] on the first night of Yule. King Hákon sprinkled the boy with water and gave him his own name. This lad grew up and afterwards became a distinguished person.

In the latter part of King Hákon's reign Eiríkr blóðøx's sons came to Norway and fought to win land and held battles with King Hákon. Hákon always had victory. Then Gamli Eiríksson fell. They fought their last battle in Hǫrðaland, at Fitjar on Storð. There Hákon was victorious and was wounded. He died at Hákonarhella—he had been born there—and he is buried in a mound at Sæheimr.

CHAPTER ELEVEN[443]

Eiríkr's sons then subjected the whole country to themselves. They promised everyone the laws that King Hákon had set up in the country. They also granted the leading men such titles as each of them had had before. But when they had established themselves in their kingdom and made themselves secure in the country, then they felt that Jarl Sigurðr in Þrándheimr had too much power. Jarl Sigurðr's brother was called Grjótgarðr. He was the younger of the two brothers and was much less respected. They incited him to kill his brother Jarl Sigurðr. They gave him support, and most people say that some of the brothers went with him. They went north into Þrándheimr and inland to Ǫgló, arrived there at night and surrounded Jarl Sigurðr's dwelling and burned him in the building with a large number of people and then went off. This was two years after King Hákon fell, according to the

---

[441] Cf. *Hákonar saga góða* (vol. I), chs 11 and 32.
[442] Sigurðr's wife Bergljót's mother was King Hákon's sister.
[443] Cf. *Haralds saga gráfeldar* (vol. I), chs 4–6, 15.

account of the priest Ari inn fróði Þorgilsson. Sigurðr's son Hákon was at this time nearly twenty years of age. He had many kinsmen and powerful ones, and his father Sigurðr was popular and beloved by everyone. Hákon found it easy to get troops because all the Þrœndr turned to him and held the land against the sons of Eiríkr so that none of them could get in through the mouth of the Þrándheimr fiord. Then the friends of both parties intervened and negotiated a settlement. So it came about by means of high-ranking people's persuasion that agreement was reached that Hákon should have the whole of the rule in Þrándheimr that his father Sigurðr had had, and be jarl over it. But Grjótgarðr and still other people, whose names Hákon put forward, were to be exiled from Norway. Hákon and Gunnhildr were sometimes on very close terms, but sometimes there were treacherous [432] dealings between them. Jarl Hákon went some summers to the eastern Baltic to raid. Then he slew Grjótgarðr and two other jarl's sons and many other people that had been at the killing of his father Jarl Sigurðr. Jarl Hákon went to see King Haraldr Gormsson of the Danes, and he was well received there and they were on the most friendly terms. At that time there was with the king of the Danes his kinsman Gull-Haraldr (Gold-), and he and Hákon became comrades. Jarl Hákon returned to Norway to his realm, and he was a powerful man and a person of great wisdom.

CHAPTER TWELVE[444]

King Tryggvi Óláfsson was a rich man and a distinguished one. The Víkverir thought he was best suited to be king and rule the whole land. He was married to Eiríkr Bjóðaskalli's daughter Ástríðr. Bjǫrn's son King Guðrøðr was also a distinguished man and was a close friend of King Tryggvi. Guðrøðr had got himself a good marriage. His son was called Haraldr. He was sent for fostering up into Grenland to Hrói inn hvíti (the White), a landed man.[445] Hrani inn víðfǫrli (the Far-Travelled) was Hrói's son. He and Haraldr were pretty much the same age and were foster-brothers. One summer, when Jarl Hákon was travelling from the south from Denmark, he had a meeting with King Tryggvi and King Guðrøðr, and they sat a long time in private talk. Then Jarl Hákon went back north. Eiríkr's sons heard about this and suspected that there must be high treason being plotted against them. The following spring they set out to go raiding, King Haraldr and his brother Guðrøðr, and they each went separately, since they were engaged in a quarrel. And when they got east to Vík, then Guðrøðr sailed eastwards across Foldin, while Haraldr

---

[444] Cf. *Haralds saga gráfeldar* (vol. I), chs 9, 11.
[445] A *lendr maðr* 'landed man' was one who held land in fief from the king. He was next in rank to a jarl in Norway.

went to Túnsberg, and there a short way up ashore was King Guðrøðr at a banquet. Then Haraldr immediately went there and surrounded the building they were in and set it on fire. King Guðrøðr went out and his troops, he fell there and many men with him. Then Guðrøðr killed King Tryggvi east by Veggirnir, betraying his trust. This was six years after Jarl Sigurðr fell. After that Eiríkr's sons subjected the Vík to themselves. Many other leading men, their kinsmen, they put to death, but some fled the land before them. Guðrøðr's son Haraldr, who was known as Haraldr inn grenski, [433] fled, first of all to Upplǫnd, and with him his foster-brother Hrani, and few other men with them. He stayed there a while with his kinsmen. Eiríkr's sons were searching hard for men who had committed offences against them, and especially for those from whom they were likely to have trouble. His kinsmen and friends advised Haraldr to leave the country.

CHAPTER THIRTEEN[446]

Haraldr grenski then went east to Svíþjóð and looked for a place for himself on a ship and for an opportunity to join a band of men who were engaged in raiding to get themselves some wealth. Haraldr was the most accomplished person. There was a man in Svíþjóð called Tósti who was one of the richest and most distinguished people in the country, of those that did not have a title of nobility. He was the greatest warrior and was for long periods on raids. He was known as Skǫglar-Tósti (Battle-). Haraldr grenski got himself into this band and spent the summer on viking raids with Tósti. Haraldr was regarded highly by everyone. Haraldr stayed with Tósti the following winter. Haraldr had been two years in Upplǫnd, and five with Skǫglar-Tósti. Tósti's daughter was called Sigríðr, young and fair and a very haughty woman.

Eiríkr's sons were very valiant men and very skilled, fierce and unforbearing in every way. In their time there were very poor harvests in Norway, both on sea and land. There was then famine and starvation all over the country. It came about that distinguished men could not put up with their loss of rights. Þórðr Hǫrða-Kárason's son Klyppr killed King Sigurðr slefa. Farmers also killed King Erlingr. Jarl Hákon remained in Þrándheimr with the support of the Þrœndr, but was sometimes south in Denmark with Haraldr Gormsson, and sometimes he went raiding in the eastern Baltic. There he and Haraldr grenski met up and in the autumn they both went to Denmark and stayed the winter with the king of the Danes. That winter they set a trap for Haraldr Eiríksson. Haraldr Gormsson sent word to Haraldr Eiríksson, inviting him to stay with him and offering him land and rule in Denmark. The following spring Haraldr

[446] Cf. *Haralds saga gráfeldar* (vol. I), chs 11, 14, 15, 16; *Óláfs saga Tryggvasonar* (vol. I), ch. 15.

travelled south to Denmark, and when he got to Limafjǫrðr, to a place called at Hálsi, there arrived there Gull-Haraldr with a large force and fought with Haraldr Eiríksson, and there Haraldr Eiríksson fell. [434] Soon afterwards Jarl Hákon arrived and captured Gull-Haraldr and hanged him on a gallows.

CHAPTER FOURTEEN[447]

Haraldr Gormsson went that summer north to Norway taking seven hundred ships. There with him then were Jarl Hákon and Haraldr grenski and many other distinguished men who had fled from their patrimonies and from Norway because of Eiríkr's sons. The king of the Danes travelled north until he got to Túnsberg, and all the people of the country submitted to him. Large numbers thronged to him. King Haraldr handed over the whole army that had come to him in Norway to Jarl Hákon and gave him to administer Rogaland, Hǫrðaland, Sogn, Firðafylki, Sunn-Mœrr, Raumsdalr, Norð-Mœrr—these seven districts he gave him to administer on the same terms as Haraldr inn hárfagri had given them to his sons, with this difference, that Hákon was also to possess there and also in Þrándheimr all the royal residences and land dues. He was also to use the royal treasury if there was an invading army in the country. King Haraldr gave Haraldr grenski Vingulmǫrk, Vestfold, Agðir as far as Líðandisnes, and the title of king, letting him have rule in every way the same as in times past his kinsmen had had and Haraldr inn hárfagri had given his sons. Haraldr grenski was then eighteen years old and afterwards became a renowned man.

Jarl Hákon took his army along the coast to the north. And when Gunnhildr and her sons heard about this, then it was hard for them to get troops. They took up the same procedure as before, sailing west to Orkney. But Jarl Hákon subjected the land to himself and ruled over it for a long time afterwards. To begin with, it went on for a long time that Gunnhildr's sons made raids on Norway and fought battles with Jarl Hákon. And meanwhile the jarl now had all the taxes that belonged to the king of the Danes for his own maintenance. But afterwards he sent the king of the Danes sometimes hawks and horses and a certain part of the tax, but sometimes nothing at all, right on until the king of the Danes complained, and eventually he got so angry that he took his army to Norway and caused there a very great deal of damage, and after that the Jarl denied him all compliance. King Haraldr kept to all his agreements with the king of the Danes, and remained thus in friendship [435] with the king as long as he lived. King Haraldr married Ásta, daughter of Guðbrandr kúla (Bump), a distinguished man.

---

[447] Cf. *Óláfs saga Tryggvasonar* (vol. I), chs 15, 16, 43.

CHAPTER FIFTEEN[448]

When King Haraldr inn hárfagri started his reign in Norway, King Eiríkr Emundarson was king at Uppsalir in Svíþjóð. He died when Haraldr was nearly twenty. After him his son Bjǫrn was king in Svíþjóð. He died of sickness. After him the kings in Svíþjóð were his sons Óláfr, father of Styrbjǫrn, and Eiríkr inn sigrsæli (the Victorious), who was king in Svíþjóð for a long time. He married Skǫglar-Tósti's daughter Sigríðr in his old age. Their son was Óláfr sœnski (the Swedish), who afterwards was king in Svíþjóð after his father Eiríkr. King Eiríkr of the Svíar died towards the end of the days of Jarl Hákon Sigurðarson. Queen Sigríðr was then at her residences, for she had residences both many and large. Sigríðr was a person of great wisdom and prophetic about many things.

CHAPTER SIXTEEN[449]

One summer, when Haraldr grenski was going to the eastern Baltic raiding to get himself wealth, then he came in to Svíþjóð. And when his foster-sister Queen Sigríðr heard about this, she sent men to him and invited him to a banquet. He did not neglect going there and took a large troop of men. There was very good entertainment there. The king and the queen sat on a high-seat and both drank together in the evening, and all his men were supplied liberally. And when the king went to bed, then the bed had been hung with splendid hangings and spread with costly coverings. There were few people in that room. And when the king was undressed and lying down, then the queen came to him and served him drink herself and enticed him hard to drink and was most agreeable. The king was pretty well drunk, indeed they both were. Then he fell asleep, and the queen then also went away to bed. The following morning there was the most plentiful banquet. And then it happened, as is generally the case where men get [436] rather heavily drunk, that the next day most men go easy with the drink. But the queen was very merry, and she and the king spoke together a great deal. She said that she valued no less the possessions she held in Svíþjóð than his kingdom that he had in Norway. At this speech the king became unhappy and took it all rather coldly and got ready to leave and was very depressed, but the queen was most cheerful and sent him off with fine gifts. Then in the autumn King Haraldr went back to Norway and stayed at home during the winter and was not very cheerful. The following summer he went to the eastern Baltic with his troops and then made for Svíþjóð and sent word to Queen Sigríðr saying that he wished to see her. She rode down to meet

[448] Cf. *Óláfs saga Tryggvasonar* (vol. I), ch. 43.
[449] Cf. *Óláfs saga Tryggvasonar* (vol. I), ch. 43.

him and they talk together. He soon raises the matter of whether Sigríðr wanted to marry him. She replies that he was talking nonsense and he is already so well married that he is by no means ill-matched. He replies, saying that Ásta is a good woman and noble.

'But she is not as high-born as I am.'

Sigríðr says: 'It may be that you are of greater descent than she. But I would have thought that the good fortune of both of you now must be with her.'

They exchanged few further words before the queen rode away. King Haraldr was very depressed. He prepared to ride up inland and see Queen Sigríðr again. Many of his men were against this, but nevertheless he went with a large troop of men and came to the residence that the queen was mistress of. The same evening another king arrived there. He was called Vísivaldr from Garðaríki in the east. The kings were both assigned to one large and ancient apartment. All the furniture of the apartment was in keeping. And there was plenty of drinking during the evening, so strong that all the men were completely drunk so that the bodyguards and the watchmen outside fell asleep. Then Queen Sigríðr had an attack made on them with both fire and weapons. The apartment there burned and the people that were inside, but those who got out were killed. Sigríðr says that thus would she make petty kings stop going from other countries to ask to marry her.

[437] CHAPTER SEVENTEEN[450]

But the previous spring Jarl Hákon had fought a battle with the Jómsvikings at Hjǫrungavágr. Hrani had stayed behind at the ships when Haraldr had made his way up inland, with the troops that were left behind, to be in charge. And when they learned that Haraldr was dead, they went away as quickly as possible and back to Norway and told about these events. Hrani went to see Ásta and told her everything that had happened on their expedition and also this, what business King Haraldr had gone to see Queen Sigríðr on. Ásta immediately went to Upplǫnd to her father when she had heard about all this, and he welcomed her, but they were both very angry about the plans that had been hatched in Svíþjóð, and also about the fact that Haraldr had planned to desert her.

CHAPTER EIGHTEEN[451]

It is said that Ásta Guðbrandsdóttir gave birth to a boy child that summer. This boy was named Óláfr when he was sprinkled with water. It was Hrani

[450] Cf. *Óláfs saga Tryggvasonar* (vol. I), chs 43–44.
[451] Cf. *Óláfs saga Tryggvasonar* (vol. I), chs 44, 60.

who sprinkled him with water. This boy was brought up there to begin with, with Guðbrandr and his mother Ásta. A few years later Ásta gave herself in marriage to Sigurðr sýr (Pig), who was then king in Hringaríki. He was son of Hálfdan, son of Sigurðr hrísi, son of Haraldr inn hárfagri. This family line had all held rule over Hringaríki. Sigurðr sýr was a man of great wisdom and a distinguished person and wealthy. He was not a fighting man, but was a good ruler, just and a moderate person in every way. Óláfr Haraldsson was brought up with his stepfather Sigurðr sýr and his mother Ásta.

One winter after King Haraldr fell, the Þrœndir took the life of Jarl Hákon and accepted Óláfr Tryggvason as king. He was son of Tryggvi Óláfsson, who was spoken of earlier. Óláfr Tryggvason was a most remarkable man and in all his abilities most like Hákon Aðalsteinsfóstri. He was Christian and was the first of the kings of Norway to hold the true faith. He introduced Christianity to the whole of Norway, and he Christianised many other countries and was a splendid king. He travelled all round the country preaching the faith to people. He arrived then at a banquet [438] at Sigurðr sýr's. Then the king, Sýr, was baptised and all his people. Then too Óláfr Haraldsson was baptised, and Óláfr Tryggvason was his godfather . . .[452]

CHAPTER NINETEEN

Óláfr Tryggvason ruled Norway for five years. He fell in battle south off Vinðland. He was then fighting with King Sveinn Haraldsson of the Danes, who was now married to Skǫglar-Tósti's daughter Sigríðr, and with King Óláfr Eiríksson of the Svíar and with Jarl Eiríkr Hákonarson. After that there ruled over Norway Jarl Eiríkr and Jarl Sveinn, sons of Hákon, and they paid taxes to the king of the Danes and the king of the Svíar. Jarl Eiríkr was married to King Sveinn of the Danes' daughter Gyða. King Sveinn's son was called Knútr. King Sveinn of the Danes took his army west to England against King Aðalráðr Játgeirsson of the English, and they fought battles and victory went now to one side, now to the other. King Sveinn of the Danes established his men in the Vík, and his power lay all on the eastern side of the fiord . . .

CHAPTER THIRTY

Now when Óláfr Tryggvason was ruling Norway, then he preached Christianity in that country, and he made slow progress in many places. To gain support for himself and to advance this religion, he took this step, he gave his sister

---

[452] The rest of this chapter corresponds to chs 1 and 2 of the version of *Óláfs saga helga* in *Heimskringla*.

Ástríðr in marriage to Erlingr Skjálgsson of Jaðarr. And because she felt it was beneath her dignity to be married to him, a man of no rank, the king then gave Erlingr an equal share to his own of the land dues and a half share with himself of all the royal revenues between Líðandisnes and Sogn. Erlingr did not wish to have the title of jarl, but he had more power than most tributary kings. Óláfr Tryggvason gave his other sister, Ingibjǫrg, in marriage to Jarl Rǫgnvaldr Úlfsson. He ruled for a long time afterwards over Vestra-Gautland. Rǫgnvaldr's father Úlfr was King Óláfr of the Svíar's mother Sigríðr in stórráða's (of the Great Undertakings') brother. After the fall of Óláfr Tryggvason, while Eiríkr and Sveinn were ruling [439] the country, Eiríkr still had his third of the land undiminished, and King Sveinn of the Danes got another third, and he had the greater part of the Vík, but Jarl Eiríkr a certain part of his share of revenues. King Óláfr inn sœnski of the Svíar got one third of the country. This comprised four districts in Þrándheimr, Sparbyggvafylki, Verdœlafylki, Skaun, Stjórdœlafylki; both parts of Mœrr; Raumsdalr; and in the east Ranríki by the national frontier. Jarl Sveinn Hákonarson was married to King Eiríkr of the Svíar's daughter Hólmfríðr, Óláfr sœnski's sister, and he held the land on behalf of the king of the Svíar and ruled over it all . . .

CHAPTER TWO HUNDRED AND THIRTY-ONE

Haraldr Sigurðarson was now[453] badly wounded. But Rǫgnvaldr Brúsason carried him to a certain farmer's during the night after the battle. This farmer received Haraldr and kept him in secret and had him cured there. Afterwards he got his son to help him away. They then went, still incognito, across the mountains and over deserted country and came out in Jamtaland. Then Haraldr spoke this:[454]

> 162. Now, with scant fame, from forest *Mork* I (*Flb*) 83
>   to forest I am slinking; *Hkr* III 69
>   Who knows I'll not be widely *Orkn* 53
>   renowned in the future? *Skald* II 44

CHAPTER TWO HUNDRED AND THIRTY-TWO

King Óláfr's brother Haraldr Sigurðarson was then fifteen years old, when King Óláfr fell. This is stated by the poet Þjóðólfr in the *drápa* that he composed about King Haraldr that is known as *Sexstefja*:[455]

---

[453] i.e. after the Battle of Stiklarstaðir.
[454] See vol. III, verse 77.
[455] See vol. III, verse 76. 32 stanzas of Þjóðólfr's poem *Sexstefja* ('Six Refrains'), recounting deeds of Haraldr harðráði, are preserved in manuscripts of *Heimskringla* and other kings' sagas, but the name of the poem only occurs here.

163. By Haugr, I heard, a shield-shower,[456] *Sexstefja* 1
sharp, drove at the ruler; *Hkr* III 68
but the burner of Bulgars[457] *Fsk* 481
his brother well supported. *Skald* II 112
Lifeless Óleifr, reluctant
he left, the princeling
at the age of twelve and three
years, helmet-stand[458] hiding.

Haraldr met Rǫgnvaldr in Jamtaland and they then went to Svíþjóð in the autumn and stayed there through the winter. The next summer they travelled east into Garðaríki to King Jarizleifr, and he welcomed them. Haraldr stayed there for a long time after that, and so did Rǫgnvaldr. The poet Bǫlverkr says this in the *drápa* that he composed about King Haraldr:[459]

164. You wiped, when you had finished *Drápa on Haraldr harð.* 1
warring, the sword's mouth,[460] ruler; *Hkr* III 69–70
you rendered the raven full of *Fsk* 227
raw meat; wolves howled on hillsides. *Skald* II 286
And, harsh prince—I've not heard of
a harmer of peace[461] more prominent
than you—the year following
you were east in Garðar.

[440] Arnórr jarlaskáld mentions this, that Rǫgnvaldr Brúsason was for a long time in charge of the defence of the land in Garðaríki, and fought many battles there:

165. So it turned out that of ancient *Rǫgnvaldsdrápa* 1
tempests of the file of graven *Orkn* 54
shields[462] the war-Njǫrðr,[463] battle-willing, *Skald* II 178–79
waged ten in Garðar.

. . .[464]

---

[456] *hlífél*: 'shield-shower', battle.
[457] *Bolgara brennir*: 'burner (i.e. enemy) of Bulgars', i.e. Haraldr.
[458] *hjalmsetr*: 'seat, support of the helmet', head.
[459] See vol. III, verse 78. In *Fsk* this verse is attributed to Valgarðr at Vǫllr.
[460] i.e. edge.
[461] i.e. warrior.
[462] *grafninga þélar él*: 'storm of the file (sword) of graven shields', battle.
[463] *gǫndlar Njǫrðr*: 'Njǫrðr (a god) of war', warrior.
[464] The miracle that is described in ch. 246 is also in *Heimskringla, Hákonar saga herðibreiðs* (vol. III), ch. 20.

CHAPTER TWO HUNDRED AND FIFTY-TWO

Magnús Óláfsson set out from the east after Yule, from Hólmgarðr down to Aldeygjuborg; they then began to prepare their ships. Arnórr jarlaskáld mentions this in *Magnússdrápa*:[465]

186. Now I mean, for well I know them,	*Magnússdrápa* 1
to name to men the exploits	*Hkr* III 3
of the strife-quick sword's-edge	*Fsk* 208–09
stainer[466]—let gold-breakers[467] listen!	*Skald* II 207–08
The serpent's home's hater[468]	
had not reached eleven winters	
fully when the bold friend of Hǫrðar[469]	
fitted warships to leave Garðar.	

Magnús set his course in the spring from the east to Svíðjóð. So says Arnorr:[470]

187. The young edge-reddener[471] called men	*Magnússdrápa* 2
out to an assembly;[472]	*Hkr* III 4
the trim troop of the eagle-feeder[473]	*Fsk* 208–09
took up, war-clad, rowing stations.	*Skald* II 209
The great king with hull rime-crusted	*Skáldsk* 94
clove, bold, the salt westwards;	
keen gales carried the surf-fire's	
quencher[474] to Sigtúnir.	

After that they travelled from the east by land to Helsingjaland. So says Arnórr in the *Hrynjandi*:[475]

188. Afterwards crimson shields you carried,	*Hrynhenda* 5
combat-Yggr,[476] through Swedish settlements.	*Hkr* III 8
No poor pick of troops you garnered.	*Skald* II 189
People of the land sought your faction.	

---

[465] See vol. III, verse 1.
[466] *hneitis eggja rjóðandi*: 'reddener of sword's edges', warrior.
[467] *seimbroti*: 'breaker, distributor of gold', generous man.
[468] *ormsetrs hati*: 'hater of the dragon's lair (treasure, on which a dragon lies)', generous man, who gives away treasure.
[469] *Hǫrðar vinr*: 'friend of people of Hǫrðaland', Norwegian king (Magnús).
[470] See vol. III, verse 2.
[471] *eggrjóðandi*: 'blade-edge reddener', warrior.
[472] Perhaps an assembly of ships or more likely a warlike expedition, a battle.
[473] *ara brædir*: 'feeder of the eagle', warrior.
[474] *brimlogs rýrir*: 'destroyer (or diminisher) of surf-fire (gold)', generous man.
[475] See vol. III, verse 7.
[476] *rimmu Yggr*: 'Óðinn of battle', warrior.

> From east you came, tongue-colourer
> of the company of wolves,[477] known to people,
> to proud meetings, picked warriors
> with pale shields and inlaid javelins.

And also this:[478]

> 189. You held west with the highest   Hrynhenda 6
> of helms of terror into Þrœndish homes;   Hkr III 8–9
> they say your foemen faltered,   Skald II 190
> feather-reddener of Yggr's seagull.[479]
> Your enemies, sater of the swarthy
> surf-of-wounds vulture,[480] felt their misery—
> they said your foemen were, fearful,
> forced to save their lives—increasing.

Here it says that Magnús came from the east over Kjǫlr into Þrándheimr and many forces thronged to him, but his enemies fled away, and also that King Sveinn immediately left the country when Magnús came into Norway. Sveinn fled to Denmark, for he could get no forces to withstand Magnús. Magnús was then accepted as king in Norway, and he subjected the whole land to himself. He was known as Magnús inn góði (the Good).

[441] CHAPTER TWO HUNDRED AND FIFTY-THREE

King Magnús had a shrine made and adorned with gold and silver and jewels. This shrine is made in both size and other aspects of shape like a coffin, but with lines of pillars underneath and up on top a lid shaped like a roof and rising up from it figureheads and a ridge. On the lid there are hinges at the back and hasps at the front, and these are locked with a key. After that King Magnús had the relics of King Óláfr placed in the shrine. Then many miracles took place there at the relics of King Óláfr. The poet Sigvatr mentions this:[481]

> 190. For him whose heart was noble   Erfidrápa Óláfs helga 24
> has a gold shrine been made, for   Hkr III 20–21
> my lord; the leader's sanctity   Skald I 693
> I laud; to God he journeyed.

---

[477] *ulfa ferðar tungu rjóðr*: 'tongue-reddener of the pack of wolves', warrior.

[478] See vol. III, verse 8.

[479] *Yggjar mós fiðrirjóðr*: 'reddener of the feathers of the seagull (raven or eagle) of Óðinn', warrior.

[480] *benja kolgu blágams fœðir*: 'feeder of the dark vulture (raven) of the wave of wounds (blood)', warrior.

[481] See vol. III, verse 21.

> Soon many a sword-tree⁴⁸² goes from
> the unsullied king's glorious
> tomb, with his sight healed,
> who had come blind thither.

Then it was made law to keep holy the anniversary of the death of King Óláfr over all Norway. That day was immediately kept there like the highest feast days. The poet Sigvatr mentions this:⁴⁸³

> 191. It befits us the feast of Ǫleifr, *Erfidrápa Óláfs helga* 25
> father of Magnús, in my dwelling *Hkr* III 21
> to celebrate—God strengthens *Skald* I 694
> the sovereign—sincerely.
> I must uphold honestly
> the holy death-day, lamented,
> of the king who fitted
> the forks of my arm⁴⁸⁴ with red gold.

CHAPTER TWO HUNDRED AND FIFTY-FOUR

The poet Sigvatr had got leave from King Óláfr to go home when the king travelled east to Garðaríki. And the next summer Sigvatr left the country and went south to Rome. Then he spoke this verse:

> 192. Weary of war, the clamour- *Erfidrápa Óláfs helga* 27
> wand⁴⁸⁵ the king gave me, wound with *Skald* I 696
> gold, I gave up, and left home on
> the good journey Romeward,
> when the precious sword, silver-hilted,
> I set down, that could lessen
> the she-wolf's husband's⁴⁸⁶ hunger,
> the hallowed staff⁴⁸⁷ to go with.

[442] And in the autumn, when Sigvatr was on his way back from the south, then he learned of the fall of King Óláfr. This was a source of the greatest grief to him. He spoke this:⁴⁸⁸

---

⁴⁸² *hrings meiðr*: 'sword's tree', warrior, man.
⁴⁸³ See vol. III, verse 22.
⁴⁸⁴ *handar tjǫlgur*: 'branches of the hand, arm', arms or fingers.
⁴⁸⁵ *gjallar vǫnd*: 'wand of clamour (battle)', sword.
⁴⁸⁶ *ylgjar verr*: 'she-wolf's husband', wolf.
⁴⁸⁷ i.e. the pilgrim's staff.
⁴⁸⁸ See vol. III, verse 11.

193. I stood on Mont,⁴⁸⁹ remembered,   *Hkr* III 14
one morning, near castles,⁴⁹⁰   *Skald* I 722
where many broad shields and masking⁴⁹¹
mailcoats flew asunder.
I recalled the king who in his
country in early bud-time⁴⁹²
once was happy; my father
was there that time, Þórrøðr.

Sigvatr was walking one day through a certain village and heard that some husband was wailing loudly, having lost his wife, beating his breast and tearing his clothes off, weeping bitterly, and he wanted very much to die. Sigvatr said:⁴⁹³

194. A man claims, if he misses   *Hkr* III 15
a maid's embrace, he's ready   *Skald* I 725
to die; love's bought dear if even
the dignified must weep for her.
But fierce tears⁴⁹⁴ the fearless,
flight-shy man sheds, bereft of
his lord; worse looks our grievous
loss to the king's servants.

Sigvatr got home to Norway and to his dwelling. He discovered that many people were criticising him and reckoned that he had been wrong to part from King Óláfr. Then he said this:⁴⁹⁵

195. May White-Christ punish me   *Hkr* III 17
if I meant to depart from   *Skald* I 728
Ǫleifr—I'm innocent
of that—with hot fire.
Such witness, plentiful as water—
I went to Rome in peril—
of others I have; from people
I shall never hide it.

---

⁴⁸⁹ *mont*: presumably the Italian *monte*, referring to either the Alps or the Appenines.

⁴⁹⁰ Each of the phrases *borgum nær* 'near castles, cities' and *of morgin* 'in the morning' could alternatively refer to the remembered battle rather than to the poet's current situation.

⁴⁹¹ *síðar*: literally 'long, hanging'.

⁴⁹² *ǫndverðan brum*: (in) the beginning of bud-time, spring; i.e. in his youth.

⁴⁹³ See vol. III, verse 12.

⁴⁹⁴ *vígtǫr*: 'battle-tears', i.e. 'tears of rage shed by a warrior in a murderous mood'.

⁴⁹⁵ See vol. III, verse 15.

After this, Sigvatr went to King Magnús's court and stayed with him, becoming one of his followers. The king was well disposed towards him.

CHAPTER TWO HUNDRED AND FIFTY-FIVE

King Sveinn Knútsson went to Denmark and there took over power with his brother Hǫrða-Knútr. Bjarni Gullbrárskáld says this in *Kálfsflokkr*:[496]

196. You helped young princes have the inheritance due to them; it's true that Sveinn could be sovereign solely over Denmark. Kálfr, to the country keen Magnús you conducted from Garðar; 'twas you gave the ruler governance of the kingdom.	*Kálfsflokkr* 6 *Hkr* III 12 *Fsk* 208 (1–4 after 5–8) *Skald* I 886

That same winter Sveinn Álfífuson died of sickness in Denmark. And Knútr inn ríki also died that winter in England on the Ides of November.[497] He had then been king over the countries of three nations, over England, Denmark, Norway for seven winters, and over England and Denmark for four and twenty winters, and first of all over Denmark alone for three winters. He was then thirty-five plus two winters of age. After him the king in England was his son Haraldr. [443] He was married to the emperor Heinrekr's daughter Gunnhildr.[498] She died childless three years later.

CHAPTER TWO HUNDRED AND FIFTY-SIX[499]

Þórir hundr left the country shortly after the fall of King Óláfr. Þórir travelled out to Jerusalem, and according to the accounts of many people, he never returned. Þórir hundr's son was called Sigurðr, father of Rannveig, who was married to Árni Árnason's son Jón. Their children were Víðkunnr in Bjarkey and Sigurðr hundr (Dog), Erlingr, Jarðþrúðr.

---

[496] See vol. III, verse 10.

[497] 13th November 1035. 12th November according to the Anglo-Saxon Chronicle.

[498] This is not correct. But Haraldr's sister Gunnhildr was married in 1036 to King Henry of Germany, who became Holy Roman Emperor (Henry III) in 1046. Gunnhildr died just over two years after her marriage. Cf. *Magnúss saga ins góða* (vol. III), ch. 17.

[499] Cf. *Magnúss saga ins góða* (vol. III), ch. 11.

CHAPTER TWO HUNDRED AND FIFTY-SEVEN[500]

Hárekr from Þjótta stayed at home at his estates, right on until Magnús Óláfsson came to the country and was king. Then Hárekr travelled south to Þrándheimr to see King Magnús. At that time Ásmundr Grankelsson was staying there with King Magnús, and as Hárekr was going ashore from his ship, then Ásmundr struck him his death-blow. Ásmundr carried out this deed with the support of King Magnús. Afterwards King Magnús gave Ásmundr a fief and stewardship in Hálogaland, and there are extensive stories about the dealings between Ásmundr and Hárekr's sons there.

CHAPTER TWO HUNDRED AND FIFTY-EIGHT[501]

Kálfr Árnason shared the government of the country with King Magnús for a certain time to begin with. Then people started to remind the king of what Kálfr had done at Stiklarstaðir. It then got more difficult for Kálfr to manage the king's moods. It came about on one occasion, when there was a crowd of people around the king and people were pleading their cases, that there came before him with urgent business a man that was mentioned earlier,[502] Þorgeirr flekkr of Súla in Veradalr. The king took no [444] notice of what he was saying, and was listening to those that were closer to him. Then Þorgeirr spoke in a loud voice, so that everyone could hear who was nearby:[503]

197.	Speak to me,	*Hkr* III 23
	Magnús king!	*Skald* II 9–10
	In your father's	
	following I was.	
	From there I carried	
	my cloven skull,	
	when they stepped over	
	the stricken king.	
	you give love to	
	the loathsome crowd	
	of lord-betrayers	
	who delighted the devil.	

Then there was an uproar, and some told Þorgeirr to go out. The king called him over to himself and his business was concluded so that Þorgeirr was well pleased, and he (the king) promised him his friendship.

[500] Cf. *Magnúss saga ins góða* (vol. III), ch. 12.
[501] Cf. *Magnúss saga ins góða* (vol. III), ch. 13.
[502] See ch. 203 above.
[503] Cf. *Magnúss saga ins góða* (vol. III), verse 23.

CHAPTER TWO HUNDRED AND FIFTY-NINE[504]

It was a little later that King Magnús was at a banquet at Haugr in Veradalr. And while the king was sitting at the tables, then there was sitting on one side of him Kálfr Árnason, and on his other side Einarr þambarskelfir. It had now come about that the king was treating Kálfr with coldness, and was now showing Einarr the greatest honour. The king said to Einarr:

'We two shall ride today to Stiklarstaðir. I want to see the traces of what happened there.'

Einarr replies: 'I cannot tell you anything about that. Let your foster-father Kálfr go. He will be able to tell about the events there.'

And when the tables were cleared away, then the king got ready to go. He said to Kálfr:

'You shall go with me to Stiklarstaðir.'

Kálfr said that this was not necessary. Then the king stood up and spoke rather angrily:

'You shall go, Kálfr.'

After that the king went out. Kálfr got his clothes on quickly and said to his servant:

'You must ride out to Egg and tell my men to have all the luggage on board ship before sunset.'

The king rode to Stiklarstaðir and Kálfr with him, and they dismounted from their horses and went to where the battle had been. Then the king spoke to Kálfr:

'Where is the place that the king fell?'

Kálfr replies, stretching out his spear-shaft: 'Here is where he lay,' he says.

The king said: 'Where were you then, Kálfr?'

He replies: 'Here, where I am standing now.'

The king spoke, and his face was now as red as blood: 'He was within range of your axe, then.'

Kálfr then leapt on his horse and rode away, and all his men, and the king rode back to Haugr. Kálfr did not stop riding until he came out to Egg. His ship was then ready by the shore and all his movable property on board and it was manned with his men. [445] They immediately made their way during the night out along the fiord. After that Kálfr travelled day and night as fast as the winds would take them. He then sailed to the west across the sea and stayed there a long time, raiding around Scotland and Ireland and the Hebrides. Bjarni Gullbrárskáld mentions this:[505]

---

[504] Cf. *Magnúss saga ins góða* (vol. III), ch. 14.
[505] See vol. III, verse 24.

198. I've heard that Haraldr's nephew *Kálfsflokkr* 7
held you dear, Þorbergr's brother; *Hkr* III 25
you earned that; it lasted *Skald* I 887–88
until men⁵⁰⁶ destroyed it.
Between you envious men
kindled constant strife.
I think Ǫleifr's heir
was harmed by this affair.

CHAPTER TWO HUNDRED AND SIXTY⁵⁰⁷

King Magnús began to grow harsher towards the farmers, so that many began to suffer heavy penalties from him both in men's lives and confiscations. Those affected most were the Þrœndir. Then the farmers began to grumble, saying among themselves:

'What can this king be intending, when he breaks the law with regard to us that King Hákon inn góði (the Good) established? Does he not remember that we have never put up with injuries to our rights? He will go the same way as his father and other rulers whom we have deprived of life when we got tired of their tyranny and lawlessness.'

This grumbling was widespread in the country. The people of Sogn had gathered together a force and were planning to fight with the king. The king's friends became aware of this, and twelve men held a conference and it was agreed between them that they should choose by lot someone to tell the king of this grumbling. And it was managed so that the lot fell to the poet Sigvatr.

CHAPTER TWO HUNDRED AND SIXTY-ONE⁵⁰⁸

Then Sigvatr composed a *flokkr*⁵⁰⁹ that is called *Bersǫglisvísur*, and it begins at first about the fact that they felt that the king was pondering too much about his plans to keep the farmers in check who were threatening to start an uprising against him. He said:⁵¹⁰

199. I've heard that south among Sygnir *Bersǫglisvísur* 1
Sigvatr has dissuaded *Hkr* III 26–27
the king from waging warfare; *Skald* II 12
I will go, if we yet must battle.

⁵⁰⁶ *herr*: 'men'. This is the reading of the main *Hkr* manuscript; others, including all manuscripts of *ÓH*, have *hann* 'he' (see *Skald* I).
⁵⁰⁷ Cf. *Magnúss saga ins góða* (vol. III), ch. 15.
⁵⁰⁸ Cf. *Magnúss saga ins góða* (vol. III), ch. 16.
⁵⁰⁹ See note 191 above.
⁵¹⁰ See vol. III, verse 25.

Let us arm, and with no
argument, defend, eager,
the lord and his lands with ring-swords;
how long till this encounter?

In the same poem there are these verses:[511]

200. He who fell at Fitjar   *Bersǫglisvísur* 5
 foremost[512] was called, and punished   *Hkr* III 27
 hostile looking, Hǫkon,   *Mork* (*Flb*) 33–34
 he was loved by people.   *Skald* II 16
 Men held fast to the most friendly
 foster-son of Aðalsteinn's
 laws later; still farmers are slow
 to relinquish what they remember.

201. I think they made just choices,   *Bersǫglisvísur* 6
 farmers and jarls also,   *Hkr* III 27–28
 for people's property was given   *Mork* (*Flb*)34
 peace by the two Óleifrs.   *Skald* II 17
 Haraldr's heir, ever trusty,
 and Tryggvi's son, supported
 leek-straight[513] laws that the namesakes
 laid down for the people.

202. King, at your counsellors you must not   *Bersǫglisvísur* 9
 become angry for plain speaking;   *Hkr* III 28
 this command of our lord will   *Mork* (*Flb*) 36
 make clear, prince, the way for glory.   *Skald* II 20
 Other laws, unless the landsmen   *Fsk* 213
 lie, the farmers say they have,
 worse than those you in Ulfasund
 once promised to people.

203. Who counsels you to cancel,   *Bersǫglisvísur* 13
 king intent on hatred—   *Hkr* III 28–29
 often you assay slender   *Mork* (*Flb*) 38–39
 swords—your promises?   *Fsk* 214
 A prosperous king of people   *Skald* II 24
 his pledges must honour.

[511] See vol. III, verses 26–33.
[512] *fjǫlgegn*: 'effective in many ways'; perhaps a periphrasis for Hákon's nickname *inn góði* 'the Good'.
[513] *laukjǫfn*: 'straight as a leek', i.e. just.

               To break your bond never,
               battle-enlarger,[514] befits you.

[446] 204. Who incites you to slay your   *Bersǫglisvísur* 11
       subjects' cattle, war-leader[515]?   *Hkr* III 29
       It is arrogance for a ruler   *Mork* (*Flb*) 37–38
       in his realm to act so.   *Fsk* 213–14
       None had earlier offered   *Skald* II 22
       a young king such counsel;
       your troops, I think, tire of plunder;
       people, prince, are angry.

     205. Take notice, thief-toppler,   *Bersǫglisvísur* 10
       of talk of men now going   *Hkr* III 29–30
       about here; the hand must be   *Mork* (*Flb*) 37
       held back by moderation.   *Fsk* 213 (first half)
       It is a friend who offers—   *Skald* II 21
       you must heed, gladdener
       of the tear-hawk of warm wounds,[516]
       what the farmers want—a warning.

     206. The threat is grave that greybeards   *Bersǫglisvísur* 12
       against the king, as I hear it,   *Hkr* III 30
       mean to rise; measures   *Mork* (*Flb*) 38
       must for that be taken.   *Fsk* 214–15
       It's harsh when thing-men hang their *Ágrip* 2008, 46–48
       heads and under mantles—   *3GT* 30, 114 (first half)
       your servants are stricken   *Skald* II 23
       with silence—stick their noses.

     207. All say the same: 'to his   *Bersǫglisvísur* 14
       subjects' ancestral properties   *Hkr* III 30–31
       my lord claims ownership';   *Mork* (*Flb*) 38
       honourable farmers turn against him. *Skald* II 25
       He who his inheritance
       hands out to king's barons
       according to rushed rulings
       will reckon that robbery.

---

[514] *hjaldrmǫgnuðr*: 'battle-increaser', warrior.
[515] *hjaldrgegnir*: 'advancer of battle', warrior.
[516] *varmra benja tármútaris teitir*: 'gladdener of the hawk (raven) of the tears of warm wounds (blood)', warrior.

After this admonishment the king reformed himself well in response. Many others also conveyed the same message to the king. So it came about that the king held talks with the wisest men and they compiled their laws. After that King Magnús had the law code that is still in Þrándheimr and is known as *Grágás* put into writing.[517] King Magnús afterwards became popular and beloved of all the people of the country. For this reason he was known as Magnús inn góði (the Good).

CHAPTER TWO HUNDRED AND SIXTY-TWO

King Magnús of Norway and King Horða-Knútr of the Danes were to begin with at odds with each other, but the population in both Norway and Denmark got tired of this. Men then intervened between them with proposals for settlement. It came about that the kings met in person at the Elfr and were reconciled and swore oaths of brotherhood, and this was a part of their agreement, that each of them was to inherit the country after the other if there was an interval between their deaths so that the other died without sons. King Haraldr Knútsson of the English died five years after the death of Knútr inn ríki. Then Horða-Knútr took over the kingdom in England and was king both there and in Denmark for two years. Then he died childless.

CHAPTER TWO HUNDRED AND SIXTY-THREE

King Magnús Óláfsson took over the kingdom in Denmark after Horða-Knútr, ruling then both Denmark and Norway. At this time the Danish realm was very subject to raids. Then Sveinn Úlfsson started trying to fight his way to the kingdom there. He fought battles with King Magnús, and Magnús always won.

[447] CHAPTER TWO HUNDRED AND SIXTY-FOUR

King Magnús gave his sister Úlfhildr Óláfsdóttir in marriage to Duke Ótta in Saxland. Their son was called Magnús. From him a great family line is descended. The dukes that have ruled over Brunswick thus trace their ancestry to Óláfr the Saint.

King Magnús took his army to Vinðland. Then he won Jómsborg and burned it and raided the country far and wide. After that he went back to Denmark. Then his army deserted him. The king was then left without a large number of men.

[517] This *Grágás* (lit. Grey Goose) is not the Lawbook known from later times in Iceland, but the name may originally have applied to this Norwegian code (the reason is not known). It was not applied to the Icelandic Lawbook until the sixteenth century, perhaps by some misunderstanding. See *Laws of Early Iceland* 1980, I 9.

CHAPTER TWO HUNDRED AND SIXTY-FIVE[518]

That same autumn Vinðr were on the move with a huge force. So when King Magnús heard about this, then he gathered an army together and went against them with the forces that he could get. Then his brother-in-law Duke Ótta came to support him. They encountered the army of Vinðr on Hlýrskógsheiðr south of Heiðabœr. King Magnús and his men lay out in the open under their shields during the night. The next day was the eve of the feast of St Michael.[519] Then his scouts reported to the king, and these men had seen the army of the Vinðr, they said the king had not a fraction of their numbers. Great fear spread through his army, men urged the king to flee. He was then very worried, for he had never taken to flight. He wanted to fight if people thought they had some chance. Duke Ótta was rather in favour of resistance. But when the king was in this state of anxiety, then he fell asleep. Then it seemed to him his father, King Óláfr the Saint, came to him and said:

'Are you all full of fear now, when heathens have a large army? You must not be afraid of that, for I shall be with you. Get [448] up and get on with the battle as soon as you hear my horn. Be confident and fearless.'

Then the king awoke. Then the sun rose. Then the king related his dream. Men were very happy at that and took heart. Then they saw the army of Vinðr. The Vinðr crossed the Skotborgará. Then all King Magnús's followers heard up in the sky above them the sound of bells, and all those who had been in Niðaróss then recognised the sound, and it was as if Glǫð was being rung. This bell was at Clemenskirkja in Kaupangr, and King Óláfr had presented it there. After that, King Magnús threw off his mailcoat and took in his hand the axe that had belonged to King Óláfr, which is called Hel, then immediately set to against the army of Vinðr. So says Arnórr jarlaskáld:[520]

| 208. | With broad axe, unwearied, went forth the ruler— sword-clash happened round the Hǫrðar's head[521]—and threw off his mailcoat, when the shaft—land was shared out by the shaping guardian of Heaven,[522] | *Magnússdrápa* 10 *Hkr* III 43–44 *Mork* (*Flb*) 65–66 *Fsk* 223 *Skald* II 219 |

---

[518] Cf. *Magnúss saga ins góða* (vol. III), chs 26–28.
[519] i.e. 28th September 1043. St Michael's day (Michaelmas) is 29th September.
[520] See vol. III, verse 41.
[521] *Hǫrða hilmir*: 'ruler of the Hǫrðar', king of Norway (Magnús)
[522] *himins skapvǫrðr*: 'the shaping-guardian of Heaven', God.

Hel[523] clove pallid craniums—
the king's two hands encircled.

Then King Magnús launched such a fierce attack that the Vinðr immediately gave way before it. Those that stood in the front line then turned in flight, but those that were in the rear stood so firmly that the others were unable to flee, and they fell one on top of the other. But the king and his men slaughtered the Vinðr like cattle. According to the accounts of learned men, this has been the greatest loss of life that has taken place in Northern lands since the coming of Christianity. Afterwards they pursued the rout and then slew a huge number of men. So says the poet Þjóðólfr:[524]

209. I hold that in a troop of a hundred *Magnússflokkr* 10
Haraldr's brother's son[525] was standing— *Hkr* III 44
the raven saw his hunger-ban *Mork* (*Flb*) 65
soon coming[526]—in the army's forefront. *Fsk* 222
Far-flung was the path of *Skald* II 72
fleeing Wends; where Magnús battled
hewn corpses came to hide the
heath a league broadly.

CHAPTER TWO HUNDRED AND SEVENTY

King Óláfr the Saint's son King Magnús inn góði was ruling over Norway, as was said above. There was with him then Jarl Rǫgnvaldr Brúsason. At this time Rǫgnvaldr's uncle Jarl Þorfinnr Sigurðarson was ruling over Orkney. Then King Magnús sent Rǫgnvaldr west to Orkney and ordered Þorfinnr to let him receive his patrimony. Þorfinnr let [449] Rǫgnvaldr have a third share of the lands with himself, for this was what his father Brúsi had had on the day he died. Jarl Þorfinnr was now married to Finnr Árnason's daughter Ingibjǫrg Mother of Jarls. Jarl Rǫgnvaldr believed he was entitled to two parts of the lands, which was what Óláfr the Saint had granted his father Brúsi and Brúsi had held during his (Óláfr's) lifetime. This was the beginning of the quarrel between the kinsmen, and there is a long story about that.[527] They fought a great battle on Péttlandsfjǫrðr. Kálfr Árnason was at that time with Jarl Þorfinnr. So said Bjarni Gullbrárskáld:[528]

[523] *Hel*: the axe owned by St Óláfr, named after the goddess of the underworld.
[524] See vol. III, verse 42. In *Mork* (*Flb*) attributed to Sigvatr.
[525] King Magnús, whose father Óláfr helgi was half-brother of Haraldr harðráði.
[526] i.e. that its food was on its way.
[527] Cf. *Orkneyinga saga*. The original version of this saga, which is no longer extant, may have been compiled round about 1200, and was doubtless known to Snorri.
[528] Cf. note 345 above (to verse 128).

210. We heard, Kálfr, in the hostility   *Kálfsflokkr* 8
how Finnr's kinsman[529] you followed, *Orkn* 67, 122
and at sea had warships   *Skald* I 889
steered at the jarl[530] quickly.
You voided the violence
of the vehement son of Brúsi,[530]
and helped—courage heated—
heedful of enmity, Þorfinnr.

King Magnús looked after the relics of King Óláfr, cutting his hair and nails. Towards the end of King Magnús's days, Haraldr Sigurðarson came to Norway. They both ruled the country for one year, until Magnús died in Jótland in Denmark. Afterwards Óláfr the Saint's brother King Haraldr ruled the country, and then King Haraldr looked after the relics of King Óláfr in the same way as King Magnús had done previously. But when King Haraldr was ready to travel from the country westwards to England, then he locked King Óláfr's shrine and threw the keys out into the Nið. But some say that he threw them overboard off Agðanes. Then had passed from the fall of King Óláfr thirty-five years, the same number of years as King Óláfr had lived here in this world. King Óláfr's shrine has never since been opened.

King Haraldr had a dream, when he [450] was lying with his army off Sólundir. King Óláfr appeared to him and he thought he spoke this verse:[531]

211. The famous king, for his advancement, *Hkr* III 178
the fat one, won most battles; *Mork* 305–06
I had, since at home I lingered, *Fsk* 277
a holy fall to earth. *Hemings þáttr* 39–40
Still I dread that death is *Skald* II 822
due, lord, to come upon you;
the greedy troll's steeds[532] you're going
to glut—God will not cause it.

King Haraldr fell in England on that expedition.

CHAPTER TWO HUNDRED AND SEVENTY-ONE

Haraldr's son was called Óláfr, his second Magnús. They were kings after King Haraldr. King Magnús was short-lived. Afterwards Óláfr was king in

---

[529] *mágr*: here, Finnr's son-in-law is Jarl Þorfinnr.
[530] i.e. Jarl Rǫgnvaldr.
[531] See vol. III, verse 152.
[532] The troll's horse is a wolf (cf. *Gylf* 46/26). The adjective 'greedy' properly belongs with *fákum* 'horses'.

Norway, a popular man and blessed with peace. He had a stone church built in Kaupangr at the place where the relics of King Óláfr were first buried, and he had this minster fully fitted out. It was consecrated Christchurch. The bishop's see was there then and Óláfr's shrine . . .[533]

CHAPTER TWO HUNDRED AND SEVENTY-THREE

King Óláfr, who was known as inn kyrri (the Peaceful), died of sickness east in Vík. His son was Magnús berfœttr (Barelegs), who was king in Norway after his father . . .[534]

CHAPTER TWO HUNDRED AND SEVENTY-FIVE

King Magnús berfœttr of Norway fell in Ireland, and then his sons Sigurðr Jórsalafari (Jerusalem-Traveller), Eysteinn, Óláfr succeeded to the kingdom . . .[535]

[451] CHAPTER TWO HUNDRED AND SEVENTY-SEVEN

Magnús berfœttr's sons, who were mentioned above, died of sickness, and Sigurðr lived longest of them. After him his son Magnús and his brother Haraldr gilli (short for Gillikristr, Servant of Christ) were kings. And after that came Haraldr gilli's sons Eysteinn, Ingi, Sigurðr . . .[536]

---

[533] The miracles that follow in this chapter and the next are also in *Heimskringla*, *Óláfs saga kyrra* (vol. III), chs 6–7.

[534] The miracles that follow in this chapter and the next are also in *Heimskringla*, *Magnúss saga berfœtts* (vol. III), chs 21–22.

[535] The miracles that follow in this chapter and the next are also in *Heimskringla*, *Magnússona saga* (vol. III), chs 30–31, in reverse order.

[536] The miracles that follow in this chapter and the next (the final chapter of the saga) are also in *Heimskringla*, *Haraldssona saga* (vol. III), chs 24–25.

Index of Names

Page references are to the page numbers of the *Íslenzk fornrit* edition, which are noted in square brackets within the text of the translation.

Aðalráðr (Æþelred II) Játgeirsson (son of Eadgar I), king of the English (978–1016) 13–16, 17 (verse), 18, 19, 22, 26, 33, 34, 274 (verse), 438; Aðalráðr's sons (Aðalráðssynir) 34.

Aðalsteinn (Æþelstan) Játvarðsson (son of Edward), king of the English (924–39) 427, 430, 445 (verse).

Aðalsteinsfóstri, nickname (foster-son of (King) Aðalsteinn) 47, 73, 97, 177, 242, 428, 437; cf. 445 (verse).

Aðils Óttarsson, king of the Swedes 361 (verse).

Afra-Fasti (Buttermilk-), a robber 349–50, 353, 370, 379.

Agðanes (Agdenes, near the entrance to Trondheimsfjord) 247, 250, 449.

Agðir (Agder, district of southern Norway) 61 (verse), 83, 191, 235, 305, 319, 346, 412, 434; Agðir dwellers (Egðir) 308 (verse). See also Norðr- and Austr-Agðir.

Agnafit (Agni's Meadow), near Stockholm in Sweden 8.

Áin helga (Helgeå, in Skáney) 278, 283, 285, 286. See also Ó en helga.

Aldeigjuborg/Aldeigja (modern Staraya Ladoga, near Lake Ladoga in Russia) 147, 148, 415, 440.

Álfhildr, King Óláfr's concubine, mother of Magnús inn góði 209.

Álfhildr daughter of Hringr Dagsson 423.

Álfífa daughter of Jarl Álfrimr (Ælfgifu of Northampton, wife of King Knútr, mother of King Sveinn) 398, 399, 401, 403–06, 410, 442.

Álfrimr, jarl, father of Álfífa 398.

Áli, a sea-king, in kennings for battle 359 (verses).

Álof daughter of Boðvarr 89.

Álof árbót (Improvement of Prosperity), daughter of Haraldr inn hárfagri 423–24.

Ámundi of Hlaupandanes on Hrossey 161, 162, 171, 174.

Ámundi Árnason 181.

Angrar (Hangran, in Bynes in Þrándheimr) 52.

Apavatn (lake in south-west Iceland) 54.

Ari father of Þorgils 127, 128.

Ari inn fróði (the Learned) Þorgilsson, priest and historian (1068–1148) 326, 410, 419, 420, 421, 431.

Ármóðr father of Árni and Arnfinnr 181, 292, 383.

Arnbjǫrn Árnason 181, 302–03, 333.

Arnfiðr/Arnfinnr Þorfinnsson, jarl in Orkney 159, 430.

Arnfinnr Ármóðsson 383.

Árni, father of Vígleikr 322.

Árni Ármóðsson 29, 181, 182, 244, 246, 247, 249, 250, 253, 292, 300, 302, 320, 321, 323, 327, 331–33, 339, 368, 372, 373, 383, 385–87, 402, 411, 412, 414, 415, 443, 444, 449; sons of 320, 327, 412.

Árni Árnason 181, 246–48, 249, 327, 402, 411, 443.

Arnkell Torf-Einarsson, jarl in Orkney (c. 946–954) 159.

Arnljótr gellini (from Gellin in Jamtaland), highwayman 258–61, 369–70, 379.

Arnórr jarlaskáld (Jarls' Poet) Þórðarson 160, 174, 208, 440, 448. See note 184.

Arnviðr blindi (the Blind), adviser of King Óláfr of the Svíar 152–54, 155–56.
Áróss (at the mouth of the river Fýri, where modern Uppsala is) 154, 344.
Ása daughter of Hákon Hlaðajarl 423.
Ásbjǫrn Selsbani (Seal-Slayer, slayer of Sel-Þórir) Sigurðarson 194–206, 212, 213, 373.
Ásgautr ármaðr (Steward) 74, 75–76.
Áskell [Ǫlmóðsson], father of Áslákr Fitjaskalli 192.
Áslákr of Finney 346, 386.
Áslákr Fitjaskalli (Baldy of Fitjar) Áskelsson 192–93, 317, 318, 322.
Áslákr son of Erlingr Skjálgsson 29, 39, 226.
Ásmundarvágr (Osmondwall on Háey (Hoy, Orkney)) 163.
Ásmundr Grankelsson 176, 177, 211, 212, 213, 253–55, 305, 443.
Ásta daughter of Guðbrandr kúla, mother of St Óláfr 3, 4, 40, 41, 42, 43, 46, 107–08, 219, 435, 436, 437. See also Ósta.
Ástríðr daughter of Eiríkr Bjóðaskalli, queen of Tryggvi Óláfsson 89, 432.
Ástríðr daughter of Njáll son of Finnr inn skjálgi 424.
Ástríðr daughter of King Óláfr of the Svíar 130, 144–46, 149, 152, 297, 327, 328, 344, 348.
Ástríðr daughter of King Sveinn tjúguskegg, wife of Jarl Úlfr 235.
Ástríðr daughter of Tryggvi Óláfsson, wife of Erlingr Skjálgsson 29, 438.
Áti, a sea king 66 (verse, in a kenning for ship).
Áttandaland/Áttundaland, an area in Uppland in eastern Sweden 110.
Atti inn dœlski (of the Dales/the Foolish) 149, 150, 153.
Austr-Agðir (Aust Agder, district in southern Norway) 82.
Austrey (Eysturoy in the Faeroes) 236, 263.
Austrfararvísur, a poem by Sigvatr Þórðarson about his journey to Gautland in late 1018 144.

Bálagarðssíða (south-west coast of Finnland) 11.
Baltic, eastern (Austrvegr) 82–84, 99, 116, 425, 432, 433, 435, 436. Cf. in the east (á austrvega) 145 (verse), see also Eystrasalt, note 176.
Bárðr, a priest from the Western Fiords of Iceland 244.
Bárðr hvíti (the White), steward 52.
Bárðr Jǫkulsson 331.
Barvík (unidentified harbour, perhaps near Baråkra in Blekinge, southern Sweden) 282.
Bear-cub (Húnn), i.e. Bersi Skáld-Torfuson 224 (verse).
Bergljót daughter of Jarl Hákon, wife of Einarr þambarskelfir 27, 192.
Bergljót daughter of Þórir þegjandi 424, 430.
Bergr, companion of the poet Sigvatr 271.
Bersi Skáld-Torfuson (son of the poet(ess) Torfa) 65, 224. See note 98.
Bersǫglisvísur (Plain-speaking Verses), a poem by Sigvatr Þórðarson 445.
Bison (the Bison), a ship, see Visundr.
Bjarkamál in fornu ('The Old Lay of Bjarki', an anonymous poem, see note 373) 361.
Bjarkey (Bjerkøy, Vestfold) 177, 194, 212, 213, 234, 250, 251, 443; Bjarkey man (Bjarkeyingr) 233.
Bjarmaland (an area somewhere round the White Sea in northern Russia, probably near modern Archangelsk) 227–29, 250, 253; Bjarmaland expedition (Bjarmalandsferð) 234.

INDEX OF NAMES

Bjarmar (people of Bjarmaland) 230, 231.
Bjarney (Bjørnøy, island off Raumsdalr) 322.
Bjarni Gullbrárskáld (Gullbrá's Poet) Hallbjarnarson 320, 333, 334, 385, 442, 445, 449. See note 345.
Bjǫrn, steward in Heiðmǫrk 297, 298, 299.
Bjǫrn digri (the Stout), King Óláfr Haraldsson's marshal 72, 79, 80, 86–92, 96, 100, 111, 113, 114, 117, 133, 327, 336–39, 384, 386.
Bjǫrn (III) Eiríksson, king of the Swedes (882–932) 116, 435.
Bjǫrn kaupmaðr (Merchant) son of Haraldr inn hárfagri 423–27, 432.
Blóðøx (Blood-Axe) nickname of Eiríkr Haraldsson 159.
Bókn (Stora Bokn, island off Rogaland) 313, 315 (verse), 320 (verse), 413.
Bolli Þorleiksson, father of Þorleikr 214. Cf. *Laxdœla saga*.
Borg (= Sarpsborg) 100, 133, 134, 144, 192, 292, 311; see Sarpsborg.
Borgund, farm in Sunn-Mœr 322.
Breiða(n), (correctly Breiðin < -vin; now Breidbygd in Upplǫnd or Dalar) 184, 185.
Breiðifjǫrðr, western Iceland 127.
Bretland (Wales) 163.
Brjánsorrosta (Battle of Clontarf in Ireland, 23rd April 1014) 160. See note 183.
Brunswick (Brúnsvík i.e. Braunschweig in Germany) 447.
Brúsi father of Klœngr 57.
Brúsi, farmer in Mærin in Valldalr 323–25.
Brúsi Sigurðarson, jarl in Orkney (1014–1030) 160, 161, 163, 165–74, 182, 327, 439, 440, 448, 449.
Brynjólfr (gamli, the old) úlfaldi (Camel), Norwegian farmer 79, 80, 82, 235.
Bulgars (Bolgarar) Bulgarians or Bulgars 439 (verse).
Bœjar (Bø) in Lesjar 182.
Bǫðvarr son of Víkinga-Kári 89.
Bǫlverkr Arnórsson, eleventh century Icelandic poet 439.
Bǫrkr father of Þórðr 214.

Canterbury (Kantaraborg, Kantarabyrgi; borg Kantara (in verse)) 20
Christ (Kristr) 124, 350, 408 (verse); Christ, man of (Kristsmaðr), Christ's men (Kristsmenn) 350, 355, 378. See also Jesus Christ and White-Christ.
Christchurch (Kristskirkja), in Niðaróss 367, 405, 450.
Clemenskirkja (St Clement's church in Niðaróss) 70, 404, 405, 448.

Dagr, father of Hringr (of Hringaríki) 423.
Dagr son of Haraldr inn hárfagri 423, 424.
Dagr son of Hringr, son of Haraldr inn hárfagri 299, 348.
Dagr son of Hringr Dagsson 348–49, 354, 357, 363, 364, 377, 383, 386, 389, 393 (verse); Dagr's storm/tempest (Dagshríð) 386, 389, 391 (verse) and note 404.
Dagr son of Rauðr 298–99, 300–01.
Dala-Guðbrandr (of the Dales) 183, 188, see Guðbrandr, lord in Dalar.
Dalar (Dales) 57, 101, 103, 107, 183, 184, 190, 209, 220; king in Dalar (Dalakonungr) 102–03, 105; see Guðbrandsdalar.
Danes (Danir) 13, 15, 19, 34, 46, 79, 120, 150, 173, 223, 270 (verse), 274 (verse), 275, 278 (verse), 288, 399 (verse); army of Danes (Danaherr) 13; king(s) of

the Danes (Danakonungr, -ar) 13, 30, 42, 44, 47, 48, 79, 97, 98, 153, 158, 221, 223, 432, 433, 434, 438, 439, 446; realm of (the) Danes, Danish realm, realm of Denmark (Danaveldi) 221, 275, 276, 303, 306, 446; Danish (people) (Danir) 12 (verse), 94 (verse); Danish maidens (danskar meyjar) 291 (verse); Danish weapons (dǫnsk vápn) 391 (verse); Danish host (danskr herr) 21 (verse); Danish (language) (Dǫnsk tunga) 39 (verse).

Denmark (Danmǫrk) 5, 6, 12, 45, 79, 83, 97, 158, 221, 223, 226, 227, 234, 235, 268, 269, 271, 274, 275, 277 (verse), 282, 284, 294, 303, 306, 308, 310 (verse), 311, 312, 333, 343, 345, 346, 398, 399, 419, 423, 432, 433, 440, 442, 446, 447, 449.

Dímon, Dímun (in the Faeroes) 218, 236, 237.

Dofrar (Dovre in Upplǫnd) 182.

Drafn (Dramsfjorden, near Oslo) 311.

Draupnir, a mythical ring, in a kenning for gold 382 (verse).

Dublin (Dyflinn) 174 (verse), 425.

Dungaðr, jarl of Katanes 159.

Dvina (Vína, River in Russia) 229.

Dœlir (people of Dalar) 184, 186, 298.

Eaðmundr (járnsíða) Aðalráðsson (Edmund Ironside, King Edmund II of the English, died 1016), 17 (Ját-, verse), 22, 26, 33.

Eaðvarðr (Eat-) (Edward the Confessor) inn góði (the Good) son of Aðalráðr, king of the English (died 1066) 22, 26, 284.

Eastern lands (Austrlǫnd), the countries on the eastern side of the Baltic 115.

Eatgeirr (Edgar) son of Aðalráðr 26.

Eatvarðr 26, 284 = Eaðvarðr.

Eatvígr (Edwig) son of Aðalráðr 26.

Edmund, St (Eaðmundr inn helgi, died 869/70) 14.

Eðla, daughter of a jarl of Vinðland 130.

Egðir (people of Agðir) 281 (verse), 321 (verse).

Egg (Egge, Sogn) 178, 181, 249, 300, 332, 402, 412, 444.

Egill, Gautish man 130.

Egill son of Síðu-Hallr 220, 240, 287.

Eið (which Eiðsvǫllr (Eidsvold) is named from; in Akershus county in south-east Norway) 104.

Eið 135 (verse), probably the same as Eiðar.

Eiðar (which Eiðaskógr is named from) 107 (verse), 135, 136 (verse).

Eiðaskógr (Eidskog, near Oslo, on the border with Sweden) 79, 136, 139 (verse), 242, 327, 328, 347.

Eikreyjar (Öckerö etc., a group of islands off Vestra-Gautland) 83, 150.

Eikund (an island off the coast of southern Norway), sound of (= Eikundasund) 309 (verse).

Eikundasund (Eikersund, off Jaðarr, south-west Norway) 235, 306, 312.

Eilífr gauzki (Gautish), steward 79–81.

Eilífr jarl, son of Jarl Rǫgnvaldr 148.

Einarr 158, see Torf-Einarr.

Einarr þambarskelfir (Bowstring-shaker) Eindriðason 27, 31, 50, 52–54, 57, 58, 65, 67, 72, 191–92, 209, 267, 307, 339, 345–46, 401–05, 411, 412, 414, 415, 444.

Einarr (Þveræingr, from Þverá) Eyjólfsson 216, 217.
Einarr rangmuðr (Twisted-Mouth) son of Sigurðr, jarl in Orkney 128, 129, 160–66, 171, 177.
Einbúi (Einbu), the highest farm in Lesjar 326.
Eindriði Einarsson (of Gimsar (Gimsan near Trondheim, Norway)) 27, 307, 345.
Eindriði Styrkársson (of Gimsar (Gimsan near Trondheim, Norway)) 27.
Eiríkr, king in Denmark 423.
Eiríkr inn sigrsæli (the Victorious) Bjarnarson, king of the Swedes (died c. 995) 98, 116, 130, 155, 156, 435, 438, 439.
Eiríkr Emundarson, king of the Swedes 115, 435.
Eiríkr Hákonarson, jarl (died c. 1023) 27, 28, 30, 31, 32, 36, 53, 55, 78, 143 (verse), 221, 226, 273 (verse), 438, 439.
Eiríkr blóðøx (Blood-Axe) Haraldsson, king of Norway (died c. 954) 159, 167, 423, 424, 425, 426, 427, 428, 429, 430, 431, 432, 433–34; sons of Eiríkr, Eiríkr's sons (Eiríkssynir) 431, 432, 433, 434.
Eiríkr (Vatnarsson?), king from Hǫrðaland 423.
Eiríkr Bjóðaskalli (Baldy of Bjóðar in Hǫrðaland) (Víkinga-Kárason?) 89, 432.
Eiríkr rauði (the Red) Þorvaldsson 126.
Eiríksdrápa (a poem by Þórðr Kolbeinsson) 30, note 55.
E(i)stland (Estland, Estonia) 115, 425.
Elfarkvíslar the delta of the Elfr 425.
Elfr (Göta älv, river in south-west Sweden) 79, 81, 85, 86, 117, 191, 235, 269, 424, 446; see Gautelfr.
Elgr, a name for the god Óðinn (in verse) 66 (in a kenning for battle).
Ella, king of Northumbria (died 867); Ella's kin (Ellu kind), i.e. the English 18 (verse).
Emma daughter of Duke Richard I of Normandy, queen of King Æþelred II and later of King Knútr inn ríki 26, 33, 275, 276.
Emundr of Skarar, lawman in Vestra-Gautland 148–53, 155, 156.
Emundr, father of King Eiríkr of the Swedes 115, 435.
Emundr Óláfsson, king of the Swedes 130.
England 13, 14, 21, 30–34, 39, 45, 83, 158, 209, 221, 223–26, 235, 249, 253, 268, 271, 274, 275, 292, 303 (verse), 311 (verse), 333, 335, 345, 401, 402, 419, 428, 430, 438, 442, 446, 449, 450; lord (i.e. king) of England (Engla dróttinn) 334 (verse).
Englandshaf (North Sea) 253.
English, the, Englishmen (Englar) 17 (verse), 19 (verse), 21 (verse), 334 (verse), 393 (verse); (enskr) 22 (verse); (enskir menn) 14; King of the English (Englakonungr) 14, 26, 33, 223, 284, 427, 430, 438, 446.
Erlendr of Gerði 346, 386.
Erlendr Torf-Einarsson, jarl in Orkney (died 954) 159.
Erlingr son of Eiríkr blóðøx 430, 433.
Erlingr Jónsson 443.
Erlingr Skjálgsson 28–30, 39, 58, 67, 70, 78, 183, 192–94, 196–98, 200, 201, 203–06, 226, 235, 244, 246, 247, 249, 268, 293, 294, 312–19, 321 (verse), 322, 339, 346, 413, 438.
Estland 425, see Eistland.
Eyjafjǫrðr in northern Iceland 215.
Eyjólfr, father of Guðmundr ríki 127, 217, 220.

Eyjólfr, father of Þorkell 214, 217.
Eyland (Öland, island in the Baltic) 84, 109.
Eynir (people of Eynafylki) 180; Eynir district (Eynafylki) (district north of Trondheimsfjord) 51.
Eyrar (= Eyrarbakki, south-west Iceland) 215.
Eyrarsund (Öresund, sound between Denmark and Sweden) 284, 286, 288, 289 (verse), 310.
Eysteinn of Heiðmǫrk, jarl 423.
Eysteinn illráði (the Evil-Doer), king 241.
Eysteinn Erlendsson, archbishop in Norway (1161–88) 405.
Eysteinn son of Haraldr gilli, king in Norway (1142–57) 451.
Eysteinn glumra (rattle) Ívarsson 158.
Eysteinn Magnússon, king in Norway (1103–23) 450.
Eysteinn orri (Black Grouse) Þorbergsson 245.
Eystra-Gautland (Östergotland, southern Sweden) 109, 148, 149.
Eystrasalt (*grœna salt*) the Baltic: see note 177.
Eystri-Dalir (a group of valleys in eastern Norway lying between the river Glomma and the Swedish border) 297, 298.
Eysýsla (Ösel/Saaremaa, island off Estonia) 9, 10; people of (Eysýslir) 9.
Eyvindr skáldaspillir (Poet-Spoiler; i.e. 'destroyer of poets' or 'plagiarist') Finnsson, Norwegian poet, tenth century 175, 421, 424.
Eyvindr úrarhorn (Aurochs Horn) 82–85, 128, 163, 171.

Faeroes, the (Færeyjar) 74, 214, 218–21, 236, 238, 240, 261, 263, 267.
Faeroese people, men (Færeyingar) 218, 219, 238.
Fenja, a giantess, in a kenning for gold 391 (verse).
Fetlafjǫrðr (fiord by Flavium Brigantium, now Betanzos, south-east of Coruna in Spain?) 24.
Fiðr see Finnr
Fife (Fífi), in Scotland 225.
Finney (Finnøy in Rogaland) 346, 386.
Finnish (Finnlendingar, i.e. Lapps) 11 (verse); (Finnar, i.e. Lapps) 383 (verse).
Finnmǫrk (Finnmark, north-east Norway) 79, 242. See also Mǫrk(in).
Finnr (Fiðr) litli (Small), from Upplǫnd 120, 121, 123.
Finnr (Fiðr) Árnason 181, 24–48, 249–53, 327, 355–56, 368, 378, 385, 387, 402, 411, 449.
Finnr inn skjálgi (the Squinter) Eyvindarson 423.
Firðafylki (Fjordane, district of western Norway) 434.
Firðir (inhabitants of Firðafylki) 375.
Firðir (= Firðafylki) 188, 423.
Fitjar (Fitje, a farm on Storð) 431, 445 (verse).
Fjaðryndaland, in Uppland, Sweden 110.
Fjalir, district in Sogn, western Norway 36.
Flæmingjaland (Flanders) 83.
Fold, Foldin (the areas round Oslofjord, Østfold and Vestfold) 40, 67, 79, 305, 306, 311, 432.
Fóli, father of Þórðr 122, 366.

INDEX OF NAMES

Frankish (valskr) 18 (verse), 62 (verse).
Frekeyjarsund (between the mainland and the islands off Raumsdalr, now Dråga) 322, 412.
Freyr, a god, in kennings for warrior 311, 382 (verses). See also Ingunar-Freyr.
Freyviðr daufi (the Deaf), adviser of King Óláfr of the Svíar 153–56.
Frísland (Frisia) 13, 82.
Fróði, a sea-king, in a kenning for sea 291 (verse).
Fróði son of Haraldr inn hárfagri 423–25.
Frosta (in Trondheimsfjord) 53.
Frostaþingslǫg (the law of Þrándheimr (Trøndelag), Nord-Mœrr, Naumudalr and Raumsdalr) 430.

Gamli Eiríksson, king 430, 431.
Gandvík (Kandalaksha Gulf or the White Sea) 232.
Garðar (= Garðaríki) 83, 334 (verse), 406 (verse), 439 (verse), 440 (verse), 442 (verse).
Garðaríki (Russia) 71, 83, 147, 148, 328, 338, 339, 341, 346, 370, 403, 415, 436, 439, 440, 441.
Gata, farm on Austrey 218, 236, 240, 263, 264, 267.
Gauka-Þórir (Cuckoo-), a robber 349–51, 353–54, 370, 379.
Gaularáss (a ridge between Gaulardalr and Strind) 57, 76, 243.
Gaulardalr (Gauldal, a valley south of Trondheimsfjord) 50, 53, 57, 76; Gaulardalr district (Gauldœlafylki, south of Trondheimsfjord) 51.
Gautar (inhabitants of Gautland) 80, 81, 85, 148, 149; the Gautish men (inir gauzku) 81. See also Vestr-Gautar.
Gautelfr (Göta älv, river in southern Sweden) 79, 150. See also Elfr.
Gauti Tófason 150.
Gautland (Östergötland and Västergötland, southern Sweden) 81, 92, 93, 97, 100, 117, 129, 133, 134, 136, 144, 145, 146, 148, 157, 235, 241, 289, 303, 310. See also Eystra- and Vestra-Gautland.
Gautr inn rauði (the Red) 236, 237, 265, 266, 267.
Geirfiðr, jarl in Spain (?) 24.
Geirsver (Gjæsvær), a little way south of North Cape, Norway 232.
Gellir Þorkelsson 220, 240–41, 255, 292, 419.
Gelmin (Gjolme), in Orkadalr 52.
Gerði (Gjerde), in Sunn-Hǫrðaland 346, 386.
Gilli, lawspeaker in the Faeroes 218–19, 236, 263, 266, 267.
Gizki (Giske), island in Sunn-Mœrr 244, 412.
Gizurr gullbrá (Golden Eyelash), Icelandic poet 358, 381.
Gizurr svarti (the Black), Icelandic poet 91, 95, 100.
Gizurr hvíti (the White) Teitsson 89.
Glǫð (Glad), a church bell 448.
Glymdrápa, a poem by Þorbjǫrn hornklofi (see vol. I n. 118) 159.
Glælognskviða, a poem by Þórarinn loftunga 399, 406. See note 413.
God (guð), the Christian God 107 (verse), 135 (verse), 188, 408 (verse), 410 (verse), 441 (verses), 450 (verse).
Gormr inn gamli (the Old), king of the Danes (c. 936–c. 958) 97, 221, 223, 272 (verse), 432, 433, 434.

Gothormr father of Þórðr 220.
Gotland, island in the Baltic 9, 84, 109, 331, 343.
Gotlanders (Gotar) 9.
Grágás, Magnús inn góði's law code 446. Cf. note 517.
Grankell/Granketill, farmer 176, 177, 211, 253–55, 372, 443.
Greece (Gríkland) 307 (verse).
Greenland (Grœnland) 126, 214; the journey to Greenland (Grœnlandsferð) 127; Greenland Sea (Grœnlandshaf) 127.
Grélǫð daughter of Dungaðr 159.
Grenland, district to the west of Vestfold 432.
Grenmarr (Langesundsfjorden, in Grenland) 58.
Gríðr, a giantess, in a kenning for wolf 321 (verse). Cf. *Gylf* 46/26.
Grímkell, King Óláfr's household bishop 72, 73, 403–05.
Grímr góði (the Good) Þorgilsson 365, 394–98, 403.
Grímsey, island off the north of Iceland 215, 216.
Gríslupollar (Castropol, on the north coast of Spain?) 23.
Grjótar, farm in Orkadalr, no longer there 51.
Grjótgarðr son of Hákon Hlaðajarl 431, 432.
Grjótgarðr Herlaugsson 423.
Grjótgarðr Ǫlvisson 302, 303, 333, 373.
Gróa daughter of Þorsteinn rauðr 159.
Grœningar (Grønning), in Valldalr 325.
Guðbrandr, lord in Dalar 183–90. See also Dala-Guðbrandr.
Guðbrandr kúla (Bump) (Óleifsson?) 51(?), 220, 435, 437.
Guðbrandsdalar (valleys in Upplǫnd) 46, 49, 57, 220, 326, 424. See also Dalar.
Guðini Úlfnaðrsson, jarl (Earl Godwine son of Wulfnoð) 284.
Guðleikr gerzki (from Garðaríki) 83, 84.
Guðmundr Eyjólfsson 127, 128, 215–17, 220.
Guðrøðr, king in Guðbrandsdalar 46, 101, 102–03, 105.
Guðrøðr (Gunnrøðr) Bjarnarson, king 425, 427–29, 432.
Guðrøðr son of Eiríkr blóðøx 430, 432.
Guðrøðr (Gunnrøðr) son of Haraldr inn hárfagri 423, 424.
Guðrøðr ljómi (Shiner), son of Haraldr inn hárfagri 423, 425.
Gulaþingslǫg (the law of the western districts Rogaland, Hǫrðaland, Sogn and Firðir) 430.
Gull-Haraldr (Gold-) son of Knútr Gormsson 432, 433, 434.
Gunnarr of Gelmin 52.
Gunnhildr daughter of Jarl Hálfdan 175, 423.
Gunnhildr daughter of the emperor Heinrekr 443.
Gunnhildr daughter of Knútr inn ríki 33.
Gunnhildr daughter of Sigurðr sýr 41, 219–20.
Gunnhildr daughter of Jarl Sveinn 39.
Gunnhildr konungamóðir (Mother of Kings) (daughter of Ǫzurr toti) 221, 425, 428, 430, 431, 434; sons of Gunnhildr, Gunnhildr's sons 47, 97, 434.
Gunnr, a valkyrie; in kennings for battle 12 (verse), 319 (verse), 382 (verse); in a kenning for eagle 56 (verse).
Gunnrøðr Bjarnarson 429, see Guðrøðr.

INDEX OF NAMES 321

Gunnrøðr son of Haraldr inn hárfagri 423, see Guðrøðr.
Gunnsteinn of Langey 211, 228, 230, 232–34, 251.
Gunnvaldsborg (in Spain?) 24.
Guthormr sindri (Flint), Norwegian poet, tenth century 426.
Guthormr son of Eiríkr blóðøx 430.
Guthormr son of Haraldr inn hárfagri 423, 424, 425.
Guthormr son of Sigurðr sýr 41, 107–08.
Guthormr Sigurðarson, jarl in Orkney (c. 890) 158.
Gyða, mother of Tryggvi Óláfsson 411.
Gyða daughter of King Eiríkr of Hǫrðaland 423.
Gyða daughter of Jarl Guðini, queen of Eatvarðr inn góði 284.
Gyða daughter of Sveinn tjúguskegg 438.
Gyða daughter of Þorgils, wife of Jarl Guðini 284.
Gǫndul, a valkyrie, in a kenning for mailcoat 63 (verse), in a kenning for swords 107 (verse).
Gǫngu-Hrólfr (Walker-) Rǫgnvaldsson (Rollo), jarl, first conqueror of Normandy (911) 26.

Hádýr (Hådyret), mountain on south-west coast of Norway 309 (verse).
Haðaland (Hadaland, a district of eastern Norway) 46, 49, 101, 102, 107, 190, 220, 424, 425.
Hákon Eiríksson, Hlaðajarl, ruler of Norway under Knútr inn ríki (died 1029–30) 31, 36–39, 45, 51, 52, 56, 78, 209, 221, 222, 226, 271, 273, 293, 295, 306, 307, 319, 321–23, 327, 330–38, 344, 345, 370, 371; cf. Hǫkon.
Hákon Grjótgarðsson, Hlaðajarl (ninth century) 423, 430.
Hákon inn góði (the Good) Aðalsteinsfóstri (foster-son of Aðalsteinn) Haraldsson, king of Norway (died c. 961) 47, 73, 97, 176, 242, 427–31, 437, 445.
Hákon inn ríki (the Great) Sigurðarson, Hlaðajarl (ruler of Norway c. 974–95) 27, 30, 47, 159, 221, 226, 419–21, 424, 431–35, 437–39.
Hákonarhella (Håkhella, in Hǫrðaland) 431.
Halarnir, points of land near Skanör in south-west Sweden 290.
Háleygr, Háleygir (man, people of Hálogaland) 175, 178, 196–98, 250, 375.
Háleyski from Hálogaland 227.
Hálfdan, jarl, son-in-law of Haraldr inn hárfagri 175, 423.
Hálfdan svarti (the Black) Guðrøðarson, king in Norway (ninth century) 421.
Hálfdan háleggr (Long-Leg) son of Haraldr inn hárfagri 158, 423, 425.
Hálfdan hvíti (the White) son of Haraldr inn hárfagri 423, 425.
Hálfdan svarti (the Black) son of Haraldr inn hárfagri 423, 425–28, 430.
Hálfdan son of Sigurðr hrísi 437.
Hálfdan son of Sigurðr sýr 41, 107–08.
Halldórr son of Brynjólfr úlfaldi 235.
Hallr Þórarinsson 420.
Hallr (of Síða, af Síðu, Síðu-Hallr) Þorsteinsson 217, 220, 240, 287, 419.
Hallvarðr from the Eastern Fiords in Iceland 165.
Hallvarðr Háreksblesi (Hárekr (from Þjótta?)'s Horse (with a blaze on his forehead)) 311. See note 329.
Hálma, mother of Þorgils 365, 394, 397.

Hálogaland (Hålogaland in northern Norway) 175–77, 211, 227, 250, 253, 291, 305, 352, 424, 443.
Háls in Limafjǫrðr 433.
Hár (the) Hard-Gripping (enn harðgreipi), one of Hrólfr kraki's men 361 (verse).
Haraldr gráfeldr (Grey-Cloak) Eiríksson (Gunnhildarson), king of Norway (died c. 975) 221, 430, 432, 433.
Haraldr Gormsson, king of the Danes (died c. 986) 14, 47, 97, 98, 221, 432–34, 438.
Haraldr Guðinason (Harold Godwineson), king of the English (died 1066) 284.
Haraldr (inn) grenski (the Grenlander) Guðrøðarson (died c. 995) 3, 4, 18 (verse), 33, 36 (verse), 46, 86, 102, 117, 174, 215, 222, 223, 270 (verse), 320 (verse), 407 (verse), 432–38, 445 (verse).
Haraldr inn hárfagri (the Fine-Haired) Hálfdanarson, king of Norway (c. 885–935) 41, 44–47, 97, 158, 159, 167, 175, 242, 348, 372, 421, 423–30, 434, 435, 437.
Haraldr (Harold Harefoot) son of Knútr inn ríki, king of the English (1035–40) 33, 442, 446.
Haraldr gilli (short for Gillikristr, Servant of Christ) Magnússon, king of Norway (1130–36) 451.
Haraldr inn harðráði (the Harsh Ruler) Sigurðarson, king of Norway (1046–66) 41, 107–08, 174, 208, 334 (verse), 347, 348, 364, 419, 439, 445 (verse), 448 (verse), 449, 450.
Haraldr son of Þorkell hávi, jarl in Denmark (died 1042) 333, 399.
Hárekr from (on) Þjótta Eyvindarson 175, 176, 181, 211, 253–55, 289, 290–91, 305, 306, 339, 345, 372–76, 386, 388, 443.
Haugasund (Høgasund, Sweden), north of the outlets of the Gautelfr 83.
Haugasund (Haugesund in Rogaland) 428.
Haugr (Haug) in Veradalr 179, 439 (verse) 444.
Haukadalr, southern Iceland 420.
Hávarðr Þorfinnsson, jarl in Orkney (c. 976–c. 991) 159.
Hávarr, father of Þorgeirr 214.
Hebrides (Suðreyjar) 174, 445.
Hedalr (Hedal, central Norway) 183.
Heðinn (Hjarrandason), a legendary king, in kenning for battle 359 (verse).
Heiðabœr (Hedeby, on the southern border of Denmark) 447.
Heiðmǫrk (Hedmark, district in eastern Norway) 46, 57, 101, 103, 107, 190, 219, 297, 300, 302, 326, 423, 424; Heiðmǫrk kings (Heinskir jǫfrar) 106 (verse).
Heiðsævislǫg, the law for the region round Lake Mjǫsa, south-east Norway) 191, 430.
Heiðsævisþing the assembly at Heiðsævi in Heiðmǫrk 191.
Heinir (people of Heiðmǫrk) 69 (verse).
Heinrekr emperor (Henry III, 1046–56) 443.
Heinrekr strjóna (Wealth or Profit) (Eadric Streona, died 1017) 33.
Hel (the name of Loki's daughter who presides over the world of the dead), King Óláfr's axe 448.
Helsingjaland (Hälsingland, on the eastern side of Sweden) 71, 241, 242, 369, 415, 440.
Helsingjar (people of Helsingjaland) 242.
Herdalar, in Lappland, not identified 10, 11 (verse).
Hereyjar (Herøy(ar), an island off Sunn-Mœrr, western Norway) 261, 321.
Hern (Hernar *ÓH*) (Hennøyar/Hernøy), in Norðr-Hǫrðaland 237.

INDEX OF NAMES 323

Hildr, a valkyrie, in a kenning for battle 362 (verse).
Hildr (or Svanhildr) daughter of Jarl Eysteinn 423.
Hísing (Hisingen, island in the estuary of the Gautelfr) 79, 83, 157.
Hjalti Skeggjason 77, 86–92, 95–100, 111–12, 128.
Hjaltland, inhabitants of (Hjaltlendingar, Shetlanders) 173 (verse); see also Shetland.
Hjǫrnagli (Tjernagel), islet (?) in Sunn-Hǫrðaland 309 (verse).
Hjǫrungavágr (Liavåg, inlet in Sunn-Mœrr) 437.
Hlaðir (Lade, near Niðaróss) 53, 430.
Hlaupandanes, in Sandvík on Hrossey 161.
Hlésey (Læsø, island between Jutland and Sweden, in the Kattegat) 150.
Hlýrskógsheiðr (Lyrskovshede, heath south of Heiðabœr) 447.
Hlǫðvir Þorfinnsson, jarl in Orkney (c. 890–c. 991) 159.
Hneitir (Striker), a sword 367.
Hof, farm in Gautland (see note 151) 136.
Hof, farm in Guðbrandsdalar 184.
Hofgarða-Refr (Refr of Hofgarðar) Gestsson, Icelandic poet, 11th century 358, 382. See note 386.
Hóll, Hólar(nir) (Dol in Brittany?) 22, 23 (verse).
Hólmfríðr daughter of King Eiríkr of the Svíar 439.
Holmfríðr daughter of King Óláfr of the Svíar 130.
Hólmgarðr (Novgorod) 84, 144, 147, 415, 440.
Holti inn frœkni (the Brave) son of Jarizleifr 148.
Hrani mjónefr (Thin-Nose) 41.
Hrani inn víðfǫrli (the Far-Travelled) Hróason, foster-brother of Haraldr grenski 3, 4, 5, 34, 36, 43, 432, 433, 437.
Hringar (people of Hringaríki) 367 (verse).
Hringaríki (Ringerike, district in south-eastern Norway) 107, 190, 220, 423, 424, 437.
Hringisakr (Ringsaker, in Heiðmǫrk) 102, 103, 105.
Hringmara heath (Hringmara heiðr; Ringmere, Norfolk) 18, 19 (verse).
Hringr Dagsson, king in Heiðmǫrk 46, 48, 102, 105, 299, 348, 354, 383, 386, 389.
Hringr Dagsson of Hringaríki 423.
Hringr son of Haraldr inn hárfagri 348, 423, 424.
Hringsfjǫrðr, in France (between the Cotentin and Brittany peninsulas?) 22.
Hringunes (Ringnes, in Heiðmǫrk) 58, 70, 104, 219.
Hróaldr father of Hersir Þórir 423.
Hrói inn hvíti (the White), landed man 432.
Hrói skjálgi (Squint-Eyed), steward of the king of the Svíar 79, 83.
Hróiskelda (Roskilde, Denmark) 284.
Hrólfr the Shooter (skjótandi), one of Hrólfr kraki's men 361 (verse).
Hrossey (Mainland, Orkney) 161.
Hrútr of Vigg 363–64.
Hrynjandi(n), a poem by Arnórr jarlaskáld, usually called *Hrynhenda* 440.
Hrœrekr Dagsson, king in Heiðmǫrk 46–48, 101–03, 105, 117–28.
Hrœrekr son of Haraldr inn hárfagri 423, 424.
Hundi son of Jarl Sigurðr 159, 160. Cf. Hvelpr.
Hundr, see Þórir hundr 384 (verses).
Hundsver, islet near Borgund (later known as Hundsverholm) 322.

Hundþorp (Hundorp), in Guðbrandsdalar) 184.
Húskarlahvǫt 'The Housecarls' Encouragement', a name given to *Bjarkamál in fornu* after its recitation at St Óláfr's last battle 362.
Hvelpr son of Jarl Sigurðr 159, see Hundi.
Hvítingsey (Kvitingsøy), island near Stavanger, south-west Norway 78, 235.
Hǫ́arr, a name for Óðinn (in a kenning for sword) 382 (verse; see note 388).
Hǫfuðlausn (Head-Ransom), a poem by Þórarinn loftunga 308.
Hǫ́kon (in verses), i.e. Hákon Eiríksson 37, 38, 272, 273; Hákon inn góði Haraldsson 445.
Hǫrða-Kári Asláksson 427, 433.
Hǫrða-Knútr ('Tough-Knot'; but according to Flateyjarbók, Hǫrða-Knútr son of Sigurðr ormr-í-auga got his name from having been born at Hǫrð in Jutland, see *Knýt* 86, note 12) son of Knútr inn ríki, king of the Danes (1035–42), king of England (1040–42) 33, 235, 275–77, 306, 442, 446.
Hǫrðaland (Hordaland, district in south-west Norway) 117, 191, 206, 235, 268, 319, 346, 412, 423–25, 431, 434. See also Sunn-Hǫrðaland.
Hǫrðar, Hǫrðalanders (people of Hǫrðaland) 295 (verse), 319 (verse), 375, 383, 440 (verse), 448 (verse).

Iceland (Ísland) 74, 77, 86, 92, 95, 125, 127, 128, 214, 215, 217, 218, 220, 240, 241, 244, 255, 261, 292, 364, 400, 419, 420–22; ship from (Íslandsfar) 55, ship for (Íslandsfar) 77; ships from (Íslandsfarar) 56; (journey) for (Íslandsferð 240).
Icelander(s) (Íslending(a)r) 166, 214, 217, 241, 364.
Icelandic eyes (*íslensk augun*) 140 (verse); Icelandic man (*íslenzkr maðr*, *maðr íslenzkr*) 54, 125, 165, 307, 331; Icelandic men (*íslenzkir menn*) 91, 220, 240; Icelandic people (*íslenzkir menn*) 422.
Ífi, a sea-king, in kenning for shields 359 (verse).
Ingi son of Haraldr gilli, king of Norway (1136 to 1161) 451.
Ingibjǫrg Mother of Jarls (jarlamóðir), daughter of Finnr Árnason 449.
Ingibjǫrg daughter of Haraldr inn hárfagri 175, 423.
Ingibjǫrg daughter of Tryggvi Óláfsson, wife of Jarl Rǫgnvaldr 85, 89–91, 96, 100, 111, 115, 148, 438.
Ingigerðr daughter of Haraldr inn hárfagri 423.
Ingigerðr daughter of King Óláfr of the Svíar 91, 95, 96, 98–100, 111, 112, 115–17, 129, 130–32, 134, 144, 146–48, 152, 328, 339, 341, 343, 415.
Ingiríðr daughter of Sigurðr sýr 41.
Ingunar-Freyr son of Njǫrðr 421. See also Freyr.
Inney (Inderøy, Trondheimsfjord, Norway) 356 (verse). Cf. Eyin iðri in vol. I.
Innþrœndir (inland Þrœndir) 70, 71, 75, 178, 180, 356 (verse), 381 (verse), 401.
Innþrœnzkr (of inner Þrándheimr) 69 (verse).
Ireland (Írland) 128, 160, 163, 174, 425, 445, 450.
Irish, king of the (Írakonungr) 128, 163.
Islands, the (Eyjar) 174, see Orkney.
Ísleifr Gizurarson, bishop at Skálholt, Iceland (1056–80) 420.
Ísríðr daughter of Guðbrandr 220.
Ívarr hvíti (the White) 285.
Ívarr Sigtryggsson 328.

INDEX OF NAMES

Jaðarr (Jæren, district in south-west Norway) 196, 198, 201, 226, 235, 247, 312, 313, 315 (verse), 319 (verse), 339, 346, 425, 438; inhabitants of (Jaðarbyggjar) 235; people of (Jaðarbyggjar) 248.
Jákob Óláfsson, king of the Svíar (1022–c. 1050) 130, 154–56; see Qnundr Óláfsson.
Jalfaðr, a name for Óðinn in kenning for warrior 390 (verse).
Jalkr, a name for Óðinn in kenning for shield 183 (verse).
James's day, eve of St (Jákobsvǫkudagr) 130.
Jamtaland (Jämtland, district in central Sweden) 71, 82, 241, 242, 255, 259, 349, 369, 370, 414, 439.
Jamtr (people of Jamtaland) 242, 255, 256.
Jarðþrúðr Jónsdóttir 443.
Jarizleifr Valdamarsson, King in Garðar 144, 147, 148, 328, 339, 343, 415, 439.
Jarlasǫgur(nar) (*Orkneyinga saga*) 173.
Járnberaland (Dalarna), in central Sweden 348.
Játgeirr (Eadgar I), father of King Aðalráðr of the English 438.
Játmundr 17 (verse), see Eaðmundr (járnsíða).
Jerusalem (Jórsalir) 339, 443; (Jórsalaheimr) 25; cf. Jórsalafari.
Jesus Christ (Jesús Kristr, cf. Christ and White Christ) 124, 369.
Jómali, the Jómali (Jómali(nn)) (the god of the Bjarmar) 230–32.
Jómsborg, viking stronghold in Wendland, southern Baltic 398, 447.
Jómsvikings (Jómsvíkingar) vikings of Jómsborg 30, 47, 437.
Jón Árnason 443.
Jórsalafari (Jerusalem-traveller) 450
Jórunn skáldmær (Poetess), Norwegian, 10th century 427.
Jótar (Jutes, people of Jótland) 272, 281, 310 (verses).
Jótland (Jutland in Denmark) 276, 278 (verse), 449.
Jótlandssíða (western shore of Jutland) 12.
Julian the Apostate (Júlíánús níðingr) Roman Emperor (361–63; for the legend of his death see *Maríu saga* 1871, 72–73 and 699–702) 14.
Jungufurða, a place in England, not identified 34.
Jǫkull Bárðarson 331, 332.
Jǫkull Ingimundarson 331.
Jǫrð, a goddess; in verse, in a kenning for a human woman 291.

Kálfr Árnason 181, 182, 247–49, 300, 301–02, 320, 321, 323, 331–35, 339, 372–78, 383–87, 402, 411, 412, 414, 415, 442 (verse), 443–45, 449.
Kálfr Arnfinnsson 383–85.
Kálfsflokkr, a poem by Bjarni Gullbrárskáld 442.
Kálfskinn, farm on Árskógsströnd in Eyjafjǫrðr, northern Iceland 128.
Kalmarnir (Kalmar, Sweden) 290.
Karl (inn) mœrski/Mœra-Karl (Karl of Mœrr/of the Mœrir) 262–67.
Karla-Magnús (Charlemagne) 210.
Karlhǫfði, a ship (the name means 'man's head', referring to the style of figurehead carved on the prow) 59, 61 (verse).
Karli of Langey, inn Háleyski (the Hálogalander) 211–13, 227–33, 250, 251, 253.
Karlsár (harbour for Cadiz?) 25.
Karmtsund (a sound by the island Kǫrmt in Rogaland, Karmsund) 77, 195, 197, 199.

Katanes (Caithness), in Scotland 159–64, 173, 335.
Kaupangr 241, 261, 403, 414, 448, 450; see Niðaróss.
Ketill Jamti (of Jamtaland or the Persistent?; cf. Jamtr) son of Jarl Ǫnundr 241.
Ketill kálfr (Calf) at (of) Hringunes 58, 70, 104–05, 219–20.
Kilir 79, 242; see Kjǫlr (of which Kilir is the plural form).
Kimbi 389–90.
Kinnlimasíða (Kinnheim, Kennemarland, the western coast of Holland) 13.
Kirjálaland (Karelia) 115.
Kjǫlr (Kjølen, mountain range in Norway) 71, 74, 241, 242, 349, 351, 370, 414, 440. Cf. Kilir.
Klyppr hersir (Lord) son of Þórðr Hǫrða-Kárason (Þorkell klyppr (= squarely built?) in *Ágrip*) 433.
Klœngr Brúsason 57. See note 81.
Knútr Knútsson, see Hǫrða-Knútr.
Knútr inn ríki (the Great) Sveinsson, king of the Danes and the English (died 1035) 30, 31, 33, 34, 39, 45, 158, 174, 209, 221–27, 234, 235, 248, 249, 253, 268–80, 283–86, 288–94, 301, 303–08, 310–12, 327, 330, 333–38, 345–47, 370–73, 398, 401, 402, 410, 411, 414, 438, 442, 446.
Knútsdrápa, a poem by Sigvatr 274.
Knýtlingar (descendants of Knútr inn ríki) 401, 412.
Kolbeinn sterki (the Strong), from Firðir 188, 189.
Kolbeinn, father of the poet Þórðr 30, 214.
Kolbjǫrn Árnason 181.
Kolr Hallsson 419.
Konofogor (Connor) king of the Irish (unidentified) 128–29, 163.
Konungahella (in Ranríki, at the mouth of the Gautelfr) 129, 157, 234, 235.
Konungssund (the King's Sound), a channel between Lǫgrinn and the Baltic 8.
Krossbrekka (Langbrekka), in Valldalr 323.
Kúrland (in the eastern Baltic area, now Latvia) 115.
Kvistsstaðir (Kvistad), on Eyin iðri (Inney, Inderøy, Trondheimsfjord) 378, 381.
Kǫrmt (Karmøy, island in south-west Norway) 195, 199, 204.

Langey (Langøy, island in Hálogaland) 211, 228, 234.
Lapp (Finnskr) 120; Lapps (Finnar) 11, 345; (the) trade (trading) with Lapps (Finnferð, Finnkaup) 175, 306, 344; Lappish (Finnskr) 423; See also Finnish.
Lappland (Finnland) 10, 115.
Leifr Eiríksson 126.
Leifr Ǫzurarson, a leading man in the Faeroes 218–19, 236, 263–67.
Leikn, a giantess, in a kenning for valkyrie 311 (verse).
Leira (the Loire in France) 26 (verse).
Lengjuvík (Lenvik in Hálogaland) 234, 250.
Lesjar (Lesja in Guðbrandsdalar) 182, 184, 323, 326.
Líðandisnes (Lindesnes, the most southerly part of Norway) 70, 117, 127, 192, 434, 438.
Liðsstaðir (Listad in Guðbrandsdalar) 186.
Limafjǫrðr (Limfjorden, in Denmark) 274, 276, 305, 308 (verse), 433.
Listi (Lista, on the south coast of Norway), in a kenning for sea (Lista is connected

INDEX OF NAMES 327

to the mainland by a narrow isthmus, and is almost an island) 93 (verse), 142 (verse), 309 (verse).
Ljárdalr (Upplǫnd, Norway) 182.
Ljótr Þorfinnsson, jarl in Orkney (c. 976–c. 991) 159.
Lóar (Lom in Upplǫnd, Norway) 182–84, 186.
Loðinn of Vigg 52.
Loðinn Erlingsson 29.
London (Lundún(ir), Lundúnaborg (City of London?)) 15, 16 (verse), 17 (verse), 31, 32 (verse), 335 (verse).
Lorudalr (Lordalen in Upplǫnd, Norway) 182.
Lucius's Church (Lúcíús-kirkja), church dedicated to St Lucius (Pope AD 253–54) in Roskilde 285.
Lund (Lundr), in Skáney 291 (verse).
Lygra, island in northern Hǫrðaland 237, 239.
Læsir, inhabitants of Lesjar 186.
Lǫgr (Lågen), river in Guðbrandsdalar 184.
Lǫgrinn (Mälaren), lake in Sweden 7, 8, 98, 154, 155, 344.

Magnús son of Haraldr inn harðráði, king of Norway (1066–69) 450.
Magnús berfœttr (Barelegs) Óláfsson, king of Norway (1093–1103) 450, 451.
Magnús inn góði (the Good) Óláfsson, king of Norway (1035–46) 209–10, 327–28, 330 (verse), 343, 410 (verse) 415, 440–49.
Magnús son of Duke Ótta, duke in Saxony (1072–1106) 447.
Magnús blindi (the Blind) Sigurðarson, king of Norway (1130–35, 1137–39) 451.
Magnússdrápa, a poem by Arnórr jarlaskáld about Magnús inn góði 440.
Markir (forests), on the boundary between Norway and Sweden (now Aremark and Øymark on the Norwegian side and Nordmark on the Swedish side) 79, 109, 134, 144.
Mary's, St, church (Máríukirkja), in Sarpsborg 81.
Masarvík (Mosvik, in Þrándheimr) 52.
Meðaldalr (Meldal), in Orkadalr 50.
Melkólmr (Malcolm II), King of the Scots (1005–34) 160.
Mercurius, St (inn helgi Merkúríús) (224–50), martyred by the Emperor Decius 14.
Michael the archangel, feast of (29th September, Michaelmas) 284, 447.
Mjǫrs (Mjøsa, lake in eastern Norway) 70.
Mont (the Alps or Appennines, see note 489) 442 (verse).
Morstangarson (son of Þóra Morstǫng) 427.
Morstr (Moster), island in Sunn-Hǫrðaland (Sunnhordland) 427.
Morstǫng see Þóra Morstǫng 427.
Múlaþing, unknown assembly-place in Sweden; perhaps for Móraþing near Uppsala 116.
Mærin (Mæren, north-east of Trondheimsfjord) 178–80.
Mœra-Karl 266, see Karl inn mœrski.
Mœrin (Muri), in Valldalr 323.
Mœrir (people of Mœrr) 26 (verse); jarl of the Mœrir (Mœrajarl) 26, 158.
Mœrr (Møre, Norð-Mœrr and Sunn-Mœrr) 76, 182, 215, 244, 261, 331, 377, 412, 439. See also Norð-Mœrr and Sunn-Mœrr.

Mǫðruvellir, in Eyjafjǫrðr (northern Iceland) 128, 215.
Mǫrk, the (Mǫrkin) 175, 228, see Finnmǫrk.
Mǫrukári Guðinason (Morkere; actually son of Ælfgar of Mercia), jarl (earl) in England 284.

Nanna, name of a goddess, wife of Baldr 140 (verse), in a kenning for a (human) woman.
Naumdœlafylki, the district of Naumudalr 176.
Naumdœlir (people of Naumudalr) 242.
Naumudalr (Namdal, central–northern Norway) 175.
Nefjólfr father of Þórarinn 125, 128, 201, 202, 215.
Nereiðr inn gamli (the Old), jarl 41.
Nes (Bynes in Þrándheimr) 52, 76.
Nes (Synste-Nes), in Lóar 183.
Nesjar (headlands between Grenmarr and Foldin (Oslofjord)) 58, 82.
Nesjavísur (the Nesjar verses), a poem by Sigvatr 61.
Nið (Nidelva, the river Nið flowing into Trondheimsfjord) 53, 54, 57 (verse), 270 (verse), 309 (verse), 449.
Niðarhólmr, island near Niðaróss 247.
Niðarnes, headland near Niðaróss 419.
Niðaróss (Trondheim) 52, 53, 57, 70, 72, 77, 174, 175, 177, 181, 209, 227, 241, 255, 261, 306, 333, 397, 448.
Nitja (Nitelva, river in Upplǫnd) 190.
Njáll son of Finnr inn skjálgi 424.
Njǫrðr, a god, father of Freyr 26 (in verse, pl., in kenning for warriors), 55 (in verse, in a kenning for warrior), 421, 440 (in verse, in a kenning for warrior).
Njǫrðungar, Njǫrðr's kin, gods, in a kenning for human beings 382 (verse).
Norð-Mœrr (Nordmøre) 424, 434.
Norðr-Agðir (people of north Agder, southern Norway) 70.
Norðreyjar (Nordoyar in the Faeroes) 263–65.
Normandy (Norðmandí) 26, 27, 33.
Northern Iceland, people of (Norðlendingar), people of the north of the country, i.e. of the Northern Quarter of Iceland 215, 216.
Northern lands (Norðrlǫnd; Scandinavia) 30, 96, 97, 152, 222, 223, 421, 448.
Northumberland (Norðimbraland) in England, the Northumbria of Saxon times 34, 430.
Norway (Nóregr) 25, 27, 29, 30, 31, 36, 38, 39, 41, 46–48, 58, 59, 71, 72, 75, 78, 79, 84, 85, 95–99, 105, 113, 114, 117, 127, 139 (verse), 146, 147, 149, 157–59, 163–66, 168, 174, 176, 182, 216, 218, 221–24, 226, 236, 239, 241, 242, 255, 267–69, 271, 275, 282, 283, 288, 289, 292, 294, 303, 305–08, 310, 311, 317, 318, 326–28, 330, 334–39, 341, 343–48, 351, 370, 398–400, 402, 403, 409–11, 415, 419, 421–23, 428, 430–38, 440–42, 446, 448–50; people of Norway (Nóregsmenn) 132, 222, 411; rulers of Norway (Nóregshofðingjar) 26; king(s) of Norway (Nóregskonung(a)r) 76, 79, 85, 96, 112, 113, 115–17, 130–32, 144, 146, 148, 149, 153, 157, 158, 175, 207, 223, 227, 256, 271, 275, 283, 419, 437, 446, 450; the realm of Norway (Nóregsveldi) 116.
Norwegians (Austmenn) 266, 267; (Nóregsmenn) 115, 217; Norwegian (Norðmaðr) 153; Norwegian person (norrœnn (maðr)) 91, 285; Norwegian stock (Norðmanna ætt) 242; Norwegians (Norðmenn) 14, 26–27, 98, 129, 173, 256, 279, 286, 289, 294, 347, 349, 400, 415; force of Norwegians (Norðmannalið) 16.

INDEX OF NAMES 329

Nýjamóða, river in England, unidentified 21 (verse).
Nyrfi (Nyrve), a small island (and the farm of the same name) in Sunn-Mœrr 322.
Næríki (Närke), district between the great lakes in Sweden 328.
Nǫrvasund (Strait of Gibraltar) 25.

Oddr Kolsson 419.
Óðinn, a god 137 (verse), in a kenning for a warrior 384 (verse); cf. Hǫarr, a name for Óðinn, in a kenning for sword 382 (verse; see note 388).
Óláfr, kinsman of Kálfr Árnason 384.
Óláfr (II) Bjarnarson, king of the Svíar (c. 970–75) 435.
Óláfr (inn) sœnski (the Swedish) Eiríksson, king of the Swedes (Svíar) (c. 995–c. 1022) 8, 45, 71, 72, 74–77, 81, 86, 89, 91–92, 95–100, 111–12, 114–17, 129–32, 144, 146, 147, 149–58, 174, 191, 242, 269, 292, 371, 435, 438, 439.
Óláfr (Geirstaðaálfr) Guðrøðarson, king in Vestfold 421.
Óláfr son of Haraldr inn hárfagri 423–28, 432, 437.
Óláfr inn helgi (the Saint), digri (the Stout) Haraldsson, king of Norway (1015–28, died 1030) 3–12, 14–16, 17 (Óleifr, verse), 18, 20–27, 33–40, 42–62, 65, 67, 68, 70–90, 92, 96–105, 107–08, 111–21, 123–34, 140, 141, 142 (verse), 143 (verse), 144–49, 152, 153, 157, 158, 163–72, 174–93, 195–97, 199–227, 232, 234–46, 248–56, 260–63, 267–72, 273 (verse), 275, 277–83, 286–306, 310–17, 319–34, 336–52, 354–58, 360–78, 380, 381, 383–85, 387, 389, 390, 393–99, 401–05, 406 (verses), 407 (verse), 408 (verses), 409–11, 415, 420–22, 437–43, 446–50; Óláfsbúðir 349 (see note 353); Óláfr's cave (Óláfshellir) 325; Óláfr's gate (Óláfshlið) 405; Óláfskirkja (St Óláfr's church in Niðaróss) 405; Óláfr's shrine (Óláfsskrín) 450.
Óláfr inn kyrri (the Peaceful) Haraldsson, king of Norway (c. 1050–93) 450.
Óláfr son of Magnús berfœttr, king of Norway (1103–15) 450.
Óláfr Tryggvason, king of Norway (995–1000) 26–30, 39, 44, 46, 47, 50, 51, 53, 78, 85, 88, 89, 98, 159, 160, 167, 177, 288, 340, 411, 413, 420, 437, 438.
Orðost (Orust), island in Ranríki 83.
Orkadalr (Orkdal, in Þrándheimr) 27, 50, 51, 57, 76, 243; Orkadalr district (Orkdœlafylki) 51.
Orkdœlar (people of Orkadalr, on the river Orkn) 52.
Orkney (Orkneyjar) 74, 128, 129, 158–61, 163, 165, 167–74, 177, 182, 214, 425, 430, 434, 448. See also Islands (the).
Orkneyingajarlar, jarls of Orkney 170, 174.
Óslóarfjǫrðr (Oslofjord) 311.
Ostrarfjǫrðr (Osterfjorden in Hǫrðaland) 207.
Ótta (Ordulf or Otto), duke in Saxony (1059–72) 447.
Ótta, river in Guðbrandsdalar 182.
Óttarr svarti (the Black), Icelandic poet, 11th century 5, 6, 16, 19, 20, 22, 25, 35, 37, 91, 95, 100, 105, 144, 172, 191, 280, 421. See note 2.

Partar, unidentified group of people in England 20 (verse). Cf. vol. III, v. 226.
Peita (in verses), Peituland (Poitou in France) 25, 26 (verse).
Péttlandsfjǫrðr (Pentland Firth, Scotland) 335, 449.

Ragnarr ryk(k)ill (Snatcher) son of Haraldr inn hárfagri 423, 424.

Ragnfrøðr son of Eiríkr blóðøx 430.
Ragnhildr daughter of Árni Armóðsson and wife of Hárekr from Þjótta 181.
Ragnhildr daughter of Dagr 298.
Ragnhildr daughter of Eiríkr, king from Denmark 423.
Ragnhildr daughter of Eiríkr blóðøx 430.
Ragnhildr daughter of Erlingr Skjálgsson 29, 244–47.
Rannveig daughter of Þórir hundr's son Sigurðr 443.
Ranríki (Bohuslän, south-east Norway, now part of Sweden) 79, 424, 429, 439.
Rauðr, farmer in Eystri-Dalir 298–99; Rauðr's sons (Rauðssynir) 298.
Raumar, people of Raumaríki 190.
Raumaríki (Romerike, district in eastern Norway) 46, 58, 101–04, 190, 191, 424.
Raumelfr (Glomma, river to the east of Oslofjord) 70, 81.
Raumsdalr (Romsdal, district in western Norway, between Norð-Mœrr and Sunn-Mœrr) 182, 261, 424–25, 434, 439.
Reinslétta, in Norð-Mœrr 426.
Rhine (Rín) river in Germany; in verse, in kennings for gold 142, 289.
Ríkarðr Ríkarðarson, jarl in Normandy (Richard II, died 1026) 26.
Ríkarðr Viljálmsson, jarl in Normandy (Richard I, died 996) 26.
Rínansey (North Ronaldsay in Orkney) 158.
Róðadrápa (Rood-drápa), a poem by Þórðr Sjáreksson 281.
Roðbert langaspjót (Longspear) Gǫngu-Hrólfsson 26 note 43.
Roðbert Ríkarðarson (Robert the Devil, died 1035), jarl in Normandy 26.
Róði, a sea king, in a kenning for the sea 60 (verse).
Rogaland (Rogaland, district in south-west Norway) 28, 58, 191, 196, 319, 346, 412, 413, 428, 434.
Rome (Rúm) 441; journey Romeward (Rúms fǫr) 441 (verse); City of Rome (Rúmaborg) 209; the road to Rome (Rúmavegr) 358; pilgrimage to Rome (Rúmferð) 32.
Rouen in Normandy (Rúðuborg) 271 (verse).
Rúða (Rouen in Normandy) 33, 34, 271; jarls of Rúða (Rúðujarlar) 26.
Rúðujarl (jarl of Rouen) 26.
Rygir (people of Rogaland) 196, 197, 375, 383.
Rýgjarbit (boundary between Agðir and the Vík, near the place now known as Gjernestangen) 306.
Rǫgnvaldr son of Jarl Brúsi, jarl in Orkney (c. 1037–c. 1045) 163, 167, 172, 327, 439, 440, 448, 449.
Rǫgnvaldr inn ríki (the Great) Eysteinsson, jarl of the Mœrir 26, 158.
Rǫgnvaldr réttilbeini (Straight-Grown) son of Haraldr inn hárfagri 423, 425.
Rǫgnvaldr Óláfsson, king in Vestfold 421.
Rǫgnvaldr Úlfsson, jarl in Vestra-Gautland 28 (verse), 85, 88–90, 94 (verse), 111–15, 117, 129, 130, 132–34, 139, 140, 142 (verse), 143 (verse), 144–48, 438.
Rǫgnvaldsey (South Ronaldsay in Orkney) 159.

Sandver (Sandvær, island in Hálogaland) 228.
Sandvík (Sandwich), on Hrossey, Orkney 161, 165.
Sarpr (Sarp, Sarpsfossen, waterfall north of the Vík) 81.
Sarpsborg (in Vingulmǫrk, eastern side of the Vík) 146, 227, 234, 291; see Borg.
Sauðungssund (Sauesund, in Fjalir, western Norway) 36, 38 (verse).

INDEX OF NAMES 331

Saurhlið (near Niðaróss) 398.
Saurr, a dog, king of the Þrœndir 241.
Saxi, unknown person 139 (verse).
Saxland (north Germany) 83, 447.
Saxons (Saxar) 120.
Scandinavian (language) (*dǫnsk tunga*) 421.
Scotland (Skotland, though this can also mean Ireland) 158, 159, 163, 173, 174, 223, 225, 445.
Scots (Skotar, though this can also mean the Irish), king of 160, 167–70.
Seal's Avenger (Selshefnir), a spear 233. Cf. Þórir selr, Sel-Þórir.
Seine (Signa), river in France 27.
Seljupollar (Cilenorum aqua, now Guardia, by the mouth of the river Minho in Spain?) 24.
Sel-Þórir (Seal-), King Óláfr's steward 193, 198, 201, 205, see Þórir selr.
Sendibítr, poem by Jórunn skáldmær (cf. vol. I, note 173) 427.
Sexstefja, poem by Þjóðólfr Arnórsson 439. See note 455.
Shetland (Hjaltland) 74, 170, 173, 174. See also Hjaltland.
Síða, south-west Iceland 419.
Síðu-Hallr, see Hallr Þorsteinsson.
Sigríðr daughter of Skjálgr (Þórólfr skjálgr), wife of Sigurðr Þórisson 194, 195, 212.
Sigríðr daughter of Jarl Sveinn Hákonarson, wife of Áslákr Erlingsson 226.
Sigríðr in stórráða (of the Great Undertakings) daughter of Skǫglar-Tósti 433, 435–38.
Sigríðr Þórisdóttir, wife of Ǫlvir at Egg and later of Kálfr Arnason 332–33, cf. 181–82.
Sigrøðr son of Haraldr inn hárfagri 423, 425, 428.
Sigtryggr, powerful man in Næríki 328.
Sigtryggr (Tryggvi) son of Haraldr inn hárfagri 423, 424.
Sigtúnir (Sigtuna in eastern Sweden) 7, 440 (verse); Old Sigtúnir (fornu Sigtúnir, Sithun, Sign(h)ildsberg or Signesberg), 4 km west of Sigtuna 7.
Sigurðr, Jarl Hákon Eiríksson's household bishop 370, 371, 398, 402.
Sigurðr, King Óláfr's bishop 184, 205.
Sigurðr hít (Paunch?), King Hrœrekr's standard-bearer 121, 123.
Sigurðr slefa (Lisp) Eiríksson 430, 433.
Sigurðr Erlingsson 29, 247, 249.
Sigurðr Eysteinsson, first jarl in Orkney 158.
Sigurðr son of Finnr inn skjálgi 424.
Sigurðr Hákonarson, Hlaðajarl (jarl of Hlaðir, died 962) 421, 428, 430–32, 435.
Sigurðr sýr (Pig; cf. Faulkes 2011, 86, note to 1/412 f.) Hálfdanarson 3, 4, 40–47, 49, 58, 68, 70, 107, 174, 219, 347, 419, 437–39, 449.
Sigurðr son of Haraldr gilli, king of Norway (1136–55) 451.
Sigurðr hrísi (Brushwood) son of Haraldr inn hárfagri 423, 437.
Sigurðr digri (the Stout) Hlǫðvisson, jarl in Orkney (991–1014) 159, 160, 161, 167, 174, 448.
Sigurðr hundr (Dog) Jónsson 443.
Sigurðr Jórsalafari (Jerusalem-Traveller) Magnússon, king of Norway (1103–30) 450, 451.
Sigurðr son of Rauðr 298, 299.
Sigurðr son of Þórir hundr 443.

Sigurðr Þórisson, brother of Þórir hundr 194.
Sigurðr Þorláksson 236, 237, 238, 239, 240, 266.
Sigvaldi son of Strút-Haraldr, jarl 12, 54.
Sigvatr skáld (Poet) Þórðarson, Icelandic poet, 11th century 7, 10–13, 17, 18, 20–24, 26, 28, 29, 33, 38, 54–56, 60–64, 68, 73, 74, 92–94, 121–22, 134, 135–40, 144, 145, 183, 209, 210, 224, 225, 267, 270–74, 277, 278, 292—97, 303, 304, 314–16, 318, 329, 358, 362, 366, 367, 377, 379, 380–84, 386, 393, 394, 405, 409, 410, 421, 441, 442, 445. See note 8.
Sil (in Guðbrandsdalar) 185.
Silund 270 (verse), see Sjáland.
Silvellir (in Guðbrandsdalar) 185.
Sjáland (Roslagen), in Uppland, Sweden 110.
Sjáland, Sjóland, Silund (Sjælland, Denmark) 269, 270 (verse), 283, 284.
Skáney/Skáni (Skåne, the southernmost part of Sweden, earlier part of Denmark) 269, 277, 278 (verse), 283, 284, 290.
Skapti Þóroddsson, lawspeaker in Iceland (1004–30) 74, 77, 127, 217, 220, 240, 243.
Skarar (Skara, Gautland) 94, 148.
Skarnsund (Skarnsund, in Þrándheimr) 52.
Skaun (Skogn; cf. Skeynir), inland in Þrándheimr 50, 75, 439.
Skerfsurð (Skjærsurd in Lesjar) 323, 324.
Skeynir (people of Skaun) 180.
Skjálgr Erlingsson 29, 193, 200–01, 203, 226, 318.
Skjálgr (Þórólfr skjálgr), father of Erlingr 28, 39, 58, 67, 70, 78, 183, 192, 194, 206, 235, 244, 268, 293, 294, 306, 312, 315 (verse), 316 (verse), 322, 413, 438.
Skot (Skotet), headland in Sunnmœrr 322.
Skotborgará (Kongeå, river in southern Denmark) 448.
Skúli Þorfinnsson, jarl in Orkney (c. 976) 159.
Skǫglar-Tósti (Battle-) 433, 435, 438.
Skǫgul, a valkyrie; in a kenning for human woman 391 (verse).
Skǫnungar (people of Skáney, i.e. Danes) 281 (verse).
Smálond (Småland, southern Sweden) 291.
Snorri goði (priest/chieftain in Iceland) Þorgrímsson 217, 220, 240, 243, 255, 420, 421.
Snæfríðr the Lappish (finnska) daughter of Svási, married to Haraldr inn hárfagri 423; Snæfríðr's sons (Snæfríðarsynir) 424.
Sogn (Sogn, western Norway) 36, 207, 424, 434, 438.
Sognsær (Sognesjø, the entrance to Sognefjorden, western Norway) 192.
Sóknarsund (Soknsund, in Rogaland) 413.
Sóleyjar (more correctly Soleyjar or Sǫleyjar?—Solør, area of eastern Norway, on the border with Sweden) 191.
Sóleyjar (i.e. Seleyjar, west of Líðandisnes) 312.
Sóli (Sole, in Jaðarr, on the south-west coast of Norway) 196, 235, 318.
Sólundir (Solundøyar, islands at the entrance to Sognefjord on the west coast of Norway) 450.
Sótasker, Sóti's skerry (Sóti's rocks) (Sotholmen, off Suðrmannaland?) 6, 7 (verse).
Sóti, viking 6.
Southwark (Súðvirki), in London 15, 16, 18 (verse).
Sparabú (Sparbu, at the northern end of Trondheimsfjord) 241.

INDEX OF NAMES 333

Sparbyggvafylki, district north-east of Trondheimsfjord 439.
Sparbyggvar, inhabitants of Sparbyggvafylki 180.
Sprakaleggr, i.e. Þorgils sprakaleggr (Break-Leg) 275.
Staðr (Stad), in Norð-Mœrr 426.
Staðr (Staden, headland at nearly the most westerly part of mainland Norway) 36, 191, 267, 306, 309 (verse), 321.
Stafabrekka (Stavbrækka, in Ljárdalr) 182.
Stafamýrar, unidentified place 353.
Stafr, farm in Veradalr (?), 353, 396.
Steig, in Guðbrandsdalar 220.
Steinavágr (Steinvåg), on the island of Heissa, Sunnmœrr 322.
Steinkell, king of the Svíar (1060–66) 424.
Steinker (Steinkjær, in the northern part of Þrándheimr) 52, 53.
Steinn (Stein), on Nes (Bynes in Þrándheimr) 76.
Steinn son of Skapti Þóroddson 220, 240, 243–49.
Stikla(r)staðir (Stiklestad, in the northern part of Þrándheimr) 363–65, 369, 376, 379 (verse), 385 (verse), 390 (verse), 396–99, 403, 415, 422, 443, 444.
Stimr [or Stim n.?] (Stemmet), mountain near the sea on the boundary of Norð-Mœrr and Raumsdalr 309 (verse).
Stjóradalr (Stjørdal, valley in Þrándheimr) 53, 75.
Stjórdœlafylki, the district of the people of Stjóradalr 439.
Stokk(s)sund, a sound (or sounds) by Stockholm 8.
Storð (Stord, an island off Hǫrðaland) 431.
Straumey (Streymoy), in the Faeroes 263, 264.
Strind (Strinda, a place in Þrándheimr) 76; Strind district (Strindafylki) in Þrándheimr 51.
Strindir (people of Strindafylki) 93 (verse).
Styrbjǫrn Óláfsson 97–99, 435.
Suðrland (Sutherland in Scotland) 160, 161.
Suðrmannaland (Södermanland in Sweden) 109.
Suðrvík (Sondervig), on the coast west of Ringkøbing in Denmark 12.
Súl (or Súla) (Sulstua), highest farm in Veradalr 352, 388, 443.
Sult (Sylte), in Valldalr 323, 331 (verse).
Sumarliði Sigurðarson, jarl in Orkney (1014–15) 160, 161.
Sunn-Hǫrðaland (south Hordaland, south-west Norway) 192, 427.
Sunn-Mœrr (Sunnmøre, western Norway) 261, 434.
Súrnadalr (Surendal, in Raumsdalr) 244.
Svanhildr (or Hildr) daughter of Eysteinn 423.
Sveinn, kinsman of King Hrœrekr 118, 119.
Sveinn Álfífuson, see Sveinn Knútsson.
Sveinn Guðinason, jarl (?Swegen Godwineson, died 1052) 284.
Sveinn Hákonarson, jarl (died 1016) 27, 39, 45, 52, 53, 54, 55, 57, 58, 59, 60 (verse), 61–63, 64 (verse), 65, 66 (verse), 67, 68 (verse), 69 (verse), 71, 72, 78, 103, 143 (verse), 191, 221, 226, 326, 371, 409, 438, 439.
Sveinn tjúguskegg (Forkbeard) Haraldsson, king of the Danes (986–1014) 13, 14, 98, 221, 235, 281 (verse), 438, 439.
Sveinn son of Knútr inn ríki and Álfífa, king of the Danes (1030–35) 345, 398–404, 406, 409–14, 440, 442.

Sveinn Úlfsson, king of Denmark (1047–74/6) 235, 277, 446.
Svíar (Swedes) 5, 7–9, 46, 79, 88, 91, 98, 99, 109, 110, 116, 130, 149, 154, 156, 242, 256, 279, 280 (verse), 282, 285, 286, 347–49, 367 (verse); Svíar army (Svíaherr) 153, 154; king(s) of the Svíar (Svíakonung(a)r) 8, 42, 44, 45, 67, 71, 72, 74–77, 79, 81, 82, 84–91, 96, 97, 99, 110–17, 129, 130, 132–34, 144–46, 148, 149, 157, 158, 174, 191, 227, 234, 242, 255, 256, 275–77, 282, 283, 289, 344, 348, 354, 371, 424, 435, 438, 439; realm of the Svíar, Swedish realm (Svíaveldi) 5, 90, 97, 109, 111, 147, 226, 327, 343, 348, 354.
Svíasker (line of rocky islands off Uppland and Suðrmannaland in Sweden) 6, 84.
Svínasund (Svinesund, on the eastern side of the Vík) 79, 424.
Svíþjóð (Sweden) 6 (verse), 7, 8, 71, 74, 84, 109, 110, 111, 114, 147, 149, 156, 191, 226, 227, 328, 344, 346–48, 370, 415, 433, 435–37, 439, 440.
Sweden (Svíþjóð) 141 (verse).
Swedes (Svíar) 280 (verse).
Swedish (sœnskr) 156, 242, 299, 440 (verse); Swedish army (sœnskr herr) 270 (verse); Swedish king (konungr (inn) sœnski, sœnski konungr) 74, 75, 87; Swedish realm, see Svíar.
Sygnir (people of Sogn) 139 (verse), 375, 445.
Sýr 438, i.e. Sigurðr sýr.
Sæheimr (Seim), in Norðr-Hǫrðaland (north Hordaland, south-west Norway) 431.
Sæla, island (Selja, in Firðir, western Norway) 36.
Sæmingr son of Ingunar-Freyr (son of Óðinn in the prologue to *Snorra Edda*) 421.
Sǫlvi klofi (Cleaver) Húnþjófsson 425.
Sǫlvi (Selva/Selven), in Norð-Mœrr, near the end of Þrándheimsfjǫrðr 426.

Teitr, the poet Sigvatr's table companion 62 (verse). Cf. note 87.
Teitr son of Bishop Ísleifr 420.
Thames (Temps), river 15, 16.
Thomas, St, the Apostle (Túmas) 312.
Tíundaland ('Tenth land', an area in Uppland in eastern Sweden) 110, 111.
Toðarfjǫrðr (Tafjord, in Sunn-Mœrr) 323, 331.
Tófi Valgautsson 287.
Torf-Einarr (Turf-) son of Rǫgnvaldr, jarl in Orkney 158, 159.
Tósti 433, see Skǫglar-Tósti.
Tósti Guðinason, jarl (Tostig Godwineson, earl of Northumberland, died 1066) 284.
Tryggvaflokkr, a poem attributed to Sigvatr (cf. note 429) 413.
Tryggvi son of Haraldr hárfagri 423, see Sigtryggr.
Tryggvi son of Óláfr son of Haraldr hárfagri, king (died 963) 26, 27, 28 (verse), 29, 30, 39, 44, 46, 47, 50, 51, 53, 78, 85, 88, 89, 98, 159, 160, 167, 177, 267 (verse), 288, 340, 411, 413, 420, 427–29, 432, 437, 438, 445 (verse).
Tryggvi son of Óláfr Tryggvason, king 411–13.
Tungur, in the most northerly part of Jaðarr (now called Tunge and Tungenes) 315 (verses).
Túnsberg (Tønsberg, Vestfold) 58, 79, 120, 123, 125, 158, 191, 192, 220, 223, 303, 306, 310, 312, 425, 428, 432, 434.
Túskaland (< Túrska-; Touraine, in France) 25 (verse).
Tǫgdrápa (Journey Poem (?), a poem by Þórarinn loftunga 308.

INDEX OF NAMES 335

Úlfasund (Ulvesund, Nordfjord), in Firðir 36, 445 (verse).
Úlfhildr daughter of Óláfr Tryggvason 327, 328, 348, 447.
Úlfkell (Ulfcytil, English aldormann, died 1016) snillingr (Master) 18, 31, 32 (verse); Úlfkell's country (Úlfkelsland), East Anglia 18.
Úlfnaðr (Wulfnoð, a South Saxon, father of Jarl Guðini) 284.
Úlfr Rǫgnvaldson, jarl 28 (verse), 143 (verses), 148.
Úlfr son of Skǫglar-Tósti 147, 438.
Úlfr son of Þorgils sprakaleggr, jarl 235, 275–77, 280, 284, 285, 446.
Úlfreksfjǫrðr (Lough Larne, in Ireland) 128, 163.
Ullarakr (district west of Fýri, near Uppsalir) 111, 112, 155.
Uppdalr (Uppdal), valley high up in the southern part of Þrándheimr 50; Uppdalr Wood (Uppdalsskógr), at the top of Orkadalr 50.
Upplendingar (people of Upplǫnd) 69 (verse) 125, 191, 208 (verse), 409, 425.
Upplǫnd (Upplanda, area of eastern Norway) 45, 49, 100, 120, 177, 182, 191, 208, 219, 227, 297, 302, 347, 354, 371, 403, 423, 425, 428, 429, 433, 437; people, men of Upplǫnd (Upplendingar) 327, 364, 424; king(s) in Upplǫnd, king(s) of the Upplendingar (Upplendingakonung(a)r) 46, 125.
Uppsalaauðr ('Uppsala wealth') 110.
Uppsalir (Uppsala) 97, 109–11, 149, 435; king(s) of (Uppsalakonung(a)r) 97, 115, 153; (the law of (Uppsalalǫg) 110, 151; the Uppsalir assembly (Uppsalaþing) 99, 114, 130, 151–53.
Uppsvíar, the Svíar (Swedes) of Uppland (the coastal area north of Stockholm) 152, 155, 156; leaders of the (Uppsvíahǫfðingjar) 155.
Útsteinn (Utstein, by the island Mosterøy in Rogaland) 317 (verse), 321 (verse).

Vágar (Vågan, on Aust-Vågøy in Lofoten, Hálogaland) 250; Vágafloti, the fleet at Vágar (i.e. the place where the merchant ships harboured?) 212; Vágastefna, meeting-place, i.e. market at Vágar 212.
Vágarǫst (Rosta, in Guðbrandsdalar) 185.
Vági (probably more correctly Vagi) (Vágá), settlement in Guðbrandsdalar 183, 184, 186.
Valdamarr 406 (verse). See next.
Valdamarr son of Jarizleifr 148; perhaps the same person 406 (verse). See note 421.
Valdi (off Valdi: perhaps on the coast below the Yorkshire Wolds, near the mouth of the Humber) 34.
Valdres (district in Upplǫnd, central Norway) 46, 207.
Valgautr, Gautish man 287.
Valland (i.e. Frakkland, Francia) 13, 26, 33, 34, 271, 292.
Valldalr (Valldal), in Sunn-Mœrr 323, 331.
Valþjófr jarl Guðinason (Walþeof was actually son of Sigurðr, jarl in Northumberland, and was probably a Dane) 284.
Vangr (Vang) in Hǫrðaland 206.
Varrandi (Guérande, just south of the Britanny peninsula, near the coast; not in Peita (Poitou)) 25, 26 (verse).
Vatsbú (Vadsbo) in Vermaland 328.
Vatsdalr, in Húnaþing, northern Iceland 331.
Veðrey (Väderø), island off Halland in Sweden 291.

Veggirnir (Vägga), southernmost farm on Sótanes in Ranríki 432.
Vegsund (sound between Sula and Yksnøy in Storfjorden, Romsdal, western Norway) 322.
Veradalr (Verdal), valley in Þrándheimr 74, 179, 363, 370, 388, 396, 443, 444.
Verdœlafylki, district around Veradalr 352, 439.
Verdœlir the people of Veradalr 180, 359 (verse), 388.
Vermaland (Värmland, district in western Sweden, on the border with Norway) 109, 149, 328, 347.
Vestfirðir (the Western Fiords of Iceland) 244.
Vestfjǫrðr (Vestfjorden, Hálogaland) 252.
Vestfold, area to the west of Oslofjord 40, 421, 423–27, 429, 434.
Vestmannaland (Västmanland), in eastern Sweden 110.
Vestra-Gautland, south-western Sweden 96, 109, 130, 132, 148, 227, 234, 287, 291, 438.
Vestrfararvísur, a poem by Sigvatr 271.
Vestr-Gautar people of Vestra-Gautland 87, 113, 115, 132, 149, 155.
Vettaland (Vettelanda in Ranríki) 82.
Víðkunnr Jónsson of Bjarkey 443.
Vigg (Vigga), a farm in Orkadalr in Þrándheimr, on the coast 52, 363.
Vígleikr Árnason 322.
Vík/the Vík (Vík/Víkin, Oslofjord and the land on both sides) 39, 57, 58, 59, 70, 79, 80, 81, 83, 86, 117, 120, 133, 158, 191, 192, 219, 220, 226, 235, 241, 291, 303, 310, 312, 399, 412, 428, 429, 432, 438, 439, 450; people of the Vík (Víkverjar) 83, 85.
Víkinga-Kári Sigurðarson 89.
Víkverir, Víkverjar (inhabitants of (the) Vík) 425, 426, 428, 430, 432.
Vilborg daughter of Gizurr hvíti 89.
Viljálmr langaspjót (William Longspear, 893–943) son of Gǫngu-Hrólfr, jarl in Normandy 26. Cf. note 43.
Viljálmr Ríkarðarson, jarl in Normandy 26. Cf. vol. III 469.
Viljálmr, Jarl, town of (Viljalms bœr, in verse) (Villamea, in northern Spain?) 23.
Vinðland (Wendland, on the southern shore of the Baltic) 130, 398, 438, 447.
Vinðr (Wends, people of Wendland) 447, 448. See also Wends.
Vingulmǫrk, district around Oslo 100, 424, 429, 434.
Vísivaldr, king from Garðaríki 436.
Vissivaldr son of Jarizleifr 148.
Visundr (the Bison), a ship 267, 268 (verses), 331.
Vitgeirr, magician 425.
Vúlgáríá (Old Great Bulgaria, on the north side of the Black Sea and eastwards between the Volga and Kuma rivers) 339.
Vænir (Lake Vänern in Sweden) 79.
Vǫrs (Voss, area in Hǫrðafylki, western Norway) 89, 206.

Wends (Vinðr) 20 (verse), 448 (verse). See also Vinðr.
White-Christ (Hvíta-Kristr, i.e. Jesus Christ; cf. Christ) 354, 369, 442 (verse).

Yggr, a name for the god Óðinn (in verses) 16 (in a kenning for battle), 17 (in a kenning for battle), 65 (in a kenning for raven), 440 (in a kenning for warrior).

Þangbrandr, Saxon priest 420.
Þelamǫrk (Telemark, southern Norway) 424.
Þingvǫllr, the site of the annual Alþingi in Iceland 214.
Þjóðólfr inn fróði (the Learned) of, from, in Hvinir (inn hvinverski), Haraldr inn hárfagri's poet 421.
Þjóðólfr Arnórsson, Icelandic poet, eleventh century 439, 448.
Þjótta (Tjøtta), island off Hálogaland 175, 176, 181, 211, 253, 289–91, 305, 306, 339, 345, 372, 375, 386, 443.
Þóra Morstǫng or Morstrstǫng (Pole of Morstr) 427.
Þóra daughter of Finnr inn skjálgi 424.
Þóra daughter of Þorbergr 245.
Þóra daughter of Þorsteinn, wife of Árni Armóðsson 181.
Þóraldi, King Óláfr's steward 179, 180.
Þórálfr Sigmundarson of Dimon 218–19, 236, 237, 238, 239.
Þorarinn loftunga (Praise-Tongue), Icelandic poet, eleventh century 307–08, 310, 399, 406, 409.
Þórarinn Nefjólfsson 125–28, 201–03, 215, 217, 218.
Þórarr, lawman in Jamtaland 255–56, 257.
Þorbergr Árnason 29, 181, 244–49, 327, 387, 402, 411, 445 (verse).
Þórðr Sigvaldaskáld (Þórrøðr in verse; Sigvaldi's Poet), father of the poet Sigvatr 54, 442 (verse).
Þórðr skotakollr (?-head) 145.
Þórðr Barkarson 214.
Þórðr Fólason, King Óláfr's standard-bearer 122, 123, 366, 380, 381.
Þórðr ístrumagi (Fat Belly) Gothormsson 186, 187, 220.
Þórðr Hǫrða-Kárason 433.
Þórðr Kolbeinsson, Icelandic poet, eleventh century 30, 31, 214.
Þórðr Sjáreksson, Icelandic poet, eleventh century 281.
Þórðr inn lági (the Short) Þorláksson 236–38, 266, 267.
Þorfinnr/Þorfiðr munnr/muðr (Mouth), poet of King Óláfr 358, 359, 381.
Þorfinnr/Þorfiðr Sigurðarson, jarl in Orkney (1020–64) 160–74, 182, 448, 449.
Þorfinnr/Þorfiðr hausakljúfr (Skull-Splitter) Torf-Einarsson, jarl in Orkney (c. 963–c. 976) 159, 430.
Þorgautr skarði (Harelip) 74–77, 84.
Þorgeirr, King Óláfr's steward 243–45.
Þorgeirr of Kvistsstaðir 378, 381.
Þorgeirr afráðskollr (Payment-Chap) 419.
Þorgeirr flekkr (Spot), a farmer 352, 443, 444.
Þorgils sprakaleggr (Break-Leg; it is thought likely that Þorgils was son of an Englishman called Spracling, and that *sprakaleggr* is a corruption of that name) 235, 275.
Þorgeirr Hávararson 214.
Þorgils Arason 127–28.
Þorgils Gellisson 326, 419, 431.
Þorgils Hálmuson, farmer at Stiklarstaðir 365, 394–98, 403.
Þorgils son of Haraldr inn hárfagri 423–25.
Þorgnýr, lawman in Tíundaland 111, 115.
Þorgnýr Þorgnýsson, lawman in Tíundaland 111, 116.

Þorgnýr son of Þorgnýr Þorgnýsson, lawman in Tíundaland 111, 113–17, 133.
Þorinn, a dwarf, in a kenning for poetry 32 (verse).
Þórir, see Gauka-Þórir.
Þórir, father of Sigurðr 194.
Þórir, man in Jamtaland 258–59.
Þórir helsingr (of Helsingjaland) 241.
Þórir langi (the Long) 80–81, 123.
Þórir selr (Seal), King Óláfr's steward 193, 195–98, 200, 201, 205, 206. See Sel-Þórir.
Þórir Erlingsson 29, 247, 249.
Þórir Guðbrandsson 51.
Þórir Hróaldsson, hersir (lord) 423.
Þórir þegjandi (Silent) son of Rǫgnvaldr Eysteinsson, jarl 424.
Þórir hundr (Dog) Þórisson, landed man 177, 194, 198, 205–06, 212, 213, 228–34, 250–53, 293–94, 300, 306, 339, 344, 345, 373–78, 383–89, 396, 397, 443; Hundr 384 (verses).
Þórir Ǫlvisson 300–02, 327, 333, 373.
Þorkell at Apavatn 54.
Þorkell fóstri (Foster-Father) Amundason 161, 162, 164–66, 169–72, 174, 177.
Þorkell Eyjólfsson 214, 217, 220, 240, 255, 292.
Þorkell (inn) hávi (the Tall) Strút-Haraldsson 12, 54, 333.
Þorlákr, father of Sigurðr and Þórðr 236, 238, 266.
Þorleikr Bollason 214.
Þormóðr Kolbrúnarskáld (Kolbrún's Poet) Bersason, Icelandic poet (997–1030) 214, 356, 358, 359, 361–62, 389, 390–93. See note 357.
Þóroddr son of Snorri goði 220, 240, 243, 255–61.
Þórr, a god 184, 187.
Þórrøðr see Þórðr Sigvaldaskáld.
Þórsbjǫrg (Torshaug), in Norð-Mœrr 426.
Þórshǫfn (Tórshavn), on Straumey (Streymoy) in the Faeroes 263.
Þorsteinn fróði (the Learned) 157.
Þorsteinn gálgi (Gallows) 181.
Þorsteinn knarrarsmiðr (merchant ship builder) 375, 385.
Þorsteinn Hallsson 217, 220.
Þorsteinn rauðr (Red) Óláfsson 159.
Þorviðr stami (Stammerer), adviser of King Óláfr of the Svíar 153–54.
Þótn (Toten, an area of Haðaland near Lake Mjǫrs) 46, 190, 208, 220, 424.
Þrándarnes (Trones, off the northern part of Hálogaland; not in Ǫmð (Andøy), but in Hinn (Hinnøy)) 194, 212.
Þrándheimr, district of northern Norway, modern Trøndelag (cf. Þrœndalǫg) 51, 52, 54, 56, 58, 70–73, 77, 82, 158, 174, 175, 177, 178, 180, 182, 192, 209. 213, 215, 234, 241, 242, 247, 250, 261, 302, 305, 306, 319, 321, 331–33, 345, 351, 352, 354, 370, 399, 401, 403, 406 (verse), 412, 423, 425–28, 430, 431, 433, 434, 439, 440, 443, 446; the mouth of (entrance to) the Þrándheimr fiord (Trondheimsfjord) (Þrándheimsmynni) 431.
Þrándr hvíti (the White) 82, 255.
Þrándr in/from Gata Þorbjarnarson, Faeroese chieftain 218, 236–37, 239, 240, 263, 264–67.

INDEX OF NAMES

Þrjótshverfi (Kverven), the most westerly part of Erlingsey (Ellingsøy), in Sunn-Mœrr 322.
Þróttr, a name for the god Óðinn, in a kenning for battle 37 (verse).
Þrœndalǫg (Trøndelag; = Þrándheimr) 27, 414.
Þrœndir, Þrœndr (people of Þrándheimr) 24 (verse), 47, 70, 72, 178, 241, 242, 359 (verse), 373, 375, 379 (verse), 403, 410, 411, 425, 426, 428, 429, 431, 433, 437, 440 (verse), 445.
Þrœndish (Þrœnzkr) from Þrándheimr 380 (verse).
Þundr, a name for the god Óðinn, in a kenning for seafarer 31 (verse), in a kenning for battle 359 (verse).
Þuríðr daughter of Snorri goði 420.
Þursasker (rocks in the sea by Thurso Bay, in the north of Caithness, Scotland?) 174 (verse).

Æsir, the Norse gods 177.

Ǫ́ en helga ('The Holy River'; Áin helga, Helgeå, in Skáney) 281 (verse). See Áin helga.
Ǫgló (Skatval district) in Stjóradalr 431.
Ǫgmundr Fólason 367 (verse).
Ǫgvaldsnes (Avaldsnes), on Kǫrmt 195, 197, 199, 201, 204–06.
Ǫleifr (in verses), i.e. Óláfr Haraldsson, inn helgi (the Saint) 10, 17, 18, 20, 21, 23, 28, 61, 134, 142, 143, 225, 268, 270, 272, 273, 281, 293, 295, 317, 330, 331, 360, 366, 367, 380, 385, 390, 393, 394, 406, 408, 409, 439, 441, 442, 445; the two Ǫleifrs (Óláfr Tryggvason and Óláfr Haraldsson (the Saint)) 445.
Ǫlvir, one of three Gautish farmers 137, 138 (verse).
Ǫlvir at Egg 178–82, 300, 302, 333, 373.
Ǫmð (Andøy), island in Hálogaland 194.
Ǫnundr jarl from Sparabú 241.
Ǫnundr (Jákob) Óláfsson, king of the Svíar (1022–c. 1050) 156, 157, 191, 226–27, 234, 235, 256, 269, 270 (verse), 275–80, 282–83, 286, 344, 347–48. See also Jákob Óláfsson.
Ǫ́sta, i.e. Ásta daughter of Guðbrandr kúla, mother of St Óláfr 139 (verse).
Ǫzurr father of Leifr 218, 236, 263, 266, 267.